METHODS IN MOLECULAR BIOLOGY

Series Editor
John M. Walker
School of Life and Medical Sciences
University of Hertfordshire
Hatfield, Hertfordshire, UK

For further volumes:
http://www.springer.com/series/7651

For over 35 years, biological scientists have come to rely on the research protocols and methodologies in the critically acclaimed Methods in Molecular Biology series. The series was the first to introduce the step-by-step protocols approach that has become the standard in all biomedical protocol publishing. Each protocol is provided in readily-reproducible step-by step fashion, opening with an introductory overview, a list of the materials and reagents needed to complete the experiment, and followed by a detailed procedure that is supported with a helpful notes section offering tips and tricks of the trade as well as troubleshooting advice. These hallmark features were introduced by series editor Dr. John Walker and constitute the key ingredient in each and every volume of the Methods in Molecular Biology series. Tested and trusted, comprehensive and reliable, all protocols from the series are indexed in PubMed.

Manuscript Instructions https://drive.google.com/file/d/1K4Az5vpAFVzYadJ3jKx2-QSo7Dqa_SNA/view?usp=sharing

AI/ML-Driven Gene Analysis

Methods and Protocols

Edited by

Y-h Taguchi

Department of Physics, Chuo University, Tokyo, Japan

Humana Press

Editor
Y-h Taguchi
Department of Physics
Chuo University
Tokyo, Japan

ISSN 1064-3745 ISSN 1940-6029 (electronic)
Methods in Molecular Biology
ISBN 978-1-0716-5283-1 ISBN 978-1-0716-5284-8 (eBook)
https://doi.org/10.1007/978-1-0716-5284-8

This Humana imprint is published by the registered company Springer Science+Business Media, LLC, part of Springer Nature.
The registered company address is: 1 New York Plaza, New York, NY 10004, U.S.A.

Preface

Recently, AI and machine learning have had a strong impact on genomics. Before these two arrived on the field, most analyses were mainly based on statistics. It was quite a passive method because it could only judge if the hypothesis was true or not, and the hypothesis must be generated by the human side. The exhaustive analysis raised concerns after the post-genomic era, so a more constructive and data-driven approach became popular. In this approach, data can derive the hypothesis by itself, and this volume presents such methods related to AI and machine learning.

In Chap. 1, we can find how we can derive the biomarker, a measure of biological and pathological processesnetwork-based methodology. In Chap. 2, we can find how we can identify drug candidate compounds from the gene expression that is deeply related to disease progression. In Chap. 3, we can find how we can infer the function of epigenetics using network based methodology. In Chap. 4, we can find that ConsRM, which is a web-based approach to predict which m6A site, which is one of the most abundant epitranscriptome modifications, is important, is useful. In Chap. 5, we can find how CellOracle can figure out which gene–gene interaction is important. In Chap. 7, we can find how well tensor decomposition can deal with massive multiomics datasets to figure out what has happened behind the massive datasets. In Chap. 8, we can find how a machine learning approach can figure out how microRNA affects the cardiovascular events. In Chap. 9, we can find how a large language model can find Non-Coding RNA Biomarker Discovery in Breast Cancer. In Chap. 10, we can find how we can deal with gene expression of bulk and single-cell measurements. In Chap. 11, we can find current gold-standard RNA structure prediction approaches and cutting-edge ML methods that can contribute to inferring RNA functions. In Chap. 12, we can find how AI/ML approaches can attack somatic variant detection in a normal human tissue. In Chap. 13, we can find a study case, including code, for the detection of CNVs, quality assessment, and identification of rare CNVs. In Chap. 14, we can find that gene embeddings are powerful tools for predicting unknown functions of genes and drugs.

Although the topics in this volume are full of variety, I hope that the readers can learn cutting-edge methodology of the current AI/ML methods applied to genomics.

Y-h Taguchi
Department of Physics
Chuo University
Tokyo, Japan

Contents

Contributors

S. Akila Parvathy Dharshini • *Department of Biotechnology, Bhupat and Jyoti Mehta School of Biosciences, Indian Institute of Technology Madras, Chennai, Tamil Nadu, India*

Benoît Aliaga • *Centre de Recherches en Cancérologie de Toulouse (CRCT), INSERM, Univ. Toulouse, CNRS, Toulouse, France*

Haydee Artaza • *Department of Clinical Science, University of Bergen, Bergen, Norway*

Ken Asada • *Division of Medical AI Research and Development, National Cancer Center Research Institute, Tsukiji, Chuo-ku, Tokyo, Japan*

Kunqi Chen • *Key Laboratory of Ministry of Education for Gastrointestinal Cancer, Fuzhou, China; Fujian Key Laboratory of Tumor Microbiology, Department of Medical Microbiology, School of Basic Medical Sciences, Fujian Medical University, Fuzhou, Fujian, China*

Yi Cong • *Information Biology Laboratory, Graduate School of Information Science and Technology, Hokkaido University, Sapporo, Japan*

Henry Cousins • *Department of Ophthalmology, Harvard Medical School, Boston, MA, USA*

Toshinori Endo • *Information Biology Laboratory, Faculty of Information Science and Technology, Hokkaido University, Sapporo, Japan*

Ryuji Hamamoto • *AI Medical and Engineering Team, RIKEN Center for Advanced Intelligenece Project, Nihonbashi, Chuo-ku, Tokyo, Japan*

Fumiya Ito • *Institute for Quantitative Biosciences, The University of Tokyo, Bunkyo City, Tokyo, Japan; Center for iPS Cell Research and Application, Kyoto University, Kyoto, Japan*

Kenji Kamimoto • *Research Institute for Microbial Diseases, The University of Osaka, Osaka, Japan; Premium Research Institute for Human Metaverse Medicine, The University of Osaka, Osaka, Japan; Bioinformatics Center, The University of Osaka, Osaka, Japan*

Risa Karakida Kawaguchi • *Center for iPS Cell Research and Application, Kyoto University, Kyoto, Japan; Graduate School of Pharmaceutical Sciences, The University of Tokyo, Bunkyo City, Tokyo, Japan*

Tamizhini Loganathan • *Saveetha Institute of Basic Medical Sciences (SIBMS), Saveetha Institute of Medical and Technical Sciences - SIMATS, SIMATS, Chennai, Tamil Nadu, India*

M. Michael Gromiha • *Department of Biotechnology, Bhupat and Jyoti Mehta School of Biosciences, Indian Institute of Technology Madras, Chennai, Tamil Nadu, India*

Luke Moat • *Center for Precision Medicine Research, Marshfield Clinic Research Institute, Marshfield, WI, USA*

Shamim Ara Mollah • *Genetics, Biomedical Informatics and Data Science, Washington University School of Medicine in St. Louis, St. Louis, MO, USA*

Satoshi Oota • *Wako, Saitama, Japan*

Vera Pancaldi • *Centre de Recherches en Cancérologie de Toulouse (CRCT), INSERM, Univ. Toulouse, CNRS, Toulouse, France*
Flavien Raynal • *Centre de Recherches en Cancérologie de Toulouse (CRCT), INSERM, Univ. Toulouse, CNRS, Toulouse, France*
Hirohide Saito • *Institute for Quantitative Biosciences, The University of Tokyo, Bunkyo City, Tokyo, Japan; Center for iPS Cell Research and Application, Kyoto University, Kyoto, Japan*
Param Sharma • *Department of Cardiology, Marshfield Clinic Health System, Marshfield, WI, USA*
Bowen Song • *Department of Public Health, School of Medicine, Nanjing University of Chinese Medicine, Nanjing, China*
Shunsuke Sumi • *Institute for Quantitative Biosciences, The University of Tokyo, Bunkyo City, Tokyo, Japan*
Y-h Taguchi • *Department of Physics, Chuo University, Tokyo, Japan*
Ruiqi Xu • *Center for iPS Cell Research and Application, Kyoto University, Kyoto, Japan*
Srinivasulu Yerukala Sathipati • *Center for Precision Medicine Research, Marshfield Clinic Research Institute, Marshfield, WI, USA*
Yuxin Zhang • *Department of Biological Sciences, Xi'an Jiaotong-Liverpool University, Suzhou, Jiangsu, China; Institute of Systems, Molecular and Integrative Biology, University of Liverpool, Liverpool, UK*

Check for updates

Chapter 1

Identification of Clinically Relevant Genes Using Machine Learning Techniques

Ken Asada and Ryuji Hamamoto

Abstract

Machine learning (ML) has demonstrated great potential and considerable effectiveness in big data analysis. It is capable of extracting novel features, including indicators or biomarkers in biology, that are unachievable with previously existing methodologies. Biomarkers are used to measure and evaluate biological and pathological processes, or pharmacological responses to assess patient status. In clinical settings, biomarkers enable the prediction and detection of many aspects, such as prognosis, drug response, and tumor recurrence. Stratification using RNA expression is the gold standard for patient prognosis in cancer. In this chapter, we describe a practical guide for identifying clinically relevant biomarkers using ML. First, integrated multi-omics data are used as input data for the analysis. Then, an autoencoder is used for dimension reduction, and a bottleneck feature space of 100 dimensions is used to extract clinically relevant features. Finally, we identify biomarkers related to the outcomes from the transcriptome data.

Keywords Biomarker, Machine learning, Autoencoder, Multi-omics analysis, Prognosis

1 Introduction

In 1998, the National Institutes of Health (NIH) Biomarker Definitions Working Group defined a biomarker as follows [1]: a characteristic that is objectively measured and evaluated as an indicator of normal biological processes, pathogenic processes, or pharmacologic responses to a therapeutic intervention. In general, biomarkers can be categorized according to their measurements [1, 2] (Fig. 1). There are specific types of biomarkers in each category; however, some might overlap depending on their unique properties.

The evolution of biomarkers has advanced from blood-based, mutation-based, and genomic-based to proteomic-based markers [3]. Therefore, the object of measurement, methodology (case handling), accuracy, and time effectiveness or consumption are important factors to gain attention in the clinical setting regarding widespread use. For example, current methodologies for assessing solid tumors include immunohistochemistry (IHC), fluorescence in situ hybridization

Y-h Taguchi (ed.), *AI/ML-Driven Gene Analysis*, Methods in Molecular Biology, vol. 3037,
https://doi.org/10.1007/978-1-0716-5284-8_1

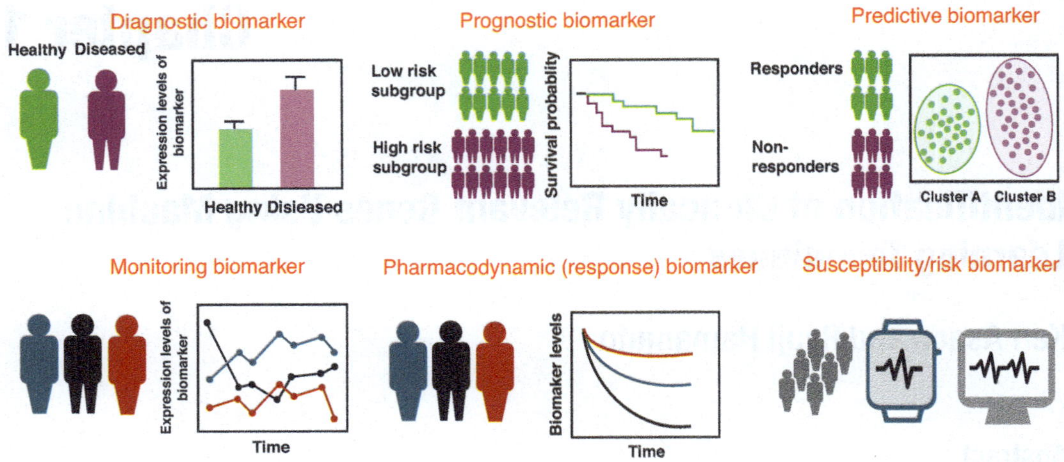

Fig. 1 Classification of biomarkers. Diagnostic biomarkers confirm, detect, or establish pathological changes in disease in the cohort. Prognostic biomarkers assess or identify the likelihood of a clinical event, such as patient prognosis, disease progression, or recurrence. Predictive biomarkers classify patients into subgroups such as drug responders and non-responders, which reflects clinical outcomes. Monitoring biomarkers measure the changes of scales of a physiological and/or pharmacological effect in a period of time to detect a typical response or to assess a status of condition. Pharmacodynamic (response) biomarkers detect a biological response to therapeutic intervention, environmental exposures or condition. Susceptibility/risk biomarkers assess the likelihood of developing a disease or medical condition

(FISH), polymerase chain reaction (PCR), next-generation sequencing (NGS), and gene expression profiling (GEP) [4, 5].

Attempts to apply genomic information to medical biology were actively pursued following the completion of the International Human Genome Project, and the concept of personalized medicine or precision oncology has attracted attention through the analysis of multi-omics data [6]. Single-nucleotide polymorphisms (SNPs) are a type of genetic variation associated with disease risk. Therefore, SNPs can be used as biomarkers to predict an individual's response to risk factors [7–9]. In cancer, DNA alterations at specific positions in specific genes are known as driver mutations, which exhibit oncogenic effects and cancer phenotypes. Because some genomic alterations are directly linked to patient outcomes or influence the response to interventions [10–12], identifying driver mutations is a high priority. Furthermore, these identified driver mutations serve as clinically attractive biomarkers and therapeutic targets. Hence, genomic testing or biomarker testing is an effective screening method for selecting patients who are expected to be sensitive to molecular targeting drugs [13].

Biomarkers are not limited to genomic alterations, including structural variation and expression of quantitative trait loci (eQTL) [14, 15]; metabolites [16, 17], bioactive compounds [18], and gene expression, and isoform expression, can also become biomarkers [19–21]. In cancer, early detection enables effective interventions and increases therapeutic opportunities, resulting in reduced mortality and morbidity [3]. The tumor mutation burden (TMB) determines the response of immune checkpoint inhibitors in tumors, indicating the potential of biomarker analysis to advance precision medicine [22].

With the advent of NGS, RNA-seq has been widely used. The methodology for RNA extraction from tissue samples is widely established. Furthermore, RNA quality checks, library preparation, sequencing, and bioinformatics are all well-pipelined. As a result, gene expression, prognosis, metastasis, and drug responses have been reported [23–27]. However, one of the long-lasting problems hampering further progress in this field is the identification of novel reliable biomarkers [28]. For example, the discovery of genes altered in coding regions in cancer could reach a plateau, or newly identified genes may be rediscovered in cancer research, which in turn limits the identification of novel marker genes [29].

To address this problem, we describe a novel methodology using machine learning (ML) to effectively and efficiently identify marker genes associated with the prognosis of patients with tumors [30, 31].

2 Materials

Linux PC or PC with multi-core threads and sufficient memory (>24 GB) is highly desirable. An environment, ideally a virtual environment to use the Python script or Tensorflow, Keras, and the application of a Visual Studio, Jupyter notebook, or terminal to execute the script, are needed in this analysis.

3 Methods

In this section, we use the publicly available lung adenocarcinoma (LUAD) dataset from The Cancer Genome Atlas (TCGA) as an example. TCGA was organized by the National Cancer Institute (NCI), United States. The NCI launched the working group in 2005, and the National Institute of Health (NIH) launched TCGA project with $100 million in the first 3 years. Since then, TCGA has collected human tissue samples, including non-tumor adjacent to the tumor (NAT). TCGA now has 33 tumor types and several omics datasets, including genomic (whole genome sequencing (WGS) and whole exome sequencing (WES)), epigenomic (DNA methylation, chromatin immunoprecipitation sequencing (ChIP-seq), and Assay for Transposase-Accessible Chromatin using sequencing (ATAC-seq)), transcriptomic (RNA-seq and miRNA-seq), and proteome data (reverse phase protein array). Summary data from TCGA are available on the website (https://portal.gdc.cancer.gov/analysis_page?app=Projects).

3.1 Preparation of Input Data Using a Tool

In this chapter, we download TCGA lung adenocarcinoma (LUAD) data using TCGA-Assembler 2 as part of the instructions. Notably, detailed instructions are available at GitHub (https://github.com/compgenome365/TCGA-Assembler-2) [32, 33]. After downloading, there are three files in the top directory: LICENSE.txt, README.md, and TCGA-Assembler folder. Under the folder, there are several files and folders; Tutorial.pdf should be initially used. For more detailed information, Manual.pdf can provide deep insight into TCGA-Assembler 2. Here, we only explain the essential part of this package for downloading the data, because the vignette includes all the necessary information. Information on study abbreviations is available in Manal.pdf or at the GDC portal (https://gdc.cancer.gov/resources-tcga-users/tcga-code-tables/tcga-study-abbreviations), which is required when using TCGA-Assembler 2 to download the multi-omics data of interest for the following analyses. Subsequently, by following the vignette, the final merged multi-omics data can be obtained in several hours, depending on how much data you would like to download for analysis. The integrated dataset obtained using TCGA-Assembler 2 is shown in Fig. 2.

3.2 Manual Data Downloading

Alternatively, data can be downloaded from TCGA data portal directly (https://portal.gdc.cancer.gov). First, TCGA-LUAD is placed in a search window (Fig. 3a–d). Next, move to the top page of PROJECT TCGA-LUAD. Under the cohort builder, you can choose which omics data you would like to download for downstream analysis. Representative dataset downloaded for RNA-seq, miRNA-seq, and DNA methylation data of LUAD from the GDC portal are shown in Fig. 3d.

When downloading data, both the omics data and the related files, including biospecimens and clinical information, should be downloaded. These files are required for the downstream Kaplan-Meier estimate in the survival analysis.

3.3 Data Preprocessing

In this step, we assume that each omics data point has already been normalized (e.g., transcripts per million (TPM) for gene expression, and continuous values between 0 and 1 in DNA methylation data). Before running a deep learning model (autoencoder), scale the data against patients using a standardization method.

3.4 Code for Autoencoder

To extract features associated with clinical outcomes from multi-omics input data, dimension reduction is conducted using an autoencoder model. You can set your own bottleneck feature space; however, we suggest 100 dimensions as the first choice.

The Example Code for the Autoencoder Model using Keras

Let us hypothetically say that the input data are 13,767-dimensional as an example for the autoencoder model. Below is an example code for Keras, and the code for PyTorch will be explained later. We implement the autoencoder with three hidden layers (500, 100, and

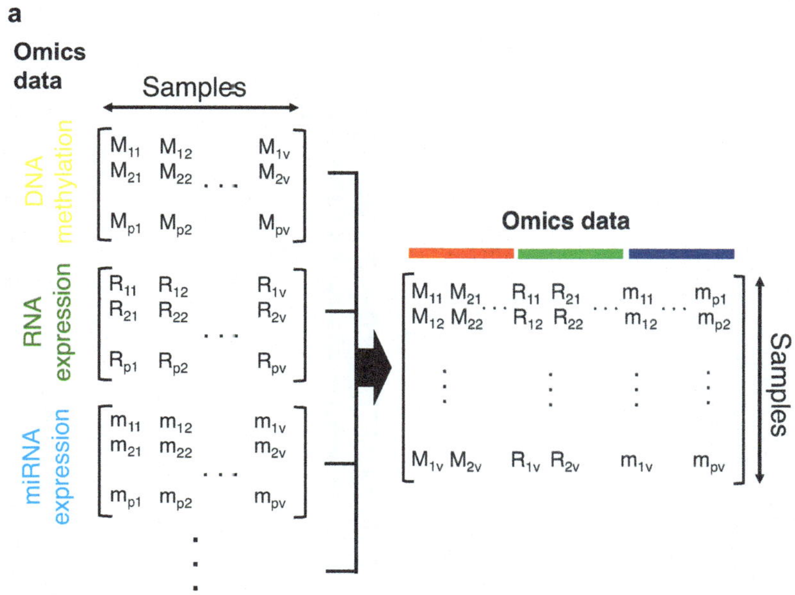

b

Example of the input data

	A	B	C	D	E	F	G	H
1	GeneSymbol	Platform	TCGA.05.439	TCGA.05.441	TCGA.05.443	TCGA.44.564	TCGA.44.614	TCGA.44.677
2	LET7A-1	miRNAExp	-0.048498	-0.0049902	0.27846776	0.0027255	0.4345504	0.27947533
3	LET7A-2	miRNAExp	0.0870425	0.15319933	0.75918695	0.16329258	1.07675232	0.7095234
4	LET7A-3	miRNAExp	-0.0470782	-0.0026739	0.27477575	0.00450102	0.4395676	0.28438352
5	LET7B	miRNAExp	0.14964684	0.15878986	1.06077973	-0.0029083	1.04507483	0.52985095
6	LET7C	miRNAExp	-0.173686	-0.1380398	-0.1614326	-0.1464179	-0.1346333	-0.0732184
7	LET7D	miRNAExp	-0.1660354	-0.1468784	-0.1627716	-0.1259291	-0.1566348	-0.1360562
8	LET7E	miRNAExp	-0.1257833	-0.1293492	-0.1230948	-0.0720909	-0.0868035	-0.0757527
9	LET7F-2	miRNAExp	0.03354311	0.07231942	0.32973252	0.33096693	0.60316424	0.40982032
10	LET7G	miRNAExp	-0.1566202	-0.1495692	-0.1795382	-0.1358793	-0.17152	-0.1291766
11	LET7I	miRNAExp	-0.1624168	-0.1355667	-0.1842837	-0.1328386	-0.1685122	-0.1328773
12	MIR100	miRNAExp	-0.06952	0.0589178	-0.0368691	-0.0772769	0.20584531	0.10033497
13	MIR101-1	miRNAExp	0.03451495	0.22574568	0.42830423	0.01660681	-0.002279	0.29347339
14	MIR101-2	miRNAExp	-0.1805923	-0.1620651	-0.2018872	-0.1540094	-0.2050405	-0.1505454
15	MIR103A-1	miRNAExp	0.39518433	0.22050347	0.90297837	0.36057275	0.58122678	0.36798645
16	MIR103A-2	miRNAExp	-0.1806198	-0.1625005	-0.2035609	-0.1539417	-0.206602	-0.1511492

Fig. 2 (**a**) Graphical interpretation of how omics data are integrated for the analysis. (**b**) Representative input data for autoencoder models

500 nodes) and the hyperparameter we use are as follows; hyperbolic tangent (tanh) is used for activation function, stochastic gradient decent (SGD) is used as an optimizer, 0.001 and 0.0001 is set for L1 and L2 regularization parameters, 0.01 for learning rate (lr), a dropout rate and epochs are set at 0.5 and 150, respectively.

```
inp = Input(shape = (13767,))
encoded = Dense(500, activation = 'tanh',
          kernel_regularizer = regularizers.l2(10e-3),
          activity_regularizer = regularizers.l1(10e-4))
             (inp)
```

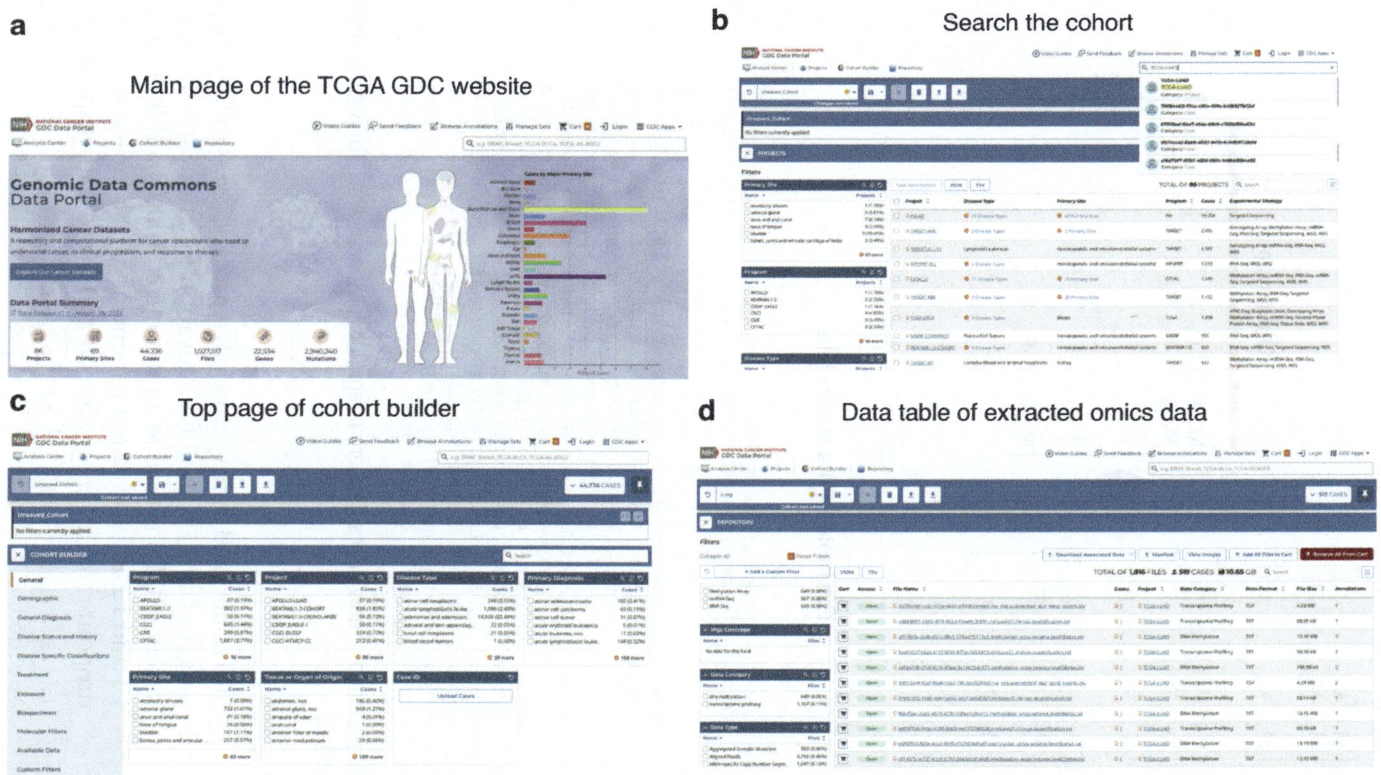

Fig. 3 The data portal of The Cancer Genome Atlas (TCGA). (**a**) Main page of the Genomic Data Common (GDC) data portal. (**b**) Finding the cohort of interest by entering keywords in the search box. (**c**) Main page of the cohort builder on the GDC data portal. (**d**) Representative data table of extracted RNA-seq, miRNA-seq, and DNA methylation omics data, filtered using the GDC data portal

```
encoded = Dropout(0.5)(encoded)
encoded = Dense(100, activation = 'tanh',
          kernel_regularizer = regularizers.l2(10e-3),
          activity_regularizer = regularizers.l1(10e-4))
(encoded)
encoded = Dropout(0.5)(encoded)
decoded = Dense(500, activation = 'tanh')(encoded)
decoded = Dense(13767, activation = 'tanh')(decoded)
autoencoder = Model(inp, decoded)
sgd = optimizers.SGD(lr = 0.01, decay = 1e-6, momentum =
0.9, Nesterov = True)
autoencoder.compile(optimizer = 'sgd',
           loss='mean_squared_error',
           metrics=['accuracy'])
history = autoencoder.fit(X, X,
            epochs = 150,
            batch_size = 1)            # 1 to 10 will
           work well.
```

Key Codes for the Autoencoder Model Using PyTorch

Here is the example code for PyTorch.

```
class AEDataset():
   def __init__(self, X, y):
     self.X = torch.Tensor(X.values)
     self.y = torch.Tensor(y.values)
   def __len__(self):
     return len(self.y)
   def __getitem__(self, idx):
     return self.X[idx], self.y[idx]
class Encoder(nn.Module):
   def __init__(self, input_size, encoding_dim):
     super().__init__()
     self.fc1 = nn.Linear(input_size, encoding_dim[0])
     self.pool1 = nn.Dropout(0.5)
     self.fc2 = nn.Linear(encoding_dim[0], encoding_
dim[1])
     self.pool2 = nn.Dropout(0.5)
   def forward(self, x):
     x = torch.tanh(self.fc1(x))
     x = self.pool1(x)
     x = torch.tanh(self.fc2(x))
     x = self.pool2(x)
     return x
class Decoder(nn.Module):
   def __init__(self, encoding_dim, input_size):
     super().__init__()
    self.fc3 = nn.Linear(encoding_dim[1],
encoding_dim[0])
     self.fc4 = nn.Linear(encoding_dim[0], input_size)
   def forward(self, x):
     x = torch.tanh(self.fc3(x))
     x = torch.tanh(self.fc4(x))
     return x
class AutoEncoder(nn.Module):
```

```
def __init__(self, input_size=13767, encoding_dim=
[500, 100]):
  super().__init__()
  self.encoder = Encoder(input_size, encoding_dim)
  self.decoder = Decoder(encoding_dim, input_size)
def forward(self, x):
  x = self.encoder(x)
  x = self.decoder(x)
  return x
```

3.5 Extraction of Survival-Associated Features from the Bottleneck Feature Space

1. In this step, clinically relevant features are extracted from a bottleneck feature space using Cox proportional hazards (CoxPH) model. The survival package in R is used to achieve this. The example code for the CoxPH analysis is as follows. Notably, statistical significance is set at $p < 0.05$.

```
# Code for CoxPH analysis.
coxph(formula = Surv(time, status) ~ Feature1, data
= df_bottleneck_feature)
```

2. If the bottlenecks feature space is 100, the CoxPH analysis should be performed 100 times. The looping code will accelerate this and minimize the effort of repeating runs.

4 Clustering

4.1 Optimal Number of Clusters

Perform cluster analysis using extracted features determined in Sect. 3.5. Hierarchical or unsupervised learning, such as *K*-means clustering method, or other methods can be applicable. Here, we use *K*-means clustering because despite the simplicity, it is vastly used and is practical in many biological data. Notably, *K*-means clustering is an unsupervised cluster analysis, and we first need to determine how many cluster numbers can be used for the analysis. From this aspect, Silhouette scores and the Calinski-Harabasz criterion can be used. After obtaining the best cluster number, do a *K*-means cluster analysis using the optimal number of K you determined.

Here, to estimate the optimized cluster number, we use Silhouette method, Calinski-Harabasz index, and Elbow plot. Each example code is as follows.

4.2 Silhouette Method

1. Below is an example code to obtain the optimal cluster number in Python.

```
from sklearn.datasets import make_blobs
from sklearn.cluster import KMeans
from sklearn.metrics import silhouette_samples,
silhouette_score
from sklearn import metrics
import matplotlib
import matplotlib.pyplot as plt
import matplotlib.cm as cm
```

```
import numpy as np
data1 = np.load("bottleneck_100.npy")
```

2. Extract and use features based on the CoxPH analysis. We use 25 features as an example.

```
data2 = data1[:,[2,6,12,15,19,25,29,35,36,38,39,40,
42,47,51,55,67,68,72,75,78,83,92,95,99]]
km = KMeans(n_clusters=10, # cluster number
     init='k-means++', # randomly select initial
cluster centroid
     n_init=10, # number of execution of K-means
with different initial centroid values
     max_iter=300, # maximum iteration of k-means
     tol=1e-04, # acceptable error for convergence
     random_state=0) # random state
y_km = km.fit_predict(data2)

cluster_labels = np.unique(y_km) # extract unique
element from the y_km
n_clusters=cluster_labels.shape[0] # return the
length of sequence
```

3. Estimate the Silhouette coefficient. The Euclidean distance is used for the estimation, and the Silhouette coefficient values for each cluster are shown in Fig. 4.

```
silhouette_vals = silhouette_samples(data2,y_
km,metric='euclidean')
y_ax_lower, y_ax_upper= 0,0
yticks = []

for i,c in enumerate(cluster_labels):
    c_silhouette_vals = silhouette_vals[y_km==c]
    c_silhouette_vals.sort()
    y_ax_upper += len(c_silhouette_vals)
    color = cm.jet(float(i)/n_clusters)
    plt.barh(range(y_ax_lower,y_ax_upper),
```

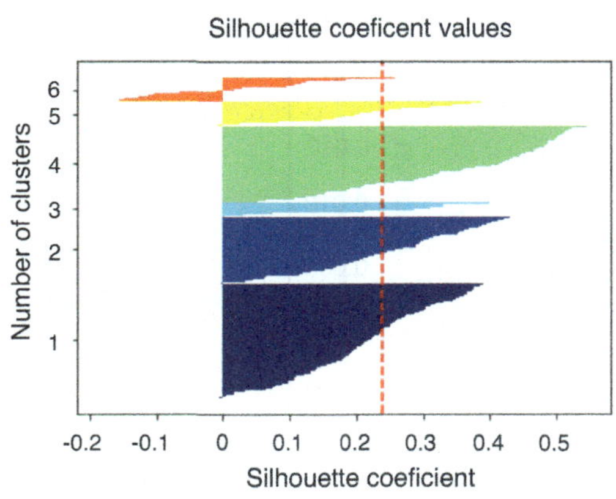

Fig. 4 Silhouette coefficient values visualized using the matplotlib package in Python

```
                    c_silhouette_vals,
                    height=1.0,
                    edgecolor='none',
                    color=color)
            yticks.append((y_ax_lower+y_ax_upper)/2)
            y_ax_lower += len(c_silhouette_vals)

        silhouette_avg = np.mean(silhouette_vals)
        plt.axvline(silhouette_avg,color="red",linestyle=
        "--")
        plt.yticks(yticks,cluster_labels + 1)       # plot
        cluster label
        plt.ylabel('Cluster')
        plt.xlabel('silhouette coefficient')
        plt.show()
```

4.3 Calinski-Harabasz Index

A larger value of the Calinski-Harabasz index indicates better clustering results. We show cluster number = 2 as an example. The analysis is repeated with orbital n_cluster until the maximum cluster number is analyzed.

```
kmeans_model = KMeans(n_clusters=2, random_state=1).
fit(data2).
labels = kmeans_model.labels_
metrics.calinski_harabaz_score(data2, labels)
print(metrics.calinski_harabaz_score(data2, labels)) #
print the result
```

4.4 Elbow Method

The Elbow method is used to determine the optimal number of clusters for a clustering algorithm, such as *K*-means. This method evaluates clustering performance (Fig. 5).

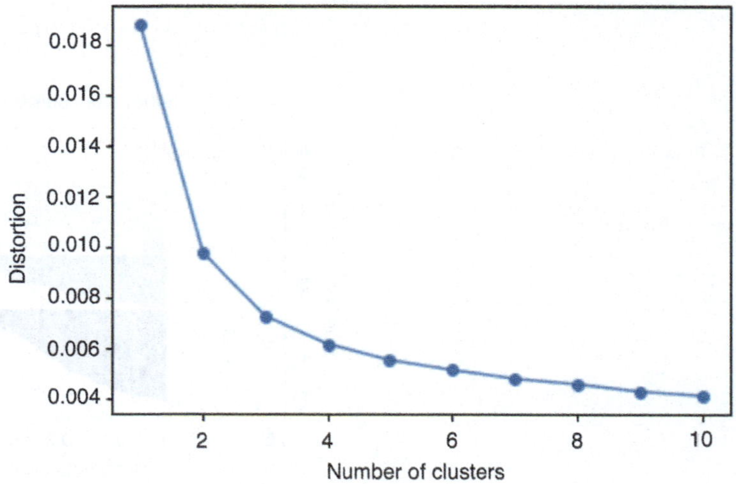

Fig. 5 Result of the Elbow method using an example dataset

```
distortions = []
for i in range(1,11):          # calculate the clusters
from 1 to 10
  km = KMeans(n_clusters=i,
        init='k-means++',       # select the initial
cluster center using k-means++ method
        n_init=10,
        max_iter=300,
        random_state=0)
  km.fit(data2)                # perform cluster analysis
  distortions.append(km.inertia_)

plt.plot(range(1,11),distortions,marker='o')
plt.xlabel('Number of clusters')
plt.ylabel('Distortion')
plt.show()
```

4.5 K-Means Clustering

Next, we perform K-means clustering with the cluster number determined in Sects. 4.2–4.4. We suggest using Python code because the autoencoder was implemented using Python. Therefore, sequential analysis is applicable. However, if one prefers to run codes in R, that will also apply.

Python Code

1. Import required packages.

```
import numpy as np
import pandas as pd
from sklearn.cluster import KMeans
from sklearn.metrics import silhouette_samples,
silhouette_score
from sklearn.datasets import make_blobs
import matplotlib
import matplotlib.pyplot as plt
import matplotlib.cm as cm
from sklearn.manifold import tSNE
```

2. Import your data for analysis.

```
data1 = np.load("bottleneck_100.npy")
```

3. The features are extracted based on the CoxPH analysis. Here, we extract 25 features as an example.

```
data2 = data1[:,[2,6,12,15,19,25,29,35,36,38,39,40,
42,47,51,55,67,68,72,75,78,83,92,95,99]]
```

4. Perform K-means cluster analysis. K = 2 is used this time based on the results from the previous Sects. (4.2–4.4).

```
kmeans = KMeans(n_clusters=2, max_iter=500, tol=
1e-04)
kmeans.fit(data2)
mylabel = kmeans.labels_
print(mylabel)
```

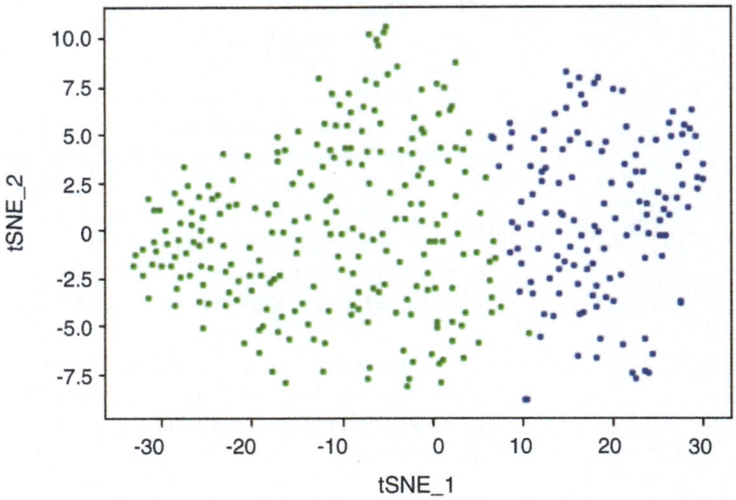

Fig. 6 Representative plot of the bottleneck feature space of 100 dimensions using tSNE

5. Visualization of the result using t-distributed stochastic neighbor embedding (tSNE) (Fig. 6).

```
X_reduced = TSNE(n_components=2, random_state=0).
fit_transform(data2)
X0 = X_reduced[mylabel == 0]
X1 = X_reduced[mylabel == 1]

plt.scatter(X0[:, 0], X0[:, 1], s=5, vmin=0.0001,
vmax=0.0001, color='green')
plt.scatter(X1[:, 0], X1[:, 1], s=5, vmin=0.0001,
vmax=0.0001, color='blue')
plt.grid()
plt.show()
```

Notably, the above-mentioned plot is a representative plot. One needs a further analysis and needs to plot the result using the extracted features by Cox-PH model in the study.

Example Code in R

1. Alternatively, R can be used for cluster analysis. An example code is shown below.

```
data1 = read.csv("Example_dataset.csv")
# Make an empty vector that we populate via our loop.
# WSS stands for the within-cluster sum of squared
errors for different values of K, and the result is
visible as an Elbow plot.
set.seed(6)
wcss = vector()
```

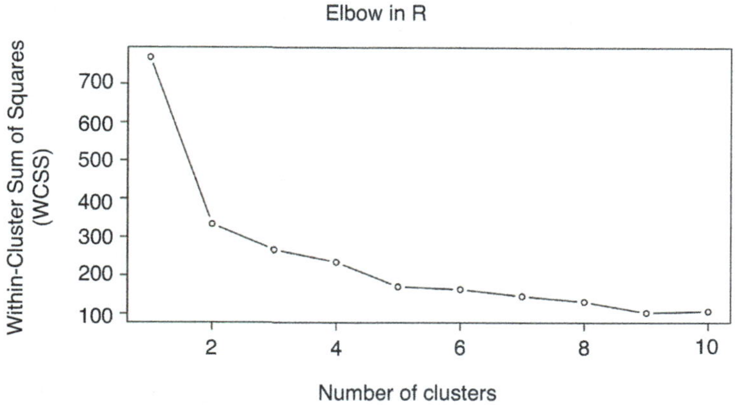

Fig. 7 Representative Elbow plot in R

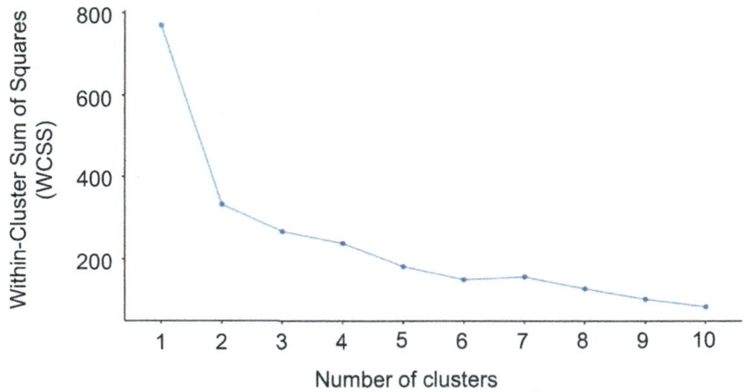

Fig. 8 Representative Elbow plot using a different code in R

2. For our 10 clusters, we start with the below code including visualization (Figs. 7 and 8).

```
for (i in 1:10) wcss[i] <- sum(kmeans(data1, i)
$withinss)
plot(1:10,
    wcss,
    type = 'b', # for lines and points
    main = paste('The Elbow Method'),
    xlab = 'Number of clusters',
    ylab = 'WCSS') # WCSS stands for within-cluster
sum of squares
fviz_nbclust(data1, kmeans, method="wss")
```

3. The Elbow plot can be plotted using ggplot2 package. Use map_dbl to run many models with varying values of K.

```
tot_withinss <- map_dbl(1:10, function(k){
  model <- kmeans(x = data1, centers = k)
  model$tot.withinss
})
```

4. Generate a data frame containing both K and tot_withinss.

```
elbow_df <- data.frame(
  k = 1:10,
  tot_withinss = tot_withinss
)
```

5. Plot the elbow plot with another code (Fig. 9).

```
ggplot(elbow_df, aes(x = k, y = tot_withinss)) +
  geom_line() + geom_point()+
  scale_x_continuous(breaks = 1:10)+
  them_bw()
```

6. Here is a Silhouette index in R (Fig. 10).

```
fviz_nbclust(data1, kmeans, method='silhouette')
```

7. The Gap Statics method calculates the goodness-of-fit of a clustering measure. Gap Statistics is used to compare the total within-cluster variations for different values of *K* with their expected values. The optimal number of clusters estimated using this method is the value that maximizes the Gap Statistics (Fig. 11).

```
set.seed(123)
gap_stat <- clusGap(data1, FUN = kmeans, nstart =
25,
               K.max = 10, B = 50)
fviz_gap_stat(gap_stat)
```

8. Here is the Caliniski-Harabasz index.

```
set.seed(3)
km2 <- kmeans(data1, 2)
km3 <- kmeans(data1, 3)
km4 <- kmeans(data1, 4)
```

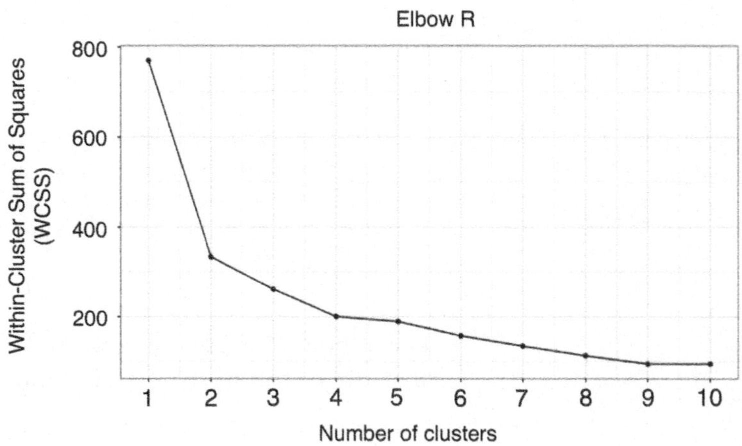

Fig. 9 Another representative Elbow plot with a different code and visualization in R

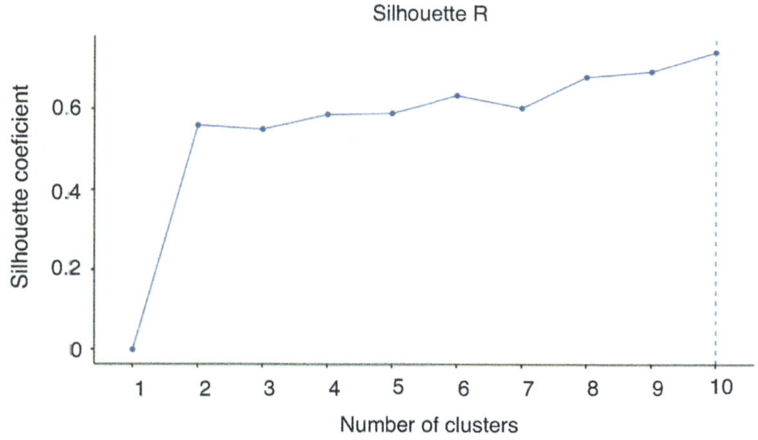

Fig. 10 Representative plot of Silhouette coefficient score in R

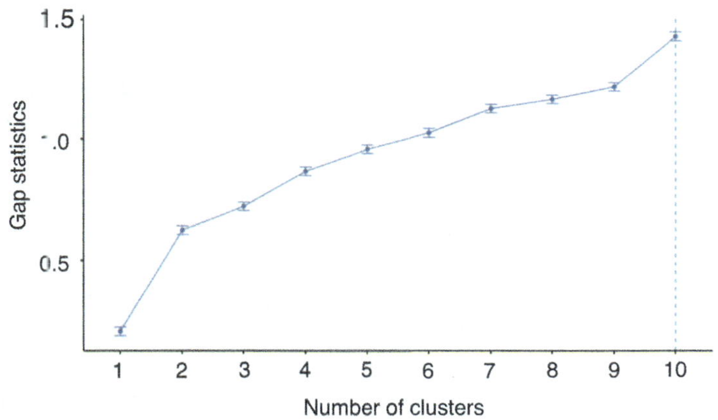

Fig. 11 Representative plot of gap statistics

```
round(calinhara(data1, km2$cluster), digits=2)
# [1] 333.33 as an example score 1

round(calinhara(data1, km3$cluster), digits=2)
#[1] 222.22 as an example score 2

round(calinhara(data1, km4$cluster), digits=2)
#[1] 111.11 as an example score 3
```

9. Finally, plot the clustering result with the best cluster number of *K*. Set a constant starting point for reproducibility. Visualization is performed using fviz_cluster function (Fig. 12).

```
d_km <- kmeans(data1, centers = 2, nstart=25)
fviz_cluster(d_km, data = data1, geom="point")
```

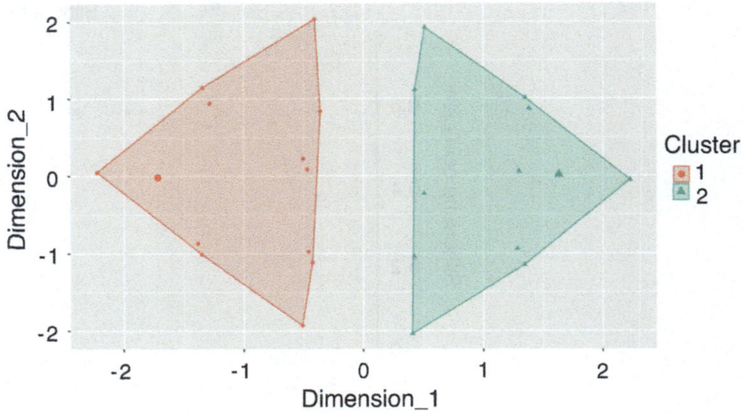

Fig. 12 Representative plot of *K*-means clustering (*K*=2) using an example dataset

Notably, there are many codes for estimating the optimal cluster number, and for visualizing scripts and packages in R. There is nothing wrong with working with one's own code to compute the analysis. You can make decisions based on what you wish to address.

5 Kaplan–Meier Survival Analysis

To examine whether the obtained cluster can achieve patient stratification, perform a Kaplan–Meier survival analysis. Python users can use lifeline packages for survival analyses. For R users, the survival package is the first choice for Kaplan–Meier analysis. Depending on the dataset, the Gehan-Wilcoxon test may be applicable for survival analysis using the survival package.

6 Differentially Expressing Gene Analysis

From Sects. 3–5, we explained how to collect the publicly available dataset that can be used for the analysis and how to extract the features that are associated with patient outcomes. If patient stratification is successfully achieved in one's cohort, the next step would be to investigate the molecular mechanisms underlying the study. In general, differentially expressing gene (DEG) analysis is performed for this purpose in high and low-risk subgroups.

DEG analysis is widely used in molecular biology. This analysis aims to identify the DEGs whose expression levels are significantly up-regulated or down-regulated between the groups (healthy vs. diseased) or conditions (treated vs. non-treated), for instance. The advantages of performing DEG analysis are as follows: (1) some

DEGs could be biomarkers or potential therapeutic targets, which enhance the attractiveness of performing DEG analysis, particularly in medical science; and (2) downstream analysis typically over-representative analysis (ORA) using DEGs reveals enriched pathways or provides insight into molecular mechanisms.

The standard methodology is to use the DESeq2 package with RNA-seq count data, and visualize DEGs as a volcano plot [34]. Notably, genes that meet the threshold of log2 Fold Change (FC) > 1 or log2 FC < −1 and fold discovery rate (FDR) < 0.05 are considered DEGs. edgeR is another reliable package for DEG analysis in R, and PyDESeq2 is available to Python users [35, 36]. Other compatible pipelines are also available for DEG analysis [37, 38].

7 Molecular Mechanisms Related to the Genes Identified

DEGs can be further analyzed to elucidate their roles in pathways by performing ORA, such as Gene Ontology (GO) analysis, Gene Set Enrichment Analysis (GSEA), and Kyoto Encyclopedia of Genes and Genomes (KEGG). ORA enables the elucidation of the molecular mechanisms in the cohort. Notably, previously published literature provides insights into how ORA can be used to profile gene expression and interpret outcomes. [39]. These sequential analyses of DEG analysis, GESA, and pathway analysis following visualization using Cytoscape are well pipelined.

8 Summary

There are several notes regarding the generality of the results. First, in this chapter, we filter the CoxPH model to extract features associated with patient survival. Theoretically, other filters can be applied to extract the features of interest. Second, we focused on overall survival (OS); however, if other clinical information, such as disease-free survival (DFS) and progression-free survival (PFS), is available, patient stratification could be performed based on DFS or PFS. Third, a classifier could be developed for predicting patient outcomes [30, 31]. In this case, a systematic approach using a grid search to determine the hyperparameters is suggested. An open-source, user-friendly, automated ML workflows, PyCaret is one option to minimize the effort required to screen reliable ML model (https://pycaret.gitbook.io/docs). Notably, we demonstrated that second-level cluster analysis reinforced the correlation associated with patient OS [40]. This is an attractive option if users encounter poor or need to improve them.

Regarding dimension reduction using the autoencoder model, the autoencoder can run independently for each omics dataset and can assemble the result later instead of using integrated input multi-omics data [31]. This strategy could be useful in some cases because the autoencoder is developed for each omics data with different hyperparameters to optimize them. However, a disadvantage of this pipeline is the multiple developments and executions required by the autoencoder.

Acknowledgments

This work was supported by BRIDGE (programs for bridging the gap between R&D and the ideal society (Society 5.0) and generating economic and social value), the AMED Innovative Cancer Medical Practice Research Project (Grant number: JP22ck0106643) to R.H.

Conflict of Interest The authors have no conflicts of interest to declare that are relevant to the content of this chapter.

References

1. Biomarkers Definitions Working G (2001) Biomarkers and surrogate endpoints: preferred definitions and conceptual framework. Clin Pharmacol Ther 69(3):89–95. https://doi.org/10.1067/mcp.2001.113989
2. Strimbu K, Tavel JA (2010) What are biomarkers?. Curr Opin HIV AIDS 5(6):463–466. https://doi.org/10.1097/COH.0b013e32833ed177
3. Srinivas PR, Kramer BS, Srivastava S (2001) Trends in biomarker research for cancer detection. Lancet Oncol 2(11):698–704. https://doi.org/10.1016/S1470-2045(01)00560-5
4. Passaro A et al (2024) Cancer biomarkers: emerging trends and clinical implications for personalized treatment. Cell 187(7):1617–1635. https://doi.org/10.1016/j.cell.2024.02.041
5. Goossens N, Nakagawa S, Sun X, Hoshida Y (2015) Cancer biomarker discovery and validation. Transl Cancer Res 4(3):256–269. https://doi.org/10.3978/j.issn.2218-676X.2015.06.04
6. Asada K et al (2021) Integrated analysis of whole genome and epigenome data using machine learning technology: toward the establishment of precision oncology. Front Oncol 11:666937. https://doi.org/10.3389/fonc.2021.666937
7. Risch N, Merikangas K (1996) The future of genetic studies of complex human diseases. Science 273(5281):1516–1517. https://doi.org/10.1126/science.273.5281.1516
8. Collins FS, Guyer MS, Charkravarti A (1997) Variations on a theme: cataloging human DNA sequence variation. Science 278(5343):1580–1581. https://doi.org/10.1126/science.278.5343.1580
9. Lander ES (1996) The new genomics: global views of biology. Science 274(5287):536–539. https://doi.org/10.1126/science.274.5287.536
10. Nguyen B et al (2022) Genomic characterization of metastatic patterns from prospective clinical sequencing of 25,000 patients. Cell 185(3):563–575.e511. https://doi.org/10.1016/j.cell.2022.01.003
11. Matsubara J et al (2023) First-line genomic profiling in previously untreated advanced solid tumors for identification of targeted therapy opportunities. JAMA Netw Open 6(7):e2323336. https://doi.org/10.1001/jamanetworkopen.2023.23336
12. Lin Y et al (2020) Genomic and transcriptomic alterations associated with drug vulnerabilities and prognosis in adenocarcinoma at the gastroesophageal junction. Nat Commun 11(1):6091. https://doi.org/10.1038/s41467-020-19949-6
13. Sakamoto T et al (2023) Biomarker testing in patients with unresectable advanced or recurrent non-small cell lung cancer. JAMA Netw Open 6(12):e2347700. https://doi.org/10.1001/jamanetworkopen.2023.47700
14. Kaneko S et al (2024) Mechanism of ERBB2 gene overexpression by the formation of super-enhancer with genomic structural abnormalities in lung adenocarcinoma without clinically actionable genetic alterations. Mol Cancer 23(1):126. https://doi.org/10.1186/s12943-024-02035-6
15. Fehrmann RS et al (2011) Trans-eQTLs reveal that independent genetic variants associated with a complex phenotype converge on

intermediate genes, with a major role for the HLA. PLoS Genet 7(8):e1002197. https://doi.org/10.1371/journal.pgen.1002197
16. Qiu S et al (2023) Small molecule metabolites: discovery of biomarkers and therapeutic targets. Signal Transduct Target Ther 8(1):132. https://doi.org/10.1038/s41392-023-01399-3
17. Karjalainen MK et al (2024) Genome-wide characterization of circulating metabolic biomarkers. Nature 628(8006):130–138. https://doi.org/10.1038/s41586-024-07148-y
18. Jaisson S, Pietrement C, Gillery P (2011) Carbamylation-derived products: bioactive compounds and potential biomarkers in chronic renal failure and atherosclerosis. Clin Chem 57(11):1499–1505. https://doi.org/10.1373/clinchem.2011.163188
19. Scherzer CR et al (2007) Molecular markers of early Parkinson's disease based on gene expression in blood. Proc Natl Acad Sci U S A 104(3):955–960. https://doi org/10.1073/pnas.0610204104
20. Su K, et al (2021) Pan-cancer analysis of pathway-based gene expression pattern at the individual level reveals biomarkers of clinical prognosis. Cell Rep Methods 1(4), 100050. https://doi.org/10.1016/j.crmeth.2021.100050
21. Demircioglu D et al (2019) A pan-cancer transcriptome analysis reveals pervasive regulation through alternative promoters. Cell 178(6):1465–1477.e1417. https://doi.org/10.1016/j.cell.2019.08.018
22. Budczies J et al (2024) Tumour mutational burden: clinical utility, challenges and emerging improvements. Nat Rev Clin Oncol 21(10):725–742. https://doi.org/10.1038/s41571-024-00932-9
23. van de Vijver MJ et al (2002) A gene-expression signature as a predictor of survival in breast cancer. N Engl J Med 347(25):1999–2009. https://doi.org/10.1056/NEJMoa021967
24. Shi X et al (2024) Mechanism insights and therapeutic intervention of tumor metastasis: latest developments and perspectives. Signal Transduct Target Ther 9(1):192. https://doi.org/10.1038/s41392-024-01885-2
25. Zhang Y, Chen F, Creighton CJ (2023) Pan-cancer molecular subtypes of metastasis reveal distinct and evolving transcriptional programs. Cell Rep Med 4(2):100932 https://doi.org/10.1016/j.xcrm.2023.100932
26. Chawla S et al (2022) Gene expression based inference of cancer drug sensitivity. Nat Commun 13(1):5680. https://doi.org/10.1038/s41467-022-33291-z
27. Jia P et al (2021) Deep generative neural network for accurate drug response imputation. Nat Commun 12(1):1740. https://doi.org/10.1038/s41467-021-21997-5
28. Sawyers CL (2008) The cancer biomarker problem. Nature 452(7187):548–552. https://doi.org/10.1038/nature06913
29. Vogelstein B et al (2013) Cancer genome landscapes. Science 339(6127):1546–1558. https://doi.org/10.1126/science.1235122
30. Asada K, et al (2020) Uncovering prognosis-related genes and pathways by multi-omics analysis in lung cancer. Biomolecules 10(4):524. https://doi.org/10.3390/biom10040524
31. Takahashi S, et al (2020) Predicting deep learning based multi-omics parallel integration survival subtypes in lung cancer using reverse phase protein array data. Biomolecules 10(10):1460. https://doi.org/10.3390/biom10101460
32. Wei L et al (2018) TCGA-assembler 2: software pipeline for retrieval and processing of TCGA/CPTAC data. Bioinformatics 34(9):1615–1617. https://doi.org/10.1093/bioinformatics/btx812
33. Zhu Y, Qiu P, Ji Y (2014) TCGA-assembler: open-source software for retrieving and processing TCGA data. Nat Methods 11(6):599–600. https://doi.org/10.1038/nmeth.2956
34. Love MI, Huber W, Anders S (2014) Moderated estimation of fold change and dispersion for RNA-seq data with DESeq2. Genome Biol 15(12):550. https://doi.org/10.1186/s13059-014-0550-8
35. Robinson MD, McCarthy DJ, Smyth GK (2010) edgeR: a bioconductor package for differential expression analysis of digital gene expression data. Bioinformatics 26(1):139–140. https://doi.org/10.1093/bioinformatics/btp616
36. Muzellec B, Telenczuk M, Cabeli V, Andreux M (2023) PyDESeq2: a Python package for bulk RNA-seq differential expression analysis. Bioinformatics 39(9), btad547. https://doi.org/10.1093/bioinformatics/btad547
37. Nagai LAE, Lee S, Nakato R (2024) Protocol for identifying differentially expressed genes using the RumBall RNA-seq analysis platform. STAR Protoc 5(1):102926. https://doi.org/10.1016/j.xpro.2024.102926
38. Costa-Silva J, Domingues D, Lopes FM (2017) RNA-Seq differential expression analysis: an extended review and a software tool. PLoS One 12(12):e0190152. https://doi.org/10.1371/journal.pone.0190152
39. Reimand J et al (2019) Pathway enrichment analysis and visualization of omics data using g:Profiler, GSEA, Cytoscape and EnrichmentMap. Nat Protoc 14(2):482–517. https://doi.org/10.1038/s41596-018-0103-9
40. Asada K et al (2024) Multi-omics and clustering analyses reveal the mechanisms underlying unmet needs for patients with lung adenocarcinoma and identify potential therapeutic targets. Mol Cancer 23(1):182. https://doi.org/10.1186/s12943-024-02093-w

Chapter 2

Drug Discovery from Gene Expression/Gene Regulation

Yi Cong and Toshinori Endo

Abstract

Gene expression and gene regulation play critical roles in understanding disease mechanisms, identifying therapeutic targets, and guiding drug discovery. Advances in high-throughput sequencing technologies, such as next-generation sequencing (NGS) and single-cell RNA sequencing (scRNA-seq), have enabled comprehensive profiling of gene expression across diverse biological contexts. Computational methods, including machine learning (ML) and deep learning (DL), have further revolutionized transcriptomic and regulatory analyses by uncovering complex gene interactions and predicting disease-associated regulatory networks. This chapter explores the integration of AI-driven approaches in gene expression analysis, focusing on differential expression analysis, clustering techniques, and gene regulatory network (GRN) inference. We discuss the role of dimensionality reduction and unsupervised learning in identifying disease subtypes and patient stratification, as well as how single-cell transcriptomics enhances our understanding of cellular heterogeneity in drug response and resistance. Furthermore, we examine network-based methodologies, highlighting the application of AI and ML in reconstructing GRNs, prioritizing regulatory targets, and facilitating drug repositioning. The emerging field of AI-assisted drug repositioning is also covered, with an emphasis on leveraging transcriptomic signatures and network-based inference to repurpose existing drugs for novel therapeutic applications. By integrating multiomics data and employing explainable AI frameworks, researchers can refine precision medicine strategies and accelerate the drug discovery process. Finally, we address current challenges in AI-driven gene analysis, including data complexity, model interpretability, and the integration of multiomics datasets. Future directions include advances in large language models (LLMs), spatial transcriptomics, and quantum-enhanced AI for predictive modeling. The convergence of AI, high-throughput sequencing, and network-based approaches promises to reshape biomedical research and optimize drug discovery pipelines for improved clinical outcomes.

Keywords Gene expression, Gene regulation, AI, Machine learning, NGS, scRNA-seq, GRNs, Drug repositioning, Precision medicine, Multiomics

1 Introduction

Advances in biomedical research have been significantly driven by high-throughput omics technologies, which provide a comprehensive view of molecular processes underlying health and disease. These technologies rely on several advanced methods and key components, critical to grasp the complex biological systems. At the center of these

Y-h Taguchi (ed.), *AI/ML-Driven Gene Analysis*, Methods in Molecular Biology, vol. 3037,
https://doi.org/10.1007/978-1-0716-5284-8_2,

technologies are data generation platforms, that enable the rapid and large-scale collection of data on different molecular entities, providing a detailed view of the biological landscape.

Among these, next-generation sequencing (NGS) has emerged as a transformative technology, enabling automated, massively parallel sequencing of vast amounts of short DNA reads. Despite the short lengths of read, NGS allows for the rapid and high-throughput acquisition of genomic data, a breakthrough in biological research. This ability to generate and analyze extensive datasets has revolutionized genomics, transcriptomics, epigenomics, and proteomics, offering unprecedented insights into gene function and regulation.

In genomics, NGS has enabled rapid sequencing of entire genomes, allowing researchers to identify genetic variations and explore evolutionary relationships [1]. However, since NGS generates vast amounts of short DNA reads, reconstructing complete genome sequences requires sequence assembly algorithms. Among these, graph-based approaches, particularly de Bruijn graphs, have been widely used to efficiently assemble fragmented short reads into contiguous genome sequences [2]. In addition, mapping NGS-generated sequences to reference genomes enables the identification of genetic variations, which has significantly advanced population genetics by facilitating large-scale analyses of genetic diversity, disease susceptibility, and evolutionary relationships. These aligned sequences also allow for population genetic analyses, selection tests, and the identification of genetic markers for further genetic mapping studies [3].

In transcriptomics, which focuses on gene expressions, RNA sequencing (RNA-Seq) utilizes NGS to profile gene expression profiles by first extracting RNA and performing reverse transcription before sequencing the RNA molecules and mapping them to the genome to generate gene expression profiles [4, 5]. This technique is crucial for quantifying gene expression levels, identifying alternative splicing events, and investigating gene regulatory networks. Single-cell RNA sequencing (scRNA-seq) extends this approach by enabling the analysis of gene expression at single-cell resolution. Early methods, such as the Tang method [6], relied on manual cell isolation followed by reverse transcription and sequencing. More recent high-throughput techniques, including Drop-seq [7] and inDrop [8], utilize droplet microfluidics to encapsulate individual cells, allowing large-scale single-cell transcriptomic analysis.

Gene regulation and chromatin accessibility studies examine chemical modifications to DNA and chromatin structures that influence gene expression without altering the DNA sequence, the genetic information. Chromatin immunoprecipitation followed by sequencing (ChIP-Seq) utilizes immunoprecipitation to selectively capture DNA fragments bound by specific proteins, such as transcription factors and histones, enabling the identification of regulatory sites and histone modifications [9]. Assay for Transposase-Accessible Chromatin using sequencing (ATAC-Seq) employs transposase to cleave open chromatin regions, enabling the identification of accessible regulatory elements and chromatin landscapes at high resolution. Its single-cell variant (scATAC-seq) extends this approach to individual cells, facilitating the study of cellular heterogeneity in gene regulation [10, 11].

Proteomics focuses on the large-scale study of proteins, their modifications, and interactions. Mass spectrometry is the primary technology used for protein identification and quantification, providing crucial insights into cellular signaling pathways and disease mechanisms. Ribosome profiling (Ribo-seq), a complementary approach, enables the direct measurement of translating mRNA fragments, offering a high-resolution view of protein synthesis and translational regulation. By sequencing ribosome-protected mRNA fragments, Ribo-seq allows researchers to study translation dynamics and identify regulatory elements influencing protein expression [12].

Metabolomics, the study of small molecules involved in metabolism, relies on techniques such as nuclear magnetic resonance (NMR) spectroscopy to analyze metabolic changes in biological system [13]. These methodologies allow researchers to explore metabolic pathways, assess physiological conditions, and identify disease biomarkers.

Ill expression of genes can cause disease phenotypes Identification of differentially expressed genes (DEGs) suggests such disease specific alteration of gene expressions, providing biomarkers for the diagnosis and prognosis. For instance, the overexpression of *MYC*, an oncogene and the loss of *TP53*, a tumor suppressor gene have been obeserved in various cancers. It has been shown that their combination is greatly accelerated tumorigenesis like behavior in vitro [14]. Single-cell analyses further uncovered the heterogeneity within tumor microenvironments, highlighting distinct immune cell states and their roles in cancer progression. Beyond cancer, altered gene expression are also implicated in neurodegenerative disorders, cardiovascular diseases, and metabolic syndromes, emphasizing the broad applicability of transcriptomic studies in medicine.

It is critical to identify the driver genes, which directly contribute to disease initiation and progression, from passenger genes, which are secondarily or incidentally expressed. Identifying driver genes within regulatory pathways provides critical targets for therapeutic intervention. For example, dysregulation of the Wnt signaling pathway has been implicated in multiple cancers, making it a focus of drug discovery efforts. The Wnt/β-catenin pathway is abnormally activated in most lung cancer tissues and is considered to be an accelerator of carcinogenesis and lung cancer progression [15]. Gene regulatory networks (GRNs) play a central role in mapping these regulatory pathways, enabling the identification of key transcription factors and regulatory hubs that could serve as potential drug targets.

Artificial intelligence (AI) and machine learning (ML) have revolutionized the analysis of gene expression and regulatory data. These technologies enable the identification of DEGs, prediction of regulatory interactions, and discovery of novel drug targets [16, 17]. For example, supervised learning algorithms like Random Forest and Support Vector Machines are employed for feature selection and classification, while unsupervised methods such as clustering and dimensionality reduction aid in uncovering patterns in complex datasets [16, 18]. Deep learning approaches, including Convolutional Neural Networks (CNNs), Deep Neural Networks (DNNs), Graph Neural Networks (GNNs), and Autoencoders, further enhance our ability to model intricate gene regulatory interactions and predict disease-specific regulatory networks [19, 20]. By integrating multiomics data, AI/ML frameworks provide a comprehensive understanding of disease mechanisms, paving the way for precision medicine and targeted drug discovery.

2 Gene Expression Data in Drug Discovery

Clustering gene expression data helps classify diseases into molecular subtypes, paving the way for personalized treatment strategies [21, 22]. Drug repositioning approaches leverage gene expression similarities to identify existing drugs with potential new applications, accelerating drug development, and reducing costs [23–25]. The following sections explore the role of differential expression analysis, gene expression clustering, and drug repositioning in advancing drug discovery.

2.1 Differential Expression Analysis in Drug Discovery

Differential expression analysis (DEA) is a fundamental approach in transcriptomics to identify genes that exhibit statistically significant expression changes between different biological conditions, such as disease versus healthy states or drug-treated versus untreated samples. DEGs are crucial for understanding disease mechanisms, discovering biomarkers, and identifying potential drug targets.

The identification of DEGs typically involves statistical methods that compare gene expression levels across conditions. RNA-Seq and microarray technologies provide genome-wide expression profiles, which are analyzed using tools, such as DESeq2 and edgeR, which apply negative binomial distribution models to detect significant expression changes [26]. Other methods, such as limma, are optimized for microarray and RNA-seq data [27]. These techniques take factors into account including read depth, normalization parameters, and statistical significance.

Interpretation of DEGs requires functional annotation to determine their biological context. Gene Ontology (GO) analysis [28] utilize the hierarchical controlled vocabulary to provide insights into the molecular functions, biological processes, and cellular components associated with DEGs, while pathway analysis such as the Kyoto Encyclopedia of Genes and Genomes (KEGG) and Reactome can reveal enriched signaling pathways related to specific diseases or drug responses [29, 30].

Furthermore, transcriptomic responses to drug treatments allow researchers to assess drug efficacy and mechanism of action. Comparative analysis of DEGs before and after drug treatment can highlight the pathways modulated by the drug, aiding in drug repositioning strategies. By integrating DEA with high-throughput screening and AI-driven approaches, novel therapeutic strategies can be developed for personalized medicine.

2.2 Clustering Gene Expression Pattern Clustering for Drug Discovery

Differential gene expression patterns reflect disease subtypes, varied drug response essential for uncovering novel therapeutic targets. The extremely high-dimensional nature of transcriptomic data consisting of expression levels of tens of thousands of genes in a genome, however, poses challenges for traditional analytical methods [31]. That is extremely high standard error, and the inherent redundancy of peripheral gene expression derived from gene regulatory network [32, 33]. Clustering techniques enable the identification of biologically relevant gene expression patterns, while dimensionality reduction methods facilitate data interpretation by reducing noise and enhancing visualization [32]. This section explores how these computational approaches contribute to disease classification, patient stratification, and single-cell transcriptomics, ultimately aiding drug discovery and precision medicine.

Dimensionality Reduction and Clustering in Transcriptomic Data

Dimensionality reduction and clustering methods provide a robust framework for analyzing high-dimensional transcriptomic data in drug discovery. By simplifying complex datasets while preserving essential biological variations, dimensionality reduction techniques such as principal component analysis (PCA) [34, 35], t-distributed stochastic neighbor embedding (t-SNE) [36], and uniform manifold approximation and projection (UMAP) [37] enhance clustering efficiency and facilitate data interpretation. These methods help reduce noise, reveal hidden structures, and improve the identification of biologically relevant clusters.

Unsupervised clustering algorithms, including k-means [38] and hierarchical clustering [39], further refine the classification of transcriptomic data. Hierarchical clustering organizes data in a tree-like structure, revealing sample relationships, while k-means partitions datasets into k clusters, optimizing intragroup homogeneity. The integration of dimensionality reduction with clustering enhances accuracy and robustness, providing a more comprehensive understanding of gene expression patterns in precision medicine.

Unsupervised Clustering for Disease Classification and Patient Stratification

Clustering methods have been instrumental in disease classification and patient stratification, particularly in drug discovery applications taking advantage in the absence of training data. By identifying molecular signatures associated with disease progression and therapeutic response, clustering-based approaches enable the classification of patient subpopulations for personalized treatment strategies. For example, hierarchical clustering has been widely used to identify molecular subtypes across various diseases. In oncology, transcriptomic clustering has revealed distinct subtypes of breast cancer, each associated with specific prognoses and treatment responses [40]. Similarly, gene expression clustering has been applied in neurodegenerative diseases and autoimmune disorders to identify patient subgroups with differential responses to therapeutic agents [41–43]. Such applications demonstrate the power of unsupervised clustering in guiding targeted treatment approaches.

Beyond disease classification, clustering techniques also play a critical role in predicting drug response and optimizing patient stratification. Tumeh et al. demonstrated that transcriptomic clustering of tumor microenvironments could predict responses to PD-1 blockade therapy, revealing a subset of patients with high pre-existing T-cell infiltration who exhibited enhanced therapeutic outcomes [44]. These findings highlight the potential of clustering-based methodologies in immunotherapy and precision medicine by enabling the selection of patients most likely to benefit from treatment.

Single-Cell Clustering for Drug Response Analysis

Unprecedented insights had been provided by single-cell RNA sequencing (scRNA-Seq) into cellular heterogeneity, offering a refined approach to drug discovery through cell-type-specific clustering. Classification of individual cells based on their transcriptomic profiles, researchers can recognize previously uncharacterized subpopulations that contributed disease progression and drug resistance [45, 46].

Xia et al. applied Seurat-based clustering to breast cancer tumor samples, identifying a tissue-resident macrophage (RTM) subpopulation associated with differential responses to immune checkpoint therapy (ICT). By employing PCA for dimensionality reduction followed by t-SNE and UMAP visualization, they extracted a 25-gene expression signature (RTM.Sig) predictive of ICT efficacy, demonstrating the potential of single-cell clustering in guiding immunotherapy strategies [47].

Clustering-based approaches have also been instrumental in elucidating mechanisms of drug resistance. Foutadakis et al. utilized scRNA-Seq to examine chemotherapy-resistant triple-negative breast cancer (TNBC) cells, uncovering transcriptional adaptations linked to epithelial-mesenchymal transition (EMT). By clustering drug-resistant and drug-sensitive populations, they identified key regulatory networks contributing to acquired resistance, offering potential therapeutic targets for overcoming treatment failure [48].

Furthermore, advanced computational approaches have significantly improved single-cell clustering for drug response prediction. Chen et al. introduced scziDesk, an algorithm integrating deep autoencoders with soft k-means clustering, enhancing the identification of subtle drug-induced transcriptional changes in heterogeneous tumor samples [49]. Such advancements facilitate the characterization of drug-sensitive and resistant cell populations, enabling the design of more effective therapeutic interventions.

A comparative evaluation by Freytag et al. assessed multiple scRNA-Seq clustering methodologies, including Seurat, Cell Ranger, CIDR, RaceID, RaceID2, RCA, SC3, SIMLR, TSCAN, ascend, countClust, and scran. The study demonstrated that the choice of clustering algorithm significantly impacts the resolution of cellular heterogeneity and drug response prediction, underscoring the importance of method selection in transcriptomic studies [50]. By leveraging the most suitable clustering approaches, researchers can optimize drug discovery pipelines and refine precision medicine strategies.

3 Gene Regulation and Network Analysis

Gene regulation is a fundamental process governing cellular behavior, proliferation and differentiation, involving intricate interactions between transcription factors (TFs), noncoding RNAs, and epigenetic modifications. Additionally, post-transcriptional and post-translational regulatory mechanisms, including RNA and protein degradation, play a crucial role in maintaining cellular homeostasis [51]. GRNs serve as a systematic framework to model these interactions, enabling the identification of key regulatory elements that influence disease phenotypes and therapeutic responses [52]. The study of GRNs is instrumental in understanding disease mechanisms, identifying biomarkers, and discovering potential drug targets.

3.1 GRN Inference

GRNs provide a systematic representation of transcriptional regulation, capturing interactions between TFs and their target genes. Understanding these regulatory mechanisms is critical for elucidating disease pathways and identifying potential drug targets. The inference of GRNs can be approached experimentally or computationally, each offering unique advantages and challenges.

High-Throughput Experimental Approaches

ChIP-Seq and ATAC-Seq are widely used techniques for mapping regulatory interactions at the genome-wide level. ChIP-Seq enables the identification of TF-binding sites and histone modifications, offering insights into regulatory elements that influence gene expression [53]. In contrast, ATAC-Seq assesses chromatin accessibility, revealing regulatory regions that may be subject to dynamic control across different cellular conditions.

MicroRNA (miRNA)-mediated regulation constitutes another layer of gene expression control, influencing post-transcriptional gene silencing. Friedman et al. demonstrated that a substantial proportion of mammalian mRNAs are conserved targets of miRNAs, highlighting the importance of integrating miRNA interactions into GRN models to capture the full spectrum of regulatory influences [54].

Computational Approaches

Inference of GRNs from high-throughput transcriptomic data has been facilitated by machine learning-based methods such as Algorithm for the Reconstruction of Accurate Cellular Networks (ARACNe) and GEne Network Inference with Ensemble of trees (GENIE3). ARACNe, an information-theoretic approach, estimates TF-target interactions based on mutual information and removes indirect effects via data processing inequality [55]. GENIE3, in contrast, employs an ensemble of regression trees to predict regulatory relationships, demonstrating robustness in handling high-dimensional data [56].

More recently, deep learning-based approaches have been integrated into GRN inference. Huang et al. introduced scGRN, a platform leveraging single-cell multiomics data to infer cell-type-specific regulatory networks, providing a valuable resource for studying dynamic gene regulation [57]. Additionally, Fang et al. developed GRNdb, a database integrating bulk and single-cell RNA-seq data to reconstruct GRNs across various physiological and pathological conditions [58]. These computational approaches have significantly improved the accuracy and scalability of GRN inference, allowing for more comprehensive modeling of regulatory interactions.

Integration of Multiomics Data with GRNs

While transcriptomic data alone provides valuable insights, incorporating additional layers such as epigenetic modifications and protein–protein interactions enhances the predictive power of GRN models. ATAC-Seq and ChIP-Seq data can be integrated to improve the identification of active regulatory elements, refining the inferred network structure. Additionally, network-based methods that incorporate post-transcriptional regulators, such as miRNAs and RNA-binding proteins, provide a more comprehensive view of gene expression control.

Fang et al. demonstrated that integrating transcriptomic and epigenomic data improves the identification of regulatory elements relevant to disease mechanisms [58]. By linking gene expression patterns to transcriptional regulatory mechanisms, these integrative approaches facilitate the identification of disease-associated regulatory pathways and potential therapeutic targets.

3.2 Network-Based Target Discovery

GRN-based analysis has proven instrumental in identifying key regulatory elements involved in disease progression and therapeutic response. Two major strategies for target identification within regulatory networks are hub gene identification and driver vs. passenger gene distinction.

Regulatory Network-Based Target Prioritization

Hub genes, characterized by a high degree of connectivity within regulatory networks, often serve as central regulators of disease processes. Driver genes, in contrast, directly contribute to disease initiation and progression by acquiring key mutations that lead to functional changes. Iorio et al. demonstrated that pharmacogenomic interactions in cancer could be mapped using GRN-based approaches, allowing for the identification of key regulatory hubs amenable to therapeutic targeting [59]. Schulze-Edinghausen et al. investigated the role of progranulin (GRN) in chronic lymphocytic leukemia (CLL), revealing its elevated expression in patient sera and its potential involvement in immune modulation [60].

Distinguishing between driver genes, which actively contribute to disease initiation and progression, and passenger genes, which accumulate mutations without functional consequences, is critical for prioritizing therapeutic targets. Network topology analysis can aid in this distinction by identifying genes with high regulatory influence. Adikusuma et al. employed a genome-wide association study (GWAS)-based genetic risk prioritization strategy integrated with GRN analysis to identify drug repositioning candidates for atopic dermatitis [61]. Their study demonstrated how integrating genetic risk loci with regulatory networks can refine target prioritization for novel therapeutic interventions.

AI/ML-Driven Advances in GRN Analysis

Artificial intelligence and machine learning have significantly advanced GRN modeling by enabling the integration of diverse data sources and improving predictive accuracy. Li et al. proposed an Operational Module Unit (OMU) system that integrates gene expression profiles, protein–protein interactions, and regulatory relationships to prioritize drug combinations based on their predicted synergistic effects [62]. This approach effectively identified novel drug combinations that could enhance therapeutic efficacy while minimizing adverse effects.

Additionally, graph neural networks (GNNs) have been applied to analyze regulatory interactions at a systems level, incorporating causal inference models to predict the impact of gene perturbations on disease phenotypes. Xu et al. introduced a Directed Acyclic Graph Neural Network (DAGNN) to model GRNs, demonstrating improved accuracy in predicting disease-associated regulatory elements [63]. By leveraging AI/ML techniques, GRN analysis continues to evolve, offering novel insights into regulatory mechanisms and enhancing drug discovery efforts.

Future directions include expanding single-cell regulatory network reconstructions, refining integration strategies for multiomics data, and improving interpretability of AI-driven predictions. These advancements hold the potential to revolutionize precision medicine by enabling a deeper understanding of gene regulation in health and disease.

4 Drug Repositioning

The identification of novel therapeutic applications for existing drugs, known as drug repositioning, has gained significant traction due to its cost-effectiveness and reduced time required for clinical translation. Traditional drug development is both costly and time-consuming, with high attrition rates in late-stage trials. By leveraging high-throughput gene expression data and GRNs, researchers can systematically identify candidate drugs that may reverse disease-associated transcriptional profiles or target key regulatory hubs. The integration of ML and AI methods has further enhanced the precision of these approaches, enabling large-scale, data-driven predictions of drug-disease associations.

4.1 Gene Expression-Based Drug Repositioning

Gene expression signatures have been extensively used to identify drugs capable of reversing disease-associated transcriptional changes. The Connectivity Map (CMap) [64] and the Library of Integrated Network-based Cellular Signatures (LINCS) [65] provide large-scale datasets linking drug-induced gene expression profiles with disease states. By comparing disease-specific gene expression signatures with drug perturbation profiles, researchers can identify compounds that may restore normal gene expression patterns and serve as potential therapeutic agents.

Sirota et al. pioneered the use of gene expression signatures for drug repositioning by identifying inverse gene expression correlations between disease states and drug responses. Their methodology involved the large-scale computational screening of gene expression profiles obtained from public repositories, aiming to match disease-specific gene expression patterns with those induced by known drugs. Through this approach, they successfully predicted novel therapeutic applications, such as the repositioning of cimetidine for lung adenocarcinoma, demonstrating the potential of transcriptomic-based screening in drug discovery [66].

Kumar et al. applied gene expression-based drug repositioning to epilepsy, utilizing CMap to retrieve drug-associated gene expression data and an in-house R script to identify 309 compounds capable of altering epilepsy-related transcriptional signatures. Molecular docking against key epilepsy targets revealed 21 compounds with superior binding affinities compared to standard antiepileptic drugs, with several candidates such as ergocalciferol and flunarizine having prior experimental support for epilepsy treatment [67].

Similarly, Cong et al. demonstrated the integration of dimensionality reduction and clustering in LINCS-based drug repositioning. By applying UMAP for dimensionality reduction and k-means clustering, they classified disease subtypes before identifying compounds capable of reversing disease-specific transcriptional signatures [68]. The corresponding analytical workflow has since been formalized into a reproducible and openly available Python implementation, facilitating standardized reuse and extension of this strategy [69]. This highlights the potential of computational approaches in refining transcriptomics-driven repurposing strategies.

Lee et al. used transcriptomic analysis to identify novel treatments for epidermolysis bullosa simplex (EBS). RNA sequencing of EBS blistered skin revealed 1276 dysregulated genes, with upregulation of proinflammatory pathways such as *IL-6*, *IL-8*, and *IL-10*. Computational screening with the Connectivity Map identified mTOR and phosphatidylinositol 3-kinase inhibitors as potential treatments. A small clinical trial with topical sirolimus demonstrated significant improvement in patients, validating the computational predictions and highlighting the clinical relevance of gene expression-based drug repositioning [70].

4.2 Network-Based Drug Repositioning

Network-based drug repositioning leverages biological network models, including GRNs, protein–protein interaction (PPI) networks, and heterogeneous biomedical graphs, to predict novel therapeutic applications for existing drugs. Unlike direct gene expression-based approaches, network-based methods integrate multiomics data to infer drug-disease associations by capturing complex molecular relationships. By analyzing network proximity, functional modules, and graph-based embeddings, these approaches enhance the identification of repositioning candidates with greater biological relevance.

Himmelstein et al. pioneered the integration of network medicine into drug repurposing through Hetionet, a comprehensive biomedical knowledge graph incorporating data from 29 distinct domains, including genetic, molecular, and clinical datasets [71]. By leveraging heterogeneous network embeddings, their study demonstrated the potential of large-scale biological data integration for prioritizing drug candidates based on system-wide interactions.

Building on this foundation, Jiménez et al. developed eXplainable Graphs for Repurposing (XG4Repo), a framework utilizing biomedical knowledge graphs to link compounds to diseases. Their model incorporates explainable paths between drugs and diseases, including intermediary nodes such as genes, pathways, and side effects, making predictions interpretable for experts [72]. This approach enhances transparency in drug repositioning and facilitates expert validation of predicted relationships.

Similarly, Zhou et al. developed a network-based drug repositioning framework that integrated human PPI networks with host–virus interaction data from coronaviruses, including SARS-CoV-2. Their approach quantified the network proximity between HCoV-associated proteins and known drug targets, leveraging a systems pharmacology model to systematically assess repositioning candidates. By integrating transcriptomic perturbation data with network-based analyses, they identified potential antiviral agents capable of disrupting key host–pathogen interactions, underscoring the power of network medicine in drug discovery [73].

In addition, Ahmed et al. proposed an integrative drug repositioning framework based on a systems biology-enabled network medicine platform. Their study constructed an HPV-induced cervical cancer protein interaction network and performed drug target network proximity analysis, identifying 142 potential anti-HPV repositionable drugs. Among these, 51 had existing cervical cancer indications, and 33 had known antiviral properties, demonstrating the utility of network-based approaches in identifying repositioning candidates for viral diseases [74].

Sadeghi et al. introduced a non-negative matrix factorization-based drug repositioning approach (NMF-DR) that integrates multiple heterogeneous drug-disease associations. Their framework combines drug similarities from different perspectives—chemical structure, target interactions, and disease phenotype relationships—into a unified recommender system [75]. By reconstructing a drug-disease adjacency matrix, they predicted novel drug indications, showcasing how machine learning techniques can enhance the efficiency and accuracy of drug repositioning.

Moreover, Li et al. introduced a novel approach utilizing directed tripartite graphs for drug repositioning, modeling drug-target-disease relationships through a heterogeneous network. Their method, known as DTD-GNN, combines graph convolutional networks (GCN), graph attention networks (GAT), and gated units to learn high-order dependencies between drugs, targets, and diseases. The model employs link prediction techniques to infer new drug-disease associations, significantly enhancing repositioning accuracy [76]. Using the BioSNAP dataset, Li et al. demonstrated the superior performance of DTD-GNN compared to traditional recommender system-based approaches, highlighting the advantage of graph neural networks in integrating heterogeneous biomedical data.

As drug repositioning strategies continue to evolve, integrating multiomics data, refining computational models, and leveraging AI-driven insights will be key to identifying novel therapeutic applications for existing drugs. The synergy between gene expression-based screening, network-driven inference, and machine learning techniques is expected to drive more precise and efficient repositioning strategies, ultimately enhancing precision medicine approaches.

5 Challenges and Future Directions

Advancements in AI-driven gene expression analysis and regulatory modeling have significantly transformed biomedical research and drug discovery. However, several key challenges remain in fully leveraging these technologies for precision medicine. These challenges include understanding the complex structure of gene expression space, integrating multiomics data, addressing the interpretability of AI models, and optimizing drug discovery pipelines. Addressing these issues requires interdisciplinary approaches and technological innovations that bridge computational biology, data science, and experimental validation.

5.1 Understanding the Complex Structure of Gene Expression Space

A fundamental challenge in computational biology is the complex structure of gene expression space, which is highly dimensional and sparsely populated. Gene expression patterns form nonuniform, high-dimensional manifolds where regulatory interactions exhibit fractal-like properties. Studies suggest that gene expression states can be modeled as a polyhedral structure, with clusters of functionally related genes forming distinct vertices that correspond to key biological functions such as differentiation, immune response, or metabolic regulation [77]. Understanding these structures is essential for developing predictive models capable of capturing the full range of biological variability. Techniques such as topological data analysis (TDA) and geometric deep learning provide promising tools to explore the organization of gene expression landscapes and improve our ability to interpret complex biological patterns [78, 79]. Further exploration of these fractal-like subspaces could contribute to generalized interaction prediction frameworks and novel approaches in drug design. Additionally, the use of spatial transcriptomics can provide valuable insights into the spatial distribution of gene expression and its relationship to drug effects.

Spatial transcriptomics is an emerging omics technology that holds immense potential in drug discovery and development [80]. It can reveal gene expression at specific locations within tissue structures and their interaction relationships, which can aid in understanding diseases and discovering new therapeutic targets and drugs. Elucidating the gene expression space can significantly contribute to interaction prediction and drug design. By analyzing gene expression profiles, researchers can identify the molecular mechanisms of action of drugs, predict drug targets, and discover new therapeutic targets [81].

5.2 Integrating Multiomics Data

Integrating multiomics data is essential for understanding biological systems and disease mechanisms, yet it remains a significant challenge in disease modeling and drug discovery. Combining proteomics, genomics, transcriptomics, metabolomics, and epigenomics enables the construction of detailed molecular networks that offer deeper insights into cellular interactions and regulatory pathways [82].

Several computational methods have been developed to facilitate multiomics integration, including Two-way Orthogonal Partial Least Squares (O2PLS) and machine learning algorithms, which provide structured frameworks for data integration and analysis [82]. Deep learning approaches, such as TransPro, enable hierarchical integration of multiomics data for pharmacological compound evaluation [83]. Graph-based learning and causal inference models have further improved the ability to infer regulatory interactions and uncover disease mechanisms. Multiomics clustering techniques have also been applied to refine the association between molecular profiles and clinical features among cancer patients, allowing for improved resolution of clustering patterns [84]. Various statistical frameworks have been developed to integrate metabolomics data with other omics layers, categorized based on hypothesis, data types, strategies, and study design [85]. Future efforts should focus on making these frameworks more interpretable and biologically relevant to enhance predictive accuracy in biomedical applications.

While genome-editing technologies, such as CRISPR-Cas9, have accelerated functional genomics, automating target validation remains a challenge. Validating target genes is still a manual and labor-intensive process, often requiring significant expertise and time, which hinders the widespread adoption of genome editing in disease modeling, drug development, and personalized medicine [86]. A standardized and scalable approach to detecting off-target effects and validating editing efficiency is needed [87]. Recent studies have demonstrated the potential of using flow cytometry-based quantification of genome editing efficiency in human cell lines, providing a precise and sensitive method for detecting genome editing events [88]. Automated systems, such as the StemCellFactory platform, integrate genome editing with high-throughput screening and analysis, facilitating the rapid and efficient validation of target genes [89]. Machine learning algorithms have also been employed to automate genome editing data analysis, identifying off-target effects and predicting editing efficiency [87]. However, ensuring the accuracy and reliability of these automated systems remains a significant challenge, as errors in genome editing can have serious consequences [90]. Developing adaptive automated systems that can integrate with different genome editing technologies and workflows will be crucial for advancing high-throughput functional genomics.

5.3 The Black-Box Problem in AI Models

The black box problem in AI models refers to the challenge of understanding the internal workings and decision-making processes of complex machine learning models, particularly those that are proprietary or highly complex [91]. Black-box evaluations of AI systems often rely on analyzing their inputs and outputs, which can limit the ability to detect hidden biases, adversarial vulnerabilities, or domain shifts in biological data [92, 93]. This is particularly problematic in healthcare, where AI models may produce the correct prediction for the wrong reason, leading to reduced generalizability and increased risks in clinical practice [93]. Addressing these issues is crucial for ensuring AI-driven decision-making is reliable and ethically sound in biomedical sciences.

Several strategies have been proposed to address the black-box problem. White-box methods involve analyzing the internal representations of AI models to enhance interpretability and reliability, and techniques such as latent space analysis enable researchers to probe deep learning models and improve worst-case performance assurances [92]. Additionally, process-based models, which integrate scientific principles into AI algorithms, offer another solution by improving robustness while maintaining predictive power [94].

Explainable AI (XAI) is gaining traction in biomedical research, particularly in clinical decision support and drug discovery. XAI techniques provide transparency in disease prediction, medical imaging, and risk assessment, making AI-driven models more understandable and actionable [95–97]. In drug discovery, XAI enhances researchers' ability to interpret AI-generated insights into molecular interactions and drug efficacy, reducing reliance on opaque deep learning models [98]. Moreover, integrating domain knowledge into AI models helps refined the explainability of predictive frameworks, ensuring they provide meaningful insights rather than black-box outputs [99].

5.4 Advancements in Large Language Models and Transformers for Gene Expression Analysis

Recent advancements in large language models (LLMs) and transformer-based architecture have led to substantial progress in the field of AI in gene expression analysis, gene regulation prediction, and drug discovery [100].

Recent approaches involve the refinement of pretrained genome foundation models, such as DNABERT [101] and Nucleotide Transformer [102], for specific genomic tasks. A comprehensive evaluation of these models by Wang et al. revealed their remarkable performance in tasks such as predicting gene-disease associations, modeling transcriptomic data, and identifying regulatory elements within noncoding regions. These models have been successfully applied to classify promoter sequences, distinguish between protein-coding and noncoding RNA regions, and predict enhancer-promoter interactions. By leveraging self-attention mechanisms, transformers can capture long-range dependencies in genomic sequences, rendering them particularly well-suited for regulatory sequence prediction [103].

Another promising application is the use of LLMs for mining biomedical literature to prioritize gene-disease associations and drug interactions [100]. Additionally, LLMs such as QuST-LLM have been integrated into spatial transcriptomics to analyze biological spatial patterns, aiding in the identification of specific single-cell clusters and regions [104].

Despite the aforementioned advancements, several challenges persist, including biases stemming from training data, substantial computational demands, and the necessity of fine-tuning for biomedical applications [105]. Moreover, it is imperative to meticulously validate LLMs to ensure that their predictions are in alignment with experimental findings and established biological knowledge [103].

Future endeavors should prioritize enhancing model generalization, developing more efficient training methodologies, and ensuring interpretability for biomedical researchers and clinicians.

5.5 Future Directions

Looking ahead, we believe that continued advancements in AI-driven gene expression analysis will likely focus on refining model generalization, interpretability, and multimodal data integration. The ability to leverage self-supervised learning techniques and few-shot learning approaches may help reduce the dependence on extensive labeled datasets, making AI models more adaptable across diverse biomedical applications. Additionally, integrating causal inference techniques into AI-driven biological models could enhance our understanding of gene regulation and disease mechanisms [106].

Another promising avenue for future research may involve the fusion of LLMs with multiomics and spatial transcriptomics data. AI-driven spatiotemporal modeling of gene expressions could uncover dynamic regulatory patterns that were previously difficult to resolve, facilitating new insights into disease progression and treatment response [107, 108]. Moreover, AI-enhanced functional genomics screens could improve precision medicine by identifying personalized therapeutic targets based on genomic and transcriptomic variability [109].

As AI models continue to evolve, their potential integration with quantum computing and synthetic biology may open new frontiers in drug discovery. Quantum-enhanced AI could accelerate molecular simulations, improving drug-target binding predictions [110], while AI-guided gene editing therapies could facilitate the development of novel therapeutic strategies tailored to specific disease phenotypes [109].

Ultimately, we anticipate that the convergence of large-scale AI models, high-throughput screening technologies, and multiomics integration will shape the next generation of biomedical research and therapeutic innovation. Future research should emphasize model transparency, reproducibility, and the ethical considerations of AI deployment in clinical and drug discovery settings to ensure responsible innovation.

Conflict of Interest

The authors have no conflicts of interest to declare that are relevant to the content of this chapter.

References

1. Mardis ER (2008) Next-generation DNA sequencing methods. Annu Rev Genom Hum Genet 9:387–402. https://doi.org/10.1146/annurev.genom.9.081307.164359
2. Compeau PEC, Pevzner PA, Tesler G (2011) How to apply de Bruijn graphs to genome assembly. Nat Biotechnol 29:987–991. https://doi.org/10.1038/nbt.2023
3. Rius M, Bourne S, Hornsby HG, Chapman MA (2015) Applications of next-generation sequencing to the study of biological invasions. Curr Zool 61:488–504. https://doi.org/10.1093/czoolo/61.3.488
4. Mortazavi A, Williams BA, McCue K et al (2008) Mapping and quantifying mammalian transcriptomes by RNA-Seq. Nat Methods 5:621–628. https://doi.org/10.1038/nmeth.1226
5. Wilhelm BT, Landry J-R (2009) RNA-seq—quantitative measurement of expression through massively parallel RNA-sequencing. Methods 48:249–257. https://doi.org/10.1016/j.ymeth.2009.03.016
6. Tang F, Barbacioru C, Wang Y et al (2009) mRNA-seq whole-transcriptome analysis of a single cell. Nat Methods 6:377–382. https://doi.org/10.1038/nmeth.1315
7. Macosko EZ, Basu A, Satija R et al (2015) Highly parallel genome-wide expression profiling of individual cells using nanoliter droplets. Cell 161:1202–1214. https://doi.org/10.1016/j.cell.2015.05.002
8. Klein AM, Mazutis L, Akartuna I et al (2015) Droplet barcoding for single-cell transcriptomics applied to embryonic stem cells. Cell 161:1187–1201. https://doi.org/10.1016/j.cell.2015.04.044
9. Johnson DS, Mortazavi A, Myers RM, Wold B (2007) Genome-wide mapping of in vivo protein-DNA interactions. Science 316:1497–1502. https://doi.org/10.1126/science.1141319
10. Buenrostro JD, Giresi PG, Zaba LC et al (2013) Transposition of native chromatin for fast and sensitive epigenomic profiling of open chromatin, DNA-binding proteins and nucleosome position. Nat Methods 10:1213–1218. https://doi.org/10.1038/nmeth.2688
11. Buenrostro JD, Wu B, Litzenburger UM et al (2015) Single-cell chromatin accessibility reveals principles of regulatory variation. Nature 523:486–490. https://doi.org/10.1038/nature14590
12. Ingolia NT, Ghaemmaghami S, Newman JRS, Weissman JS (2009) Genome-wide analysis in vivo of translation with nucleotide resolution using ribosome profiling. Science 324:218–223. https://doi.org/10.1126/science.1168978
13. Nicholson JK, Connelly J, Lindon JC, Holmes E (2002) Metabonomics: a platform for studying drug toxicity and gene function. Nat Rev Drug Discov 1:153–161. https://doi.org/10.1038/nrd728
14. Felsher DW, Zetterberg A, Zhu J et al (2000) Overexpression of *MYC* causes *p53* -dependent G 2 arrest of normal fibroblasts. Proc Natl Acad Sci U S A 97:10544–10548. https://doi.org/10.1073/pnas.190327097
15. Shen X, Gao C, Li H et al (2023) Natural compounds: Wnt pathway inhibitors with therapeutic potential in lung cancer. Front Pharmacol 14:1250893. https://doi.org/10.3389/fphar.2023.1250893
16. Abbas M, EL-Manzalawy Y (2020) Machine learning based refined differential gene expression analysis of pediatric sepsis. BMC Med Genomics 13: 122. https://doi.org/10.1186/s12920-020-00771-4
17. Niazi S (2023) The coming of age of AI/ML in drug discovery, development, clinical testing, and manufacturing: the FDA perspectives. Drug Des Devel Ther 17:2691–2725. https://doi.org/10.2147/DDDT.S424991
18. Ching T, Himmelstein DS, Beaulieu-Jones BK et al (2018) Opportunities and obstacles for deep learning in biology and medicine. J R Soc Interface 15:20170387. https://doi.org/10.1098/rsif.2017.0387
19. Zou J, Huss M, Abid A et al (2019) A primer on deep learning in genomics. Nat Genet 51:12–18. https://doi.org/10.1038/s41588-018-0295-5
20. Gaudelet T, Day B, Jamasb AR et al (2021) Utilizing graph machine learning within drug discovery and development. Brief Bioinform 22:bbab159. https://doi.org/10.1093/bib/bbab159
21. Freeman TC, Goldovsky L, Brosch M et al (2007) Construction, visualisation, and clustering of transcription networks from microarray expression data. PLOS Comput Biol 3:e206. https://doi.org/10.1371/journal.pcbi.0030206
22. van Dam S, Võsa U, van der Graaf A et al (2017) Gene co-expression analysis for functional classification and gene–disease predictions. Brief Bioinform 19(4):575. https://doi.org/10.1093/bib/bbw139
23. Low ZY, Farouk IA, Lal SK (2020) Drug repositioning: new approaches and future prospects for life-debilitating diseases and the COVID-19 pandemic outbreak.

Viruses 12:1058. https://doi.org/10.3390/v12091058
24. Cong Y, Nakagawa S, Ogura A et al (2026) AI and ML-driven strategies for drug repurposing: techniques, applications, and challenges. In: Lavecchia A (ed) Applied artificial intelligence for drug discovery. Springer Nature, New York, 689-735. https://doi.org/10.1007/978-3-031-98022-0_23
25. Cong Y, Endo T (2022) Multi-omics and artificial intelligence-guided drug repositioning: prospects, challenges, and lessons learned from COVID-19. Omics 26:361–371. https://doi.org/10.1089/omi.2022.0068
26. Anders S, Huber W (2010) Differential expression analysis for sequence count data. Genome Biol 11: R106. https://doi.org/10.1186/gb-2010-11-10-r106
27. Smyth GK (2004) Linear models and empirical bayes methods for assessing differential expression in microarray experiments. Stat Appl Genet Mol Biol 3:1–25. https://doi.org/10.2202/1544-6115.1027
28. Ashburner M, Ball CA, Blake JA et al (2000) Gene ontology: tool for the unification of biology. Nat Genet 25:25–29. https://doi.org/10.1038/75556
29. Kanehisa M (2000) KEGG: Kyoto encyclopedia of genes and genomes. Nucleic Acids Res 28:27–30. https://doi.org/10.1093/nar/28.1.27
30. Yin H, Duo H, Li S et al (2024) Unlocking biological insights from differentially expressed genes: concepts, methods, and future perspectives. J Adv Res 76:135. https://doi.org/10.1016/j.jare.2024.12.004
31. Braun R, Leibon G, Pauls S, Rockmore D (2011) Partition decoupling for multi-gene analysis of gene expression profiling data. BMC Bioinformatics 12: 497. https://doi.org/10.1186/1471-2105-12-497
32. Zhang S, Li X, Lin Q et al (2020) Uncovering the key dimensions of high-throughput biomolecular data using deep learning. Nucleic Acids Res 48:e56–e56. https://doi.org/10.1093/nar/gkaa191
33. Mulas R, Casey MJ (2021) Estimating cellular redundancy in networks of genetic expression. Math Biosci 341:108713. https://doi.org/10.1016/j.mbs.2021.108713
34. Pearson K (1901) On lines and planes of closest fit to systems of points in space. Lond Edinb Dublin Philos Mag J Sci 2:559–572. https://doi.org/10.1080/14786440109462720
35. Hotelling H (1933) Analysis of a complex of statistical variables into principal components. J Educ Psychol 24:417–441. https://doi.org/10.1037/h0071325
36. van der Maaten L, Geoffrey H (2008) Visualizing data using t-SNE. J Mach Learn Res 9:2579–2605
37. McInnes L, Healy J, Melville J (2018) UMAP: uniform manifold approximation and projection for dimension reduction. J Open Source Softw 3(29):861
38. Macqueen J (1967) Some methods for classification and analysis of multivariate observations. Proceedings of the 5th Berkeley Symposium on mathematical statistics and probability, volume 1: statistics. University of California Press, Berkeley, 281–297
39. Johnson SC (1967) Hierarchical clustering schemes. Psychometrika 32:241–254. https://doi.org/10.1007/BF02289588
40. Perou CM, Sørlie T, Eisen MB et al (2000) Molecular portraits of human breast tumours. Nature 406:747–752. https://doi.org/10.1038/35021093
41. Deokar A (2020) Stratification of systemic lupus erythematosus patients with gene expression data reveals expression of distinct immune pathways. medRxiv: 2020.08.25.20181578. https://doi.org/10.1101/2020.08.25.20181578
42. Tian M, Shen J, Qi Z et al (2023) Bioinformatics analysis and prediction of Alzheimer's disease and alcohol dependence based on Ferroptosis-related genes. Front Aging Neurosci 15:1201142. https://doi.org/10.3389/fnagi.2023.1201142
43. Lindholm Carlström E, Niazi A, Etemadikhah M et al (2021) Transcriptome analysis of post-mortem brain tissue reveals up-regulation of the complement cascade in a subgroup of schizophrenia patients. Genes (Basel) 12:1242. https://doi.org/10.3390/genes12081242
44. Tumeh PC, Harview CL, Yearley JH et al (2014) PD-1 blockade induces responses by inhibiting adaptive immune resistance. Nature 515:568–571. https://doi.org/10.1038/nature13954
45. Wang L, Hu S, Zhou B (2022) Deciphering cardiac biology and disease by single-cell transcriptomic profiling. Biomolecules 12:566. https://doi.org/10.3390/biom12040566
46. Qiu X, Nair MG, Jaroszewski L, Godzik A (2024) Deciphering abnormal platelet subpopulations in COVID-19, sepsis and systemic lupus erythematosus through machine learning and single-cell transcriptomics. Int J Mol Sci 25:5941. https://doi.org/10.3390/ijms25115941
47. Xia Z-A, Zhou Y, Li J, He J (2022) Integrated analysis of single-cell and bulk RNA-sequencing reveals a tissue-resident macrophage-related signature for predicting immunotherapy response in breast cancer patients. Cancers (Basel) 14:5506. https://doi.org/10.3390/cancers14225506
48. Foutadakis S, Kordias D, Vatsellas G, Magklara A (2024) Identification of new

chemoresistance-associated genes in triple-negative breast cancer by single-cell transcriptomic analysis. Int J Mol Sci 25:6853. https://doi.org/10.3390/ijms25136853
49. Chen L, Wang W, Zhai Y, Deng M (2020) Deep soft K-means clustering with self-training for single-cell RNA sequence data. NAR Genom Bioinform 2:lqaa039. https://doi.org/10.1093/nargab/lqaa039
50. Freytag S, Tian L, Lönnstedt I et al (2018) Comparison of clustering tools in R for medium-sized 10x Genomics single-cell RNA-sequencing data. F1000Res 7:1297. https://doi.org/10.12688/f1000research.15809.2
51. Pashler AL, Towler BP, Jones CI et al (2021) Genome-wide analyses of XRN1-sensitive targets in osteosarcoma cells identify disease-relevant transcripts containing G-rich motifs. RNA 27:1265–1280. https://doi.org/10.1261/rna.078872.121
52. Narang V, Ramli MA, Singhal A et al (2015) Automated identification of core regulatory genes in human gene regulatory networks. PLOS Comput Biol 11:e1004504. https://doi.org/10.1371/journal.pcbi.1004504
53. Buenrostro JD, Wu B, Litzenburger UM et al (2015) Single-cell chromatin accessibility reveals principles of regulatory variation. Nature 523:486–490. https://doi.org/10.1038/nature14590
54. Friedman RC, Farh KK-H, Burge CB, Bartel DP (2009) Most mammalian mRNAs are conserved targets of microRNAs. Genome Res 19:92–105. https://doi.org/10.1101/gr.082701.108
55. Margolin AA, Nemenman I, Basso K et al (2006) ARACNE: an algorithm for the reconstruction of gene regulatory networks in a Mammalian cellular context. BMC Bioinformatics 7: S7. https://doi.org/10.1186/1471-2105-7-S1-S7
56. Huynh-Thu VA, Irrthum A, Wehenkel L, Geurts P (2010) Inferring regulatory networks from expression data using tree-based methods. PLOS One 5:e12776. https://doi.org/10.1371/journal.pone.0012776
57. Huang X, Song C, Zhang G et al (2024) scGRN: a comprehensive single-cell gene regulatory network platform of human and mouse. Nucleic Acids Res 52:D293–D303. https://doi.org/10.1093/nar/gkad885
58. Fang L, Li Y, Ma L et al (2021) GRNdb: decoding the gene regulatory networks in diverse human and mouse conditions. Nucleic Acids Res 49:D97–D103. https://doi.org/10.1093/nar/gkaa995
59. Iorio F, Knijnenburg TA, Vis DJ et al (2016) A landscape of pharmacogenomic interactions in cancer. Cell 166:740–754. https://doi.org/10.1016/j.cell.2016.06.017
60. Schulze-Edinghausen L, Dürr C, Öztürk S et al (2019) Dissecting the prognostic significance and functional role of progranulin in chronic lymphocytic leukemia. Cancers (Basel) 11:822. https://doi.org/10.3390/cancers11060822
61. Adikusuma W, Irham LM, Chou W-H et al (2021) Drug repurposing for atopic dermatitis by integration of gene networking and genomic information. Front Immunol 12:724277. https://doi.org/10.3389/fimmu.2021.724277
62. Li J, Xu H, McIndoe RA (2022) A novel network based linear model for prioritization of synergistic drug combinations. PLOS One 17:e0266382. https://doi.org/10.1371/journal.pone.0266382
63. Xu T, Zhao J, Xiong M (2023) Graphical learning and causal inference for drug repurposing. medRxiv: 2023.07.29.23293346. https://doi.org/10.1101/2023.07.29.23293346
64. Lamb J, Crawford ED, Peck D et al (2006) The connectivity map: using gene-expression signatures to connect small molecules, genes, and disease. Science 313:1929–1935. https://doi.org/10.1126/science.1132939
65. Subramanian A, Narayan R, Corsello SM et al (2017) A next generation connectivity map: L1000 platform and the first 1,000,000 profiles. Cell 171(1437–1452):e17. https://doi.org/10.1016/j.cell.2017.10.049
66. Sirota M, Dudley JT, Kim J et al (2011) Discovery and preclinical validation of drug indications using compendia of public gene expression data. Sci Transl Med 3:96ra77. https://doi.org/10.1126/scitranslmed.3001318
67. Kumar P (2022) Drug repositioning for idiopathic epilepsy using gene expression signature data. Bioinformation 18:845–852. https://doi.org/10.6026/97320630018845
68. Cong Y, Shintani M, Imanari F et al (2022) A new approach to drug repurposing with two-stage prediction, machine learning, and unsupervised clustering of gene expression. Omics 26:339–347. https://doi.org/10.1089/omi.2022.0026
69. Cong Y, Osada N, Endo T (2026) Reproducible and multi-study transcriptomic integration with disint, disease integration and clustering toolkit, and application to drug repositioning. Omics 30:71. https://doi.org/10.1177/15578100251413812
70. Lee GH, Lekwuttikarn R, Tafoya E et al (2022) Transcriptomic repositioning analysis identifies mTOR inhibitor as potential therapy for epidermolysis bullosa simplex.

J Invest Dermatol 142:382–389. https://doi.org/10.1016/j.jid.2021.07.170
71. Himmelstein DS, Lizee A, Hessler C et al (2017) Systematic integration of biomedical knowledge prioritizes drugs for repurposing. Elife 6:e26726. https://doi.org/10.7554/eLife.26726
72. Jiménez A, Merino MJ, Parras J, Zazo S (2024) Explainable drug repurposing via path based knowledge graph completion. Sci Rep 14: 16587. https://doi.org/10.1038/s41598-024-67163-x
73. Zhou Y, Hou Y, Shen J et al (2020) Network-based drug repurposing for novel coronavirus 2019-nCoV/SARS-CoV-2. Cell Discov 6:14. https://doi.org/10.1038/s41421-020-0153-3
74. Ahmed F, Yang YJ, Samantasinghar A et al (2023) Network-based drug repurposing for HPV-associated cervical cancer. Comput Struct Biotechnol J 21:5186–5200. https://doi.org/10.1016/j.csbj.2023.10.038
75. Sadeghi S, Lu J, Ngom A (2022) A network-based drug repurposing method via non-negative matrix factorization. Bioinformatics 38:1369–1377. https://doi.org/10.1093/bioinformatics/btab826
76. Li W, Ma W, Yang M, Tang X (2024) Drug repurposing based on the DTD-GNN graph neural network: revealing the relationships among drugs, targets and diseases. BMC Genomics 25:584. https://doi.org/10.1186/s12864-024-10499-5
77. Grange P, Bohland JW, Okaty BW et al (2014) Cell-type–based model explaining coexpression patterns of genes in the brain. Proc Natl Acad Sci U S A 111:5397–5402. https://doi.org/10.1073/pnas.1312098111
78. Mar JC, Quackenbush J (2009) Decomposition of gene expression state space trajectories. PLOS Comput Biol 5:e1000626. https://doi.org/10.1371/journal.pcbi.1000626
79. Thévenin A, Ein-Dor L, Ozery-Flato M, Shamir R (2014) Functional gene groups are concentrated within chromosomes, among chromosomes and in the nuclear space of the human genome. Nucleic Acids Res 42:9854–9861. https://doi.org/10.1093/nar/gku667
80. Cao J, Li C, Cui Z et al (2024) Spatial transcriptomics: a powerful tool in disease understanding and drug discovery. Theranostics 14:2946–2968. https://doi.org/10.7150/thno.95908
81. Neary B, Qiu P (2024) Characterization of expression-based gene clusters gives insights into variation in patient response to cancer therapies. Cancer Inform 23:11769351241271560. https://doi.org/10.1177/11769351241271560
82. Vitorino R (2024) Transforming clinical research: the power of high-throughput omics integration. Proteomes 12:25. https://doi.org/10.3390/proteomes12030025
83. Jain M, Dhariwal R, Patil N et al (2023) Unveiling the molecular footprint: proteome-based biomarkers for Alzheimer's disease. Proteomes 11:33. https://doi.org/10.3390/proteomes11040033
84. Heo YJ, Hwa C, Lee G-H et al (2021) Integrative multi-omics approaches in cancer research: from biological networks to clinical subtypes. Mol Cells 44:433–443. https://doi.org/10.14348/molcells.2021.0042
85. Jendoubi T (2021) Approaches to integrating metabolomics and multi-omics data: a primer. Metabolites 11:184. https://doi.org/10.3390/metabo11030184
86. Nießing B, Breitkreuz Y, Elanzew A et al (2024) Automated CRISPR/Cas9-based genome editing of human pluripotent stem cells using the StemCellFactory. Front Bioeng Biotechnol 12:1459273. https://doi.org/10.3389/fbioe.2024.1459273
87. Zhang Z, Bao X, Lin C-P (2023) Progress and prospects of gene editing in pluripotent stem cells. Biomedicines 11:2168. https://doi.org/10.3390/biomedicines11082168
88. Hasan MN, Hyodo T, Biswas M et al (2023) Flowcytometry-based quantification of genome editing efficiency in human cell lines using the L1CAM gene. PLOS One 18:e0294146. https://doi.org/10.1371/journal.pone.0294146
89. Nießing B, Breitkreuz Y, Elanzew A et al (2024) Automated CRISPR/Cas9-based genome editing of human pluripotent stem cells using the StemCellFactory. Front Bioeng Biotechnol 12:1459273. https://doi.org/10.3389/fbioe.2024.1459273
90. Naqvi RZ, Mahmood MA, Mansoor S et al (2024) Omics-driven exploration and mining of key functional genes for the improvement of food and fiber crops. Front Plant Sci 14:1273859. https://doi.org/10.3389/fpls.2023.1273859
91. Nazat S, Arreche O, Abdallah M (2024) On evaluating black-box explainable AI methods for enhancing anomaly detection in autonomous driving systems. Sensors 24:3515. https://doi.org/10.3390/s24113515
92. Casper S, Ezell C, Siegmann C et al (2024) Black-box access is insufficient for rigorous AI audits. In: The 2024 ACM conference on fairness, accountability, and transparency. ACM, New York, NY, USA, pp 2254–2272
93. Rudin C, Chen C, Chen Z et al (2022) Interpretable machine learning: Fundamental principles and 10 grand challenges. Stat Surv 16:1. https://doi.org/10.1214/21-SS133

94. Karpatne A, Jia X, Kumar V (2024) Knowledge-guided machine learning: current trends and future prospects. arXiv: 2403.15989. https://doi.org/10.48550/arXiv.2403.15989
95. Stubbin A, Chyrikov T, Zhao J, Chajo C (2024) The limits of perception: analyzing inconsistencies in saliency maps in XAI. arXiv: 2403.15684. https://doi.org/10.48550/arXiv.2403.15684
96. Alizadehsani R, Oyelere SS, Hussain S et al (2024) Explainable artificial intelligence for drug discovery and development: a comprehensive survey. IEEE Access 12:35796–35812. https://doi.org/10.1109/ACCESS.2024.3373195
97. Metta C, Beretta A, Pellungrini R et al (2024) Towards transparent healthcare: advancing local explanation methods in explainable artificial intelligence. Bioengineering 11:369. https://doi.org/10.3390/bioengineering11040369
98. Jiménez-Luna J, Grisoni F, Schneider G (2020) Drug discovery with explainable artificial intelligence. Nat Mach Intell 2:573–584. https://doi.org/10.1038/s42256-020-00236-4
99. Xin Teoh Y, Othmani A, Li Goh S et al (2024) Deciphering knee osteoarthritis diagnostic features with explainable artificial intelligence: a systematic review. IEEE Access 12:109080–109108. https://doi.org/10.1109/ACCESS.2024.3439096
100. Zheng Y, Koh HY, Yang M et al (2024) Large language models in drug discovery and development: from disease mechanisms to clinical trials. Patterns 6:101346
101. Ji Y, Zhou Z, Liu H, Davuluri RV (2021) DNABERT: pre-trained bidirectional encoder representations from transformers model for DNA-language in genome. Bioinformatics 37:2112–2120. https://doi.org/10.1093/bioinformatics/btab083
102. Dalla-Torre H, Gonzalez L, Mendoza-Revilla J et al (2025) Nucleotide transformer: building and evaluating robust foundation models for human genomics. Nat Methods 22:287–297. https://doi.org/10.1038/s41592-024-02523-z
103. Wang W, Hou Z, Liu X, Peng X (2024) Exploring the potentials and challenges of using large language models for the analysis of transcriptional regulation of long non-coding RNAs. arXiv: 2411.03522. https://doi.org/10.48550/arXiv.2411.03522
104. Huang CH (2024) QuST-LLM: integrating large language models for comprehensive spatial transcriptomics analysis. arXiv: 2406.14307. https://doi.org/10.48550/arXiv.2406.1430
105. Lyu Y, Wu Z, Zhang L et al (2024) GP-GPT: large language model for gene-phenotype mapping. arXiv: 2409.09825. https://doi.org/10.48550/arXiv.2409.09825
106. Chen Y, Mao R, Xu J et al (2024) A causal regulation modeling algorithm for temporal events with application to *Escherichia coli's* aerobic to anaerobic transition. Int J Mol Sci 25:5654. https://doi.org/10.3390/ijms25115654
107. Kenchanmane Raju SK (2022) Machine learning models reveal the importance of time-point specific cis-regulatory elements in *Arabidopsis thaliana* wounding response. Plant Cell 34:716–717. https://doi.org/10.1093/plcell/koab288
108. Venkatraman S, Basu S, Clark AG et al (2021) An empirical bayes approach to estimating dynamic models of co-regulated gene expression. Data Sci Sci 2:2219707
109. Dixit S, Kumar A, Srinivasan K et al (2024) Advancing genome editing with artificial intelligence: opportunities, challenges, and future directions. Front Bioeng Biotechnol 11:1335901. https://doi.org/10.3389/fbioe.2023.1335901
110. Niazi SK, Mariam Z (2023) Computer-aided drug design and drug discovery: a prospective analysis. Pharmaceuticals 17:22. https://doi.org/10.3390/ph17010022

Chapter 3

AI-Based 3D Heterogeneous Network Model for Functional Prediction of Epigenetics

Shamim Ara Mollah

Abstract

Human biology and diseases are the result of constantly evolving processes within an intricately complex molecular network of interactions, such as epigenetic regulation. Epigenetics refers to heritable changes in gene expression that occur without alterations to the underlying DNA sequence. These changes, driven by mechanisms such as DNA methylation, histone modifications, and noncoding RNAs, play critical roles in regulating chromatin structure and gene activity. Epigenetic regulation offers valuable insights into biological systems, and when integrated with sophisticated analyses, it enables us to gain insights into gene regulation and cellular behavior. Here, we describe an artificial intelligence (AI)-based model that is capable of generating 3-dimensional (3D) heterogeneous network by integrating multimodal data for the functional prediction of epigenetic mechanisms, emphasizing its applications in medicine, developmental biology, and personalized therapeutics. Heterogeneous networks in biology are powerful tools for understanding the complex interactions and interdependencies within biological systems. Key advancements in AI and multiomics data integration have propelled this field, offering new insights into disease mechanisms, biomarker discovery, and therapeutic interventions.

Keywords Epigenetics, 3D network, Heterogeneous network, Aartificial intelligence, Functional prediction, Proteomics, Functional genomics, Multiomics integration, Histone modifications

1 Introduction

Epigenetics is the study of heritable changes in gene expression that do not involve alterations in the DNA sequence. These changes are driven by chemical modifications such as DNA methylation, histone modifications, and noncoding RNA interactions, which collectively influence chromatin structure and gene expression. Functional prediction in epigenetics seeks to understand the biological impact of these modifications, linking them to cellular processes, phenotypic outcomes, and disease states.

With advancements in high-throughput sequencing technologies and computational tools, the functional prediction of epigenetic modifications has become a cornerstone of modern biology. Here,

Y-h Taguchi (ed.), *AI/ML-Driven Gene Analysis*, Methods in Molecular Biology, vol. 3037,
https://doi.org/10.1007/978-1-0716-5284-8_3,

we describe a computational approach for a real-world application of functional prediction in epigenetics. Biological data are often interdependent, forming intricate relationships that can be best captured using network structures. Complex biological systems, such as gene regulation and protein–protein interactions, can be effectively modeled as networks. Examples include protein–protein interaction networks, gene regulatory networks, and many others [1–4]. These networks provide an intuitive representation of relational structures, making them a powerful tool for analyzing interconnected data. A typical network model can be represented as $G=(V, E)$, where $V \in R^n$ is a set of n unique vertices and $E \in R^{n \times n}$ is a set of edges capturing the pairwise relationships among vertices. Compared to unstructured, also known as linkage-free data, network-based models provide several significant advantages: (i) explicit representation of relationships, where networks naturally capture complex dependencies and relevance relationships between data instances. This explicit linkage enables a more accurate representation of system dynamics [1]; (ii) propagation of information across structures, where, in addition to directly connected entities, networks facilitate the modeling of implicit correlations, allowing insights into indirect associations that may not be immediately obvious [5]; (iii) structural similarity and relational inference, where entities with similar structural properties in a network—such as having common neighbors or similar connectivity patterns—are often functionally related. This principle is widely used in link prediction, recommendation systems, and functional genomics [5]; (iv) support for machine learning applications such as clustering [6], classification [7], prediction [8], and visualization [9], leveraging network structures for improved analytical performance.

In recent years, a considerable body of research has focused on transforming linkage-free data into network-structured data, a process commonly referred to as "network construction" [10]. This approach has garnered particular attention in the biomedical domain. For instance, gene regulatory network construction aims to model the complex regulatory activities between genes by analyzing gene expression data [11, 12]. Gene coexpression network construction aims to establish pairwise associations between gene transcripts by calculating their coexpression values [13, 14]. Protein–protein interaction network construction seeks to uncover high-confidence correlation relationships among proteins in various organisms using high-throughput technologies [15, 16]. A common characteristic of these network construction methods is that they derive a 2 Dimensional (2D) homogeneous network model from a single data object, such as gene expression or protein interaction data, meaning that all nodes represent the same type of biological entity (e.g., genes or proteins). However, this approach fails to account for cases in which two distinct but correlated data objects are involved, such as biological systems that often involve multiple interacting components, necessitating the development of 3 Dimensional (3D) heterogeneous networks, thereby enabling a richer representation of complex systems [17]. In general, the challenge of constructing a 3D network model from two distinct but correlated data objects is twofold: (i) the characterization of relationships between each data object and shared factors, and (ii) the characterization of relationships between the two data objects in a unified network model [18, 19].

To address these challenges, recent advances have proposed novel methods for constructing 3D heterogeneous networks by incorporating multiple data types and shared factors using multimodal network learning approaches, which have led to enhanced representation learning and better predictive performance [20]. Graph Neural Networks (GNNs) have been developed to dynamically learn multitype relationships, allowing for deeper insights into complex biological and computational systems. However, GNN suffers from black-box problem, i.e., lack of interpretability. To address this challenge, we introduce gen3DNet, a generalized multimodal network learning framework that can integrate diverse data sources, such as genomic, proteomic, clinical, and any other datasets, to provide interpretable, richer, and more robust predictive models. As an example of a functional prediction of epigenetic system, we demonstrate the utility of gen3DNet in the functional prediction of histone regulations mediated by phosphoprotein when treated with therapeutic agents in breast cancer using mass spectrometry datasets. These datasets can be viewed as two separate data objects that are causally mediated by shared therapeutic agents or factors.

Here, we extend the iPhDNet [4] model (capturing the interactions among peptides, histones, and drugs) to gen3DNet, encapsulated in an R package capable of generating 3D heterogeneous network models from any modes of two input data objects with shared factors. Figure 1 shows the high-level implementation scheme of the proposed gen3DNet, which takes two data objects as inputs. First, it performs the clustering on the first data object, e.g., using Non-negative Matrix Factorization (NMF) [21], to obtain the linkage coefficients between samples from the first object and shared factors, where k clusters (e.g., C_1, C_2, ..., C_k) are generated for all samples and shared factors, respectively. We implemented three methods to determine the optimal selection of K, including NbClust [22], Cophenetic [23], and Silhouette [24]–based techniques and evaluation metrics. Additionally, the linkage coefficients between samples from the two different objects are obtained based on the Partial Least Squares Regression (PLSR) model [25]. Finally, the two interaction networks generated in above two steps are integrated into a single 3D network.

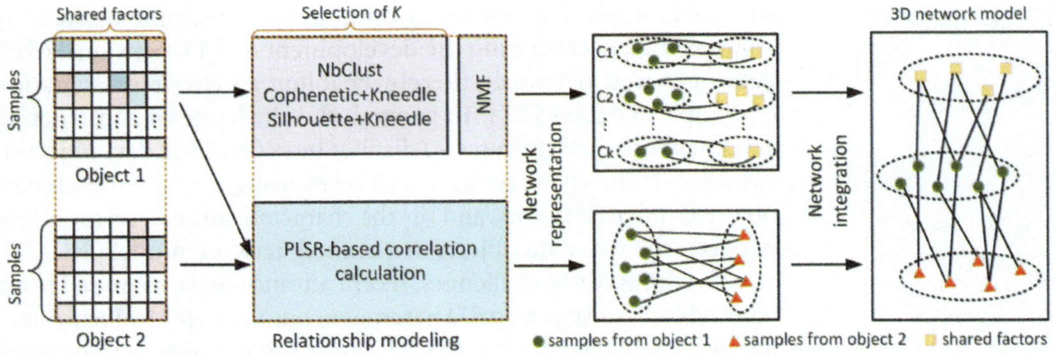

Fig. 1 Implementation framework of the proposed AI-based three-dimensional (3D) heterogeneous network, gen3DNet. Depicting an integrative model consists of an unsupervised learning component: Non-negative Matrix Factorization (NMF) and a supervised learning component: Partial Least Squares Regression (PLSR)

2 Materials

2.1 Data Sources for Epigenetic Studies

The experimental data were generated by the NIH Library of Integrated Network-Based Cellular Signatures (LINCS) Proteomic Characterization Center for Signaling and Epigenetics (PCCSE) repository (https://panoramaweb.org/LINCS). Data were collected for MCF7 breast cancer cell line. Level 3 (log2-normalized) mass spectrometry (MS)-based targeted Phosphoproteomics assay (P100) against 96 phosphopeptides data, and level 3 (log2-normalized) (*see* **Note 13**) MS-based Global Chromatin Profiling assay (GCP) against 60 probes that monitor combinations of posttranslational modification on histones data after treatment with 31 established drugs (serine and threonine kinase inhibitors) are used in this study (*see* **Note 1**).

2.2 Data Preprocessing

For each of the 31 drugs in the proteomic assays (P100 and GCP), there were three biological replicates available at 24 h. Replicates were used to impute missing data by taking their weighted average values during the preprocessing step (*see* **Notes 1 and 2**). Sparse data (containing many zero values) were replaced by very small values (*see* **Note 2**). Differential histone modifications and phosphorylation changes were computed by taking fold changes of each perturbed phosphopeptide and histone code with respect to the control (DMSO), log-transformed and centered (*see* **Note 6**). These resulted in two data matrices: (i) phosphoprotein profiles consisting of 96 phosphopeptides × 31 drugs and (ii) global chromatin profiles consisting of 60 histone modifications × 31 drugs. Prior to modeling, P100 data were normalized with respect to the mean and standard deviation of the respective variables. Histone codes and phosphoproteins with extreme values or single replicates (outliers) were purged from the datasets (*see* **Note 7**).

3 Methods

3.1 Quantification and Statistical Analysis

1. Let the two input data objects (GCP and P100) be represented as $M_1 \in R^{m \times f}$ and $M_2 \in R^{n \times f}$ respectively, where m and n are the numbers of samples from the first (M_1) and second (M_2) data objects, respectively, and f is the number of shared factors between these two data objects. First, the relationships between the samples and shared factors are calculated from the M_1, which involves a non-negative matrix factorization performed as:

$$M_1 \approx WH^T \tag{1}$$

$$W,\ H \geq 0$$

where samples and shared factors are mapped in a k-dimensional latent space represented in $W \in R^{m \times k}$ and $H \in R^{n \times k}$, respectively. Similar to vector quantization methods such as Principal Components Analysis (PCA) [26] and Singular Value Decomposition (SVD) [27], the objective of NMF is to explain the observed data using a compact number of latent features, i.e., basis components (W), which, when combined with loading/mixture components (H), approximate the original data (M_1) as accurately as possible. Since the objective is to reduce the dimension of the original data M_1, the factorization rank k is often chosen such that $k \ll (n, m)$. We used an NMF version that minimizes the divergence function (KL divergence) given by Brunet et al. [28] as the loss function. Therefore, NMF finds the solution of the following:

$$\begin{aligned} &\min D(M_1 \| WH^T) \\ &= \sum_{i=1}^{n} \sum_{j=1}^{m} \left(M_{1_{ij}} \log \frac{A_{ij}}{(WH^T)_{ij}} - M_{1_{ij}} + (WH^T)_{ij} \right) \end{aligned} \tag{2}$$

where D is the loss function, via an iterative process [21]. Since Eq. 1 is a non-convex optimization problem with respect to W and H, there is no guarantee of reaching a local minimum. Additionally, iterative update rules are known for slow convergence, requiring more iterations, with a complexity of $O(mnk^2 N_i N_o)$, where N_i represents the number of inner iterations for solving the non-negative linear model, and N_o denotes the number of outer iterations alternating between W and H updates. As a result, initializing the factor matrices (W, H) is a crucial aspect of designing effective NMF methods

[21]. We employed a robust initialization strategy using a seeding algorithm based on non-negative double Singular Value Decomposition (nndSVD) [29] (*see* **Note 5**). This approach makes the process deterministic, requiring only a single execution, thereby reducing the complexity to $O(mnk^2 N_i + N_o)$. In our NMF formulation, both the matrix representing the basis components (histone signatures) and the matrix of mixture coefficients (drug prototypes) are constrained to have non-negative values. To guarantee the non-negativity constraint, M_1 was log-transformed (*see* **Note 3**). Then, all samples are grouped into k clusters based on W, in which each sample is assigned with a cluster with the largest membership value across the k latent dimensions, i.e., each of the k latent space dimensions corresponds to a cluster. The same clustering process applies to all shared factors based on H. Finally, samples and shared factors from the identical clusters build the pairwise edge connections, where the weights on the edges are given by the corresponding coefficient values in H, i.e., assume sample s_i and factor p_j are in the kth cluster, then the connection weight between s_i and p_j equals to $H_{j,k}$.

2. Then, the relationships between samples from M_1 and M_2 are calculated based on the PLSR model as follows:

$$M_1 = W_{\text{coef}} M_2 + E \tag{3}$$

where $W_{\text{coef}} \in R^{m \times n}$ is the coefficient matrix revealing the contributions of the second object M_2 to the formulation of the first object M_1, and E is the residual or error matrix for the PLSR model. We then build the connection between samples from M_1 and M_2, where the edge weights are given by W_{coef}. PLSR is a multivariate regression method used to construct predictive models when the number of predictor variables (phosphopeptides, in our case) exceeds the number of dependent variables (histone marks) and collinearity is present, as phosphopeptides are often correlated with one another. One of the key challenges in PLSR is determining the optimal number of latent variables (components). Using too few components can result in underfitting, whereas too many can lead to overfitting and reduced generalizability. We determined the optimal model parameters using tenfold cross-validation on the training data (*see* **Note 8**). Predictive performance was evaluated by calculating the Residual Sum of Squares (RSS) error on the test set. To ensure accurate model prediction, we selected the optimal number of latent variables or Principal Components (PCs) based on an RSS value <0.05 (*see* **Note 9**). After generating the coefficients W_{coef}, we retained only the significant peptides (p-value < 0.0001) using a t-test, where the degrees of freedom (DOF) were computed as:

$$\text{DOF} = \min(\text{column of } M_2, \text{ row of } M_2) - \text{PC} - 1 \tag{4}$$

The general idea behind PLSR is to try to extract latent factors, accounting for as much of the observed variation as possible while modeling the responses well. In this formulation, we are predicting the strength of each phosphopeptide (predictor) mediation contributing to the modulation of histones (responses) in breast cancer when treated by the same drugs. PLSR assumes a linear relationship between the latent variables and the response. For datasets with significant nonlinearities, such as intricate interactions or complex patterns, PLSR may struggle to capture these nuances effectively unless modified (e.g., using kernel methods). To address this shortcoming, we introduced a kernel function that can be applied for those datasets. By default, the kernel function is set to 0 to reflect linearity of PLSR but can be set 1 to capture nonlinearity of datasets (*see* **Note 11**).

Lastly, by integrating the output networks from the NMF and PLSR models, a 3D heterogeneous network model is finally generated. The heterogeneous 3D drug–phosphoprotein–histone interactome network is shown in Fig. 2. This network can be used to gain mechanistic insights into epigenetic regulations, where the identified histone signatures mediated by specific significant phosphoproteins can serve as potential biomarkers for experimental validations and further drug efficacy studies in breast cancer.

3.2 Default k -Selection Algorithm

Determining the number of clusters in a dataset is a crucial aspect of gen3DNet, yet no single domain-based method exists for selecting this parameter. To address this, we evaluated several common k-selection algorithms to identify the most generalizable approach. We generated hundreds of synthetic/simulated datasets, each with a predefined number of clusters, applied the candidate algorithms, and analyzed the correlation between true and predicted k values under varying conditions. Based on these findings, we selected a combination of the Ward clustering algorithm and the Krzanowski–Lai (KL) index (implemented in the NbClust library) as the optimal/default k-selection method for gen3DNet (*see* **Note 4**). Each dataset was generated by placing k cluster centers (k ranging from 2 to 10) and adding data points around each center following a Gaussian distribution, with the standard deviations (values ranging from 1, 3, 5, 7, 9, and 11) as a key parameter. Another important parameter, number of dimensions (columns) in the dataset was varied from 2, 4, 8, 16, and 32. Both of these parameters were varied across these values. The number of samples (rows) in each simulated dataset was left constant (at 1000).

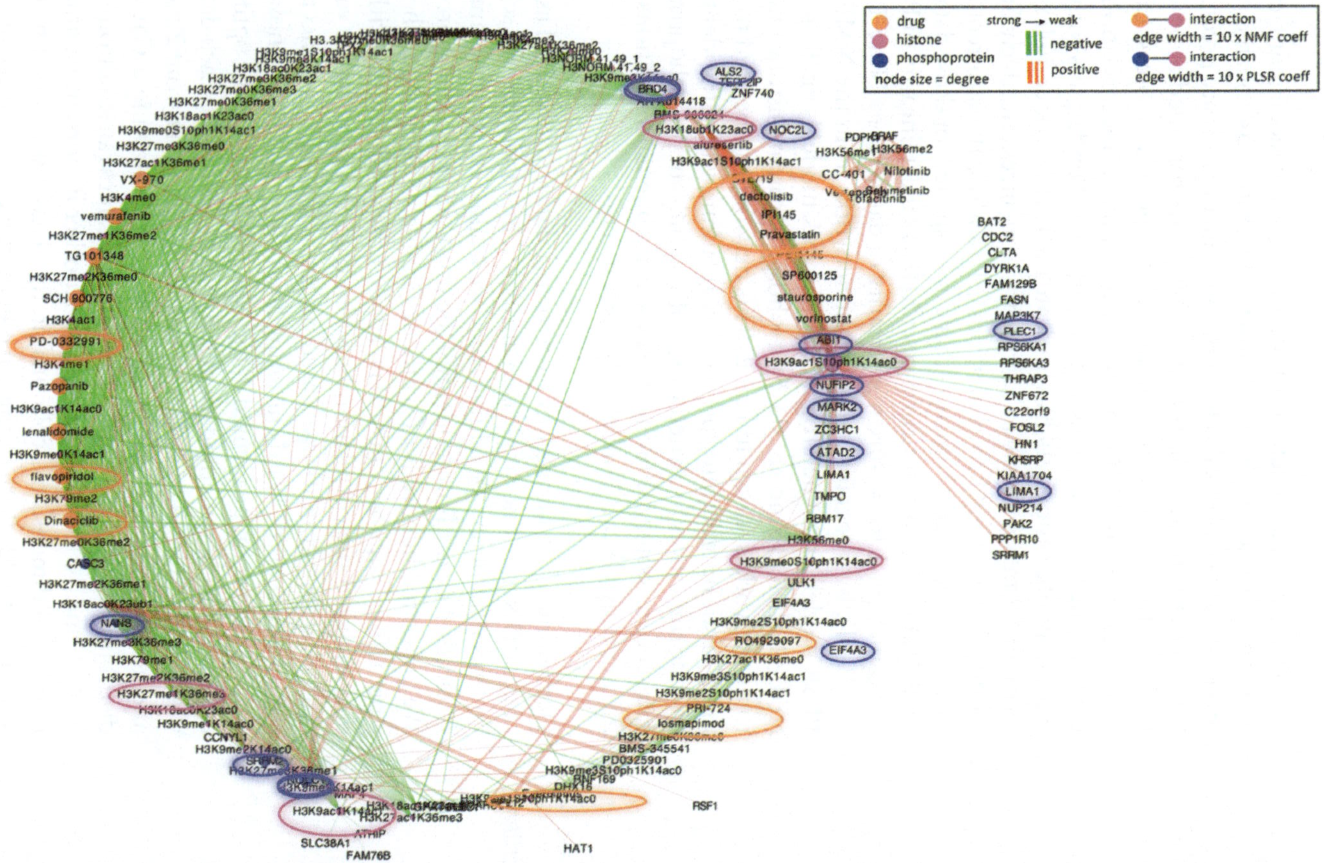

Fig. 2 3D heterogeneous network view of drug–phosphoprotein–histone interactome generated by gen3DNet. The network shows histone regulations highlighting enriched histone codes acting as highly connected nodes (hub) mediated by significantly enriched phosphoproteins treated by various drugs. The strength of an interaction is captured by the thickness of an edge

The following candidate k-selection methods are used:

1. **Cophenetic correlation:** In hierarchical classification, the cophenetic correlation measures the relationship between true distances and dendrogrammatic distances for each pair of data points. As the number of clusters increases, this correlation improves, making its maximum value biased toward the highest possible cluster count. To address this, a separate algorithm is needed to identify the "knee"—the point beyond which increasing k provides little benefit. We used the Kneedle algorithm [30] for this purpose. Since the knee often forms an "L" shape, the algorithm draws a line from the upper left to the lower right and identifies the point farthest from this line, marking the bend of the "L" shape.
2. **Silhouette:** The silhouette score for an individual point ranges from −1 to +1, measuring how well it fits within its assigned cluster compared to other clusters. For a given point i, let $a(i)$ represents the average distance between i and other points in its cluster, and $b(i)$ denote the average distance between i and the nearest neighboring cluster. The silhouette score for i is then calculated as:

$$\frac{b(i) - a(i)}{\max\{a(i), b(i)\}} \tag{5}$$

   For an entire dataset, the silhouette is the average over all points. This method is also combined with the Kneedle algorithm for knee detection.
3. **Ward KL:** This k-selection method uses the Krzanowski–Lai (KL) index [31] to determine the optimal number of clusters, with cluster assignments performed using the Ward algorithm [32]. The Ward algorithm is a hierarchical clustering method that minimizes within-cluster variance, measured as the squared Euclidean distance between points. Initially, each point is treated as an individual cluster, and at each iteration, the pair of clusters with the smallest within-cluster distance is merged. We used the "ward.D2" implementation from the NbClust library.

To apply this clustering method for k-selection, the NbClust library evaluates cluster solutions for k values ranging from 1 to 32, selecting the one with the highest KL index score.

The KL index is based on the quantity $k^{2/p}\widetilde{S}_k$, where p is the number of columns, and $\widetilde{S}_k$ is the trace of the pooled within-group covariance matrix. The difference between a given value of k and the previous value is then referred to as DIFF_k.

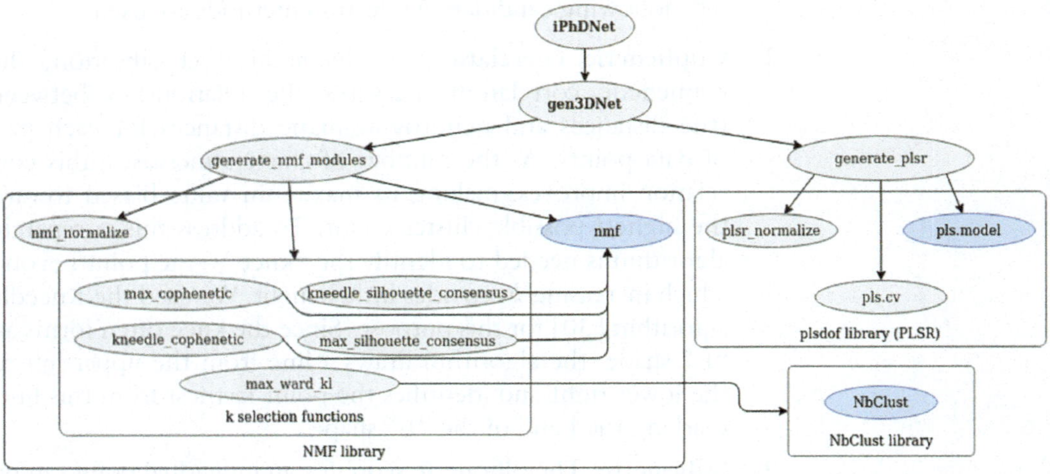

Fig. 3 The dependency relations between modules in the gen3DNet package. The package is optimized by generalizing iPhDNet model to include robust *k* selection functions

Finally, the KL index itself is defined as:

$$\mathrm{KL}(k) = \left| \frac{\mathrm{DIFF}_k}{\mathrm{DIFF}_{k+1}} \right| \tag{6}$$

Therefore, the KL index will be maximized when the change from adding the next cluster ($|\mathrm{DIFF}_{k+1}|$) is the smallest compared with the change from adding the previous cluster ($|\mathrm{DIFF}_k|$). The detailed dependency relations between modules in gen3DNet are depicted in Fig. 3.

Test Case

We demonstrate an application of gen3DNet to build a 3D network model linking phosphoproteins, histones, and drugs data obtained from the study by Mollah and Subramaniam [4] and compare the results with iPhDNet [4]. Gen3DNet results are in perfect agreement with iPhDNet results. This includes significance evaluation of coefficients of phosphoproteins attributing to histone signatures generated by PLSR model using optimal components (*see* **Note 10**) and significance evaluation of loading coefficients of drugs attributing to histone signatures generated by NMF. The meaningful biological significance of these results is also evaluated by LINCS consortium (*see* **Note 14**).

Evaluation

To evaluate gen3DNet model, 20 datasets were simulated for each combination of (n_{rows}, standard deviation within/standard deviation between) specified in determining default *k* section. Each of the three *k*-selection methods was applied to the datasets. The results for a pair of settings are shown in Fig. 4, depicting true *k* on the *x*-axis and the

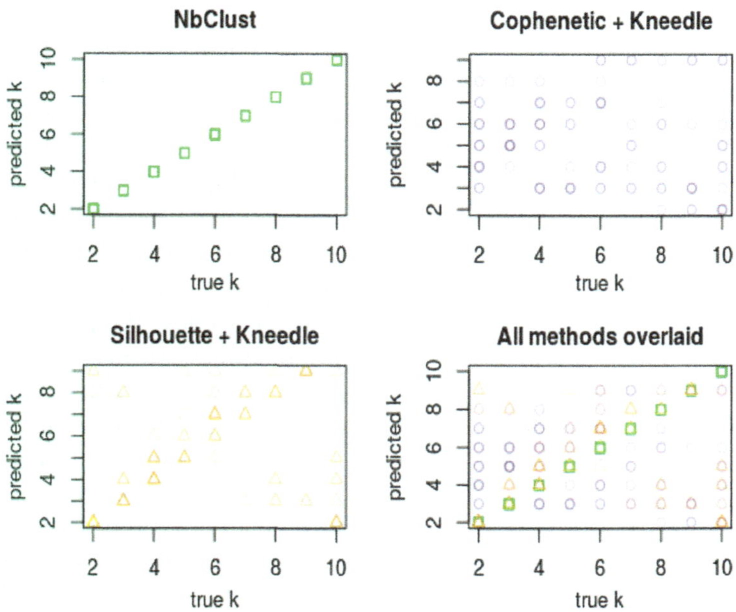

Fig. 4 Comparison of the three adopted methods for identifying the optimal number of clusters (*k*). NbClust (Ward algorithm) performed the best, showing the perfect correlation between the true number of clusters and the prediction (45° angle/diagonal line), while it is weaker for the other methods: Cophenetic + Kneedle and Silhouette + Kneedle (scattered throughout)

predicted *k* on the *y*-axis. The correlation between the true number of clusters and the Ward (NbClust) prediction is perfect (diagonal or 45° angle line), while it is weaker for the other methods: Cophenetic + Kneedle and Silhouette + Kneedle (scattered throughout). These analyses were run on high-performance computing clusters (*see* **Note 12**).

3.3 gen3DNet R Package Installation

The package can be installed in two ways:

1) The release version from CRAN:

```
install.packages("gen3DNet")
or 2) Directly from GitHub:
install.packages("gen3DNet")
remotes::install_github("MollahLab/gen3DNet")
```

4 Notes

1. **Data preprocessing, normalization, and data heterogeneity:** Preprocessing steps such as normalization and batch correction are critical to ensure that the NIH LINCS data are consistent across experiments. LINCS provides a variety

of data types, including gene expression, protein abundance, and cellular phenotypic responses, across different experimental conditions. Variations in experimental protocols or technical artifacts can lead to significant noise, making it challenging to interpret and integrate data from different sources. Use level 3 or higher preprocessed and normalized datasets from LINCS or appropriate normalization methods for other datasets to ensure consistency and comparability.

2. **Handling sparse and missing data:** NMF is typically less effective when applied directly to sparse data. In many cases (e.g., in genomics, proteomics), data matrices are sparse (containing many zero values), and NMF might struggle to produce meaningful factorization without additional modifications to the algorithm. PLSR does not inherently handle missing data. When there are missing values in the predictor or response matrices, preprocessing steps such as imputation must be performed. Incorrect handling of missing data can lead to biased or inaccurate models. Eliminate data features (histones or phosphoproteins) with only one replicate to allow proper data imputation. Impute data using weighted average of the fold change values of both P100 and GCP datasets or use imputation methods for other datasets.
3. **Difficulty with negative values:** NMF assumes non-negativity in the data, meaning that all data points must be positive. However, many real-world datasets (such as those gene expression or protein abundance) may contain negative values, which complicates the direct application of NMF and therefore requires data preprocessing or transformation. Use proper log transformation on the datasets to satisfy the non-negativity constraint.
4. **Choosing the correct rank (number of components):** One of the primary challenges of NMF is determining the appropriate rank (the number of components) for factorization. A poor choice of rank can lead to either overfitting (if the rank is too high) or underfitting (if the rank is too low), which may not accurately capture the underlying structure of the data. Use default/Ward algorithm when running gen3DNet to determine the optimal rank.
5. **Initialization:** The initialization of the pair of factors (W, H) is considered an important component in the design of successful NMF methods. A robust initialization strategy using the seeding algorithm based on a non-negative double singular value decomposition (nndSVD) was used to make the process deterministic and reduce the complexity from $O(mnk^2 N_i N_o)$ to $O(mnk^2 N_i + N_o)$, where N_i is the number of

inner iterations to solve the non-negative linear model and N_o is the number of outer iterations to alternate W and H steps.

6. **Scaling and centering data:** Proper scaling and centering of the predictor variables are crucial in PLSR. Without appropriate preprocessing, variables with larger ranges can dominate the analysis, leading to biased results. Ensure all predictors are on the same scale using log transformation or other scaling methods on the datasets.
7. **Sensitivity to outliers:** PLSR can be sensitive to outliers in the data. If outliers are not properly detected and handled, they can distort the model by affecting the estimation of the latent variables, leading to inaccurate predictions. Outliers were identified during preprocessing step and purged from the datasets prior to data analyses.
8. **Complexity of model validation:** Validating the performance of a PLSR model can be difficult, especially when the number of latent variables is large. Cross-validation and other techniques can help, but the results can be highly sensitive to the choice of validation method, the number of components, and other hyperparameters. Identification of optimal principal components (PCs) with residual square sum (RSS) value <0.05 was used to predict the model accurately and validated using tenfold cross-validation.
9. **Selecting optimal number of latent variables:** One of the main challenges in PLSR is selecting the optimal number of latent variables (components). If too few components are used, the model may underfit the data, while using too many components may lead to overfitting and loss of generalizability. Optimal number of latent variables or principal components (PCs) was identified by setting residual square sum (RSS) value <0.05.
10. **Interpretation of model coefficients:** Interpreting the coefficients of the PLSR model can be difficult. Unlike linear regression, where coefficients are directly interpretable, the latent variables in PLSR do not correspond directly to the original variables, making it hard to understand the specific influence of each predictor on the response. Careful attention to preprocessing, model selection, and validation is essential for obtaining reliable and interpretable results.
11. **Difficulty with non-linear relationships:** PLSR assumes a linear relationship between the latent variables and the response. For datasets where nonlinearities play an important role, such as interactions or complex patterns, PLSR may not capture these nuances effectively without modifications (e.g., kernel methods). Gen3DNet is implemented with kernel

methods; however, by default the option is set to 0 (turned off). Make sure it is set to 1 (turned on).

12. **Computational resources:** Building and analyzing large-scale 3D heterogeneous networks that integrate multiomics data requires significant computational power, which can be a bottleneck for researchers without access to high-performance computing resources. Gen3DNet analyses run more efficiently on high-performance computing clusters as well as on personal computer with adequate memory and CPU power.
13. **Reproducibility and consistency:** The reproducibility of results from multiomics data is often dependent on how the data are preprocessed, analyzed, and integrated. Small changes in methodology or data handling can lead to varying results, making it challenging to ensure consistent and reproducible outcomes when working with the LINCS dataset.
14. **Interpretation of biological signatures:** LINCS data are designed to generate molecular signatures for various perturbations, but interpreting these signatures in a meaningful biological context is not always straightforward. The molecular responses to perturbations may be highly context-dependent, and linking these signatures to specific biological processes or diseases requires deep domain knowledge.

Acknowledgments

This work was supported by NIH NHGRI grant U01HG013227-01 and Washington University School of Medicine in St. Louis Department of Genetics funds.

Conflict of Interest The authors have no conflicts of interest to declare that are relevant to the content of this chapter.

References

1. Newman MEJ, Park J (2003) Why social networks are different from other types of networks. Phys Rev E Stat Nonlin Soft Matter Phys 68(3 Pt 2):036122
2. Franceschini A, Szklarczyk D, Frankild S, Kuhn M, Simonovic M, Roth A et al. (2013) STRING v9.1: protein-protein interaction networks, with increased coverage and integration. Nucleic Acids Res 41(Database issue):D808–D815
3. Hartwell LH, Hopfield JJ, Leibler S, Murray AW (1999) From molecular to modular cell biology. Nature 402(6761 Suppl):C47–C52
4. Mollah SA, Subramaniam S (2020) Histone signatures predict therapeutic efficacy in breast cancer. IEEE Open J Eng Med Biol 1:74–82
5. Boccaletti S et al. (2006) Complex networks: structure and dynamics. Phys Rep 424(4):175–308
6. Tang L., Wang X, Liu H (2009) Uncovering groups via heterogeneous interaction analysis. In: 2009 Ninth IEEE international conference on data mining. IEEE, pp 503–512
7. Zhang D, Wang Y, Zhou L, Yuan H, Shen D (2011) Multimodal classification of Alzheimer's

disease and mild cognitive impairment. Neuroimage 55(3):856–867
8. Scarselli F et al. (2009) The graph neural network model. IEEE Trans Neural Netw 20(1):61–80
9. Ribeiro LF et al. (2017) A survey on network-based learning in the biomedical domain. IEEE Trans Knowl Data Eng 29(4):847–860
10. Tao C et al. (2013) The challenge of constructing large-scale biological networks. Bioinformatics 29(1):120–126
11. Zhang X et al. (2019) Gene regulatory network inference based on gene expression data: a review. Artif Intell Med 96:81–92
12. Alon U (2007) Network motifs: theory and experimental approaches. Nat Rev Genet 8(6):450–461
13. Langfelder P, Horvath S (2008) WGCNA: an R package for weighted correlation network analysis. BMC Bioinform 9(1):559
14. Horvath S et al. (2011) WGCNA: an R package for weighted correlation network analysis. BMC Bioinform 9:559
15. Szklarczyk D et al. (2019) STRING v11: protein-protein association networks with increased coverage, supporting functional discovery in genome-wide experimental datasets. Nucleic Acids Res 47(D1):D607–D613
16. von Mering C, Jensen LJ, Snel B, Hooper SD, Krupp M, Foglierini M, Jouffre N, Huynen MA, Bork P (2005) STRING: known and predicted protein–protein associations, integrated and transferred across organisms. Nucleic Acids Res 33(Database issue):D433–D437
17. Jiang J et al. (2018) Construction of heterogeneous networks in biological and computational systems. Comput Biol Chem 76:118–127
18. Liu X et al. (2015) Network-based learning methods for bioinformatics applications. Front Genet 6:47
19. Chen Z et al. (2020) A survey on network-based learning in biological systems. Comput Biol Chem 84:107224
20. Wang H, Wang J, Wang J, Zhao M, Zhang W, Zhang F, Xie X, Guo M (2018) GraphGAN: Graph representation learning with generative adversarial nets. In: Proceedings of the AAAI conference on artificial intelligence, vol 32, No. 1
21. Lee DD, Seung HS (1999) Learning the parts of objects by non-negative matrix factorization. Nature 401:788–791
22. Charrad M, Ghazzali N, Boiteau V, Niknafs A (2014) NbClust: an R package for determining the relevant number of clusters in a data set. J Stat Softw 61(6):1–36.
23. Saraçli S, Doğan N, Doğan İ (2013) Comparison of hierarchical cluster analysis methods by cophenetic correlation. J Inequalities Appl 2013:1–8. 2013:203
24. Shahapure KR, Nicholas C (2020) Cluster quality analysis using silhouette score. In: 2020 IEEE 7th international conference on data science and advanced analytics (DSAA). IEEE
25. Krämer N, Sugiyama M (2011) The degrees of freedom of partial least squares regression. J Am Stat Assoc 106:697–705
26. Jolliffe IT (2002) Principal component analysis. In: Springer series in statistics. Springer.
27. Eckart C, Young G (1936) The approximation of one matrix by another of lower rank. Psychometrika 1(3):211–218
28. Brunet J-P, Tamayo P, Golub TR, Mesirov JP (2004) Metagenes and molecular pattern discovery using matrix factorization. Proc Natl Acad Sci U S A 101:4164–4169
29. Boutsidis C, Gallopoulos E (2008) SVD based initialization: a head start for nonnegative matrix factorization. Pattern Recognit 41:1350–1362
30. Satopaa V, Albrecht J, Irwin D, Raghavan B (2011) Finding a "kneedle" in a haystack: detecting knee points in system behavior. In: 2011 31st international conference on distributed computing systems workshops. IEEE
31. Krzanowski WJ, Lai YT (1988) A criterion for determining the number of groups in a data set using sum-of-squares clustering. Biometrics 44:23
32. Murtagh F, Legendre P (2011) Ward's hierarchical clustering method: clustering criterion and agglomerative algorithm. arXiv [stat.ML]

Chapter 4

Functional Prediction of Epitranscriptome

Yuxin Zhang, Bowen Song and Kunqi Chen

Abstract

N6-methyladenosine (m6A) is one of the most prevalent and well-studied RNA modifications, playing a pivotal role in many biological processes. With the recent advances in high-throughput sequencing technologies, tens of thousands of m6A sites have been reported. However, not all m6A sites are important or functionally significant, highlighting the need to distinguish biologically relevant m6As from non-functional or technically artefactual ones. Here, we describe ConsRM, which is a web-based resource that was designed to evaluate the importance of m6As from an evolutionary perspective. It introduced a novel scoring framework for quantifying the conservation degree of m6As in humans. Its web interface includes a database of 177998 distinct human m6A sites along with their calculated conservation score, and allows users to analyze their own data via the web server. ConsRM is freely accessible at: http://180.208.58.19/conservation/browser.html.

Keywords Conservation analysis, N6-methyladenosine (m6A), Machine learning, Genome analysis, Scoring framework, Evolutionary

1 Introduction

To date, more than 170 modifications have been reported on RNA molecules [1–4]. Among them, N6-methyladensone (m6A) is one of the most abundant and studied one [5, 6]. Studies have revealed its critical roles in modulating RNA metabolism, such as splicing, stability, translation, and degradation [7]. It is dynamically regulated by m6A "writers" (methyltransferase), "erasers" (demethylases), and "readers" (binding proteins), which collectively regulate gene expressions and thus influence many biological processes, such as cell differentiation, tissue homeostasis, and normal development [8–15].

With the advances of high-throughput sequencing techniques, various techniques are available for the identification of m6A modifications with single-base resolution, including m6A-CLIP, miCLIP, PA-m6A-seq, m6ACE-seq, m6A-REF-seq, and m6A-Label-seq [16–23]. Tens of thousands of m6A sites were reported by these experimental techniques and can be queried from various databases

Y-h Taguchi (ed.), *AI/ML-Driven Gene Analysis*, Methods in Molecular Biology, vol. 3037,
https://doi.org/10.1007/978-1-0716-5284-8_4,

or other sources [24, 25]. However, it is increasingly evident that not all m6A sites are important or functionally significant. While some m6A modifications play critical roles in regulating translation efficiency, RNA splicing, and decay, others may have very limited effect. This heterogeneity underscores the need for further research to distinguish functional m6A sites from non-functional sites or sites that may arise as false positives due to technical limitations.

To evaluate the functional importance of m6A sites, various resources can be used and integrated. Some studies infer potential roles of sites by linking them to their potential target genes, functional elements, and diseases. Examples include m6A2Target, RMBase, Met-DB, and REPIC [26–29]. In addition, multi-omics data can provide insight into the functional roles of sites. For example, m6A-express integrates m6A data with gene expression data to predict the functional outcomes [30]. In this project, we seek to address the challenge from evolutionary perspective. It was known that positive selection acts to preserve traits that confer a survival advantage, ensuring that beneficial features are maintained across generations [31, 32]. This suggests that evolutionarily advantageous elements, such as functionally important m6A sites, are likely to be more conserved across species. Here, we describe ConsRM, a resource for conservation analysis of m6A modification sites, which aims to identify functional m6A sites in humans from an evolutionary perspective [33]. It is a web-based, user-friendly resource, which provides a novel scoring framework for quantifying the conservation of individual m6A sites and a collection of 177998 human m6A sites along with their conservation scores. Also, users are allowed to evaluate their own m6A sites with the consRM server.

2 Materials

2.1 m6A Sites

177,998 distinct m6A sites in human and 110,959 sites in the mouse transcriptome were collected from 46 datasets covering 17 tissues or cells. The collected sites were derived from six different m6A detection techniques.

2.2 Software and Programming Language

1. R and Rstudio.
2. UCSC LiftOver tool: http://genome.ucsc.edu/cgi-bin/hgLiftOver
3. R language interface: LIBSVM.
4. R packages: phastCons100way.UCSC.hg19, ANNOVAR.

2.3 Functional Annotation Data

1. Mutations: 37094832 germline mutations and 2684788 somatic mutations collected from dbSNP and the TCGA database[34, 35].

2. RBP binding sites: RNA-binding protein (RBP) binding sites collected from SATBASE2[36].
3. miRNA binding sites.
4. RNA splicing sites.

3 Methods

Here we describe the development of ConsRM scoring mechanism and how to perform conservation analysis with the ConsRM web-server.

3.1 Evaluating Conservation of m6A Site with ConsRM Score

The ConsRM scoring mechanism integrates information from six sources, including positional mapping, tissue-specific mapping, support from multiple studies, sequence similarity, machine learning modeling, and genome conversion. The ConsRM score for individual m6A sites is calculated by taking the average of the above six elements.

Positional Mapping

Positional mapping inspects whether RNAs transcribed from conserved loci in human and mouse are equally m6A modifiable.

1. Transfer the 177,998 collected human m6A sites to the mouse assembly using the UCSC LiftOver tool.
2. For a human m6A site, if its corresponding mouse coordinate is also m6A, assign a score of one to the human site.
3. Due to potential imprecise conversion, if its corresponding mouse site is not m6A but an m6A site can be found within 1, 2, 3, 4 bp nearby, assign scores of 0.8, 0.6, 0.4, or 0.2, respectively, to it.

Tissue-Specific Mapping

Tissue-specific mapping evaluates whether RNAs transcribed from conserved locus of human and mouse are equally modifiable across tissues. Assign one score to m6A sites observed in both human and mouse tissues. For example, if the m6A sites appear at both human and mouse liver tissue, its Tissue-specific mapping score is 1.

Supports from Multiple Studies

Support from multiple studies concerns whether m6A sites can be detected by different m6A profiling experiments. The collected sites cover six different m6A profiling techniques. Thus, assign 1, 0.8, 0.6, 0.4, or 0.2 mark to a human m6A site if it was detected by 6, 5–6, 2–4, 2, or only one technique.

Sequence Similarity

Sequence similarity score examines the similarity between the nearby sequence of human m6A sites and their corresponding mouse sites.

1. Extract the sequence of 11 bp window centered by human m6A sites and corresponding mouse sites.

2. Use the motif-specific scoring matrix (MSSM) (*see* **Note 1**) to evaluate the similarity between human and mouse sequences [37].
3. Assign the cumulative scores (ranging from 0 to 1) obtained from the MSSM to human m6A sites.
4. Assign a zero mark to human m6A sites if their corresponding mouse coordinates are not adenosine.

Machine Learning Model

Train a machine learning model to predict the conservation of m6A sites (i.e., whether the m6A site is conserved or not).

1. Use domain knowledge, including sequence features (i.e., chemical properties and nucleotide density (*see* **Note 2**) and genomic features (*see* **Note 3**), to computationally represent each human m6A sites [38–40].
2. Select sites modified in both the human and mouse transcriptome as a positive dataset.
3. Select a negative dataset with PU (positive-unlabeled) learning (*see* **Note 4**) methods from the rest of m6A sites [41].
4. Use Support Vector Machine algorithm with LIBSVM platform to train the machine learning model.
5. Use 5-fold cross-validation plus the AUROC (Area Under Receiver Operating Curve), sensitivity, specificity, accuracy, and Matthew's correlation coefficients metrics to evaluate the model performance (*see* **Note 5**).
6. For each individual m6A sites, use the proposed SVM model to predict the probability of being conserved m6A sites. Assign the probability value as the score to m6A sites.

Genome Conversion

Genome conversion examines whether the m6A sites are evolutionarily conserved across species.

1. Calculate the phastCons 100-way conservation score based on the genome-wide alignments of human and other 99 vertebrate species with R package phastCons100way.UCSC.hg19 [42] (*see* **Note 6**).
2. Assign the phastCons scores to human m6A sites to indicate their conservation degree.

Functional Annotation of Human m6A Sites

1. Use R ANNOVAR package to perform basic annotations of human m6A sites, including gene symbol and gene region (e.g., CDS or 3'UTR).
2. Indicate the RBP binding, miRNA targets and RNA splicing information for human m6A sites.

3. Indicate the genetic mutations, including germline and somatic mutations, for m6A sites to suggest their association to diseases.

3.2 Conservation Analysis with ConsRM

A user-friendly web interface was constructed for ConsRM. It is composed of two main parts: (1) a database of collected human m6A sites along with their ConsRM score and functional annotations, and (2) a server that allows users to perform conservation analysis for their own data. The website is freely accessible at: http://180.208.58.19/conservation/browser.html.

Usage of Database

1. Find collected human m6A sites on the Database page.
2. Query m6A sites by Cell line or Technology: users could query the m6A sites from certain cell lines or tissues, or sites derived from different profiling techniques (Fig. 1).
3. Sort results by ConsRM score: users could sort the queried m6A sites by their consRM scores (Fig. 1).
4. See detailed information for individual m6A sites: users could find detailed information by clicking the ID of sites, including the detailed conservation scores (Fig. 2a), basic information and annotations (Fig. 2b), information of corresponding coordinate in mouse transcriptome (if any) (Fig. 2c), etc.

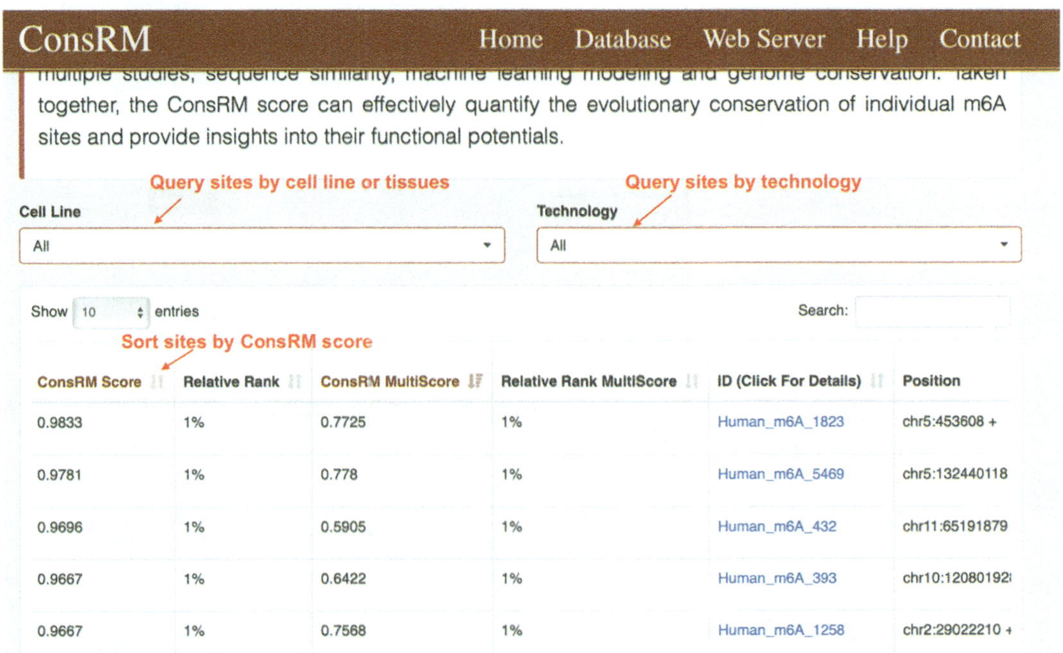

Fig. 1 Query human m6A sites

Fig. 2 Detailed information on individual m6A site. (**a**) Conservation degree of example human m6A site, (**b**) basic information of example human m6A site, (**c**) information of the corresponding site in the mouse transcriptome

5. Genome Browser view of individual m6A sites: by clicking the JBrowse button, users can get an integrated view of reference sequences, modification site information, related RBP binding, splicing, miRNA binding event, and associated mutation information (Fig. 3).

Usage of Web Server

1. Input data: Users could enter their data in the rectangle or upload files n tab-delimited TXT format. The data should be in exactly four columns and separated by tab characters. The four columns should contain the chromosome (e.g., 1, 2, or X), start position, end position, and strand, in the exact order. Each row represents a single site of interest (Fig. 4).
2. Specify the genome assembly used and cell line or tissues for uploaded m6A sites (Fig. 4).

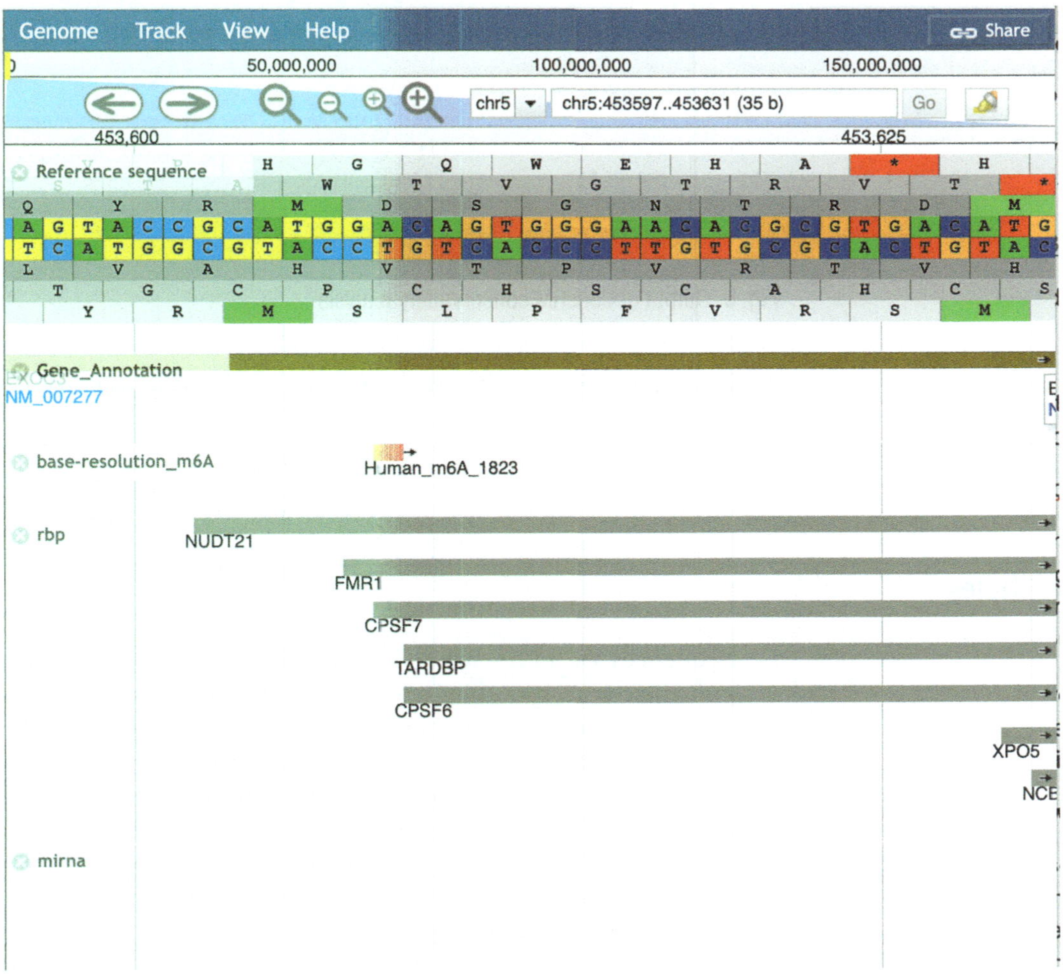

Fig. 3 Genome Browser view of an individual m6A site

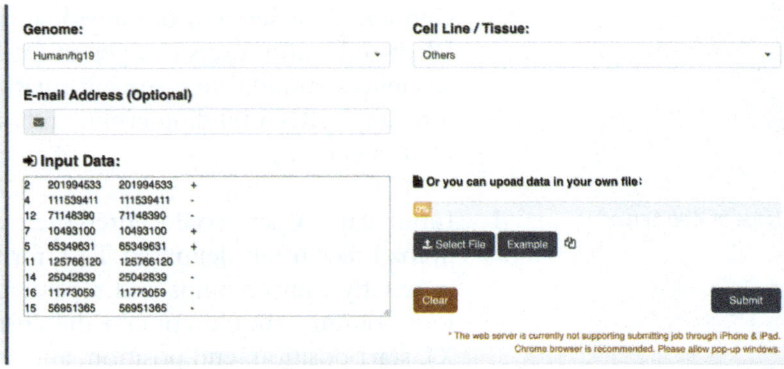

Fig. 4 Input for ConsRM conservation analysis

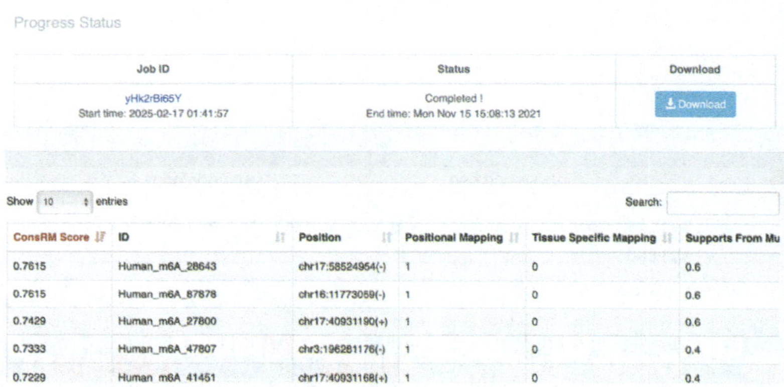

Fig. 5 Output of ConsRM conservation analysis

3. Click submit to run the job and wait for the server to finish the job.
4. Retrieve the results with JobID (Fig. 5).

4 Notes

1. Sequences of 11 bp window centered by human m6A sites and their corresponding coordinates at the mouse transcriptome are extracted. The motif-specific scoring matrix (MSSM) is used to measure the sequence similarity between them (Table 1). Different alignments will receive different scores or penalties, and the m6A-related DRACH motif will receive a higher score. The maximum alignment score is 2*6+5*4=32. Taking the human m6A sites (chr15:77,776,162, plus strand) for demonstration, the sequence of 11 bp centered by it and its corresponding mouse coordinates are TGTAAACAGAG and GGCAGAGAGGG, respectively. The alignment score of these

Table 1
Motif-specific scoring matrix

Positions	−5	−4	−3	−2	−1	0	1	2	3	4	5
Motif				D	R	A	C	H			
No change (I)	2	2	2	4	4	4	4	4	2	2	2
Transition (S)	1	1	1	3	3	3	3	3	1	1	1
Transversion(V)	0	0	0	0	0	0	0	0	0	0	0

Transition refers to the A to G, or C to T mismatch. Transversion refers to A to C or G to T mismatch

two sequences is: 0+2+1+4+3+4+0+4+2+1+2=23. Thus, the sequence similarity score of this human m6A site is 23/32=0.71875.

2. When training the machine learning model for conservation prediction, sequence features, i.e., chemical property and nucleotide density, are used. In terms of chemical property features, the four nucleotides are encoded by three distinct chemical properties, including ring structure, functional groups and hydrogen bonds. Therefore, the A, C, G, U can be encoded as a vector of three features, (1,1,1), (0,1,0), (1,0,0) and (0,0,1). In terms of nucleotide density feature, the cumulative nucleotide frequency is calculated for each nucleotide position. The density of the i-th position of nucleotide (d_i) is calculated the as the total number of occurrences of that nucleotide up to the i-th position in the sequence. Then, the cumulative frequency (f_i) is calculated as di/i. Using the sequence AUGGACACU for demonstration, the cumulative frequency for adenosine is 1 (1/1). 0.4 (2/5) and 0.43 (3/7) at the first, fifth and seven position, respectively. Finally, this sequence can be represented as a vector of nine features (1, 0.5, 0.33, 0.5, 0.4, 0.17, 0.43, 0.33, 0.11).
3. 60 genomic features are included to the machine learning to facilitate the conservation prediction. Detailed explanation of genomic features used can be found from Table 2.
4. When training the machine learning model, m6A sites modified on both human and mouse tissues are considered as conserved (positive). Due to the possible false negative issues, the rest of samples (excluding the positive samples) should be considered as unlabeled data rather than negative. The positive-unlabeled learning strategy is applied to select the most reliable negative data from unlabeled data. Firstly, same number of negative samples N as the positive dataset P are selected from the unlabeled dataset U. A temporary SVM model will be trained with these two datasets and used to predict the probabilities

Table 2
Genomic features used for conservation prediction

ID	Name	Description	Note
1	UTR5	5′ UTR	Dummy variables indicating whether the site overlaps with the topological region of the major RNA transcript.
2	UTR3	3′ UTR	
3	Cds	Coding sequence	
4	Stop_codons	Stop codons flanked by 100 bp	
5	Start_codons	Start codons flanked by 100 bp	
6	TSS	Downstream 100 bp of TSS	
7	TSS_A	Downstream 100 bp of TSS on A	
8	exon_stop	Exons containing stop codons	
9	alternative_exon	Alternative exons	
10	constitutive_exon	Constitutive exons	
11	internal_exon	Internal exons	
12	long_exon	Long exons (exon length >=400 bp)	
13	last_exon	5′ last_exon	
14	last_exon_400 bp	5′ 400 bp of the last exons	
15	last_exon_sc400	5′ 400 bp of the last exons containing stop codons	
16	intron	Intron	
17	pos_UTR5	Relative position on 5′UTR	Relative position in the region
18	pos_UTR3	Relative position on 3′UTR	
19	pos_cds	Relative position on coding sequence	
20	pos_exons	Relative position on exon	
21	dist_sj_5_p2000	Distance to the 5′ splicing junction	Nucleotide distances toward the splicing junctions
22	dist_sj_3_p2000	Distance to the 3′ splicing junction	
23	length_UTR3	3′UTR length	The region length in bp
24	length_UTR5	5′UTR length	
25	length_cds	Coding sequence length	
26	length_gene_exon	Gene length on exon	
27	length_gene_full	Full gene length	
28	length_tx_exon	Mature transcript length	
29	length_tx_full	Full transcript length	

Table 2
Continued

ID	Name	Description	Note
30	clust_f1000	Count of neighboring input site at 1001 bp	Clustering information
31	clust_f100	Count of neighboring input site at 101 bp	
32	clust_A_f1000	Count of neighboring A within a 2001 nt window	
33	clust_A_f100	Count of neighboring A within a 201 nt window	
34	dist_nearest_ p2000	istance to the closest neighboring input site at 2001 bp	
35	dist_nearest_ p200	distance to the closest neighboring input site at 201 bp	
36	dist_A_p2000	Distance to the closest neighboring A at 2001 bp	
37	dist_A_p200	Distance to the closest neighboring A at 201 bp	
38	PC_1bp	PhastCons scores of the nucleotide	Scores related to evolutionary conservation
39	PC_101bp	Average phastCons scores within the flanking 101 bp	
40	FC_1bp	FitCons scores of the nucleotide	
41	FC_101bp	Average fitCons scores within the flanking 101 bp region	
42	struct_hybridize	Predicted RNA hybridized region	RNA secondary structures
43	struct_loop	Predicted RNA loop region	
44	HNRNPC_ eCLIP	eCLIP data of HNRNPC RNA binding sites	Attributes of the genes or transcripts
45	miR_targeted_ genes	miRNA targeted genes	
46	TargetScan	Predicted miRNA targeted sites by TargetScan	
47	Verified_ miRtargets	miRNA targeted sites verified by experiment	
48	METTL3_TREW	Overlapped with binding regions of METTL3	
49	METTL14_ TREW	Overlapped with binding regions of METTL14	
50	WTAP_TREW	Overlapped with binding regions of WTAP	
51	METTL16_CLIP	Overlapped with binding regions of METTL16	
52	ALKBH5_ PARCLIP	Overlapped with binding regions of ALKBH5	
53	FTO_CLIP	Overlapped with binding regions of FTO	

(continued)

Table 2
Continued

ID	Name	Description	Note
54	sncRNA	sncRNA	Genomic properties
55	lncRNA	lncRNA	
56	isoform_num	Number of isoform	
57	exon_num	Number of exon	
58	HK_genes	Housekeeping genes	
59	GC_cont_genes	GC composition of genes	
60	GC_cont_101bp	GC composition of 101 bp	

for unlabeled dataset U. The top 1% of the unlabeled dataset U with highest positive probabilities are considered to be uncovered positive samples, and thus are excluded from dataset U. Above process are repeated for 10 times and the retained dataset U and positive dataset P were used for the final model training.

5. Sensitivity (Sn), Specificity (Sp), Accuracy (Acc) and Matthews correlation coefficient (MCC) are calculated as:

$$\mathrm{Sn} = \mathrm{TP}/(\mathrm{TP}+\mathrm{FN})$$

$$\mathrm{Sp} = \mathrm{TN}/(\mathrm{TN}+\mathrm{FP})$$

$$\mathrm{MCC} = (\mathrm{TP} * \mathrm{TN} - \mathrm{FP} * \mathrm{FN})/\surd \left((\mathrm{TP} + \mathrm{FP})*(\mathrm{TP} + \mathrm{FN})(\mathrm{TN} + \mathrm{FP})(\mathrm{TN} + \mathrm{FN})\right)$$

$$\mathrm{Acc} = (\mathrm{TP} + \mathrm{TN})/(\mathrm{TP} + \mathrm{TN} + \mathrm{FP} + \mathrm{FN})$$

Where TP, FP, TN, and FN are the number of true positive, false negative, true negative and false negative

6. The phastCons 100-way conservation score is a metric used in genomics to measure the evolutionary conservation of DNA sequences across multiple species. It is derived from a statistical model called phastCons, which is part of the PHAST (Phylogenetic Analysis with Space/Time models). The score ranges from 0 to 1, where 0 indicates no conservation (the

sequence is highly variable across species), and 1 indicates perfect conservation. Intermediate scores reflect varying degrees of conservation.

Conflict of Interest

The authors have no conflicts of interest to declare that are relevant to the content of this chapter.

References

1. Boccaletto P, Machnicka MA, Purta E, Piatkowski P, Baginski B, Wirecki TK, de Crécy-Lagard V, Ross R, Limbach PA, Kotter A, Helm M, Bujnicki JM (2018) MODOMICS: a database of RNA modification pathways. 2017 update. Nucleic Acids Res 46(D1):D303–D307. https://doi.org/10.1093/nar/gkx1030
2. Wang X, Zhang Y, Chen K, Liang Z, Ma J, Xia R, de Magalhães JP, Rigden DJ, Meng J, Song B (2024) m7GHub V2.0: an updated database for decoding the N7-methylguanosine (m7G) epitranscriptome. Nucleic Acids Res 52(D1):D203–d212. https://doi.org/10.1093/nar/gkad789
3. Huang J, Wang X, Xia R, Yang D, Liu J, Lv Q, Yu X, Meng J, Chen K, Song B, Wang Y (2024) Domain-knowledge enabled ensemble learning of 5-formylcytosine (f5C) modification sites. Comput Struct Biotechnol J 23:3175–3185. https://doi.org/10.1016/j.csbj.2024.08.004
4. Zhang Y, Yan H, Wei Z, Hong H, Huang D, Liu G, Qin Q, Rong R, Gao P, Meng J, Ying B (2024) NanoMUD: Profiling of pseudouridine and N1-methylpseudouridine using Oxford Nanopore direct RNA sequencing. Int J Biol Macromol 270(Pt 2):132433. https://doi.org/10.1016/j.ijbiomac.2024.132433
5. Dominissini D, Moshitch-Moshkovitz S, Schwartz S, Salmon-Divon M, Ungar L, Osenberg S, Cesarkas K, Jacob-Hirsch J, Amariglio N, Kupiec M, Sorek R, Rechavi G (2012) Topology of the human and mouse m6A RNA methylomes revealed by m6A-seq. Nature 485(7397):201–206. https://doi.org/10.1038/nature11112
6. Zhang Y, Huang D, Wei Z, Chen K (2022) Primary sequence-assisted prediction of m(6)A RNA methylation sites from Oxford nanopore direct RNA sequencing data. Methods 203:62–69. https://doi.org/10.1016/j.ymeth.2022.04.003
7. Wang X, Zhao BS, Roundtree IA, Lu Z, Han D, Ma H, Weng X, Chen K, Shi H, He C (2015) N(6)-methyladenosine modulates messenger RNA translation efficiency. Cell 161(6):1388–1399. https://doi.org/10.1016/j.cell.2015.05.014
8. Liu J, Yue Y, Han D, Wang X, Fu Y, Zhang L, Jia G, Yu M, Lu Z, Deng X, Dai Q, Chen W, He C (2014) A METTL3-METTL14 complex mediates mammalian nuclear RNA N6-adenosine methylation. Nat Chem Biol 10(2):93–95. https://doi.org/10.1038/nchembio.1432
9. Schwartz S, Mumbach MR, Jovanovic M, Wang T, Maciag K, Bushkin GG, Mertins P, Ter-Ovanesyan D, Habib N, Cacchiarelli D, Sanjana NE, Freinkman E, Pacold ME, Satija R, Mikkelsen TS, Hacohen N, Zhang F, Carr SA, Lander ES, Regev A (2014) Perturbation of m6A writers reveals two distinct classes of mRNA methylation at internal and 5' sites. Cell Rep 8(1):284–296. https://doi.org/10.1016/j.celrep.2014.05.048
10. Ping XL, Sun BF, Wang L, Xiao W, Yang X, Wang WJ, Adhikari S, Shi Y, Lv Y, Chen YS, Zhao X, Li A, Yang Y, Dahal U, Lou XM, Liu X, Huang J, Yuan WP, Zhu XF, Cheng T, Zhao YL, Wang X, Rendtlew Danielsen JM, Liu F, Yang YG (2014) Mammalian WTAP is a regulatory subunit of the RNA N6-methyladenosine methyltransferase. Cell Res 24(2):177–189. https://doi.org/10.1038/cr.2014.3
11. Jia G, Fu Y, Zhao X, Dai Q, Zheng G, Yang Y, Yi C, Lindahl T, Pan T, Yang YG, He C (2011) N6-methyladenosine in nuclear RNA is a major substrate of the obesity-associated FTO. Nat Chem Biol 7(12):885–887. https://doi.org/10.1038/nchembio.687
12. Haussmann IU, Bodi Z, Sanchez-Moran E, Mongan NP, Archer N, Fray RG, Soller M (2016) m(6)A potentiates Sxl alternative pre-mRNA splicing for robust Drosophila sex determination. Nature 540(7632):301–304. https://doi.org/10.1038/nature20577
13. Meyer KD, Jaffrey SR (2017) Rethinking m(6)A readers, writers, and erasers. Annu Rev Cell Dev Biol 33:319–342. https://doi.org/10.1146/annurev-cellbio-100616-060758

14. Zhou J, Wan J, Gao X, Zhang X, Jaffrey SR, Qian SB (2015) Dynamic m(6)A mRNA methylation directs translational control of heat shock response. Nature 526(7574):591–594. https://doi.org/10.1038/nature15377
15. Xia R, Yin X, Huang J, Chen K, Ma J, Wei Z, Su J, Blake N, Rigden DJ, Meng J, Song B (2024) Interpretable deep cross networks unveiled common signatures of dysregulated epitranscriptomes across 12 cancer types. Mol Ther Nucleic Acids 35(4):102376. https://doi.org/10.1016/j.omtn.2024.102376
16. Gjoneska E, Pfenning AR, Mathys H, Quon G, Kundaje A, Tsai LH, Kellis M (2015) Conserved epigenomic signals in mice and humans reveal immune basis of Alzheimer's disease. Nature 518(7539):365–369. https://doi.org/10.1038/nature14252
17. Linder B, Grozhik AV, Olarerin-George AO, Meydan C, Mason CE, Jaffrey SR (2015) Single-nucleotide-resolution mapping of m6A and m6Am throughout the transcriptome. Nat Methods 12(8):767–772. https://doi.org/10.1038/nmeth.3453
18. Chen K, Lu Z, Wang X, Fu Y, Luo GZ, Liu N, Han D, Dominissini D, Dai Q, Pan T, He C (2015) High-resolution N(6) -methyladenosine (m(6) A) map using photo-crosslinking-assisted m(6) A sequencing. Angew Chem Int Ed Engl 54(5):1587–1590. https://doi.org/10.1002/anie.201410647
19. Kunitski M, Eicke N, Huber P, Köhler J, Zeller S, Voigtsberger J, Schlott N, Henrichs K, Sann H, Trinter F, Schmidt LPH, Kalinin A, Schöffler MS, Jahnke T, Lein M, Dörner R (2019) Double-slit photoelectron interference in strong-field ionization of the neon dimer. Nat Commun 10(1):1. https://doi.org/10.1038/s41467-018-07882-8
20. Zhang Z, Chen LQ, Zhao YL, Yang CG, Roundtree IA, Zhang Z, Ren J, Xie W, He C, Luo GZ (2019) Single-base mapping of m(6)A by an antibody-independent method. Sci Adv 5(7):eaax0250. https://doi.org/10.1126/sciadv.aax0250
21. Chen K, Song B, Tang Y, Wei Z, Xu Q, Su J, de Magalhães JP, Rigden DJ, Meng J (2021) RMDisease: a database of genetic variants that affect RNA modifications, with implications for epitranscriptome pathogenesis. Nucleic Acids Res 49(D1):D1396–d1404. https://doi.org/10.1093/nar/gkaa790
22. Meyer KD (2019) DART-seq: an antibody-free method for global m(6)A detection. Nat Methods 16(12):1275–1280. https://doi.org/10.1038/s41592-019-0570-0
23. Shu X, Cao J, Cheng M, Xiang S, Gao M, Li T, Ying X, Wang F, Yue Y, Lu Z, Dai Q, Cui X, Ma L, Wang Y, He C, Feng X, Liu J (2020) A metabolic labeling method detects m(6)A transcriptome-wide at single base resolution. Nat Chem Biol 16(8):887–895. https://doi.org/10.1038/s41589-020-0526-9
24. Zhang Y, Jiang J, Ma J, Wei Z, Wang Y, Song B, Meng J, Jia G, de Magalhães JP, Rigden DJ, Hang D, Chen K (2023) DirectRMDB: a database of post-transcriptional RNA modifications unveiled from direct RNA sequencing technology. Nucleic Acids Res 51(D1):D106–d116. https://doi.org/10.1093/nar/gkac1061
25. Liang Z, Ye H, Ma J, Wei Z, Wang Y, Zhang Y, Huang D, Song B, Meng J, Rigden DJ, Chen K (2024) m6A-Atlas v2.0: updated resources for unraveling the N6-methyladenosine (m6A) epitranscriptome among multiple species. Nucleic Acids Res 52(D1):D194–d202. https://doi.org/10.1093/nar/gkad691
26. Deng S, Zhang H, Zhu K, Li X, Ye Y, Li R, Liu X, Lin D, Zuo Z, Zheng J (2021) M6A2Target: a comprehensive database for targets of m6A writers, erasers and readers. Brief Bioinform 22(3). https://doi.org/10.1093/bib/bbaa055
27. Sun WJ, Li JH, Liu S, Wu J, Zhou H, Qu LH, Yang JH (2016) RMBase: a resource for decoding the landscape of RNA modifications from high-throughput sequencing data. Nucleic Acids Res 44(D1):D259–D265. https://doi.org/10.1093/nar/gkv1036
28. Liu H, Flores MA, Meng J, Zhang L, Zhao X, Rao MK, Chen Y, Huang Y (2015) MeT-DB: a database of transcriptome methylation in mammalian cells. Nucleic Acids Res 43(Database issue):D197–D203. https://doi.org/10.1093/nar/gku1024
29. Liu S, Zhu A, He C, Chen M (2020) REPIC: a database for exploring the N(6)-methyladenosine methylome. Genome Biol 21(1):100. https://doi.org/10.1186/s13059-020-02012-4
30. Zhang T, Zhang SW, Zhang SY, Gao SJ, Chen Y, Huang Y (2021) m6A-express: uncovering complex and condition-specific m6A regulation of gene expression. Nucleic Acids Res 49(20):e116. https://doi.org/10.1093/nar/gkab714
31. Graur D, Zheng Y, Azevedo RB (2015) An evolutionary classification of genomic function. Genome Biol Evol 7(3):642–645. https://doi.org/10.1093/gbe/evv021
32. Tu G, Wang X, Xia R, Song B (2024) m6A-TCPred: a web server to predict tissue-conserved human m(6)A sites using machine learning approach. BMC Bioinformatics 25(1):127. https://doi.org/10.1186/s12859-024-05738-1
33. Song B, Chen K, Tang Y, Wei Z, Su J, de Magalhães JP, Rigden DJ, Meng J (2021) ConsRM: collection and large-scale prediction of the evolutionarily conserved RNA methylation sites, with implications for the functional epitranscriptome. Brief Bioinform

22(6):bbab088. https://doi.org/10.1093/bib/bbab088

34. Sherry ST, Ward MH, Kholodov M, Baker J, Phan L, Smigielski EM, Sirotkin K (2001) dbSNP: the NCBI database of genetic variation. Nucleic Acids Res 29(1):308–311. https://doi.org/10.1093/nar/29.1.308
35. Tomczak K, Czerwińska P, Wiznerowicz M (2015) The cancer genome atlas (TCGA): an immeasurable source of knowledge. Contemp Oncol (Pozn) 19(1a):A68–A77. https://doi.org/10.5114/wo.2014.47136
36. Li JH, Liu S, Zhou H, Qu LH, Yang JH (2014) starBase v2.0: decoding miRNA-ceRNA, miRNA-ncRNA and protein-RNA interaction networks from large-scale CLIP-Seq data. Nucleic Acids Res 42(Database issue):D92–D97. https://doi.org/10.1093/nar/gkt1248
37. Malik R, Nigg EA, Körner R (2008) Comparative conservation analysis of the human mitotic phosphoproteome. Bioinformatics 24(12):1426–1432. https://doi.org/10.1093/bioinformatics/btn197
38. Chen K, Wei Z, Zhang Q, Wu X, Rong R, Lu Z, Su J, de Magalhães JP, Rigden DJ, Meng J (2019) WHISTLE: a high-accuracy map of the human N6-methyladenosine (m6A) epitranscriptome predicted using a machine learning approach. Nucleic Acids Res 47(7):e41. https://doi.org/10.1093/nar/gkz074
39. Chen W, Feng P, Yang H, Ding H, Lin H, Chou KC (2018) iRNA-3typeA: identifying Three Types of Modification at RNA's Adenosine Sites. Mol Ther Nucleic Acids 11:468–474. https://doi.org/10.1016/j.omtn.2018.03.012
40. Chen W, Feng P, Tang H, Ding H, Lin H (2016) RAMPred: identifying the N(1)-methyladenosine sites in eukaryotic transcriptomes. Sci Rep 6: 31080. https://doi.org/10.1038/srep31080
41. Zeng X, Zhong Y, Lin W, Zou Q (2020) Predicting disease-associated circular RNAs using deep forests combined with positive-unlabeled learning methods. Brief Bioinform 21(4):1425–1436. https://doi.org/10.1093/bib/bbz080
42. Siepel A, Bejerano G, Pedersen JS, Hinrichs AS, Hou M, Rosenbloom K, Clawson H, Spieth J, Hillier LW, Richards S, Weinstock GM, Wilson RK, Gibbs RA, Kent WJ, Miller W, Haussler D (2005) Evolutionarily conserved elements in vertebrate, insect, worm, and yeast genomes. Genome Res 15(8):1034–1050. https://doi.org/10.1101/gr.3715005

Chapter 5

Inference of Gene–Gene Interaction and Its Function

Kenji Kamimoto

Abstract

The complex functions of cells are achieved through the interactions of diverse molecules and genes, and the analysis of gene interactions is essential to understanding the circuit of biological systems. Computational biology, machine learning, and artificial intelligence are becoming increasingly crucial for extracting insight into complex gene interactions from large-scale and complex data. In this chapter, we introduce computational methods for inferring gene–gene interactions and analyzing the function of genes. First, we briefly review the approaches and characteristics of gene–gene interaction inference algorithms. Then, we present a step-by-step protocol for gene network construction and analysis using CellOracle. This method learns regulatory patterns from single-cell gene expression and epigenomic data to construct transcriptional gene–gene association network models. One of the unique features of this method is the simulation of cell differentiation, which we call "in silico gene perturbation." This approach allows simulation of the dynamics of cell identity upon gene perturbation, facilitating the utilization of gene network models and interpretation of gene function.

Keywords Gene regulatory network, Modeling, Simulation, Single-cell omics, In silico perturbation

1 Introduction

1.1 Definitions and Interpretations of Inferred Gene–Gene Interaction

Gene–gene interactions can be directly measured through experimental methods or inferred from large-scale omics data. This chapter focuses on the computational methodology to infer gene–gene interaction from large-scale observational data. It is also essential to clarify the meaning of the term "interaction" because it can be interpreted in various ways. Here, we focus on methods that utilize transcriptomics data, such as RNA sequencing (RNA-seq), to infer the transcriptional gene–gene interaction [1, 2]. Accordingly, the inferred relationships between genes should not be taken as evidence of physical interactions—for example, protein–protein binding, phosphorylation-based signal transduction, or intercellular interactions such as ligand–receptor binding. If we want to infer protein–protein physical binding, for example, another methodology, such as AlphaFold [3], is required, but we do not cover such topics in this chapter.

Y-h Taguchi (ed.), *AI/ML-Driven Gene Analysis*, Methods in Molecular Biology, vol. 3037,
https://doi.org/10.1007/978-1-0716-5284-8_5,

Before describing our analysis method, we briefly overview general approaches to infer relationships between genes from transcriptome data [1, 2]. Because these approaches attempt to infer relationships among an enormous number of genes, the analysis output is inherently complex, making large networks. Networks inferred from transcriptional data are often called gene regulatory networks (GRNs)—although not all GRNs necessarily represent transcriptional regulation—and the construction process is generally known as GRN inference. Historically, the inference method of gene–gene interaction has progressed with the advancement of omics technology. The early gene network studies used microarray data [4]; more recently, RNA-seq and single-cell RNA-seq have been employed, leading to the development of numerous methods [5, 6]. GRN inference methods rest on the premise that if a biological relationship exists between genes, it will be reflected in the gene expression data. In other words, we can infer the large-scale gene–gene connections, which are primarily unmeasurable directly, by analyzing the observational data with some algorithms. This premise is exploited by statistical, mathematical, or machine learning techniques applied to sample-by-gene expression matrices or cell-by-gene matrices, where each gene's expression is quantitatively measured for each sample.

One common approach computes pairwise correlation between genes, assuming that significant correlations suggest an underlying interaction [4]. Alternatively, regression models are built to predict the expression of a target gene based on other genes; a significant predictor–response relationship is then interpreted as an interaction [6]. It is important to note that neither approach guarantees a causal relationship or a directional hierarchy in the underlying gene regulatory mechanisms. Inferring such causality from transcriptome data falls under the domain of causal inference, which cannot be adequately addressed by correlation analysis alone. While numerous methods exist for inferring gene associations or GRNs, each method has specific assumptions and inherent limitations. Careful interpretation is essential for each technique.

1.2 Utilization of Genomic and Cellular Information in Gene Interaction Inference

In addition to general statistical methods such as correlation and regression analyses, methods tailored to specific biological phenomena have also been developed [1, 7,8]. As noted above, causal inference from observational data is generally challenging and is a problem that extends beyond biology into statistics and informatics. However, incorporating additional information about gene regulation makes it possible to mitigate or even circumvent some of the challenges in statistical causal inference [8]. In GRN inference from transcriptome data, for example, integration of genomic information is helpful in inferring regulation between genes. Generally, transcription factors and RNA polymerase bind to transcriptional regulatory regions of genomic DNA—such as promoters and enhancers—to initiate mRNA synthesis. Thus, it is possible to narrow down candidate regulators for a given gene by incorporating such transcription machinery information. GRN inference algorithms, such as SCENIC, were developed to integrate cis-regulatory genomic DNA sequence and transcription factor binding information to refine GRN models [7, 8].

Another approach is to use the temporal information of biological phenomena. For example, if we have gene expression matrix data as time series, we can apply ordinary differential equations (ODEs) to make GRN models [9]. This approach constructs GRN models to explain the temporal dynamics of gene expression and enables inference of directed graphs.

Moreover, some algorithms elegantly consider the structure of transcriptional machinery by considering RNA splicing to provide temporal dynamics of gene expression for each gene, enabling detailed modeling of gene expression [10]. Because mRNA is subject to splicing after transcription, modeling the ratio of spliced to unspliced mRNA enables the estimation of transcriptional kinetics. Like the ODE approach, we can infer the directed network edge if we acquire temporal dynamics information from RNA splicing. Machine learning methods were developed to integrate the RNA splicing information and GRN inference [11].

The overarching concept in the example above is that effective integration of biological domain knowledge into the modeling strategy can lead to accurate and feasible causal inference. Biological events are complex and large, requiring flexible and scalable algorithm development. Machine learning is promising for flexibly integrating biological domain knowledge with a modeling algorithm.

1.3 Modeling Gene Regulation Using Machine Learning

Machine learning approaches for modeling gene regulatory networks (GRNs) have taken various forms. As a prominent method of early machine learning-based GRN inference algorithms, we briefly introduce GENIE3, which is based on tree-based regression [12]. As an ensemble method—employing techniques such as Random Forest and Extra-Trees—GENIE3 has proven effective at detecting gene connections in simulated gene expression and experimentally measured datasets [13]. Unlike correlation-based analyses that consider only pairwise relationships, multifactor models are essential to consider conditional regulation made by many genes. Also, nonlinear models effectively capture complex biological regulation. GENIE3 outperformed another statistical method on the Dialogue for Reverse Engineering Assessment and Methods (DREAM) challenge, where GRN inference algorithms are benchmarked with a simulated dataset [12, 14]. As highlighted above, one of the strengths of machine learning-based algorithms is their robustness. Biological experimental data are always noisy, and the ensemble method, such as Random Forest, is one of the good ways to deal with it. It is also promising to use probabilistic modeling approaches [1]. Initially developed for the

DREAM challenge, where an algorithm can use only limited uniform data input, GENIE3 was designed without incorporating biological information except the gene expression matrix. Nevertheless, its underlying approach has served as the foundation for subsequent methods such as SCENIC, which integrates genomic regulatory region data to enhance the inference of regulatory relationships [15].

In recent years, large-scale single-cell RNA-seq technologies have spurred the development of more sophisticated AI/machine learning models [1, 5, 6, 13, 16]. Training models with many parameters requires vast amounts of data; obtaining transcriptome data from thousands to millions of cells in a single experiment is now possible with a large-scale scRNA-seq technique. The rapid expansion of accessible scRNA-seq databases and increased computational resources has further accelerated the advancement of machine learning-based gene interaction inference methods. Moreover, the development of large machine learning models, called foundation models, is emerging to solve various biological research tasks, including gene–gene interaction analysis [17–21]. These models typically use large-scale transformer architectures to capture gene associations across different cell types or states [19]. The disadvantage of the generalized foundation model is that it employs very large deep neural network models, and a single gene–gene connection edge cannot simply be represented by a single weight, making interpretation more challenging. Thus, while machine learning offers powerful tools for modeling gene regulatory circuits, an inherent trade-off remains between model complexity and interpretability. Advancing methods to analyze internal model structures and to interpret their biological mechanism will be crucial for the continued progress of this field.

1.4 Summary of Method

In the second half of this chapter, we introduce CellOracle, our method for GRN inference and analysis [22]. CellOracle first constructs a cell type-specific GRN model by integrating single-cell gene expression and epigenomic data.

As discussed above, inferring gene–gene interactions from observational data is challenging, and understanding the functional implications of the inferred network is even more complex. Even when a network model is obtained through GRN inference, biological networks' sheer scale and intricacy make their interpretation nontrivial. Consequently, much of previous GRN research has made significant efforts for network structure analysis, such as applying graph theory and performing community detection analyses.

In contrast, CellOracle is designed not only for structural analysis of GRNs but also for utilizing network models to simulate cell dynamics and gene functions (Fig. 1). A distinctive feature of CellOracle is its "in silico gene perturbation analysis," which uses the GRN model as a simulator to predict cellular responses to gene perturbations. This simulation-based approach enables the interpretation of gene function. The underlying founding assumptions of this

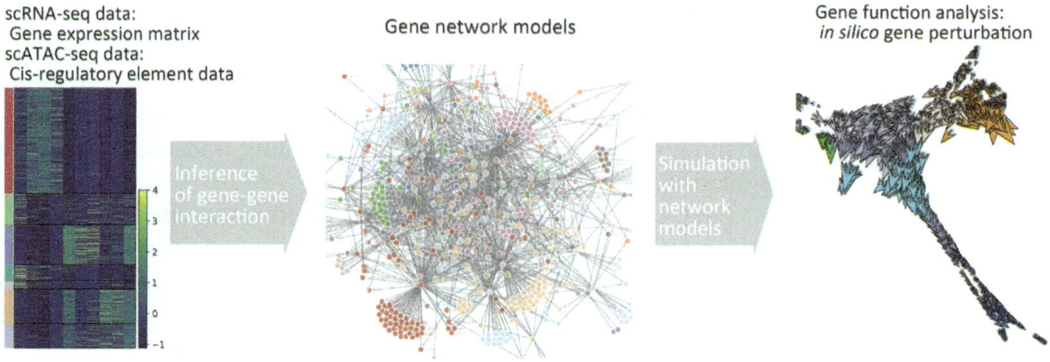

Fig. 1 An overview of gene–gene connection analysis and gene function analysis using CellOracle

approach are twofold: (1) a GRN represents a blueprint of cellular design, and if it adequately models the biological regulatory circuit, it should be capable of simulating resultant biological phenomenon of interest such as cell differentiation; and (2) in the analysis of transcription factors, the cascade-like propagation of regulatory effects is critical, and simulating transcription cascades using the inferred network model can reveal the functional roles of transcription factors.

CellOracle integrates scRNA-seq data, single-cell ATAC-seq (scATAC-seq) data, and transcription factor DNA-binding motif information for network construction. The resulting output is a weighted, directed network model. This model can be analyzed using graph theory and standard network visualization tools. Subsequently, CellOracle performs cell fate simulations based on the inferred GRN. These simulations estimate the impact of transcription factor perturbations on downstream genes at a single-cell resolution. This calculation, termed "signal propagation," leverages the gene connectivity within the network as a differentiable function; when a target gene is perturbed, we compute the partial derivatives to the downstream genes in the network. Finally, the simulated gene shift vectors are converted to cell identity embedding vectors. The outputs are visualized in a two-dimensional landscape of cell differentiation (Fig. 1, right).

1.5 Outline of Theory: Modeling and Analysis of Transcriptional GRN with CellOracle

CellOracle is specifically designed to model and predict transcriptional regulation. As mentioned earlier, the interpretation of gene–gene interactions depends on their definitions, the types of data used, and the algorithms employed. In CellOracle, our focus is on modeling transcriptional control; therefore, gene–gene connections are represented as directed network graphs linking transcription factors to their target genes. Incorporating directionality is essential for analyzing gene function.

Unlike many GRN inference strategies that solely rely on statistical or computational causal inference from gene expression data,

CellOracle intentionally avoids statistical causal inference. Instead, it integrates multiple omics datasets—including scRNA-seq and scATAC-seq—with protein–DNA binding motif data and genomic annotation to embed biological knowledge directly into the model, enriching it with causal information regarding transcriptional gene regulation.

First, scATAC-seq data and transcription start site (TSS) information are analyzed to extract active promoter and enhancer regions. ATAC-seq exploits the preferential insertion of Tn5 transposase into areas of open chromatin, which are indicative of active transcription [23, 24]. These enriched signals reflect cell state-dependent and genome-wide information about transcriptionally active regulatory regions. Besides, we use Cicero to infer distal cis-regulatory elements among scATAC-seq peaks. Cicero uses co-accessibility information between scATAC-seq peaks [25].

CellOracle comprehensively searches for transcription factor binding motifs within these active cis-regulatory regions. This analysis generates a candidate list of regulatory transcription factors for each gene. By applying this procedure to all genes, an unweighted, directed graph representing transcriptional regulatory relationships is constructed—the base GRN—which serves as the input for subsequent modeling steps.

Next, the base GRN is converted into a quantitative predictive network model using scRNA-seq data. In this step, a regression model is developed where the expression data of candidate transcription factors serve as the explanatory variables, and the target gene's expression level is the predictor variable. In addition, several computational strategies are incorporated in this process: (1) The scRNA-seq data are first clustered into smaller groups to model cell state-specific quantitative relationships among genes. (2) Regularization is applied to the base GRN to remove inactive connections, which also helps stabilize the regression model when dealing with a limited input sample size. (3) Bagging modeling techniques are used to estimate the weights of gene–gene connections as probability distributions. Here, we can select Bayesian regression models instead of bagging. Finally, a threshold is set to prune weak connections from the network. Because the network calculation is performed separately for each cell cluster, a distinct network is generated for each cluster, enabling cell state-specific modeling.

The regression model is employed for gene perturbation simulations to predict the directional changes in downstream gene expression following the modulation of an upstream transcription factor. This process involves propagating partial derivatives through the GRN; rather than predicting absolute gene expression levels, the model simulates the relative changes that spread through the network. To facilitate this, gene–gene interactions need to be formulated as differentiable functions. Consequently, a vector representing the differential changes in downstream genes upon gene perturbation is obtained for each cell. Finally, these predicted changes are projected onto a two-dimensional trajectory space—using analogous visualization methodologies inspired by RNA velocity—to provide a 2D vector representation of the anticipated cellular movement. For additional details on the principle of this method and its practical applications, please refer to the original CellOracle publication and application papers [22, 26–28].

1.6 Outline of Major Procedures of the Protocol

CellOracle consists of several sections. The relationship between these procedures is illustrated in Fig. 2.

1. To set up a computational environment, install the CellOracle package on your computer from pypi.org and ensure all dependencies are met. Alternatively, you can skip installation and use a prebuilt Docker image.
2. Process single-cell ATAC-seq data to identify open chromatin regions and extract active promoter and enhancer regions. This step uses the R package, Cicero.
3. Peaks in scATAC-seq data are scanned to make a base GRN.

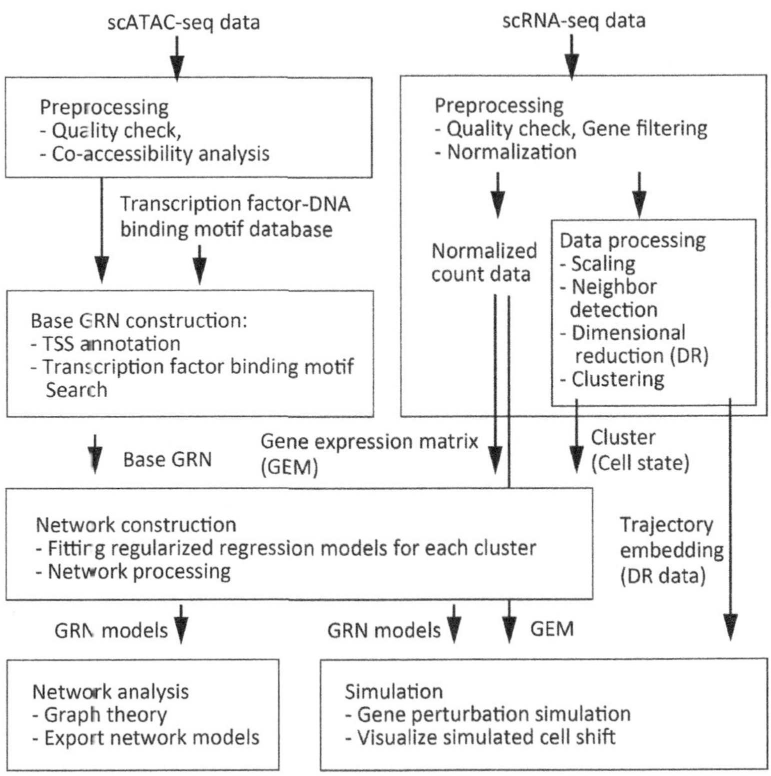

Fig. 2 Outline of major procedures of the protocol

4. Preprocess single-cell RNA-seq data to normalize expression levels, perform clustering, and prepare quantitative gene expression matrices.
5. Refine the base GRN using scRNA-seq data by applying regression models to estimate connection weights and derive cell-specific networks.
6. The structure of reconstructed GRN models is analyzed using graph analysis tools.
7. Perform in silico gene perturbation analyses using GRN models to analyze gene function.

2 Materials

2.1 Computational Resources

CellOracle was implemented as a Python package. First, we must prepare a computational environment where Python can be installed. We recommend installing CellOracle on Linux or macOS. However, it cannot be installed on Windows because some dependent packages cannot be built on Windows. The required memory size depends on the size of the scRNA-seq data to be handled. A CPU with many cores is recommended since it determines the speed of GRN calculations (*see* **Notes 1 and 2**).

2.2 Anaconda

Anaconda (anaconda.org) is an open-source program distribution platform for Python and R. Anaconda is highly recommended for installing the CellOracle package. Although we use the "pip install" command to install CellOracle, creating a new Anaconda environment and installing some dependent packages with "conda install" is recommended to avoid package version conflicts. Anaconda is available at anaconda.org.

2.3 CellOracle and Related Packages

CellOracle

The CellOracle source code is available in the GitHub repository (https://github.com/morris-lab/CellOracle). However, in this protocol, we install CellOracle via pypi.org, and users do not need to download CellOracle source code from the GitHub repository manually.

Python Packages Required for CellOracle

CellOracle has some dependent packages shown below. We listed them for clarification purposes. Manual downloading is usually unnecessary because these can be installed automatically with pip or `conda` commands. If there is an installation error, installing the package with the "`conda install`" command before CellOracle installation may circumvent the installation error.

numpy, pandas, h5py: Python libraries for efficient mathematical calculation, data manipulation, and storage. https://numpy.org, https://pandas.pydata.org, https://www.h5py.org.

matplotlib, seaborn: Libraries for data visualization. https://matplotlib.org, https://seaborn.pydata.org.

jupyter: jupyter is a web-based interactive coding environment. https://jupyter.org.

scikit-learn: scikit-learn is a general machine learning library. https://scikit-learn.org.

velocyto: velocyto is a Python implementation of RNA velocity analysis [10]. CellOracle uses the visualization functions of velocyto's code. However, CellOracle does not use RNA velocity and splicing information for GRN calculation. http://velocyto.org.

Scanpy and AnnData: Scanpy is a toolkit for scRNA-seq data analysis [29]. It includes data processing, plotting, and many downstream analysis functions. The core of scRNA-seq data management is performed with AnnData. The AnnData package efficiently handles structured gene expression matrix data and related metadata. https://scanpy.readthedocs.io/, https://anndata.readthedocs.io/

gimmemotifs, genomepy: gimmemotifs is a transcription factor motif analysis python package [30]. https://gimmemotifs.readthedocs.io/ genomepy is a tool for handling genomic DNA sequence data. https://vanheeringen-lab.github.io/genomepy/.

igraph: igraph is a toolkit for network analysis and visualization. https://igraph.org.

2.4 Cicero

Cicero is an R package for analyzing scATAC-seq data [25]. It can be found at https://cole-trapnell-lab.github.io/cicero-release/. We use Cicero to process scATAC-seq data, extracting cell state-specific active cis-regulatory elements. Since Cicero is not part of the CellOracle package, it can be installed independently. Please see Sect. 3 for the installation procedure.

2.5 Transcription Factor Motif Database

CellOracle includes transcription factor motif data. The default motif for the mouse and human is **gimme.vertebrate.v5.0**. (https://gimmemotifs.readthedocs.io/en/master/overview.html), an integrated and curated motif data in gimmemotif package. CellOracle uses motif data from the Cis-BP database (https://cisbp.ccbr.utoronto.ca) for other species.

2.6 Input Data

scATAC-seq Data

For the analysis of ATAC-seq data with CellOracle, the reference genome used to generate the ATAC-seq data must match the TSS dataset employed by CellOracle. This correspondence is required to map ATAC-seq peaks to transcription start sites accurately. Furthermore, because the method utilizes a transcription factor binding motif database, analyses cannot be performed for species lacking transcription factor binding data. In this protocol, we show an analysis example using mouse scATAC-seq data from 10x Genomics; however, scATAC-seq data from other platforms can also be used, provided they are in a format compatible with Cicero, the initial input step for scATAC-seq analysis.

scRNA-seq Data

CellOracle can be applied to various scRNA-seq datasets for network construction, provided several criteria are met. First, the gene symbols in the gene expression matrix must follow the same format as those used in the scATAC-seq data. Second, the gene expression matrix must consist of unscaled count data; in this chapter, we describe the preprocessing steps. Third, the scRNA-seq data must be compatible with Scanpy for data loading. In addition, for in silico perturbation analysis, the scRNA-seq data must capture a continuous developmental process. CellOracle's cell fate simulation relies on the assumption of gradual and continuous cellular transitions. Please refer to the original publication [22] for further details on these principles. In this chapter, we utilize Scanpy's data loading function to download scRNA-seq data of mouse hematopoiesis [31]—a typical phenomenon that embodies a continuous developmental process.

3 Method

3.1 Preparation of the Computational Environment for CellOracle Analysis

We recommend using Linux, specifically Ubuntu, to install and run the analysis described in this chapter. Here, we used Ubuntu 20.04.6 LTS for the following procedures. The Python and R environments required for installing CellOracle are created using Anaconda, and all commands should be executed in the terminal unless otherwise specified. This protocol uses Python 3.10; versions for other dependent Python packages are automatically determined. R and Cicero can be installed separately from CellOracle, as they are not used simultaneously.

1. Create a new virtual environment for installing CellOracle by executing the following commands in the terminal:

```
conda create -n celloracle_env python=3.10 -y
conda activate celloracle_env
```

2. Install CellOracle dependencies. Although the later step, running "pip install celloracle," can automatically install all dependencies, it is recommended to preinstall some packages via conda to avoid compile errors:

```
conda install cython numpy pytest -c conda-forge
conda install gimmemotifs==0.17.2 -c bioconda
```

3. Install bedtools. CellOracle's scATAC-seq analysis uses the Pybedtools package, which depends on Bedtools [32].

Although Pybedtools is installed automatically in Step 4, Bedtools may not be, so install it in advance:

```
sudo apt-get install bedtools
```

4. Install CellOracle along with any remaining dependencies. For troubleshooting, please also *see* **Notes 3 and 4**.

```
pip install celloracle
```

3.2 Installation of Cicero

1. Create a new virtual environment for R and install R using the following commands:

```
conda create -n cicero_env -y
conda activate cicero_env
conda install r-base==4.1.3 r-essential -y
conda install r-hmisc r-pkgdown r-units r-sf -c
conda-forge
```

2. Launch R and install the necessary dependency packages for Cicero.

```
if (!requireNamespace("BiocManager", quietly =
TRUE))
install.packages("BiocManager")
BiocManager::install(c("Gviz", "GenomicRanges",
"rtracklayer"))
```

3. Install Cicero by executing the following commands in R:

```
install.packages("devtools")
devtools::install_github("cole-trapnell-lab/cice-
ro-release", ref = "monocle3")
```

If you have trouble with the Cicero installation process, *see* **Note 5** for an alternative solution.

3.3 scATAC-seq Data Processing with Cicero

scATAC-seq data are loaded to extract sample-specific cis-regulatory connections between scATAC-seq peaks. The output of this analysis is used for the CellOracle motif analysis to construct base GRN.

1. Run the code below in the R console to start the scATAC-seq data analysis. This step includes downloading demo data (*see* **Note 6**). In this protocol, we download and use 10x Genomics scATAC-seq data made with mm10 mouse reference genome.

```
library(cicero)
library(monocle3)

# Create a folder to store data and download a demo
scATAC-seq data.
dir.create("data")
download.file(url =
```

```
"http://cf.10xgenomics.com/samples/cell-atac/1.1.0/
atac_v1_E18_brain_fresh_5k/atac_v1_E18_brain_
fresh_5k_filtered_peak_bc_matrix.tar.gz",
destfile = "data/matrix.tar.gz")
system("tar -xvf data/matrix.tar.gz -C data")

# You can substitute the data path below for your
scATAC-seq data.
data_folder <- "data/filtered_peak_bc_matrix"

# Create a folder to save results
output_folder <- "cicero_output"
dir.create(output_folder)

# Read scATAC-seq data
indata <- Matrix::readMM(paste0(data_folder, "/ma-
trix.mtx"))
# Cicero also requires genome information data.

download.file(url =
"https://raw.githubusercontent.com/morris-lab/
CellOracle/master/docs/demo_data/mm10_chromosome_
length.txt",

        destfile = "./mm10_chromosome_length.txt")
chromosome_length <- read.table("./mm10_chromosome_
length.txt")
```

2. Run the code below to perform scATAC-seq data preprocessing.

```
# Binarize the matrix, adjust the data format
indata@x[indata@x > 0] <- 1
cellinfo <- read.table(paste0(data_folder, "/bar-
codes.tsv"))
row.names(cellinfo) <- cellinfo$V1
names(cellinfo) <- "cells"
peakinfo <- read.table(paste0(data_folder, "/peaks.
bed"))
names(peakinfo) <- c("chr", "bp1", "bp2")
peakinfo$site_name <- paste(peakinfo$chr, peakin-
fo$bp1, peakinfo$bp2, sep="_")
row.names(peakinfo) <- peakinfo$site_name
row.names(indata) <- row.names(peakinfo)
colnames(indata) <- row.names(cellinfo)
# Make CDS
input_cds <- suppressWarnings(new_cell_data_set(in-
data, cell_metadata = cellinfo, gene_metadata =
peakinfo))
input_cds <- monocle3::detect_genes(input_cds)
#Ensure there are no peaks included with zero reads
input_cds <- input_cds[Matrix::rowSums(exprs(input_
cds))!= 0,]
```

3. Run the code below for the quality check and dimensional reduction with scATAC-seq data. The threshold for max_count and min_count should be adjusted to your data.

```
# Visualize scATAC-seq peak count per cell
hist(Matrix::colSums(exprs(input_cds)))
# Filter cells by peak_count
max_count <- 15000
min_count <- 2000
input_cds <- input_cds[,Matrix::colSums(exprs(in-
put_cds)) >= min_count]
input_cds <- input_cds[,Matrix::colSums(exprs(in-
put_cds)) <= max_count]
# Data preprocessing
set.seed(2017)
input_cds <- detect_genes(input_cds)
input_cds <- estimate_size_factors(input_cds)
input_cds <- preprocess_cds(input_cds, method =
"LSI")
# Dimensional reduction with umap
input_cds <- reduce_dimension(input_cds, reduction_
method = 'UMAP',

                    preprocess_method = "LSI")
umap_coords <- reducedDims(input_cds)$UMAP
cicero_cds <- make_cicero_cds(input_cds, reduced_
coordinates = umap_coords)
```

4. Run Cicero to make a peak-to-peak co-accessibility peak table (Fig. 3). We use these data to identify cis-regulatory elements.

```
# Run Cicero
conns <- run_cicero(cicero_cds, chromosome_length) #
Takes a few minutes to run
# Check results
head(conns)
# Save Cicero co-access peak table.
all_peaks <- row.names(exprs(input_cds))
```

	Peak1	Peak2	coaccess
	<fct>	<fct>	<dbl>
2	chr1_3094484_3095479	chr1_3113499_3113979	-0.316289004
3	chr1_3094484_3095479	chr1_3119478_3121690	-0.419240532
4	chr1_3094484_3095479	chr1_3399730_3400368	-0.050867246
5	chr1_3113499_3113979	chr1_3094484_3095479	-0.316289004
7	chr1_3113499_3113979	chr1_3119478_3121690	0.370342744
8	chr1_3113499_3113979	chr1_3399730_3400368	-0.009276026

Fig. 3 A peak-to-peak co-access peak table made by Cicero analysis

```
write.csv(x = all_peaks, file = paste0(output_folder,
"/all_peaks.csv"))
write.csv(x = conns, file = paste0(output_folder, "/
cicero_connections.csv"))
```

3.4 Base GRN Construction with CellOracle

First, the co-accessibility peak is processed to annotate TSS and the corresponding gene. Then, we will scan the transcription factor binding motifs, generating the list of regulatory candidate transcription factors for each target gene. This process is repeated genome-wide. From this step, we use Python with Jupyter Notebook.

1. Load and process scATAC-seq peak data and co-accessibility data.

```
import pandas as pd
from celloracle import motif_analysis as ma
# Load scATAC-seq peak list and Cicero analysis re-
sults. These were made in the Method 3.3.
peaks = pd.read_csv("all_peaks.csv", index_col=0)
peaks = peaks.x.values
cicero_connections  =  pd.read_csv("cicero_connec-
tions.csv", index_col=0)
```

2. Annotate the scATAC-seq peak with TSS information built with CellOracle. Then, pick up peaks that are related to the TSS peaks using Cicero co-accessibility data (*see* **Note 7**).

```
# TSS annotation
tss_annotated   =   ma.get_tss_info(peak_str_list=
peaks, ref_genome="mm10")
# Check results of TSS annotation
tss_annotated.tail()
# Merge the TSS annotated peak file with Cicero
results.
integrated = ma.integrate_tss_peak_with_cicero(tss_
peak=tss_annotated,
cicero_connections=cicero_connections)
integrated.head()
# Filtering
peak = integrated[integrated.coaccess >= 0.8]
peak = peak[["peak_id", "gene_short_name"]].reset_
index(drop=True)
peak.head()
# Save the processed peak data, representing a list
of cis-regulatory elements for each target gene.
peak.to_csv("processed_peak_file.csv")
```

3. Install reference genome data using genomepy. For the transcription factor motif scan, CellOracle requires reference genome data (Fig. 4 and *see* **Note 8**).

```
# We can check the installation status
ref_genome = "mm10"
genome_installation  =  ma.is_genome_installed(ref_
genome=ref_genome,
```

```
genomes_dir=None)
print(ref_genome,         "installation:         ",
genome_installation)
# Install reference genome if it is not found on the
computer.
if not genome_installation:
    import genomepy
    genomepy.install_genome(name=ref_genome, provid-
er="UCSC", genomes_dir=None)
else:
    print(ref_genome, "is installed.")
```

In [5]:
```
ma.SUPPORTED_REF_GENOME
```

Out [5]:

	species	ref_genome	provider
0	Human	hg38	UCSC
1	Human	hg19	UCSC
2	Mouse	mm39	UCSC
3	Mouse	mm10	UCSC
4	Mouse	mm9	UCSC
5	S.cerevisiae	sacCer2	UCSC
6	S.cerevisiae	sacCer3	UCSC
7	Zebrafish	danRer7	UCSC
8	Zebrafish	danRer10	UCSC
9	Zebrafish	danRer11	UCSC
10	Xenopus tropicalis	xenTro2	UCSC
11	Xenopus tropicalis	xenTro3	UCSC
12	Xenopus laevis	Xenopus_laevis_v10.1	NCBI
13	Rat	rn4	UCSC
14	Rat	rn5	UCSC
15	Rat	rn6	UCSC
16	Drosophila	dm3	UCSC
17	Drosophila	dm6	UCSC
18	C.elegans	ce6	UCSC
19	C.elegans	ce10	UCSC
20	Arabidopsis	TAIR10	Ensembl
21	Chicken	galGal4	UCSC
22	Chicken	galGal5	UCSC
23	Chicken	galGal6	UCSC
24	Guinea_Pig	Cavpor3.0	Ensembl
25	Pig	Sscrofa11.1	Ensembl
26	Axolotl	AmexG_v6.0-DD	Axolotl-omics.org

Fig. 4 How to check the supported reference genome in CellOracle

4. Search for TF binding motifs. The input data, peaks, are prepared as described in Step 2. If the number of peaks is large, the motif scan step may take several hours.

```
# Quality check and filter peaks if needed.
peaks = ma.check_peak_format(peaks, ref_genome, ge-
nomes_dir=None)
# Instantiate TFinfo object
tfi = ma.TFinfo(peak_data_frame=peaks, ref_genome=
ref_genome)
# Scan motifs.
tfi.scan(fpr=0.02, motifs=None, verbose=True)
# Save tfinfo object
tfi.to_hdf5(file_path="test1.celloracle.tfinfo")
# Post processing
tfi.reset_filtering()
tfi.filter_motifs_by_score(threshold=10)
tfi.make_TFinfo_dataframe_and_dictionary(verbose=
True)
# Convert the results as a data frame and save it.
df = tfi.to_dataframe()
df.to_parquet("base_GRN_dataframe.parquet")
```

3.5 scRNA-seq Data Preprocessing for CellOracle Analysis

scRNA-seq data need preprocessing, including variable gene selection, normalization, clustering, and dimensional reduction.

1. Load libraries and scRNA-seq data. In this protocol, we use mouse hematopoiesis scRNA-seq data [31] (*see* **Note 9**).

```
import matplotlib.pyplot as plt
import scanpy as sc
# Configuration for jupyter notebook
%matplotlib inline
%config InlineBackend.figure_format = 'retina'
# Configuration
adata = sc.datasets.paul15()
```

2. Perform filtering, normalization, variable gene detection, and transformation (*see* **Note 10**).

```
# Filter genes and select the top 2000 highly-vari-
able genes
sc.pp.filter_genes(adata, min_counts=1)
sc.pp.normalize_per_cell(adata,
key_n_counts='n_counts_all')
# Select the top 2000 highly-variable genes
filter_result = sc.pp.filter_genes_dispersion(adata.X,
flavor='cell_ranger',
n_top_genes=2000,
log=False)
# Subset the genes
adata = adata[:, filter_result.gene_subset]
sc.pp.normalize_per_cell(adata)
```

```
# keep raw cont data before log transformation
adata.raw = adata
adata.layers["raw_count"] = adata.raw.X.copy()
# Log transformation and scaling
sc.pp.log1p(adata)
sc.pp.scale(adata)
```

3. Perform PCA, neighbor calculations, and cell clustering. This is a typical workflow of scRNA-seq analysis. A parameter, n_neighbors, can be increased when you use a larger scRNA-seq data.

```
# PCA
sc.tl.pca(adata, svd_solver='arpack')
# Diffusion map
sc.pp.neighbors(adata, n_neighbors=4, n_pcs=20)
sc.tl.diffmap(adata)
# Calculate neighbors again based on the diffusion map
sc.pp.neighbors(adata, n_neighbors=10, use_rep='X_diffmap')
# Cell clustering
sc.tl.louvain(adata, resolution=0.8)
```

4. Perform dimensional reduction to get 2D embedding of scRNA-seq data representing a continuous developmental process (Fig. 5). This step is critical. If we cannot get biologically meaningful cell embedding that recapitulates cell differentiation trajectory, downstream simulation analysis cannot be interpreted well. Please *see* **Notes 11– 13**.

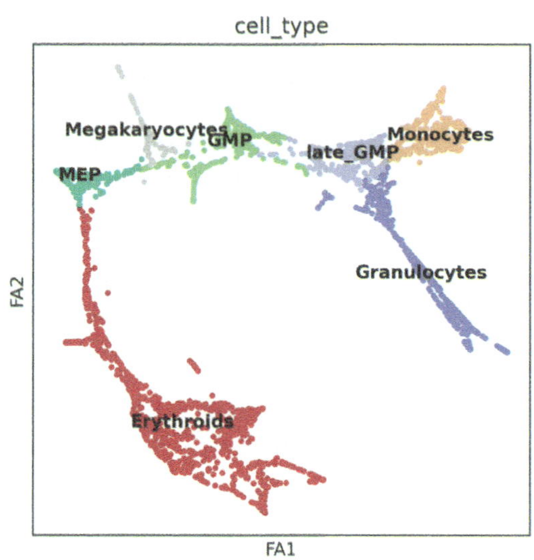

Fig. 5 A typical dimensional reduction plot representing a continuous cell differentiation trajectory

```
# PAGA graph construction
sc.tl.paga(adata, groups='louvain')
sc.tl.draw_graph(adata, init_pos='paga', random_
state=123)
# check result
sc.pl.draw_graph(adata, color='louvain', legend_
loc='on data')
# Save processed data
adata.write_h5ad("Paul_etal_15.h5ad")
```

3.6 GRN Model Construction and Network Structure Analysis with CellOracle

CellOracle constructs cluster-wise GRN models using base GRN and scRNA-seq data. GRN models can be analyzed with general graph/network analysis tools. This protocol shows how to use network analysis functions built in CellOracle. The network model can also be used for in silico gene perturbation analysis described in Sect. 3.7.

1. Load processed scRNA-seq data with a CellOracle data loading function (*see* **Note 14**).

```
# 0. Import
import os
import sys
import matplotlib.pyplot as plt
import numpy as np
import pandas as pd
import scanpy as sc
import seaborn as sns
import celloracle as co
# Configuration for plotting
%config InlineBackend.figure_format = 'retina'
%matplotlib inline
save_folder = "figures"
os.makedirs(save_folder, exist_ok=True)
# Load processed anndata
adata = co.data.load_Paul2015_data()
adata
```

2. Downsampling cells to reduce the required computational resources if the data include more than 30,000 cells.

```
n_cells_downsample = 30000
if adata.shape[0] > n_cells_downsample:
   # Let's downsample into 30K cells
   sc.pp.subsample(adata, n_obs=n_cells_downsample,
random_state=123)
```

3. Load base GRN, which was calculated in Sect. 3.4, or load CellOracle's pre-built base GRN (*see* **Note 15**).

```
# Load TF info, which was made from the mouse cell
atlas dataset.
base_GRN=co.data.load_mouse_scATAC_atlas_base_GRN()
```

4. Make an Oracle object. Oracle is a custom class for preprocessing, data handling, and network construction (*see* **Note 16** and Fig. 6).

```
# Instantiate Oracle object
oracle = co.Oracle()
# We use the unscaled mRNA count.
adata.X = adata.layers["raw_count"].copy()
# Load anndata with the cluster name and dimensional
reduction data name.
oracle.import_anndata_as_raw_count(adata=adata,
cluster_column_name="louvain_annot",
embedding_name="X_draw_graph_fa")
# Load TF info dataframe with the following code.
oracle.import_TF_data(TF_info_matrix=base_GRN)
# Perform PCA. The PCA data is required for knn
imputation.
oracle.perform_PCA()
# Calculate parameters for knn imputation
plt.plot(np.cumsum(oracle.pca.explained_variance_
ratio_)[:100])
n_comps = np.where(np.diff(np.diff(np.cumsum(oracle.
pca.explained_variance_ratio_))>0.002))[0][0]
n_comps = min(n_comps, 50)
n_cell = oracle.adata.shape[0]
k = int(0.025*n_cell)
# Perform knn imputation
oracle.knn_imputation(n_pca_dims=n_comps, k=k, bal-
anced=True, b_sight=k*8,
            b_maxl=k*4, n_jobs=4)
```

```
[6]: oracle = co.data.load_tutorial_oracle_object()
     oracle

[6]: Oracle object

     Meta data
         celloracle version used for instantiation: 0.10.0
         n_cells: 2671
         n_genes: 1999
         cluster_name: louvain_annot
         dimensional_reduction_name: X_draw_graph_fa
         n_target_genes_in_TFdict: 21259 genes
         n_regulatory_in_TFdict: 1093 genes
         n_regulatory_in_both_TFdict_and_scRNA-seq: 90 genes
         n_target_genes_both_TFdict_and_scRNA-seq: 1850 genes
         k_for_knn_imputation: 66
     Status
         Gene expression matrix: Ready
         BaseGRN: Ready
         PCA calculation: Done
         Knn imputation: Done
         GRN calculation for simulation: Not finished
```

Fig. 6 How to check the metadata and calculation status of GRN in the Oracle object

In [28]:
```
links.links_dict["Ery_0"]
```

Out [28]:

	source	target	coef_mean	coef_abs	p	-logp
0	Elf1	0610007L01Rik	0.003746	0.003746	1.440512e-03	2.841483
1	Mef2c	0610007L01Rik	-0.007328	0.007328	1.365241e-04	3.864791
2	Chd2	0610007L01Rik	-0.010170	0.010170	4.160059e-06	5.380900
3	Irf7	0610007L01Rik	-0.009342	0.009342	2.462105e-06	5.608693
4	Stat3	0610007L01Rik	-0.008464	0.008464	1.636075e-04	3.786197
...	...	...	...	...	...	...
74932	Nfkb1	Zyx	0.015513	0.015513	6.787753e-06	5.168274
74933	Zbtb4	Zyx	0.000247	0.000247	8.890848e-01	0.051057
74934	Klf4	Zyx	-0.005566	0.005566	9.731835e-08	7.011805
74935	Nfia	Zyx	-0.026013	0.026013	2.981702e-10	9.525536
74936	Rel	Zyx	-0.002867	0.002867	1.196048e-01	0.922251

Fig. 7 Network nodes, edges, and weights are calculated for each cell cluster

5. Construct network models. The alpha is a parameter for L-2 regularization. The network is stored in a custom object, Links (Fig. 7). *See* **Note 17** for an alternative downstream analysis option.

```
# Calculate GRN for each population in the "louvain_
annot" clustering unit.
# This step may take some time. (~30minutes)
links = oracle.get_links(cluster_name_for_GRN_unit=
"louvain_annot", alpha=10,
                     verbose_level=10)
# An example: Check network edge weights for the
"Ery_0" cluster.
links.links_dict["Ery_0"]
# Save Links object.
links.to_hdf5(file_path="links.celloracle.links")
```

6. Remove the weak edges before doing network structure analysis.

```
links.filter_links(p=0.001,       weight="coef_abs",
threshold_number=2000)
```

7. Analyze network structures based on network degree (k), the number of edges for each node. Here, we investigate the degree distribution $P(k)$, the fraction of the network node with degree k (Fig. 8). The linear relationship between log$k$ and log $P(k)$ is used to measure the scale-free feature of the network. *See* **Note 18** to save plots.

```
# Show degree distribution.
Links.plot_degree_distributions(plot_model=True)
```

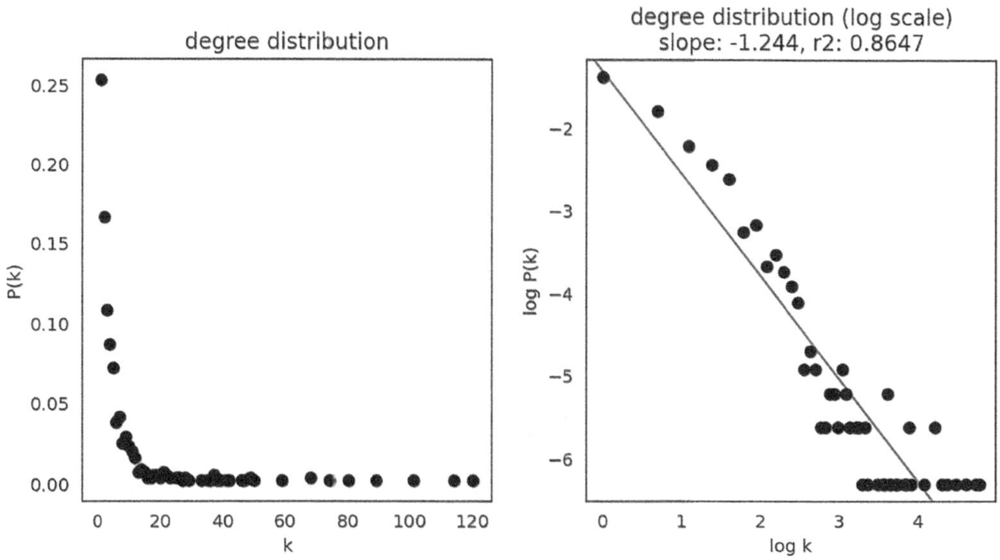

Fig. 8 Checking the degree distribution in the inferred GRN

8. Visualize network score dynamics. Links object calculates several scores for network structure, including degree centrality, betweenness centrality, and eigenvector centrality. Here are examples of how to use the plotting function (Figs. 9 and 10).

```
# Visualize top n-th genes with high scores.
links.plot_scores_as_rank(cluster="MEP_0", n_gene=
30, save=f"{save_folder}/ranked_score")
# Compare GRN score between two clusters
links.plot_score_comparison_2D(value=
"eigenvector_centrality",
cluster1="MEP_0",
cluster2="GMP1_0",
percentile=98,
save=f"{save_folder}/score_comparison")
# Visualize Gata2 network score dynamics
links.plot_score_per_cluster(goi="Gata2", save=
f"{save_folder}/network_score_per_gene/")
# Plot degree_centrality
plt.subplots_adjust(left=0.15, bottom=0.3)
plt.ylim([0,0.040])
links.plot_score_discributions(values=
["degree_centrality_all"],
                      method="boxplot",
                      save=f"{save_folder}")
```

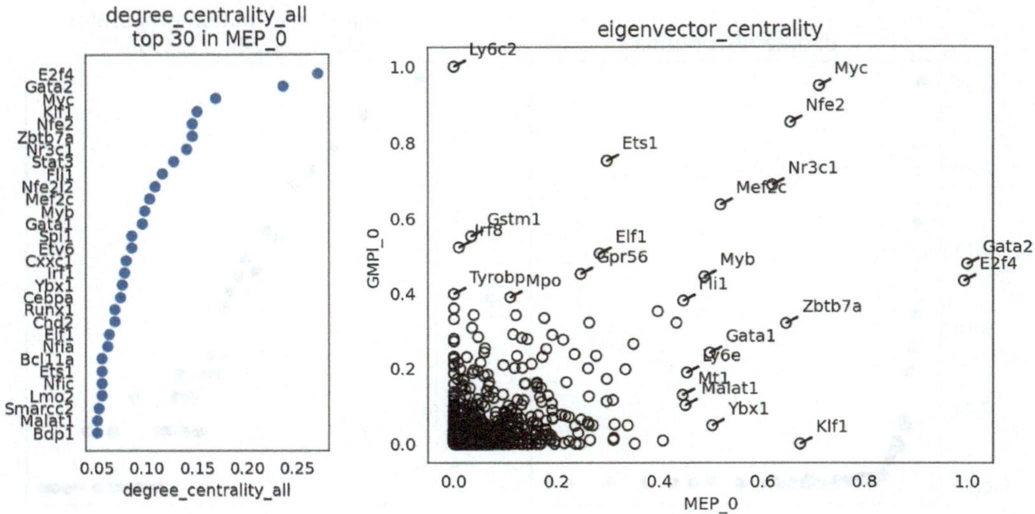

Fig. 9 Examples of network structure analysis: Top 30 genes with degree centrality score (left), comparison of centrality score between clusters (right)

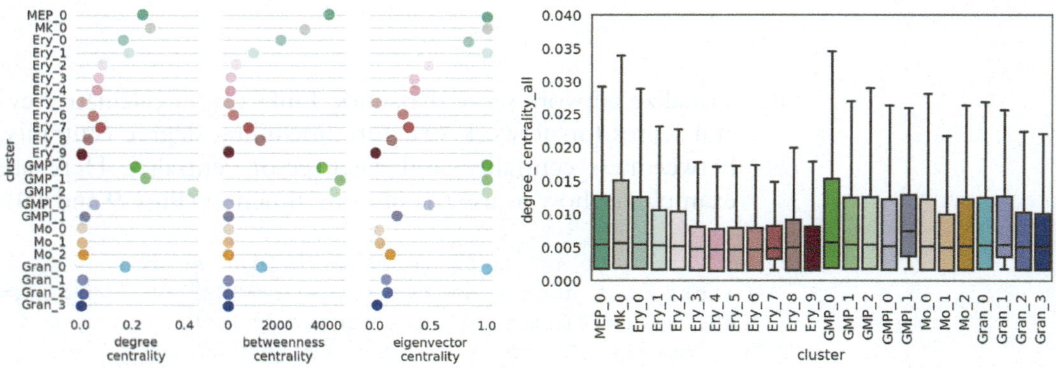

Fig. 10 Examples of network structure analysis: Gata2 network score across clusters (left), distribution of degree centrality across clusters (right)

3.7 Gene Function Analysis Using in silico Gene Perturbation

We introduce how to perform in silico gene perturbation analysis. The input data for this analysis are an Oracle object and Links object made in the network construction protocol described in Sect. 3.6. The output is 2D vectors representing the simulated shift in cell identity on the scRNA-seq trajectory space (Fig. 11). We can predict cell type-specific transcription factor function regarding cell differentiation.

1. Import libraries and load data.

```
import os
import matplotlib.pyplot as plt
import numpy as np
import scanpy as sc
```

Fig. 11 Visualization of gene perturbation simulation results upon Irf8 KO. The right panel is a random control

```
import celloracle as co
# Plotting configuration
%config InlineBackend.figure_format = 'retina'
%matplotlib inline
# Make a folder to save plots
save_folder = "figures"
os.makedirs(save_folder, exist_ok=True)
# Load the tutorial oracle and links object.
oracle = co.data.load_tutorial_oracle_object()
links = co.data.load_tutorial_links_object()
```

2. Perform data preprocessing for simulation.

```
links.filter_links()
oracle.get_cluster_specific_TFdict_from_Links(links_
object=links)
oracle.fit_GRN_for_simulation(alpha=10, use_cluster_
specific_TFdict=True)
```

3. Perform in silico transcription factor perturbation analysis. Here, we need to specify perturbation conditions (*see* **Note 19**). The results are stored in the Oracle object; no plot is shown at this step.

```
# Check gene expression before the analysis.
goi = "Irf8"
sc.pl.draw_graph(oracle.adata, color=[goi, oracle.
cluster_column_name],
layer="imputed_count", use_raw=False, cmap=
"viridis")
# Plot gene expression in histogram
sc.get.obs_df(oracle.adata, keys=[goi], layer="im-
puted_count").hist()
plt.show()
# Enter perturbation conditions to simulate.
```

```
oracle.simulate_shift(perturb_condition={goi: 0.0},
n_propagation=3)
# Get transition probability and calculate cell iden-
tity shift vector
oracle.estimate_transition_prob(n_neighbors=200,
                    knn_random=True,
                    sampled_fraction=1)
oracle.calculate_embedding_shift(sigma_corr=0.05)
```

4. Visualize the results. The simulated cell state shift vector is projected onto the 2D cell embedding (Fig. 11). Seek to find the optimal scale parameter based on your data (*see* **Note 20**).

```
# Check gene
fig, ax = plt.subplots(1, 2, figsize=[6,13])
scale = 35
# Show quiver plot
oracle.plot_quiver(scale=scale, ax=ax[0])
ax[0].set_title(f"Simulated cell identity shift vec-
tor: {goi} KO")
# Show a quiver plot that was calculated with a ran-
domized graph.
oracle.plot_quiver_random(scale=scale, ax=ax[1])
ax[1].set_title(f"Randomized simulation vector")
plt.show()
```

5. Interpret results. The 2D vector generated by the CellOracle in silico gene perturbation suggests that gene perturbation may cause a shift in cell identity upon gene perturbation. Although this analysis provides intuitive guidance to interpret GRN models, there are several limitations and cautions (*see* **Notes 21–24**). We also recommend reading the original paper of CellOracle for more information [22].

4 Notes

1. We use several machine learning algorithms that implement parallel calculations. The more CPU cores available, the faster the calculations can be. We also recommend using a computational environment with at least 16 GB of memory. The memory usage depends on the number of cells in the scRNA-seq data. In particular, the simulation step requires a lot of memory and can cause memory errors if you do not have enough memory.
2. The minimum computing resources requirement may change as algorithms are updated or added. Please refer to CellOracle's web documentation for the latest information (https://morris-lab.github.io/CellOracle.documentation/index.html).

3. Installing errors related to velocyto on macOS may occur due to the default compiler. Switching the compiler resolves the issue if errors are encountered on macOS.
4. We do not recommend installing CellOracle on Windows OS or using WSL. Although installing CellOracle on a Windows Subsystem for Linux is possible, the calculations may be extremely slow on WSL.
5. Installing Cicero (and monocle3) requires many dependency packages, and compilation errors may occur depending on the user's operating system and compiler settings. If you are not experienced with troubleshooting R package installations, we recommend using Docker. For instance, the Docker prebuilt image "ShortCake" (https://hub.docker.com/r/rnakato/shortcake) provides a preconfigured environment with numerous single-cell analysis tools, including Cicero and CellOracle.
6. When you analyze your data, please replace the "data/filtered_peak_bc_matrix" with the path to your scATAC-seq data.
7. Here, we filter the co-accessibility peak with a threshold of 0.8. This means that cis-regulatory elements with scores greater than 0.8 are considered cis-regulatory elements and used for the CellOracle base GRN construction. The threshold value can be adjusted according to your data.
8. The list of supported reference genomes can be checked with `ma.SUPPORTED_REF_GENOME` (Fig. 4).
9. Please change `"adata = sc.datasets.paul15()"` to `"adata = sc.read_10x_mtx(PATH)"` to read your scRNA-seq data.
10. Although clustering and dimensional reduction use data after log transformation, CellOracle GRN calculation requires gene expression data before log transformation. We keep gene expression data in adata.raw before transformation and scaling.
11. The dimensionality reduction step requires careful consideration for a CellOracle analysis. Make sure the dimensionality reduction results recapitulate the continuous cellular transition of interest for a successful analysis.
12. This protocol uses the Force-Atlas algorithm [33] in conjunction with PAGA [34] as the initial points. A scanpy tutorial originally introduced this trick. Alternatively, another dimensional reduction algorithm, such as UMAP, or a trajectory inference method, such as CellRank [35], can be employed.
13. Cell type annotation is not necessary but recommended after the cell clustering. By checking and naming the cell state

for each cluster, downstream analysis and interpretation are enhanced. However, the cell type annotation requires substantial biological knowledge about the data, and we skip the cell annotation step in this protocol.

14. When loading your data, substitute `"adata = co.data.load_Paul2015_data()"` with `"adata = sc.read_h5ad("DATAPATH")"`.
15. CellOracle package provides several prebuilt base GRN data made with scATAC-seq atlas [36]. These pre-built base GRN data are helpful as an alternative to the sample-specific base GRN when scATAC-seq data are unavailable. Base GRN made from various cell types includes many gene–gene connections. If you have scATAC-seq data and calculated a base GRN as shown in Sect. 3.4, Step 4, please load and use the data frame file here.
16. Summary of data content and calculation state can be checked by calling the Oracle object (Fig. 6).
17. If the user wants to analyze the network models using a different network analysis method, you can do so after exporting the network data in the links.links_dict to a CSV file.
18. The plots can be saved as files in PNG and PDF formats. Enter the folder path in the "save" argument to save figures.
19. The target gene expression value for the perturbation should be set between zero and twofold as the observed value. We cannot do the simulation outside the range.
20. It is necessary to adjust the scale parameter, which controls the scale of the quiver plot. Smaller-scale parameters generate large arrows. It is helpful to check randomized results to find the optimal scale value (Fig. 11, right). If you see vectors with substantial size in the random plot, it suggests the scale parameter is too small.
21. This method simulates the effects of gene perturbation on cellular identity using network models. Consequently, it cannot analyze the functions of genes not represented as nodes within the constructed network models. Moreover, only the transcription factors defined in the base GRN possess outgoing edges and can be simulated because the method focuses on transcriptional regulation. The list of active transcription factors in the network models can be accessed via Oracle.active_regulatory_genes.
22. A transcription factor of interest may be absent from the constructed GRN, preventing its analysis. This can occur for several reasons, as follows. (1) The gene is not detected in the scRNA-seq data. (2) The gene is excluded during the highly variable gene selection step in scRNA-seq preprocessing due

to low detection rates, low expression levels, or uniformly expressed patterns that provide little information. (3) The transcription factor is missing from the base GRN because its DNA-binding information is unavailable in the database.

23. CellOracle explicitly focuses on modeling transcription, and it is essential to acknowledge the assumptions and limitations. First, scRNA-seq data typically contain noise and dropout events, and the method may fail to detect some gene edges; therefore, the absence of a detected connection in the GRN model should not be interpreted as evidence of a lack of gene function. Second, the method does not account for cell division, cell death, intercellular communication, or mechanical forces. Therefore, it is unsuitable for analyzing biological phenomena predominantly driven by factors other than transcription.

24. CellOracle predicts "small-scale changes" derived from the model built on the input data. Since these subtle perturbation vectors are projected onto an overall continuous map of cell differentiation, the vector map can visualize the large-scale flow of cell identity shift. However, the prediction unit, each single-cell simulation vector, cannot be interpreted as a long-term cell transformation. Accordingly, the method should not be used for long-term transformation. It is also inappropriate to simulate to induce cell types not present in the input data (e.g., simulating terminally differentiated cells using only iPSC scRNA-seq data). Also, it is not recommended to simulate genes with expression levels that deviate significantly from the distribution observed in the input data. If a user enters such values for the simulation parameter, CellOracle will produce an error message.

Acknowledgement

This study was funded by the research grant of JSPS KAKENHI JP24K23187, JP25H01358, Shimadzu Science Foundation, The Naito Foundation, The Nakajima Foundation, Inoue Foundation for Science, The Sumitomo Foundation, and Astellas Foundation for Research on Metabolic Disorders.

Conflict of Interest The authors have no conflicts of interest to declare that are relevant to the content of this chapter.

References

1. Mercatelli D, Scalambra L, Triboli L, Ray F, Giorgi FM (2020) Gene regulatory network inference resources: a practical overview. Biochim Biophys Acta Gene Regul Mech 1863
2. Marbach D, Costello JC, Küffner R, Vega NM, Prill RJ, Camacho DM, Allison KR, Kellis M, Collins JJ, Aderhold A, Stolovitzky G, Bonneau R, Chen Y, Cordero F, Crane M, Dondelinger F, Drton M, Esposito R, Foygel R, De La Fuente A, Gertheiss J, Geurts P, Greenfield A, Grzegorczyk M, Haury AC, Holmes B, Hothorn T, Husmeier D, Huynh-Thu VA, Irrthum A, Karlebach G, Lèbre S, De Leo V, Madar A, Mani S, Mordelet F, Ostrer H, Ouyang Z, Pandya R, Petri T, Pinna A, Poultney CS, Rezny S, Ruskin HJ, Saeys Y, Shamir R, Sîrbu A, Song M, Soranzo N, Statnikov A, Vega N, Vera-Licona P, Vert JP, Visconti A, Wang H, Wehenkel L, Windhager L, Zhang Y, Zimmer R (2012) Wisdom of crowds for robust gene network inference. Nat Methods 9:796–804. https://doi.org/10.1038/nmeth.2016
3. Ronneberger O, Tunyasuvunakool K, Bates R, Žídek A, Ballard AJ, Cowie A, Romera-paredes B, Nikolov S, Jain R, Adler J, Back T, Petersen S, Reiman D, Clancy E, Zielinski M, Steinegger M, Pacholska M, Berghammer T, Bodenstein S, Silver D, Vinyals O, Senior AW, Kavukcuoglu K (2021) Highly accurate protein structure prediction with AlphaFold. Nature 596:583–589. https://doi.org/10.1038/s41586-021-03819-2
4. Langfelder P, Horvath S (2008) WGCNA: an R package for weighted correlation network analysis. BMC Bioinformatics 9. https://doi.org/10.1186/1471-2105-9-559
5. Akers K, Murali TM (2021) Gene regulatory network inference in single-cell biology. Curr Opin Syst Biol 26:87–97
6. Kim D, Tran A, Kim HJ, Lin Y, Yang JYH, Yang P (2023) Gene regulatory network reconstruction: harnessing the power of single-cell multi-omic data. NPJ Syst Biol Appl 9
7. Bravo González-Blas C, De Winter S, Hulselmans G, Hecker N, Matetovici I, Christiaens V, Poovathingal S, Wouters J, Aibar S, Aerts S (2023) SCENIC+: single-cell multiomic inference of enhancers and gene regulatory networks. Nat Methods 20:1355–1367. https://doi.org/10.1038/s41592-023-01938-4
8. Aibar S, González-Blas CB, Moerman T, Huynh-Thu VA, Imrichova H, Hulselmans G, Rambow F, Marine JC, Geurts P, Aerts J, Van Den Oord J, Atak ZK, Wouters J, Aerts S (2017) SCENIC: single-cell regulatory network inference and clustering. Nat Methods 14:1083–1086. https://doi.org/10.1038/nmeth.4463
9. Yang B, Chen Y (2020) Overview of gene regulatory network inference based on differential equation models. Curr Protein Pept Sci 21:1054–1059. https://doi.org/10.2174/1389203721666200213103350
10. La Manno G, Soldatov R, Zeisel A, Braun E, Hochgerner H, Petukhov V, Lidschreiber K, Kastriti ME, Lönnerberg P, Furlan A, Fan J, Borm LE, Liu Z, van Bruggen D, Guo J, He X, Barker R, Sundström E, Castelo-Branco G, Cramer P, Adameyko I, Linnarsson S, Kharchenko PV (2018) RNA velocity of single cells. Nature 560:494–498. https://doi.org/10.1038/s41586-018-0414-6
11. Wang W, Hu Z, Weiler P, Mayes S, Lange M, Fountain DM, Haug JO, Wang J, Xue Z, Sauka- Spengler T, Theis FJ (2026) RegVelo: Gene-regulatory-informed dynamics of single cells. Cell 189:3773–3800. https://doi.org/10.1016/j.cell.2026.04.022
12. Huynh-Thu VA, Irrthum A, Wehenkel L, Geurts P (2010) Inferring regulatory networks from expression data using tree-based methods. PLOS One 5. https://doi.org/10.1371/journal.pone.0012776
13. Pratapa A, Jalihal AP, Law JN, Bharadwaj A, Murali TM (2020) Benchmarking algorithms for gene regulatory network inference from single-cell transcriptomic data. Nat Methods 17:147–154. https://doi.org/10.1038/s41592-019-0690-6
14. Greenfield A, Madar A, Ostrer H, Bonneau R (2010) DREAM4: Combining genetic and dynamic information to identify biological networks and Dynamical Models. PLOS One 5. https://doi.org/10.1371/journal.pone.0013397
15. Aibar S, González-Blas CB, Moerman T, Huynh-Thu VA, Imrichova H, Hulselmans G, Rambow F, Marine JC, Geurts P, Aerts J, van den Oord J, Atak ZK, Wouters J, Aerts S (2017) SCENIC: Single-cell regulatory network inference and clustering. Nature Methods 14(11):1083–1086. https://doi.org/10.1038/nmeth.4463
16. Chen Y, Li Y, Narayan R, Subramanian A, Xie X (2016) Gene expression inference with deep learning. Bioinformatics 32:1832–1839. https://doi.org/10.1093/bioinformatics/btw074
17. Yang X, Liu G, Feng G, Bu D, Wang P, Jiang J, Chen S, Yang Q, Miao H, Zhang Y, Man Z, Liang Z, Wang Z, Li Y, Li Z, Liu Y, Tian Y, Liu W, Li C, Li A, Dong J, Hu Z, Fang C, Cui L, Deng Z, Jiang H, Cui W, Zhang J, Yang Z, Li H, He X, Zhong L, Zhou J, Wang Z, Long Q, Xu P, X-Compass Consortium, Wang H, Meng Z, Wang X, Wang Y, Wang Y, Zhang S, Guo J, Zhao Y, Zhou Y, Li F, Liu J, Chen Y, Yang G, Li X (2024) GeneCompass: deciphering universal gene regulatory mechanisms with a knowledge-informed cross-species foundation

model. Cell Res 34:830–845. https://doi.org/10.1038/s41422-024-01034-y
18. Hao M, Gong J, Zeng X, Liu C, Guo Y, Cheng X, Wang T, Ma J, Zhang X, Song L (2024) Large-scale foundation model on single-cell transcriptomics. Nat Methods 21:1481–1491. https://doi.org/10.1038/s41592-024-02305-7
19. Szałata A, Hrovatin K, Becker S, Tejada-Lapuerta A, Cui H, Wang B, Theis FJ (2024) Transformers in single-cell omics: a review and new perspectives. Nat Methods 21:1430–1443. https://doi.org/10.1038/s41592-024-02353-z
20. Cui H, Wang C, Maan H, Pang K, Luo F, Duan N, Wang B (2024) scGPT: toward building a foundation model for single-cell multi-omics using generative AI. Nat Methods 21:1470–1480. https://doi.org/10.1038/s41592-024-02201-0
21. Chen Y, Zou J (2024) GenePT: a simple but effective foundation model for genes and cells built from ChatGPT. bioRxiv. https://doi.org/10.1101/2023.10.16.562533
22. Kamimoto K, Stringa B, Hoffmann CM, Jindal K, Solnica-Krezel L, Morris SA (2023) Dissecting cell identity via network inference and in silico gene perturbation. Nature 614:742–751. https://doi.org/10.1038/s41586-022-05688-9
23. Buenrostro JD, Giresi PG, Zaba LC, Chang HY, Greenleaf WJ (2013) Transposition of native chromatin for fast and sensitive epigenomic profiling of open chromatin, DNA-binding proteins and nucleosome position. Nat Methods 10:1213–1218. https://doi.org/10.1038/nmeth.2688
24. Buenrostro JD, Wu B, Litzenburger UM, Ruff D, Gonzales ML, Snyder MP, Chang HY, Greenleaf WJ (2015) Single-cell chromatin accessibility reveals principles of regulatory variation. Nature 523:486–490. https://doi.org/10.1038/nature14590
25. Pliner HA, Packer JS, McFaline-Figueroa JL, Cusanovich DA, Daza RM, Aghamirzaie D, Srivatsan S, Qiu X, Jackson D, Minkina A, Adey AC, Steemers FJ, Shendure J, Trapnell C (2018) Cicero predicts cis-regulatory DNA interactions from single-cell chromatin accessibility data. Mol Cell 71:858–871.e8. https://doi.org/10.1016/j.molcel.2018 06.044
26. Kamimoto K, Adil MT, Jindal K, Hoffmann CM, Kong W, Yang X, Morris SA (2023) Gene regulatory network reconfiguration in direct lineage reprogramming. Stem Cell Reports 18:97–112. https://doi.org/10.1016/j.stemcr.2022.11.010
27. Amrute JM, Lai L, Ma P, Koenig AL, Kamimoto K, Bredemeyer A, Shankar TS, Kuppe C, Kadyrov FF, Schulte LJ, Stoutenburg D, Kopecky BJ, Navankasattusas S, Visker J, Morris SA, Kramann R, Leuschner F, Mann DL, Drakos SG, Lavine KJ (2023) Defining cardiac functional recovery in end-stage heart failure at single-cell resolution. Nat Cardiovasc Res 2:399–416. https://doi.org/10.1038/s44161-023-00260-8
28. Bocchi VD, Conforti P, Vezzoli E, Besusso D, Cappadona C, Lischetti T, Galimberti M, Ranzani V, Bonnal RJP, De Simone M, Rossetti G, He X, Kamimoto K, Espuny-Camacho I, Faedo A, Gervasoni F, Vuono R, Morris SA, Chen J, Felsenfeld D, Pavesi G, Barker RA, Pagani M, Cattaneo E (2021) The coding and long noncoding single-cell atlas of the developing human fetal striatum. Science 372. https://doi.org/10.1126/science.abf5759
29. Wolf FA, Angerer P, Theis FJ (2018) SCANPY: Large-scale single-cell gene expression data analysis. Genome Biol 19. https://doi.org/10.1186/s13059-017-1382-0
30. Bruse N, van Heeringen SJ (2018) GimmeMotifs: an analysis framework for transcription factor motif analysis. bioRxiv. https://doi.org/10.1101/474403
31. Paul F, Arkin Y, Giladi A, Jaitin DA, Kenigsberg E, Keren-Shaul H, Winter D, Lara-Astiaso D, Gury M, Weiner A, David E, Cohen N, Lauridsen FKB, Haas S, Schlitzer A, Mildner A, Ginhoux F, Jung S, Trumpp A, Porse BT, Tanay A, Amit I (2015) Transcriptional heterogeneity and lineage commitment in myeloid progenitors. Cell 163:1663–1677. https://doi.org/10.1016/j.cell.2015.11.013
32. Quinlan AR, Hall IM (2010) BEDTools: a flexible suite of utilities for comparing genomic features. Bioinformatics 26:841–842. https://doi.org/10.1093/bioinformatics/btq033
33. Jacomy M, Venturini T, Heymann S, Bastian M (2014) ForceAtlas2, a continuous graph layout algorithm for handy network visualization designed for the Gephi software. PLOS One 9. https://doi.org/10.1371/journal.pone.0098679
34. Wolf FA, Hamey FK, Plass M, Solana J, Dahlin JS, Göttgens B, Rajewsky N, Simon L, Theis FJ (2019) PAGA: graph abstraction reconciles clustering with trajectory inference through a topology preserving map of single cells. Genome Biol 20:1–9. https://doi.org/10.1186/s13059-019-1663-x
35. Weiler P, Lange M, Klein M, Pe'er D, Theis F (2024) CellRank 2: unified fate mapping in multiview single-cell data. Nat Methods 21:1196–1205. https://doi.org/10.1038/s41592-024-02303-9
36. Cusanovich DA, Hill AJ, Aghamirzaie D, Daza RM, Pliner HA, Berletch JB, Filippova GN, Huang X, Christiansen L, DeWitt WS, Lee C, Regalado SG, Read DF, Steemers FJ, Disteche CM, Trapnell C, Shendure J (2018) A single-cell atlas of in vivo mammalian chromatin accessibility. Cell 174:1309–1324.e18. https://doi.org/10.1016/j.cell.2018.06.052

Chapter 6

Analysis of Chromatin Structure Using Network Approaches: A Step-by-Step Guide

Benoît Aliaga, Flavien Raynal and Vera Pancaldi

Abstract

Chromosome Conformation Capture assays, such as High-throughput Chromosome Conformation Capture (Hi-C) and Promoter Capture Hi-C (PCHi-C), have transformed our comprehension of 3D genome organization in the nucleus. However, these techniques require computational expertise to analyze the data and extract interpretable biological signals, and a number of dedicated tools have therefore been developed. In this chapter, we present a step-by-step guide to ChAseR, an R package to analyze chromatin architecture using network-based approaches. Chromatin contact data are represented as a graph in which nodes correspond to genomic fragments and edges to physical interactions. ChAseR can add diverse genomic and epigenomic features to nodes (e.g., histone marks from ChIP-seq, chromatin accessibility from ATAC-seq, or gene expression from RNA-seq). ChAseR uses chromatin assortativity (ChAs), which provides information on the 3D organization of the nucleus by quantifying the 3D clustering of distinct genomic and epigenomic features. We illustrate the workflow on a promoter-centered chromatin network derived from human monocytes.

Keywords Chromatin interaction networks, 3D Genome organization, Promoter capture Hi-C (PCHi-C), ChAseR, Chromatin assortativity, Epigenomic features, Network randomization, Z-score

1 Introduction

Cells are life's fundamental units, and throughout evolution, they became more specialized, acquiring specific roles in multicellular organisms, with phenotypes as diverse as those of neurons, heart, and skin cells. This diversity leads us to question the definition of **cell identity** or **cell type**, which corresponds to the biological characteristics that define a cell's phenotype and specific function in an organism [1, 2]. Biologically, cell type can be described at different levels, including the genome, epigenome, including gene expression, proteome, tissue histology, and physiology. For example, a neuron expresses specific genes that are not expressed in other cell types, for example, in muscle cells. While a cell's identity remains relatively stable, its **phenotype** can be flexible or plastic. Under environmental

Y-h Taguchi (ed.), *AI/ML-Driven Gene Analysis*, Methods in Molecular Biology, vol. 3037,
https://doi.org/10.1007/978-1-0716-5284-8_6,

stress, some cells can change their behavior or other traits without losing their identity. For instance, a macrophage can exist in two **phenotypic states**: pro-inflammatory and anti-inflammatory. We can define the pro- or anti-inflammatory response as a **function** of macrophages. Developing biotherapies in regenerative medicine and disease research requires a better understanding of the mechanisms that explain the cell type, identity, function, and phenotypic plasticity.

Conrad Waddington, the father of epigenetics, proposed a conceptual model of an **epigenetic landscape** to explain how development determines cell fate [3]. Valleys and hills shape this landscape, which is reminiscent of energy potential landscapes in physics. At the top of this landscape, a group of stem cells, with high "potential" to move on this landscape, given their high energy state, will move downward and encounter branching valleys, representing different possible cell fates (e.g., muscle, neuron, or liver cells). The motion of cells in this landscape tends to bring them to these valleys, and cells in the wells or troughs will have less "potential" energy and will not be able to move far. Waddington also described an important notion: *canalization* [4]. *Canalization* depicts the developmental ability to produce consistent phenotypes despite genetic or environmental variability, which corresponds to saying that there are a few wells in which all cells will end up, much fewer than the initial locations in which the cells can be found before differentiation. Waddington used the formation of deep valleys in his landscape to represent a high degree of canalization. In other words, if the valleys are deep, switching to another cell type is difficult or expensive for the cells. The depth represents the degree of canalization.

In the last decades, it has been broadly accepted that epigenetics plays a basic role in **defining** and **stabilizing** cellular identity by **regulating** gene expression without modifying the DNA sequence [5, 6]. Four epigenetic carriers exist: (i) histone posttranslational modifications, (ii) DNA methylation, (iii) noncoding RNAs, and (iv) proteins that modify the chromatin structure, such as those forming the Polycomb or the SAGA complexes. The first three are able to write, erase, and read epigenetic information. Histone posttranslational modifications, with Polycomb complexes, can alter the chromatin structure via alteration of its physical structure and modify gene expression programs [6–10]. These epigenetic marks can act as a biological memory of the cell identity [11, 12].

Several techniques exist to investigate chromatin architecture at different scales. These techniques are classified into two main categories: chromosome conformation capture-based methods and imaging techniques. We will start by focusing on the first category, a group of molecular biology methods designed to analyze the spatial organization of chromatin in the nucleus by detecting physical contacts between DNA regions using DNA sequencing. These techniques use crosslinking with formaldehyde to "freeze" chromatin physical interactions. Then, restriction enzymes digest the DNA within the chromatin. The DNA fragments are ligated to form hybrid molecules, which are then sequenced.

The original method, Chromosome Conformation Capture (3C), detects one-to-one interactions between selected loci. More advanced techniques, such as High-throughput Chromosome Conformation Capture (Hi-C), enable genome-wide (all-to-all) mapping of chromatin interactions. Several specialized variants of Hi-C have been developed to enrich for specific types of interactions. For example, Promoter Capture Hi-C (PCHi-C) and the broader family of Capture-C approaches are designed to detect interactions involving targeted regions such as gene promoters or other genomic loci of interest, allowing a focused view of regulatory contacts. Another important advancement is Micro-C, a technique that uses micrococcal nuclease (MNase) digestion instead of restriction enzymes, enabling the detection of chromatin contacts at nucleosome resolution. The evolution of these techniques—from single-locus studies to comprehensive, potentially genome-wide, contact maps—has been reviewed by Goel and Hansen [13].

With techniques such as ChIP-seq or CUT&Run, it is possible to determine where specific transcription factors (TFs) and complexes bind to the genome or to map the location of histone modifications. A combination of HiC with ChIPseq allows us to map 3D contacts specifically mediated by a protein of interest, leading to the Chromatin Interaction Analysis by Paired-End Tag Sequencing (ChIA-PET) and HiChIP assays.

Like other genome-wide next-generation sequencing–based methods, Hi-C and its derived techniques generate large quantities of data that require specialized computational methods for processing, analysis, and interpretation. In this chapter, we will present some specific approaches to perform processing and analysis of chromatin conformation capture datasets and give examples of how to extract biological insight from them using chromatin network approaches. These tools are also applicable to datasets produced by other assays that identify 3D chromatin structure interactions, provided that the genomic coordinates of the contacting chromatin fragments are known [14].

2 Chromatin Conformation Capture Data Preprocessing

Starting from the sequencing results obtained after a Hi-C or derived protocol, the workflow begins with read alignment to a reference genome using tools such as Bowtie2 [15] or BWA-MEM [16], followed by the filtering out of invalid Hi-C read pairs such as self-ligated and uninformative pairs. The next steps involve normalization and bias correction. Hi-C data contain systematic biases arising from restriction enzyme cutting sites, GC content, and sequence mappability differences. For Hi-C data, methods such as ICE and KR are commonly used to correct systematic biases, whereas CHiCAGO [17] and HiCapTools [18] are algorithms specifically employed for processing Capture Hi-C data to distinguish signals from background noise [17].

For Hi-C data, contact matrices are constructed at different resolutions (e.g., 1, 10, 100 kb) to identify key features such as topologically associated domains (TADs), chromatin loops, A/B compartments, Frequently Interacting REgions (FIREs), and several others. TAD detection methods rely on insulation scores or directionality indices, while algorithms such as HiCCUPS [19] and Fit-Hi-C [20] are used to identify chromatin loops. For functional annotation, tools such as Genomic Regions Enrichment of Annotations Tool (GREAT) [21], HOMER [22], and CHiCAGO (for PCHi-C datasets) [17] help link promoter–chromatin interactions to gene regulation and biological pathways.

These tools are frequently used in 3D chromatin structure studies. In the following, we explain step-by-step how to process and interpret chromatin structure datasets within a network theory framework.

3 ChAseR, an Example of a Chromatin Network Construction and Analysis Tool

The previous tools focused on specific spatial interactions on 3D chromatin structure studied by Hi-C and PCHi-C, such as loops, topologically associating domains (TADs), and compartments. In contrast, chromatin network approaches also allow us to consider chromatin organization at a global statistical level, employing a broader concept of chromatin organization and emphasizing the patterns in chromatin interactions across the genome. A chromatin network is a graph representation of the physical interactions between different genomic regions in the three-dimensional space of the nucleus, which has been proposed by several authors as a useful framework to study epigenome organization, as reviewed in Pancaldi [14]. This chapter presents an R package called ChAseR, which uses a network to model 3D chromatin organization, in which nodes represent chromatin fragments that are characterized by several epigenomic/genomic features, such as gene expression levels, histone modifications, DNA methylation levels, transcription factor binding sites, or any other characteristic of the genomic sequence or associated genes [23, 24]. Here, we will provide some elements of network theory that will be needed to understand how this framework can help us extract insight from chromatin conformation capture datasets.

The terms "graph" and "network" are commonly used in the literature but may be interchangeable depending on the context. "Graph" is employed in mathematical contexts to describe the theoretical object, while "network" is used in applied fields such as sociology, biology, and computer science as we discuss specific instances of a graph. A "graph" or a "network" contains a set of vertices (or nodes) and links (or edges) that connect pairs of vertices/nodes. For example, a node represents entities, like cities in a transportation system, and an edge can represent a road between two cities. In chromatin networks, a node is a sequenced DNA fragment representing a genomic locus such as a promoter, an enhancer, or other chromatin region. Edges represent physical interactions between these genomic regions, as detected by chromosome conformation capture techniques (Hi-C and derived techniques, GAM, SPRITE, etc.) [25]. In this context, the number of contacts between specific genomic regions in a population of cells can be used as a weight, reflecting the strength of interaction between the corresponding nodes in the network.

Since genome-wide chromatin structure datasets produced by Hi-C started being represented as matrices, drawn as heatmaps, showing essentially the number of contacts between all possible pairs of chromatin regions, they were quickly interpreted as adjacency matrices of a chromatin contact network.

Early work in this direction includes Botta et al. [26], which modeled chromatin as a network to explore genome folding mechanisms. Boulos et al. further extended this idea in a series of physics-based studies [27, 28], investigating network properties and scaling behaviors of chromatin contacts. Morlot et al. (2016) also developed polymer-based models consistent with network interpretations of Hi-C data [29].

Several recent studies and tools now explicitly treat chromatin as a biological network. For example, Chovanec et al. [30] introduced a web platform to visualize and analyze chromatin contact networks. Other computational methods include GRAAL [31], which reconstructs genome architecture using network-based optimization, and HMM-based methods [32] that integrate chromatin state information into network models.

These examples show how network theory provides a powerful abstraction for interpreting chromatin structure beyond simple spatial maps, enabling the integration of diverse biological data and identifying functionally relevant topological features.

At present, several web servers allow the visualization of chromatin as networks.

We will focus specifically on Promoter Capture Hi-C (PCHi-C) datasets since they allow us to specifically explore genes and other chromatin regions in contact with them. Note that, generally, the regions close to coding genes are very sparse in the genome, which is mostly dominated by large repetitive regions devoid of any coding potential.

First, ChAseR constructs a chromatin interaction network using chromatin conformation capture data (such as Hi-C or PCHi-C). Next, users can integrate feature data (ChIP-seq, ATAC-seq, bulk RNA-seq) onto network nodes. Each feature is associated with a specific chromatin region and is represented by a numerical or categorical value. Chromatin assortativity (ChAs)is a measure that evaluates the extent to which chromatin regions with the same characteristics (histone modifications, DNA methylation, gene expression, gene function, etc.) tend to preferentially interact in 3D. It is an application of the concept of assortativity of attributes, or homophily, initially defined in network science and especially in social networks [33]. ChAs is defined as a correlation value of node features across all node pairs in the network. It indicates whether regions with a specific characteristic tend to establish preferential 3D contacts within the nucleus, essentially identifying whether specific regions "'cluster" on the network:

- ChAs > 0: regions with the same characteristic interact more often than expected at random (positive assortativity).
- ChAs = 0: contacts between regions carrying the studied characteristic are randomly distributed (no assortativity).
- ChAs < 0: regions with the studied characteristic avoid associating with each other and interact with regions with other characteristics (negative assortativity or disassortativity).

ChAs is a useful metric in chromatin interaction networks but is limited to global chromatin interaction. For example, if a feature is very rare, even a high ChAs may be due to a random effect. If a feature is ubiquitous, it becomes difficult to tell whether its 3D clustering is specific or simply due to its prevalence. We need another metric to account for the features to avoid interpretation bias. Abundance was developed to measure how many chromatin fragments carry a feature in an interaction network [23]. The comparison ChAs vs. Abundance analysis is essential to understand how a feature is distributed on the 3D network in the nucleus. Generally, we plot ChAs vs. Abundance to understand how strongly a feature is associated to the 3D chromatin organization. We can have three cases:

- Low abundance + high ChAs
- High abundance + high ChAs
- Intermediate abundance + variable ChAs

In the first case, the feature is rare but very strongly clustered in specific domains (e.g., Polycomb-repressed chromatin clusters). In the second case, the feature is very present and dominant in the 3D organization of the genome (e.g., active euchromatic compartment). In the third case, it is necessary to analyze whether the characteristic is homogeneous or whether it presents structured subsets.

Plotting ChAs vs. Abundance is useful for understanding chromatin functional organization. Low abundance but high ChAs indicates a strong association between the feature and the 3D structure. High abundance with high ChAs suggests large-scale functional compartmentalization. It also helps to compare different cells or conditions. For example, a feature may have similar abundance but different ChAs between two cell types, indicating a difference in chromatin organization.

To evaluate the significance of ChAs values for specific node characteristics, we evaluate whether randomizing the assignment of node attributes to network nodes produces comparable values of ChAs. Clearly, ChAs values of one attribute will depend on the frequency or abundance of nodes with that attribute, and this randomization procedure, which preserves the attribute abundance, will help us identify attributes that are more assortative than expected purely based on their average values across nodes or their frequency.

To be able to assess whether the clustering patterns are stronger than what would be expected given the feature's abundance, another metric needs to be defined, namely the ChAs Z-score, which assesses whether an observed ChAs value significantly differs from what would be expected by chance. It is obtained by comparing the ChAs value calculated for a given feature with a distribution of ChAs values obtained by shuffling the assignment of feature value to the network nodes in a randomization procedure.

The Z-score is a statistical metric that quantifies the distance away from the mean of a distribution expressed as a number of standard deviations. With the ChAs Z-score, we will evaluate the statistical significance of ChAs. If the observed ChAs is much higher than the random ChAs' average, the studied feature forms significant preferential contacts in 3D. In other cases, if the ChAs is close to the random values, the feature is randomly distributed in the nuclear space. A Z-score below −2 or above 2 corresponds to a significance p-value of 0.05.

The ChAs Z-score allows a comparison of the different features with each other. Some epigenetic marks may naturally have higher or lower ChAs values. The Z-score allows for standardized comparisons and identifies which features are most strongly associated with chromatin organization. The ChAs Z-score can also identify chromatin contacts specific to particular cell types or conditions. A feature with a high ChAs but a low Z-score may indicate that it is common but not particularly organized in 3D. In other cases, a feature with medium ChAs but a high Z-score may reveal a specific chromatin organization, which is not expected by chance and might be biologically relevant or even functional.

For some features, the presence of clusters on the network might depend on the fact that contiguous regions of chromatin have that feature, for example, this is the case for large Polycomb-bound domains. In chromatin networks, we are likely to have contacts between genomic regions that are close in 3D simply because they are also close along the genome in 1D. In these cases, high ChAs might just be due to the clustering of regions with the feature along the chromosome, with no impact of 3D "distal" contacts.

For this reason, a second type of randomization can be performed, this time trying to preserve the genomic distance between regions that are found in the 3D contact. We can thus calculate a Z-score of ChAs based on the comparison of the observed value with the value obtained with the distance-preserving randomization. Nodes with features with significant Z-scores in a distance-preserving randomization are more clustered in 3D space than what would be expected based on their clustering along the chromosome.

Given these basic definitions of ChAs and ChAs Z-score, we will now give some examples of how to interpret ChAs results for different features. For example, H3K27me3 has a high ChAs Z-score, indicating that regions enriched in H3K27me3 tend to associate in 3D and form well-defined epigenetic domains (e.g., Polycomb-repressed regions). Some epigenetic marks, such as H3K4me3 (associated with active promoters), can show high ChAs in promoter–promoter (PP) networks, suggesting that active promoters preferentially interact with each other. High values of ChAs Z-scores are found for H3K9me3, suggesting the clustering of heterochromatic regions, and extremely high values of ChAs Z-scores are found for replication timing, suggesting that chromatin regions that are replicated at similar times in the replication program are associating in 3D [24]. Significant positive ChAs Z-scores of replication origin efficiency suggest that regions containing origins that fire with similar frequency in a population form preferential interactions in the 3D nucleus [34].

Since its first publication in 2016 [23], ChAseR has been successfully applied in several published studies. Here, we present three examples. First, in Jodkowska et al., the authors explored the relationship between 3D chromatin connectivity and replication origin efficiency in mouse embryonic stem cells [34]. By integrating replication initiation data with high-resolution chromatin interaction maps, they demonstrated that replication origin efficiency correlates with the number of chromatin contacts, suggesting that spatial genome organization plays a crucial role in the regulation of DNA replication. Second, in Tomás-Daza et al., the authors examined 3D genome organization across hematopoietic differentiation by integrating chromatin interaction data with epigenomic features [35]. This network-based approach revealed how the spatial configuration of chromatin contributes to lineage-specific gene regulation. Third, in Raynal et al., the authors investigated global chromatin reorganization during oncogenesis [36]. ChAseR was used to track changes in chromatin assortativity of specific gene sets based on gene ages and chromatin marks across different stages of cancer progression, revealing key epigenomic features associated with tumor-specific 3D genome rewiring. The study highlighted how oncogenic transformation impacts spatial genome architecture, particularly at Polycomb-regulated regions.

In the following, we will present a typical workflow to perform a ChAs analysis using ChAseR with files from several datasets.

4 ChAseR Pipeline Overview

- The ChAseR pipeline is structured into five main steps (Fig. 1).
- First, chromatin interaction data are loaded with genomic or epigenomic features, such as gene expression levels or histone modifications.
- The second step consists of building a chromatin interaction network in which these features are associated with the corresponding nodes.
- Third, chromatin assortativity analysis is performed to evaluate the tendency of connected nodes to share similar features.
- Fourth, randomization procedures are applied to assess the statistical significance of the observed patterns.
- Finally, ChAs Z-scores are computed to evaluate the statistical significance of assortativity, taking into account the abundance of each feature.

5 Materials

5.1 Input Data

As a practical example, we will show how to compute chromatin assortativity for various genomic features on a promoter-centered chromatin network derived from human monocytes using PCHiC. To do so, we will integrate several datasets, whose references are provided in Table 1.

5.2 Set Up Your Environment

Before using ChAseR, it is important to organize the folders correctly. That is the key to efficient and reproducible research [37]. We suggest to start by creating a main project directory, which will be subdivided into four subfolders: data/ (for raw and processed datasets), scripts/ (for analysis code), results/ (for output files and figures), and docs/ (for metadata, tutorial, README files, and other files).

```
setwd("/Your/Working/Directory/Path")
# Define the main project directory
project_name <- "Bioinformatics_Project"
dir.create(project_name)
# Define subdirectories
subdirs <- c("Data", "Scripts", "Results",
"Docs")
# Create each subdirectory
sapply(file.path(project_name, subdirs), dir.
create, recursive = TRUE)
```

Move your data into the data/ folder and ensure that it is in one of the required file formats; see Table 2.

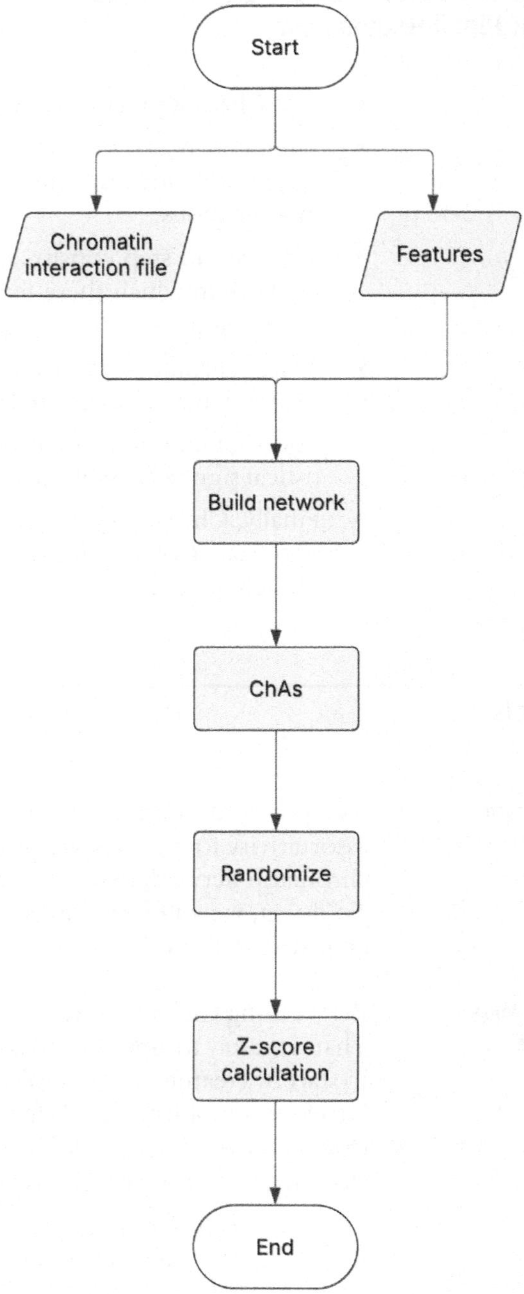

Fig. 1 ChAseR pipeline

5.3 Install ChAseR Package

To install ChAseR, you will need the devtools package, which simplifies installing packages from GitHub (especially for packages not available on CRAN). If you have not installed it yet, you can install and load it as follows:

```
install.packages("devtools")
library(devtools)
```

Table 1
Input datasets used to build the promoter-centered chromatin interaction network and associated genomic features in human monocytes

File type	Target	Cell type	Database	Dataset ID
PCHi-C	Promoter-centered chromatin interactions	Monocyte	GEO	Javierre et al. [38] DATA S1
ChIP-seq	H3K4me1	Monocyte	ENCODE	ENCSR400VWA
ChIP-seq	H3K4me3	Monocyte	ENCODE	ENCSR796FCS
ChIP-seq	H3K27ac	Monocyte	ENCODE	ENCSR012PII
ChIP-seq	H3K36me3	Monocyte	ENCODE	ENCSR244XWL
ChIP-seq	H3K27me3	Monocyte	ENCODE	ENCSR080XUB
ChIP-seq	H3K9me3	Monocyte	ENCODE	ENCSR236JVK
RNA-seq	Gene expression	Monocyte	GEO	GSE147310
ATAC-seq	Open chromatin region	Monocyte	GEO	GSE87218

Most of these datasets have also been explored in Madrid-Mencia et al. [24] and Raynal et al. [36]

Table 2
Required input file types supported by ChAseR

File type	Description	Formats	Category
Promoter capture Hi-C	Defines pairs of 3D interacting fragments from PCHi-C (e.g., CHiCAGO output file)	.tsv, .bedpe, .ibed	Network
ChIP-seq, ATAC-seq	Associates chromatin characteristics with fragments overlapping peaks	.bed, .tsv, .txt	Features
RNA-seq	Associates expression levels with promoters from count matrix	.tsv, .txt	Features

You can start a new R script.

Next, install ChAseR in your R environment and load it:

```
devtools::install_bitbucket("eraineri/chaser")
library(chaser)
```

Your R environment is ready to work with ChAseR.

5.4 Load Graphics Package

To continue, install and load ggplot2, a commonly used package for visualizing data in R.

```
install.packages("ggplot2")
library(ggplot2)
```

Everything is now installed in your R environment, and you can start using ChAseR.

5.5 Build Network

ChAseR can load chromatin interaction networks directly from text-like file formats. The resulting chromatin network nodes represent genomic fragments, and edges represent physical contacts.

In this example, we will use a promoter capture Hi-C (PCHiC) dataset from monocytes, processed with the CHiCAGO pipeline, which detects significant chromatin interactions based on di-tag sequencing signal strength.

The CHiCAGO tool gives a score to each potential interaction in order to estimate the probability that a given interaction is true, taking into account genomic distance and background noise. A threshold of 5, recommended by the authors (Cairns et al. [17]), ensures reproducibility and helps filter out artifacts. Interactions above this cutoff are more likely to represent biologically meaningful contacts, such as promoter–enhancer or promoter–promoter interactions.

```
# Load the chromatin interactions file
pchic = read.table(file.path(input_path,"PCHiC_
peak_matrix_Monocyte.txt"), header = T)

# Filter interactions to keep scores >= 5 only
mono = pchic[which(pchic$Mon >= 5),]
```

Here, we focus only on promoter–promoter interactions, excluding any contacts involving non-promoter regions. In typical annotation conventions, DNA fragments overlapping gene promoters are named after the corresponding gene(s), whereas fragments corresponding to distal regulatory elements are labeled with a dot ("."). By removing such entries, we focus the analysis specifically on interactions between gene promoters. However, depending on the biological question and dataset features, you may choose to include regulatory region interactions as well.

```
# Keep only Promoter-Promoter interactions
mono = mono[which(!(mono$oeName == ".")),]
```

Note: Ensure chromosome naming is consistent across datasets (e.g., "chr1" vs. "1").

To build the chromatin network, we only need the genomic coordinates (chromosome, start, end) of each pair of interacting fragments. In our dataset, these are columns 1, 2, 3 and 6, 7, 8, respectively. The `make_chromnet()` function uses these coordinates to generate the chromatin interaction network.

```
# Load the Monocyte chromatin network on ChAser
net = make_chromnet(mono[,c(1,2,3,6,7,8)])
```

5.6 Associating Features to Nodes

Once the chromatin network is loaded, ChAseR allows the assignment of various genomic features (e.g., histone modifications, gene expression levels, DNA methylation, open chromatin regions) to the network nodes. Each feature corresponds to a specific chromatin region and can have a numerical or categorical value.

In this chapter, we will use the six most commonly studied histone marks and one protein peak files (output of the MACS2 peak calling program). To evaluate the genome-wide distribution of chromatin accessibility, an ATAC-seq dataset will be used. In addition, low- and high-expressed genes, defined based on RNA-seq quantification, will also be included as features.

- H3K4me1: All enhancers
- H3K4me3: Active gene promoters
- H3K9me3: Constitutive heterochromatin
- H3K27ac: Active enhancers
- H3K27me3: Facultative heterochromatin
- H3K36me3: Actively transcribed gene body
- CTCF: Genome architectural protein
- ATAC-seq: Open chromatin regions
- RNA-seq: Gene expression quantification (Low.Exp and High.Exp)

First, import all the feature datasets into R:

```
#Load features on R
CTCF = read.table(file.path(input_path, "CTCF_
Monocyte_peaks.bed"))
H3K4me1 = read.table(file.path(input_path, "H3K4me1_
Monocyte_peaks.bed"))
H3K4me3 = read.table(file.path(input_path, "H3K4me3_
Monocyte_peaks.bed"))
H3K9me3 = read.table(file.path(input_path, "H3K9me3_
Monocyte_peaks.bed"))
H3K27ac = read.table(file.path(input_path, "H3K27ac_
Monocyte_peaks.bed"))
H3K27me3 = read.table(file.path(input_path, "H3K27me3_
Monocyte_peaks.bed"))
H3K36me3 = read.table(file.path(input_path, "H3K36me3_
Monocyte_peaks.bed"))
Low_exp = read.table(file.path(input_path, "Lowly_
expressed_genes_Monocyte.bed"), header = T)
High_exp = read.table(file.path(input_path, "Highly_
expressed_genes_Monocyte.bed"), header = T)
ATAC = read.table(file.path(input_path, "ATAC-
Seq_Monocyte_peaks.bed"), header = T)
```

Then, associate each dataset as a chromatin feature on the network using the `load_features()` function from ChAseR:

```
# Load features on the network with ChAseR
net = load_features(net, CTCF, type = "bed6",
missingv = 0, auxfun = mean, featnames = "CTCF")
net = load_features(net, H3K4me1, type =
"bed6", missingv = 0, auxfun = mean, featnames
= "H3K4me1")
```

```
net = load_features(net, H3K4me3, type =
"bed6", missingv = 0, auxfun = mean, featnames
= "H3K4me3")
net = load_features(net, H3K9me3, type =
"bed6", missingv = 0, auxfun = mean, featnames
= "H3K9me3")
net = load_features(net, H3K27ac, type =
"bed6", missingv = 0, auxfun = mean, featnames
= "H3K27ac")
net = load_features(net, H3K27me3, type =
"bed6", missingv = 0, auxfun = mean, featnames
= "H3K27me3")
net = load_features(net, H3K36me3, type =
"bed6", missingv = 0, auxfun = mean, featnames
= "H3K36me3")
net = load_features(net, Low_exp, type =
"features_table", missingv = 0, auxfun = mean,
featnames = "Low.Exp")
net = load_features(net, High_exp, type =
"features_table", missingv = 0, auxfun = mean,
featnames = "High.Exp")
net = load_features(net, ATAC, type = "features_
table", missingv = 0, auxfun = mean, featnames
= "ATAC.Seq")
```

6 Chromatin Assortativity (ChAs)

Once all features have been successfully mapped to the chromatin network, we can compute chromatin assortativity (ChAs) for each feature using the chas() function from ChAseR.

```
# Compute ChAs
chas_net <- chas(net,"chas")
```

To visualize the results, we can generate a simple bar plot showing the ChAs values (Fig. 2):

```
# Plot ChAs values
nb_features = ncol(net$features)
m = chas_net[order(chas_net,decreasing = T)]
b = barplot(m,col=rainbow(nb_features), ylab="",
     main="Chromatin Assortativity - Monocyte
     Network",
     ylim=c(0,.4), xaxt="n", axes=0, border =
     "white")
pos = ifelse(m>0, round(m,2),"")
neg = ifelse(m<0, round(m,2),"")
text(b, m, labels = pos, cex = 1.2, pos = 3)
text(b, m, labels = neg, cex = 1.2, pos = 1)
mtext("ChAs", side = 2, line = 2,cex = 1.4)
axis(2, at = c(0,.4), las = 2, cex.axis = 1.4,
lwd = 1.2, font = 1)
```

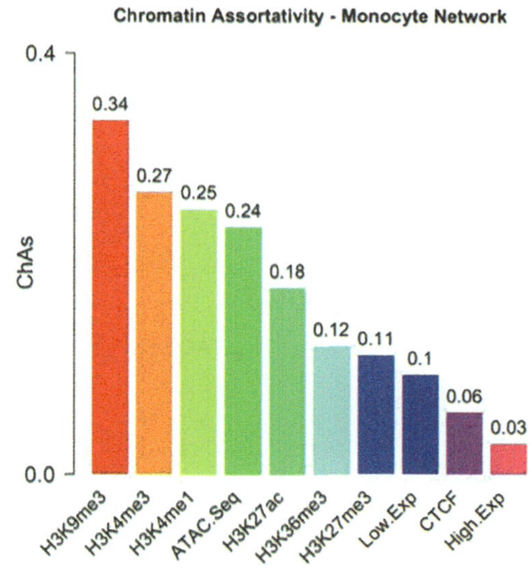

Fig. 2 Resulting ChAs values for each feature

```
text(cex=1.2, x = b+.1, y = -0.02, names(m),
xpd = T, srt = 45, pos = 2)
```

Each bar represents the assortativity value for a given feature. Positive values indicate that regions with similar feature levels tend to interact more frequently.

7 Randomizations

To evaluate the statistical significance of ChAs values, we perform randomizations of the chromatin network using the `randomize()` function from the ChAseR package. This function shuffles the assignment of features across nodes while preserving their global abundance, allowing us to compute Z-scores.

```
# Compute randomizations
random_hic_net=chaser::randomize(net  =  net,
nrandom = 100, dist.match = T)
# Compute ChAs of randomizations
chas_random_hic_net=vector()
for (i in 1:length(random_hic_net))
{
chas_random_hic_net=c(chas_random_hic_
net,chas(random_hic_net[[i]],"chas"))
}
```

Next, we organize the results into a data frame to compare ChAs values from both the randomized and real networks:

```
# Build random ChAs data.frame
```

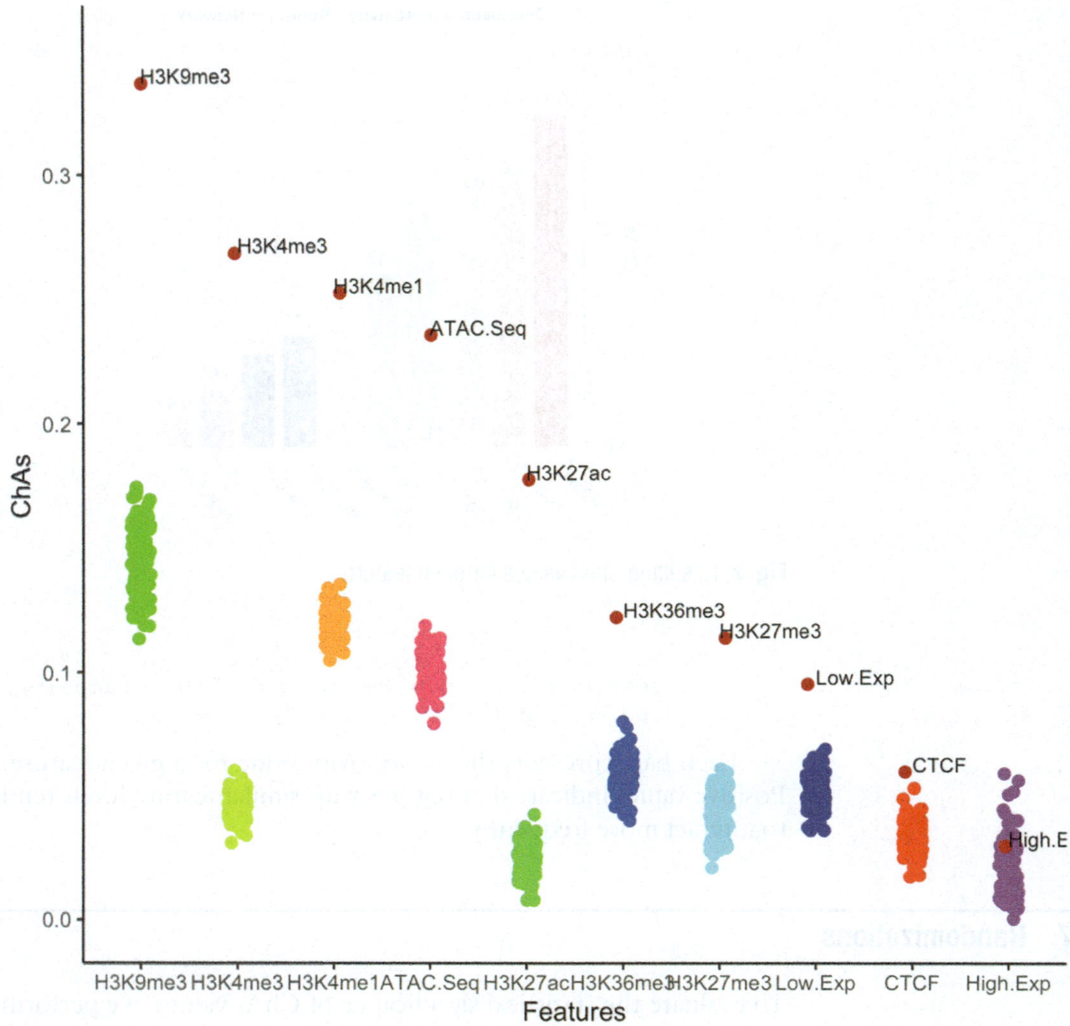

Fig. 3 Dot plot with observed ChAs (dark red) and expected ChAs (colored)

```
df_random_hic_net=data.frame(Value=
chas_random_hic_net,
      Sample=names(chas_random_hic_net))
df_random_hic_net$Value=as.numeric(as.
character(df_random_hic_net$Value))
# Build real ChAs data.frame
df_chas_hic_net=data.frame(Value=chas_net,
      Sample=names(chas_net))
df_chas_hic_net$Value=as.numeric(as.
character(df_chas_hic_net$Value))
df_hic_net=rbind(df_random_hic_net,df_chas_
hic_net)
#Manage colors and labels
all_color=rainbow(ncol(net$features))
color=c(rep(all_color,nrow(df_random_hic_
net)/nrow(df_chas_hic_net)),
    rep("#CC0000",nrow(df_chas_hic_net)))
labels=vector()
```

```
labels=c(rep("",nrow(df_hic_net)-
(length(unique(df_hic_net$Sample)))),
     as.character(df_hic_net$Sample[(nrow(df_
hic_net)-
                      length(unique(df_hic_
net$Sample))+1):nrow(df_hic_net)]))
df_hic_net$Sample=factor(df_hic_net$Sample,
                    levels=names(chas_
net[order(chas_net,decreasing = T)]))
```

We can now visualize the ChAs values from the original network and compare to those obtained from the randomized networks (Fig. 3):

```
p <- ggplot(data=df_hic_net, aes(x=Sample, y=
Value, group=Sample),show.legend=F) +
  ylim(0,.35) +
  ylab("ChAs") +
  xlab("Features") +
  geom_jitter(colour=color,width = 0.1, size=
2) +
  geom_text(aes(label=labels),hjust=0, vjust=
0,size=3) +
  theme_classic() +
  ggtitle("")
print(p)
```

Colored dots represent ChAs value levels expected by chance for each feature. Features with ChAs values significantly higher than those observed in randomized networks are likely to exhibit biologically meaningful assortativity patterns, supported by high Z-scores.

7.1 ChAs Z-Scores

We now compute the Z-score for each feature by comparing the observed ChAs values from the real network to the distribution of ChAs values obtained from randomized networks. This involves calculating the mean and standard deviation of the randomized ChAs values for each feature.

```
# Compute mean and standard deviation from
randomization ChAs distribution
test = df_hic_net
nb_features = ncol(net$features)
nb_randomizations = length(random_hic_net)
test_random = df_hic_net[1:(nb_features*nb_
randomizations),]
test_chas = df_hic_net[-(1:(nb_features*nb_
randomizations)),]
mean_random <- aggregate(. ~ Sample, data =
test_random, mean)
sd_random <- aggregate(. ~ Sample, data = test_
random, sd)
```

Then, we simply apply the Z-score formula:

$$Z = \frac{(X - \mu)}{\sigma}$$

where X is the observed ChAs value, μ is the mean of the randomized ChAs values, and σ is the corresponding standard deviation.

```
# Apply Z-score formula
zscore = vector()
for(i in mean_random$Sample){
    zscore=c(zscore,   (test_chas[which(test_
chas$Sample == i),1]-
            mean_random[which(mean_
random$Sample == i),2])/
        sd_random[which(sd_random$Sample   ==
i),2])
}
names(zscore) = mean_random$Sample
```

We can now visualize the computed Z-scores using a bar plot (Fig. 4).

```
# ChAs Z-scores barplot
m = zscore[order(zscore, decreasing = T)]
b  =  barplot(m,  col  =  rainbow(nb_features),
ylab = "",
      main   =   "Chromatin   Assortativity   -
Monocyte Network",
      ylim   =   c(0,75),   xaxt   =   "n",axes   =
0,border = "white")
pos = ifelse(m>0, round(m,1), "")
neg = ifelse(m<0, round(m,1), "")
text(b, m, labels = pos, cex = 1.2,pos = 3)
```

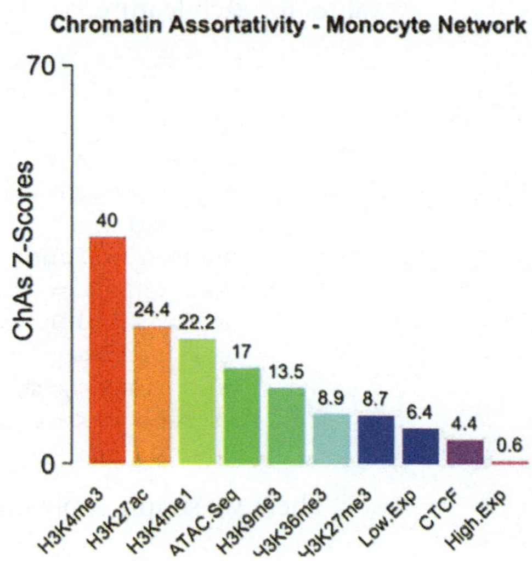

Fig. 4 ChAs Z-scores bar plot

```
text(b, m, labels = neg, cex = 1.2,pos = 1)
mtext("ChAs Z-Scores", side = 2, line = 2,cex
= 1.4)
axis(2,     at=c(0,70),las=2,cex.axis=1.4,lwd=
1.2,font=1)
text(cex=1.2, x=b+.1, y=-5, names(m), xpd=T,
srt=45,pos=2)
```

Each bar represents the assortativity Z-score for a given feature. A Z-score greater than 2 indicates that the observed ChAs value for this feature is higher than at least 95% of the values obtained from the randomized networks. In such cases, the ChAs can be considered statistically significant.

8 Conclusion

It is important to decipher the chromatin organization and the different functions of chromatin structures to understand the origin of cell identity, plasticity, and function. In the last two decades, techniques have evolved quickly, making it easier to study how chromatin is organized in 3D. Chromosome conformation capture approaches, such as Hi-C and PCHi-C, are essential for deciphering the three-dimensional organization of the genome and understanding how chromatin structure participates in gene regulation. Chromatin networks emerged as a new computational method for studying 3D chromatin structure. In this chapter, we present how ChAseR works and how to use it with R. ChAseR allows the visualization of chromosomal contact networks with GARDEN-NET [24] and quantifies interactions between different epigenetic marks, proteins, or gene expression levels. Metrics such as the chromatin assortativity (ChAs) and its Z-score thus help to differentiate fortuitous contacts from those that reflect true functional or structuring mechanisms. By integrating quantitative information on epigenetic marks—such as H3K27me3 or H3K4me3—and comparing their genome-wide abundance with their assortativity scores, one can infer their spatial distribution and functional role in genome organization, whether associated with repressive (heterochromatic) or active (euchromatic) domains.

Acknowledgments

The authors thank Emanuele Raineri for co-developing ChAseR. This work benefited from support provided by the Agence Nationale de la Recherche (ANR) through project ANR-23-CE12-0023 (supporting Flavien Raynal, engineer) and project ANR-24-CE52-0683 (supporting Benoît Aliaga, postdoctoral researcher).

Conflict of Interest The authors have no conflicts of interest to declare that are relevant to the content of this chapter.

References

1. Morris SA (2019) The evolving concept of cell identity in the single cell era. Development 146:dev169748. https://doi.org/10.1242/dev.169748
2. Zeng H (2022) What is a cell type and how to define it?. Cell 185:2739–2755. https://doi.org/10.1016/j.cell.2022.06.031
3. Waddington CH (1957) The strategy of the genes
4. Waddington CH (1942) Canalization of development and the inheritance of acquired characters. Nature 150:563–565. https://doi.org/10.1038/150563a0
5. Berger SL, Kouzarides T, Shiekhattar R, Shilatifard A (2009) An operational definition of epigenetics. Genes Dev 23:781–783. https://doi.org/10.1101/gad.1787609
6. Chen Y, Liang R, Li Y et al. (2024) Chromatin accessibility: biological functions, molecular mechanisms and therapeutic application. Signal Transduct Target Ther 9:340. https://doi.org/10.1038/s41392-024-02030-9
7. Ito T (2007) Role of histone modification in chromatin dynamics. J Biochem (Tokyo) 141:609–614. https://doi.org/10.1093/jb/mvm091
8. Gelato KA, Fischle W (2008) Role of histone modifications in defining chromatin structure and function. bchm 389:353–363. https://doi.org/10.1515/BC.2008.048
9. Bannister AJ, Kouzarides T (2011) Regulation of chromatin by histone modifications. Cell Res 21:381–395. https://doi.org/10.1038/cr.2011.22
10. Ito S, Umehara T, Koseki H (2024) Polycomb-mediated histone modifications and gene regulation. Biochem Soc Trans 52:151–161. https://doi.org/10.1042/BST20230336
11. D'Urso A, Brickner JH (2014) Mechanisms of epigenetic memory. Trends Genet 30:230–236. https://doi.org/10.1016/j.tig.2014.04.004
12. Duran-Ferrer M, Clot G, Nadeu F et al. (2020) The proliferative history shapes the DNA methylome of B-cell tumors and predicts clinical outcome. Nat Cancer 1:1066–1081. https://doi.org/10.1038/s43018-020-00131-2
13. Goel VY, Hansen AS (2021) The macro and micro of chromosome conformation capture. WIREs Dev Biol 10:e395. https://doi.org/10.1002/wdev.395
14. Pancaldi V (2023) Network models of chromatin structure. Curr Opin Genet Dev 80:102051. https://doi.org/10.1016/j.gde.2023.102051
15. Langmead B, Salzberg SL (2012) Fast gapped-read alignment with Bowtie 2. Nat Methods 9:357–359. https://doi.org/10.1038/nmeth.1923
16. Li H, Durbin R (2010) Fast and accurate long-read alignment with Burrows-Wheeler transform. Bioinformatics 26:589–595. https://doi.org/10.1093/bioinformatics/btp698
17. Cairns J, Freire-Pritchett P, Wingett SW et al. (2016) CHiCAGO: robust detection of DNA looping interactions in Capture Hi-C data. Genome Biol 17: 127. https://doi.org/10.1186/s13059-016-0992-2
18. Anil A, Spalinskas R, Åkerborg Ö, Sahlén P (2018) HiCapTools: a software suite for probe design and proximity detection for targeted chromosome conformation capture applications. Bioinformatics 34:675–677. https://doi.org/10.1093/bioinformatics/btx625
19. Wingett SW, Ewels P, Furlan-Magaril M et al. (2015) HiCUP: pipeline for mapping and processing Hi-C data. F1000Research 4:1310. https://doi.org/10.12688/f1000research.7334.1
20. Ay F, Bailey TL, Noble WS (2014) Statistical confidence estimation for Hi-C data reveals regulatory chromatin contacts. Genome Res 24:999–1011. https://doi.org/10.1101/gr.160374.113
21. McLean CY, Bristor D, Hiller M et al. (2010) GREAT improves functional interpretation of cis-regulatory regions. Nat Biotechnol 28:495–501. https://doi.org/10.1038/nbt.1630
22. Heinz S, Benner C, Spann N et al. (2010) Simple combinations of lineage-determining transcription factors prime cis-regulatory elements required for macrophage and B cell identities. Mol Cell 38:576–589. https://doi.org/10.1016/j.molcel.2010.05.004
23. Pancaldi V, Carrillo-de-Santa-Pau E, Javierre BM et al. (2016) Integrating epigenomic data and 3D genomic structure with a new measure of chromatin assortativity. Genome Biol 17: 152. https://doi.org/10.1186/s13059-016-1003-3
24. Madrid-Mencía M, Raineri E, Cao TBN, Pancaldi V (2020) Using GARDEN-NET and ChAseR to explore human haematopoietic 3D chromatin interaction networks. Nucleic Acids Res 48:4066–4080. https://doi.org/10.1093/nar/gkaa159
25. Pancaldi V (2021) Chromatin network analyses: towards structure-function relationships

in epigenomics. Front Bioinform 1:742216. https://doi.org/10.3389/fbinf.2021.742216
26. Botta M, Haider S, Leung IXY et al. (2010) Intra- and inter-chromosomal interactions correlate with CTCF binding genome wide. Mol Syst Biol 6:426. https://doi.org/10.1038/msb.2010.79
27. Boulos RE, Arneodo A, Jensen P, Audit B (2013) Revealing long-range interconnected hubs in human chromatin interaction data using graph theory. Phys Rev Lett 111:118102. https://doi.org/10.1103/PhysRevLett.111.118102
28. Boulos RE, Julienne H, Baker A et al. (2014) From the chromatin interaction network to the organization of the human genome into replication N/U-domains. New J Phys 16:115014. https://doi.org/10.1088/1367-2630/16/11/115014
29. Morlot J-B, Mozziconacci J, Lesne A (2016) Network concepts for analyzing 3D genome structure from chromosomal contact maps. EPJ Nonlinear Biomed Phys 4: 2. https://doi.org/10.1140/epjnbp/s40366-016-0029-5
30. Chovanec P, Collier AJ, Krueger C et al. (2021) Widespread reorganisation of pluripotent factor binding and gene regulatory interactions between human pluripotent states. Nat Commun 12: 2098. https://doi.org/10.1038/s41467-021-22201-4
31. Marie-Nelly H, Marbouty M, Cournac A et al. (2014) High-quality genome (re)assembly using chromosomal contact data. Nat Commun 5: 5695. https://doi.org/10.1038/ncomms6695
32. Tan ZW, Guarnera E, Berezovsky IN (2018) Exploring chromatin hierarchical organization via Markov State modelling. PLoS Comput Biol 14:e1006686. https://doi.org/10.1371/journal.pcbi.1006686
33. Newman MEJ (2003) Mixing patterns in networks. Phys Rev E 67:026126. https://doi.org/10.1103/PhysRevE.67.026126
34. Jodkowska K, Pancaldi V, Rigau M et al. (2022) 3D chromatin connectivity underlies replication origin efficiency in mouse embryonic stem cells. Nucleic Acids Res 50:12149–12165. https://doi.org/10.1093/nar/gkac1111
35. Tomás-Daza L, Rovirosa L, López-Martí P et al. (2023) Low input capture Hi-C (liCHi-C) identifies promoter-enhancer interactions at high-resolution. Nat Commun 14: 268. https://doi.org/10.1038/s41467-023-35911-8
36. Raynal F, Sengupta K, Plewczynski D et al. (2025) Global chromatin reorganization and regulation of genes with specific evolutionary ages during differentiation and cancer. Nucleic Acids Res 53:gkaf084. https://doi.org/10.1093/nar/gkaf084
37. Noble WS (2009) A quick guide to organizing computational biology projects. PLoS Comput Biol 5:1–5. https://doi.org/10.1371/journal.pcbi.1000424
38. Javierre BM, Burren OS, Wilder SP et al. (2016) Lineage-specific genome architecture links enhancers and non-coding disease variants to target gene promoters. Cell 167:1369–1384.e19. https://doi.org/10.1016/j.cell.2016.09.037

Check for updates

Chapter 7

Tensor Decomposition-Based Unsupervised Feature Extraction Applied to Bioinformatics

Y-h Taguchi

Abstract

Genomic research frequently encounters "large p small n" problems, where the number of variables significantly outweighs the number of samples. To address this challenge, this chapter presents tensor decomposition (TD)-based unsupervised feature extraction (FE) as a robust framework for feature selection in bioinformatics. By employing Tucker decomposition via higher-order singular value decomposition (HOSVD), multidimensional omics data are decomposed into low-dimensional latent spaces. Relevant features are identified using singular value vectors associated with specific biological conditions, with statistical significance assessed through an empirical Gaussian null hypothesis. A novel optimization method is introduced to refine the null hypothesis by maximizing the flatness of the P-value distribution. The utility of TD-based unsupervised FE is demonstrated across diverse scenarios, including multiomics integration, temporal data analysis—where it detects patterns like periodicity without prior knowledge—drug repositioning, and biomarker identification. To support practical implementation, two Bioconductor packages, TDbasedUFE and TDbasedUFEadv, are introduced. This methodology provides a versatile and effective approach for extracting meaningful biological insights from complex, high-dimensional datasets.

Keywords Tensor decomposition, Multiomics, Gene expression, Histone modification, DNA methylation

1 Introduction

In genomic research, so-called large p small n problems, i.e., a small number of samples associated with many numbers of variables, is very common. For example, consider a typical RNA-seq analysis. The number of genes, which corresponds to the number of variables, p, is as many as 10^4 whereas the number of samples, n, is typically at most 10^2; this is a typical situation of large p small n problem. Thus, to address large p small n problems is a critical issue in genomic research. Needless to say explicitly, there are no ways to address large p small n problems in the general aspect. Large p small n problems can be addressed only from the specific points of aspect. In this chapter, we aim to address large p small n problems, specifically in genomic research.

Y-h Taguchi (ed.), *AI/ML-Driven Gene Analysis*, Methods in Molecular Biology, vol. 3037,
https://doi.org/10.1007/978-1-0716-5284-8_7,

Tensor decomposition (TD)-based unsupervised feature extraction (FE) [1] is used for this purpose in this chapter. TD-based unsupervised FE was proposed in 2017 and was applied to a wide range of problems. I summarize how we can apply TD-based unsupervised FE to various problems.

2 TD-Based Unsupervised FE

In this section, we review what TD-based unsupervised FE is.

2.1 What is Tensor?

Tensor is an extension of a matrix that has only two indices corresponding to row and column, respectively. A typical tensor has more than two indices, each of which represents distinct features/samples. For example, consider when gene expression profiles are measured at multiple tissues of some human subjects. The gene expression profiles are naturally expressed as a three-way tensor, $x_{ijk} \in \mathbb{R}^{N \times M \times K}$, which represents expression of the ith gene of jth subject's kth tissue where N, M, and K represents the number of genes, number of subjects, and the number of tissues. Generally, not restricted to gene expression profiles, all of omics data sets measured in multiple experimental conditions are naturally formatted as a tensor rather than a matrix.

2.2 What are the Advantages of the Usage of Tensors in Genomic Science?

Nowadays, it is usual that the measurement of genomic features fits with tensors. For example, suppose that we observed gene expression of multiple tissues of multiple human subjects. In that case, it is natural to express gene expression as a tensor, x_{ijk}, which represents the expression of the ith gene of the jth tissue of the kth human subject. If more conditions are added, e.g., time dependence and the treatment of drugs, more indices are naturally added. More complex conditions are used, more indices are required. Thus, it is very reasonable to employ tensors to represent expression of multiple omics data sets.

2.3 Tensor Decomposition

What is the additional benefit of representing omics profiles as tensors? It is a tensor decomposition (TD). TD is an extension of PCA or SVD applied to a matrix. As PCA and SVD can generate low-dimensional representation of a matrix, TD can generate low-dimensional representation of a tensor. This kind of low-dimensional representation is often denoted as a latent variable in a context of data science. Such a low-dimensional representation is expected to express hidden important features, e.g., clustering, which is difficult to identify if TD is not available.

In contrast to SVD or PCA, which is a unique way to have low-dimensional representation, there are no unique low-dimensional representations in tensors at all [1]. For example, there are multiple well-known TDs, e.g., CP decomposition, Tucker decomposition, and tensor train decomposition. These TDs have their own pros and cons, which are discussed in detail in my book [1]. In this chapter, I employ Tucker decomposition that is performed specifically by higher order singular value decomposition (HOSVD) algorithms, which turns out to work very well. In Tucker decomposition, a tensor, x_{ijk}, can be decomposed as:

$$x_{ijk} = \sum_{l_1=1}^{N} \sum_{l_2=1}^{M} \sum_{l_3=1}^{K} G(l_1 l_2 l_3) u_{l_1 i} u_{l_2 j} u_{l3k},$$

where $G \in \mathbb{R}^{N\times M\times K}$ is a core tensor that represents a contribution of $u_{l_1 i} u_{l_2 j} u_{l_3 k}$ toward x_{ijk}, $u_{l_1 i} \in \mathbb{R}^{N\times N}$, $u_{l_2 j} \in \mathbb{R}^{M\times M}$, and $u_{l_3 k} \in \mathbb{R}^{K\times K}$ are singular value matrices and are orthogonal matrices. Individual vectors with the fixed l_1, l_2 or l_3 of the singular value matrices are expected to represent latent vectors coincident with low-dimensional structures hidden in tensors.

2.4 Feature Selection

We select features (typically genes) using the above TD. Suppose that i represents a feature and j and k represent the properties of samples. In the above example where j and k represent subjects and tissues, respectively, thus $u_{l_2 j}$ and u_{l3k} represent the dependence of x_{ijk} upon j and k. For example, when subjects composed of healthy controls and disease patients, it is expected that some $u_{l_2 j}$ is distinct between healthy controls and disease patients. Similarly, it is expected that some $u_{l_3 k}$ has tissue-specific values. If so, it is an evidence that some genes have the expression distinct between healthy controls and disease patients in the tissue-specific manner. Otherwise, there are no ways to find $u_{l_2 j}$ and $u_{l_3 k}$ associated with such a dependence.

The problem is which genes are associated with expression distinct between healthy controls and disease patients in the tissue-specific manner. To this end, we develop some manner to identify such genes. At first, we need to specify which $u_{l_1 i}$ is associated with $u_{l_2 j}$ and $u_{l_3 k}$ associated with such a dependence. This problem can be solved by investigating G. Since singular value vectors are unit vectors, G has all the weight that describes the interaction among $u_{l_1 i}$, $u_{l_2 j}$, and $u_{l_3 k}$. Thus, $u_{l_1 i}$ that is associated with $u_{l_2 j}$ and $u_{l_3 k}$ associated with such dependence has the largest absolute values of G with the specified l_2 and l_3. This allows us to select $u_{l_1 i}$ to be used for feature (gene) selection.

The way by which we can select *is* based upon $u_{l_1 i}$ is as follows. At first, we attribute the null hypothesis to $u_{l_1 i}$ so as to identify $u_{l_1 i}$ associated with $u_{l_2 j}$ and $u_{l_3 k}$ associated with such a dependence. Unfortunately, since there are no known null hypothesis when x_{ijk} is purely random numbers, we empirically assume that $u_{l_1 i}$ obeys Gaussion. Although it is purely empirical, it works pretty well as can be seen below. Using this, we try to find $u_{l_1 i}$ that have too large absolute values if the null hypothesis stands. Since Gaussian distribution has very small probabilities for absolutely larger values, we can deny the null hypothesis for such $u_{l_1 i}$ s. To do this, we employ the cumulative χ^2 distribution as:

$$P_i = P_{\chi^2}\left[> \left(\frac{u_{l_1 i}}{\sigma_{l_1}} \right)^2 \right],$$

where $P_{\chi^2}[>x]$ is the cumulative χ^2 distribution that represents the probability that the argument is larger than x. P_i is corrected by Benjamini–Hochberg (BH) criterion [1], one of multiple comparison correction methods, which estimate the true rejection probability to reject the null hypothesis (in this case, "$u_{l_1 i}$ obeys Gaussian"). This is required since P_i equal to $1/N$ can appear by chance when the number of genes is N; if we do not correct P_i, we reject the null hypothesis wrongly (i.e., more frequently than expected), and we get the wrong (i.e., too many) number of genes supposed not to obey Gaussian.

After correcting P_is, we selected genes associated with P-values less than threshold value, say 0.01. The examples of the application to real examples can be found in the previous studies [2, 3].

2.5 Optimization of σ_{l_1}

It is not a good idea to estimate σ_{l_1} with considering all of N genes, since those not obeying Gaussian should be excluded from computing σ_{l_1}. Nevertheless, before computing σ_{l_1}, we cannot compute P_is used to select genes to be excluded to compute σ_{l_1}. To avoid this contradiction, we compute histogram of P_is, say h_s that represents the number of is within the sth bin, and require h_s as flat as possible since h_s should be constant when the null hypothesis is fully satisfied. This means that the optimal set of genes to be excluded can be estimated with requiring flatness of h_s as much as possible. To do this, we compute the standard deviation of h_s as

$$\sigma_{h_s} = \sqrt{\frac{\sum_{s=1}^{S} (h_s - \overline{h_s})^2}{S}}$$

$$\overline{h_s} = \frac{\sum_{s=1}^{S} h_s}{S}$$

where S is the total number of bins. The actual algorithm is as follows:

1. Set tentative σ_{l_1}.
2. Compute P_is and correct them with BH criterion.

3. Exclude is associated with adjusted P_i less than threshold P-value, say 0.01.
4. Compute h_s using not excluded P_is and σ_{h_s} as well.
5. Update σ_{l_1} so us to decrease σ_{h_s}.
6. Go to Step 2.
7. Repeat until σ_{h_s} is minimized.

To demonstrate how well the above algorithm works, we apply the above procedure to the following data set.

$$x_i \sim N(0,1),\ 1 \le i \le 9500$$

$$, \sim N(4,1), 9500 < i \le 10000$$

where $N(\mu,\sigma)$ is the Gaussian distribution with the mean of μ and the standard deviation of σ. Here, the null hypothesis is that $x_i \sim N(0,)$, i.e., x_i obeys Gaussian distribution with zero mean and standard deviation of 1.

Figure 1 shows the result. As can be seen, σ_{h_s} has the minimum value, when σ=1 as expected. Histogram of P_i excluding is is flat as

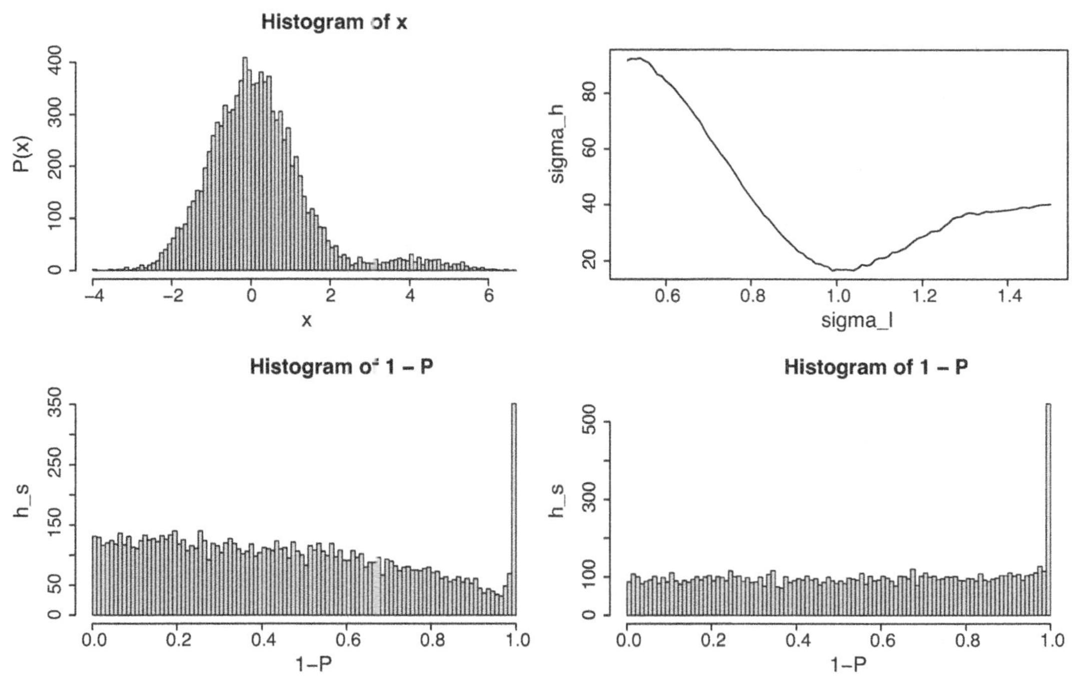

Fig. 1 The demonstration how well the above algorithm can select is not obeying Gaussian of $N(0,1)$ (i.e. i> 9500). Top left: Distribution of x_i. Top right: The dependence of σ_{h_s} on σ. Bottom left: Histogram of P_i with using σ using all x_i. Bottom right: Histogram of P_i with using $\sigma = 1$

Table 1
Confusion matrix when the above procedure applied to x_i

	$1 \leq i \leq 9500$	$9500 < i \leq 10000$
Adjusted $P > 0.01$	9494	193
Adjusted $P \leqq 0.01$	6	307

expected. Thus, the above workflame works well to exclude variables not obeying the null hypothesis.

Table 1 shows the confusion matrix. Among 500 *i*s not obeying the null hypothesis, 307 *i*s are correctly selected, and only the six *i*s are wrongly selected. Thus, the above workframe works pretty well to select *i*s not obeying the null hypothesis.

The examples of the application to real data sets can be found in the previous studies [4–7].

Here is a source code to perform this analysis.

```
R code No. 1
x <- rnorm(10000)
x[9501:10000] <- rnorm(500,4)
data <- NULL
for (i in 1:100)
{
cat(i, " ")
sigma <- 0.5+0.01*i
P <- pchisq((x-mean(x))^2/sigma^2,1,lower.tail=F)
index <- p.adjust(P,"BH")<0.01
hc <- hist(1-P[!index],plot=F,breaks=100)
data <- rbind(data,c(sigma,sd(hc$count)))
}
par(mfrow=c(2,2))
hist(x,breaks=100,xlab="x",ylab="P(x)",cex.axis=
2,cex.axis=1.5)
plot(data,type="l",xlab="sigma_l",ylab=
"sigma_h",cex.axis=2,cex.axis=1.5)
sigma <- sd(x)
P <- pchisq((x-mean(x))^2/sigma^2,1,lower.tail=F)
hist(1-P,breaks=100,xlab="1-P",ylab="h_s",cex.
axis=2,cex.axis=1.5)
sigma <- 1
P <- pchisq((x-mean(x))^2/sigma^2,1,lower.tail=F)
hist(1-P,breaks=100,xlab="1-P",ylab="h_s",cex.
axis=2,cex.axis=1.5)
par(mfrow=c(1,1))
table(p.adjust(P,"BH")<0.01,10000:1<=500)
```

3 Various Application

TD-based unsupervised FE can be applied to various cases not dealing with a single tensor.

3.1 Multiple Omics Data Set Not Sharing Features

It is very usual to analyze multiomics data sets not sharing features, e.g., integrated analysis of gene expression, methylation, and the expression of microRNAs. Here, we consider the case where the multiple omics profiles, which naturally have distinct numbers of features, are measured for the same sample. For example, we have K omics profiles, x_{ijk}, which represents the expression of ith feature of kth omics of jth sample and the numbers of features depend upon k as N_k. To integrate x_{ijk} as a tensor, we compute the product of x_{ijk} as:

$$x_{jj'k} = \sum_{i=1}^{N_k} x_{ijk} x_{ij'k}$$

and with applying HOSVD to the above, we get,

$$x_{jj'k} = \sum_{l_1=1}^{M} \sum_{l_2=1}^{M} \sum_{l_3=1}^{K} G(l_1 l_2 l_3) u_{l_1 j} u_{l_2 j'} u_{l_3 k},$$

where $G \in \mathbb{R}^{N]M \times M \times K}$ is a core tensor that represents a contribution of $u_{l_1 j} u_{l_2 j'} u_{l_3 k}$ toward $x_{jj'k}$, $u_{l_1 j} \in \mathbb{R}^{M \times M}$, $u_{l2j'} \in \mathbb{R}^{M \times M}$, and $u_{l_3 k} \in \mathbb{R}^{K \times K}$ are singular value matrices and are orthogonal matrices.

With this procedure, we can deal with multiple omics profiles as a tensor and TD-based unsupervised FE can be applied to multiomics profiles. The examples of applications can be seen at the various previous studies [8, 9].

3.2 The Alternative Ways dealing with Multiple Omics Data Set Not Sharing Features

Although the method described in the previous section is very useful, when the number of samples is huge, the methods require the memory size of the square of sample size. For example, when we consider a single cell multiomics data set, the number of samples can be huge since the number of samples in this case is equal to the total number of cells. In this case, we need alternative methods: the usage of singular value decomposition (SVD) applied to individual profiles. Suppose, we have multiomics profiles as described in the previous subsection, x_{ijk}. Before applying HOSVD to x_{ijk}, SVD is applied to individual profiles as:

$$x_{ijk} = \sum_{l=1}^{L_k} \lambda_l u_{li} v_{lj},$$

where $u_{li} \in \mathbb{R}^{L_k \times N_k}$ and $v_{lj} \in \mathbb{R}^{L_k \times M}$ are singular value matrices and $\lambda_l \in \mathbb{R}^{L_k}$ are singular values. L_k is equal to $\min(N_k, M)$. After that, with selecting L as the smallest value within L_k, we get $x_{ljk} \in \mathbb{R}^{L \times M \times K}$ and applying HOSVD to x_{ljk}, we get,

$$x_{ljk} = \sum_{l_1=1}^{L} \sum_{l_2=1}^{M} \sum_{l_3=1}^{K} G(l_1 l_2 l_3) u_{l_1 l} u_{l_2 j} u_{l_3 k},$$

where $G \in \mathbb{R}^{L \times M \times K}$ is a core tensor that represents a contribution of $u_{l_1 l} u_{l_2 j} u_{l_3 k}$ toward x_{ljk}, $u_{l_1 l} \in \mathbb{R}^{L \times L}$, $u_{l_2 j} \in \mathbb{R}^{M \times M}$, and $u_{l_3 k} \in \mathbb{R}^{K \times K}$ are singular value matrices and are orthogonal matrices.

The downstream analysis is as follows. Once $u_{l_2 j}$ and/or $u_{l_3 k}$ of interest are identified, we compute the singular value vector attributed to features, is, as,

$$u_{l_1 ik} = \sum_{j=1}^{M} u_{l_1 j} x_{ijk}$$

and $u_{l_1 ik}$ is used to select is in kth omics data. The example of application of this method can be found in previous studies [10, 11].

3.3 When Only Two Omics Profiles are Available

In this section, we assume that there are only two profiles, not generally K profiles.

At first, we consider the case that the common omics profiles are measured between two distinct profiles, associated with distinct sample indices, j and k, respectively. In this case, we generate a tensor from two matrices as,

$$x_{ijk} = x_{ij} x_{ik} \in \mathbb{R}^{N \times M \times K},$$

where x_{ij} and x_{ik} represent ith feature's value of jth and kth sample, respectively. Here, we assume the same omic profiles are measured for jth and kth samples, respectively. The downstream analysis is the same as the case where x_{ijk} represents expression of ith feature of kth and jth conditions. The application of this procedure can be found in the previous study [12].

The problem of this approach is to require a huge memory as large as $N \times M \times K$. To reduce required memory, we can take the summation of i as,

$$x_{jk} = \sum_{i=1}^{N} x_{ijk} \in \mathbb{R}^{M \times K}.$$

Then, SVD is applied to x_{jk} and we get,

$$x_{jk} = \sum_{l=1}^{L} \lambda_l u_{lj} v_{lk}.$$

This enables us to investigate the dependance of j and k upon labeling/classification. Once, we can identify u_{lj} and v_{lk} of interest, we can compute singular value vectors attributed to is as,

$$u_{li} = \sum_{j=1}^{M} u_{lj} x_{ij}$$

and

$$u_{li} = \sum\nolimits_{k=1}^{K} v_{lk} x_{ik}.$$

Although we have two distinct u_{li}, it is not bad at all, since we can validate the efficiency of the analysis by investigating the overlap between two gene sets selected using two distinct u_{li}. The examples of application of this procedure can be found in the previous studies [13, 14].

On the other hand, when there are two distinct omics profiles sharing samples, the problem is not so easy. Suppose that, we have two matrices that represent two distinct omics profiles, $x_{ij} \in \mathrm{R}^{N \times M}$ and $x_{kj} \in \mathrm{R}^{K \times M}$, which represent ith and kth omics profiles of jth sample. In this case, if we generate a tensor with the product of x_{ij} and x_{kj} as

$$x_{ijk} = x_{ij} x_{kj} \in \mathbb{R}^{N \times M \times K},$$

which requires a huge memory since the numbers of features, N and K, are generally very large. To suppress this difficulty as much as possible, we take the summation of j as,

$$x_{ik} = \sum_{j=1}^{M} x_{ijk} \in \mathbb{R}^{N \times K}$$

that reduces the required memory size to $1/M$.

In this formulation, index j, which is used to identify to see if dependence of classification/labeling exists, is missing. To recover j, we do

$$u_{lj} = \sum_{i=1}^{N} u_{li} x_{ij}$$

and

$$u_{lj} = \sum_{k=1}^{K} v_{lk} x_{kj},$$

where

$$x_{ik} = \sum_{l=1}^{L_k} \lambda_l u_{li} v_{lk}.$$

Now, we have two singular value vectors attributed to samples. *j*, computed from *i*th and *k*th feature (omics profile), respectively.

It is not bad at all, since we can now validate the success of the analysis by checking consistency between two u_{lj}s. If there are pairs of u_{lj}s, which are consistent with each other, this suggests that the analysis is successful. Once we can confirm that the analysis is successful, then we can select features *i* and *k* as usual using u_{li} and v_{lk}, respectively. The examples of application of this procedure is also found in the previous studies [15, 16].

3.4 Substitution to Network Analysis

In this subsection, we discuss how we can apply TD-based unsupervised FE to a data set with only features or samples. The core idea of TD-based unsupervised FE is as follows. At first, singular value vectors attributed to samples are investigated. Next, the singular value vectors attributed to samples of interest, e.g., distinct between controls and treated samples, are identified. Then with selecting the core tensor with the largest absolute values with fixing indices attributed to samples as those identified, we can decide that singular value vectors attribute to features are used for feature selection. Finally, we can attribute *P*-values to features and select features associated with adjusted *P*-values less than threshold values. At a glance, we need both features and samples to perform TD-based unsupervised FE. Nevertheless, we can make use of TD-based unsupervised FE even when we can have only samples or features.

Suppose we have tensors like $x_{ii'k} \in \mathrm{R}^{N \times N \times K}$ or $x_{jj'k} \in \mathrm{R}^{M \times M \times K}$. The former represents the *k*th interaction between *i*th and *i'*th features, whereas the latter represents the *k*th interaction between *j*th and *j'*th samples. The former example is protein–protein interaction and that of the latter is cell–cell interactions. The way we can make use of TD-based unsupervised FE is simple. Simply applying HOSVD to $x_{ii'k}$ or $x_{jj'k}$ and we get,

$$x_{ii'k} = \sum_{l_1=1}^{N} \sum_{l_2=1}^{N} \sum_{l_3=1}^{K} G(l_1 l_2 l_3) u_{l_1 i} u_{l_2 i'} u_{l_3 k},$$

where $G \in \mathbb{R}^{N \times N \times K}$ is a core tensor that represents a contribution of $u_{l_1 i} u_{l_2 i'} u_{l_3 k}$ toward $x_{ii'k}$, $u_{l_1 i} \in \mathbb{R}^{N \times N}$, $u_{l_2 i'} \in \mathbb{R}^{N \times N}$, and $u_{l_3 k} \in \mathbb{R}^{K \times K}$ are singular value matrices and are orthogonal matrices or

$$x_{jj'k} = \sum_{l_1=1}^{M} \sum_{l_2=1}^{M} \sum_{l_3=1}^{K} G\left(l_1 l_2 l_3\right) u_{l_1 j} u_{l_2 j'} u_{l_3 k}.$$

where $G \in \mathbb{R}^{M \times M \times K}$ is a core tensor that represents a contribution of $u_{l_1j}u_{l_2j'}u_{l_3k}$ toward $x_{jj'k}$, $u_{l_1j} \in \mathbb{R}^{M \times M}$, $u_{l_2j'} \in \mathbb{R}^{M \times M}$, and $u_{l_3k} \in \mathbb{R}^{K \times K}$ are singular value matrices and are orthogonal matrices. Since we can get singular value vectors attributed to features immediately for $x_{ii'k}$, we can select features using the standard procedure of TD-based unsupervised FE. Although one might wonder how we can make use of this procedure, the successful example can be found in the previous study [17], where useful cancer drug candidate compounds were identified.

It is also useful when applied to Hi-C data [18].

For $x_{jj'k}$, it is unclear how we can make use of it. Nevertheless, if we can have additional omics profile, x_{ij}, we can have,

$$u_{l_1i} = \sum_{j=1}^{M} x_{ij}u_{l_1j} \in \mathbb{R}^{N \times N}$$

and select features as usual.

4 Various Actual Applications

Apart from the previous section about the variety of analysis methods, we discuss about what kind of problems can be analyzed with TD-based unsupervised FE.

4.1 Temporal Data Analysis

One possible useful application of TD-based unsupervised FE is analysis of temporal data. For example, suppose that $x_{ijt} \in R^{N \times M \times T}$ represent the expression of *i*th gene of *j*th sample at *t*th time point. With simply applying HOSVD to x_{ijt}, we get,

$$x_{ijt} = \sum_{l_1=1}^{N} \sum_{l_2=1}^{M} \sum_{l_3=1}^{T} G\left(l_1 l_2 l_3\right) u_{l_1i}u_{l_2j}u_{l_3t},$$

where $G \in \mathbb{R}^{\times M \times T}$ is a core tensor that represents a contribution of $u_{l_1j}u_{l_2j}u_{l_3t}$ toward x_{ijt}, $u_{l_1i} \in \mathbb{R}^{N \times N}$, $u_{l_2j} \in \mathbb{R}^{M \times M}$, and $u_{l_3t} \in \mathbb{R}^{T \times T}$ are singular value matrices and are orthogonal matrices. With investigating u_{l_3t}, we can know what kind of temporal patterns are hidden in x_{ijt} without assuming something a priori. The remarkable point is that TD-based unsupervised FE does not require preassumed temporal patterns, e.g., periodicity, monotonic derease/increase, etc., which usual temporal analyses methods require. Because of this advantage, we can find nonpresumed temporal patterns in x_{ijt}.

To demonstrate how well TD-based unsupervised FE can detect periodic motion without preknowledge, we apply TD-based unsupervised FE to the following data set $x_{ijt} \in \mathbb{R}^{10000 \times 10 \times 100}$ as

$$x_{ijt} = \sin\left(\mathrm{mod}(10j+t, 100)\frac{2\pi}{100}\right) + \epsilon, \quad 9500 < i \leq 10000$$

$$= \mathit{permuted}\ \sin\left(\frac{2\pi t}{100}\right) + \epsilon, \quad 1 \leq i \leq 9500,$$

where $\epsilon \in N(0,1)$ and mod is modular function and permuted is permutation (randomization). With applying HOSVD to the above data set, we can have the following (Fig. 2). Although even x_{ijt} for i>9500, which is supposed to have periodicity, apparently does not represent any periodicity because of added noises, ϵ, (top left panel of Fig. 2), u_{1t} and u_{2t} exhibit clear periodicity (top right panel of Fig. 2). u_{1j} and u_{2j} exhibit the effect of phase shift ($10j$ in the definition of x_{ijt}) and u_{1i} and u_{2i} for $9500 < i \leq 10000$ exhibits larger values than others as expected. To select $9500 < i \leq 10000$, we optimize standard deviation and attribute P_i as

$$P_i = P_{\chi^2}\left[> \sum_{l_1=1}^{2} \left(\frac{u_{l_1 i}}{\sigma_{l_1}}\right)^2 \right].$$

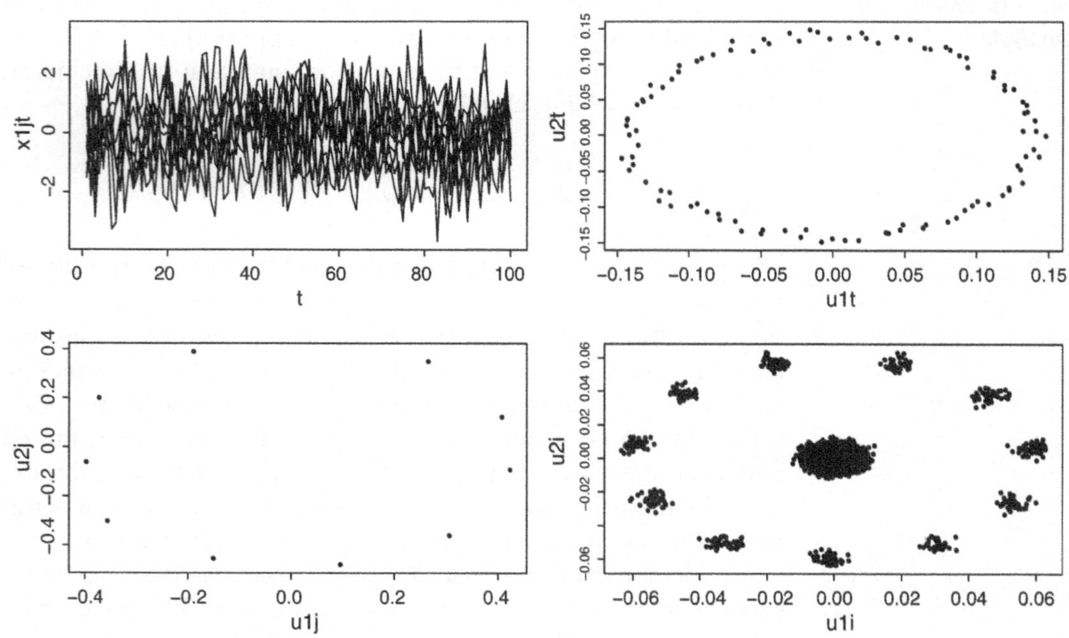

Fig. 2 Top left: x_{9501jt} Top right: Scatter plot of u_{1t} and u_{2t}. Bottom left: Scratter plot of u_{1j} and u_{2j}. Bottom right: Scratterr plot of u_{1i} and u_{2i}

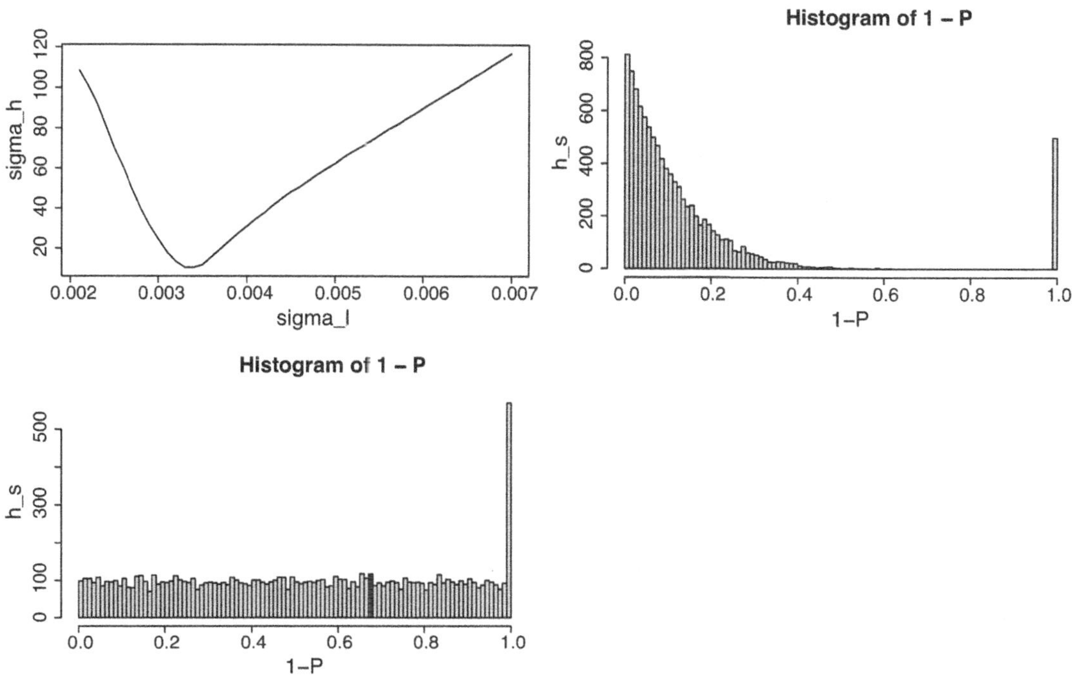

Fig. 3 Top left: The dependence upon σ_{h_s} on σ. Top right: Histogram of P_i with using σ using all $u_{l_1 i}$. Bottom left: Histogram of P_i with using the optimized σ

Table 2
Confusion matrix when the above procedure applied to u_{1i} and u_{2i}

	$1 \leq i \leq 9500$	$9500 < i \leq 10000$
Adjusted P > 0.01	9495	0
Adjusted P ≦ 0.01	5	500

Figure 3 shows the result. Top left panel of Fig. 3 shows the dependence of the standard deviation of the histogram of $1\text{-}P_i$, σ_h, upon $\sigma_{1i} = \sigma_{2i}$. As expected, there is $\sigma_{1i} = \sigma_{2i}$ that minimizes σ_h. Top right panel of Fig. 3 shows the histogram of $1\text{-}P_i$ without the optimization of $\sigma_{1i} = \sigma_{2i}$ and bottom left panel of Fig. 3 shows the histogram of $1\text{-}P_i$ with the optimization of $\sigma_{1i} = \sigma_{2i}$. It is obvious that the latter is more consistent with the null hypothesis that u_{1i} and u_{2i} obey Gaussian.

Table 2 shows the confusion matrix that shows the excellent performance. TD-based unsupervised FE can detect periodic motion without preknowledge.

Successful application of temporal data analysis can be found in the previous studies [19, 20]. Here is a source code to perform this analysis

```
R code No.2
x <- sin(seq(0,2*pi,length=100))
x0 <- x
for (i in c(1:10)){x <- cbind(x,x0[(10*i+
c(1:100))%%100+1])}
x <- array(x,c(100,10,10000))
x[,,1:9500] <- apply(x[,,1:9500],1:2,sample)
x <- x+rnorm(100*10*10000)
HOSVD <- hosvd(as.tensor(x),c(2,2,2))
pdf(file="fig2.pdf")
par(mfrow=c(2,2))
matplot(x[,,9501],type="l",col=1,lty=1,xlab=
"t",ylab="x1jt")
plot(HOSVD$U[[1]][,1:2],pch=16,xlab="u1t",ylab=
"u2t")
plot(HOSVD$U[[2]][,1:2],pch=16,xlab="u1j",ylab=
"u2j")
plot(HOSVD$U[[3]][,1:2],pch=16,xlab="u1i",ylab=
"u2i")
par(mfrow=c(1,1))
dev.off()
xx <- HOSVD$U[[3]][,1:2]
data <- NULL
for (i in 1:50)
{
cat(i, " ")
sigma <- 0.002+0.0001*i
P <- pchisq(rowSums((xx - apply(xx,2,mean))^2)/
sigma^2,2,lower.tail=F)
index <- p.adjust(P,"BH")<0.01
hc <- hist(1-P[!index],plot=F,breaks=100)
data <- rbind(data,c(sigma,sd(hc$count)))
}
pdf(file="fig3.pdf")
par(mfrow=c(2,2))
plot(data,type="l",xlab="sigma_l",ylab=
"sigma_h",cex.axis=2,cex.axis=1.5)
sigma <- sd(xx)
P <- pchisq(rowSums((xx - apply(xx,2,mean))^2)/
sigma^2,2,lower.tail=F)
hist(1-P,breaks=100,xlab="1-P",ylab="h_s",cex.
axis=2,cex.axis=1.5)
sigma <- data[which.min(data[,2]),1]
P <- pchisq(rowSums((xx - apply(xx,2,mean))^2)/
sigma^2,2,lower.tail=F)
hist(1-P,breaks=100,xlab="1-P",ylab="h_s",cex.
axis=2,cex.axis=1.5)
par(mfrow=c(1,1))
dev.off()
table(p.adjust(P,"BH")<0.01,c(1:10000)>9500)
```

4.2 Drug Repositioning

Drug repositioning from gene expression is yet another way possible by TD-based unsupervised FE. Suppose we have gene expression of healthy controls and patients, respectively. TD-based unsupervised FE can identify genes whose expression differs between healthy controls and patients. If we need only to investigate the distinction between healthy controls and patients, it is not required to employ tensors but matrices. Nevertheless, it is usual to have more complicated experimental setups. For example, the experiments are performed using various kind of cell lines, gene expression profiles are naturally formatted as a tensor, x_{ijk}, which represents the expression of the ith gene of jth cell lines under the kth condition (e.g., $k=1$: control and $k=2$: infected) [21]. Or alternatively, we can consider the case where multiple tissues are treated by multiple drug compounds [22]. In that case, gene expression is also formatted as a tensor, x_{ijk}, which represents the expression of the ith gene of jth tissues treated by kth compounds. Although these are only a few examples, in any case, drugs whose treatments affect the expression of genes selected by TD-based unsupervised FE can be regarded as candidate drug compounds. In more complicated cases, gene expression of healthy controls and patients can be integrated with that of tissues treated by drug compounds. Suppose that x_{ij} represents the expression of ith gene between healthy controls and patients (e.g., $j \leqq M/2$: healthy controls and $j > M/2$: patients where M is the total number of subjects) and x_{ik} represents the expression of ith gene between tissues treated or not treated tissues (e.g., $k \leqq K/2$: treated and $k > K/2$: not treated where K is total number of tissues), we can have $x_{ijk} = x_{ij}x_{ik}$ and proceed the same analysis as cases when x_{ijk} is initially given [12]. Thus, drug repositioning is one of useful applications that can be performed by TD-based unsupervised FE.

4.3 Biomarker Identification

Biomarker identification is yet another application that can be performed by TD based unsupervised FE. Suppose we have gene expression of ith gene at the jth sample, x_{ij}. If samples are composed of healthy controls and patients, genes whose expression is distinct between patients and healthy controls are selected and can be biomarkers that can diagnose diseases. Of course, we do not need tensors if we have these kinds of simple setups. Nevertheless, more complicated things are often considered. For example, we might be forced to analyze tissue dependence and/or time course data sets. TD-based unsupervised FE can even treat the tensors with seven indices [22]. Therefore, TD-based unsupervised FE is fitted with biomarker identification under more complicated conditions.

5 Bioconductor Packages

To let readers perform TD-based unsupervised FE easily, we introduce two Bioconductor packages here [23].

5.1 TDbasedUFE

TDbasedUFE [24] is a basic package that can perform simple gene expression analysis formatted as a tensor and multiomicsanalysis where samples are shared. The reason why we provide it is because it is easier for readers to learn two basic and frequently used implementations of TD-based unsupervised FE to understand basic concepts. Since practically more advanced implementation is required, readers can try the second Bioconductor package below.

5.2 TDbasedUFEadv

Yet, another package to perform TD-based unsupervised FE is TDbasedUFEadv [25]. In this package, readers can learn more complicated implementations of TD-based unsupervised FE not included in TDbasedUFE. Only readers who need more complicated and advanced usage can try it. It also includes some examples to perform enrichment analysis using genes selected by TD-based unsupervised FE.

Conflict of Interest

The authors have no conflicts of interest to declare that are relevant to the content of this chapter.

References

1. Taguchi Y-h (2024) Unsupervised feature extraction applied to bioinformatics: A PCA based and TD based approach. 2nd Ed. Springer International Publishing, Cham
2. Taguchi Y-H (2017) Tensor decomposition-based unsupervised feature extraction identifies candidate genes that induce post-traumatic stress disorder-mediated heart diseases. BMC Med Genom 10: 67. https://doi.org/10.1186/s12920-017-0302-1
3. Taguchi Y (2019) Drug candidate identification based on gene expression of treated cells using tensor decomposition-based unsupervised feature extraction for large-scale data. BMC Bioinformatics 19: 388. https://doi.org/10.1186/s12859-018-2395-8
4. Taguchi Y-h, Turki T (2022) Adapted tensor decomposition and PCA based unsupervised feature extraction select more biologically reasonable differentially expressed genes than conventional methods. Sci Rep 12: 17438. https://doi.org/10.1038/s41598-022-21474-z
5. Taguchi Y-H, Turki T (2023) Principal component analysis- and tensor decomposition-based unsupervised feature extraction to select more suitable differentially methylated cytosines: optimization of standard deviation versus state-of-the-art methods. Genomics 115:110577. https://doi.org/10.1016/j.ygeno.2023.110577
6. Turki T, Roy SS, Taguchi Y-H (2023) Optimized tensor decomposition and principal component analysis outperforming state-of-the-art methods when analyzing histone modification chromatin immunoprecipitation profiles. Algorithms 16:401. https://doi.org/10.3390/a16090401
7. Taguchi Y-H, Turki T (2023) Tensor decomposition discriminates tissues using scATAC-seq. Biochim Biophys Acta BBA–Gen Subj 1867:130360. https://doi.org/10.1016/j.bbagen.2023.130360
8. Taguchi Y, Turki T (2022) Novel feature selection method via kernel tensor decomposition for improved multi-omics data analysis. BMC Med Genom 15: 37. https://doi.org/10.1186/s12920-022-01181-4
9. Taguchi Y-h, Komaki S, Sutoh Y et al. (2023) Integrated analysis of human DNA methylation, gene expression, and genomic variation in iMETHYL database using kernel tensor decomposition-based unsupervised feature extraction. PLOS One 18:e0289029. https://doi.org/10.1371/journal.pone.0289029
10. Taguchi Y-h, Turki T (2021) Tensor-decomposition-based unsupervised feature extraction in single-cell multiomics data analysis.

Genes 12:1442. https://doi.org/10.3390/genes12091442
11. Taguchi Y-h, Turki T (2022) A tensor decomposition-based integrated analysis applicable to multiple gene expression profiles without sample matching. Sci Rep 12: 21242. https://doi.org/10.1038/s41598-022-25524-4
12. Taguchi Y-h (2017) Identification of candidate drugs using tensor-decomposition-based unsupervised feature extraction in integrated analysis of gene expression between diseases and DrugMatrix datasets. Sci Rep 7: 13733. https://doi.org/10.1038/s41598-017-13003-0
13. Taguchi Y-h, Turki T (2019) Tensor decomposition-based unsupervised feature extraction applied to singlecell gene expression analysis. Front Genet 10:864. https://doi.org/10.3389/fgene.2019.00864
14. Taguchi Y-h (2017) Tensor decomposition-based unsupervised feature extraction applied to matrix products for multi-view data processing. PLOS One 12:e0183933. https://doi.org/10.1371/journal.pone.0183933
15. Ng K-L, Taguchi Y-H (2020) Identification of miRNA signatures for kidney renal clear cell carcinoma using the tensor-decomposition method. Sci Rep 10:15149. https://doi.org/10.1038/s41598-020-71997-6
16. Roy SS, Taguchi Y-H (2021) Identification of genes associated with altered gene expression and m6A profiles during hypoxia using tensor decomposition based unsupervised feature extraction. Sci Rep 11:8909. https://doi.org/10.1038/s41598-021-87779-7
17. Taguchi Y-h, Turki T (2024) Novel artificial intelligence-based identification of drug-gene-disease interaction using protein-protein interaction. BMC Bioinformatics 25:377. https://doi.org/10.1186/s12859-024-06009-9
18. Taguchi Y-H, Turki T (2025) Novel AI-powered computational method using tensor decomposition for identification of common optimal bin sizes when integrating multiple Hi-C datasets. Sci Rep 15:7459. https://doi.org/10.1038/s41598-025-91355-8
19. Taguchi Y, Turki T (2019) Neurological disorder drug discovery from gene expression with tensor decomposition. Curr Pharm Des 25:4589–4599. https://doi.org/10.2174/1381612825666191210160906
20. Taguchi Y-H, Turki T (2021) Application of tensor decomposition to gene expression of infection of mouse hepatitis virus can identify critical human genes and effective drugs for SARS-CoV-2 infection. IEEE J Sel Top Signal Process 15:746–758. https://doi.org/10.1109/JSTSP.2021.3061251
21. Taguchi Y-h, Turki T (2020) A new advanced in silico drug discovery method for novel coronavirus (SARS-CoV-2) with tensor decomposition-based unsupervised feature extraction. PLOS One 15:e0238907. https://doi.org/10.1371/journal.pone.0238907
22. Taguchi Y-h, Turki T (2020) Universal nature of drug treatment responses in drug-tissue-wide model-animal experiments using tensor decomposition-based unsupervised feature extraction. Front Genet 11:695. https://doi.org/10.3389/fgene.2020.00695
23. Taguchi Y-h, Turki T (2023) Application note: TDbasedUFE and TDbasedUFEadv: bioconductor packages to perform tensor decomposition based unsupervised feature extraction. Front Artif Intell 6, 1237542. https://doi.org/10.3389/frai.2023.1237542
24. TDbasedUFE. In: Bioconductor. http://bioconductor.org/packages/TDbasedUFE/. Accessed 13 June 2026
25. TDbasedUFEadv. In: Bioconductor. http://bioconductor.org/packages/TDbasedUFEadv/. Accessed 13 June 2026

Check for updates

Chapter 8

Circulating MicroRNAs as Biomarkers for Cardiovascular Events: Bioinformatics and Machine Learning Approaches

Srinivasulu Yerukala Sathipati , Luke Moat and Param Sharma

Abstract

MicroRNAs (miRNAs) have emerged as key regulators of gene expression, influencing various biological processes, including those implicated in cancer and cardiovascular diseases (CVDs). These small, noncoding RNAs modulate gene functions by targeting messenger RNAs, thereby playing a critical role in disease progression. Increasing evidence suggests that circulating miRNAs hold great promise as minimally invasive biomarkers for early detection and risk assessment of cardiovascular conditions. This chapter provides a comprehensive overview of protocols for leveraging circulating miRNAs as predictive biomarkers for cardiovascular events, with a particular focus on postoperative atrial fibrillation (POAF). We outline methodologies encompassing sample collection, miRNA extraction, data preprocessing, biomarker identification, and predictive modeling using bioinformatics and machine learning approaches. By integrating computational and experimental techniques, we highlight strategies to enhance early cardiovascular disease detection and discuss challenges related to standardization and clinical translation of miRNA-based diagnostics.

Keywords miRNA profiling, Atrial fibrillation, Aardiovascular diseases, Machine learning, Bioinformatics approach

1 Introduction

MicroRNAs (miRNAs) are short, noncoding RNA molecules, typically 20–24 nucleotides in length, that regulate gene expression at the posttranscriptional level by targeting complementary sequences on messenger RNAs (mRNAs), leading to mRNA degradation or translational repression [1]. These regulatory molecules are involved in a wide range of physiological and pathological processes, including cell differentiation, proliferation, apoptosis, and stress responses [1, 2].

In cardiovascular diseases (CVDs), miRNAs play a crucial role in maintaining cardiac homeostasis, influencing processes such as cardiac development, vascular integrity, and myocardial remodeling [2]. Dysregulation of specific miRNAs has been linked to key pathological mechanisms, including cardiac hypertrophy, fibrosis,

Y-h Taguchi (ed.), *AI/ML-Driven Gene Analysis*, Methods in Molecular Biology, vol. 3037,
https://doi.org/10.1007/978-1-0716-5284-8_8,

and arrhythmogenesis [3, 4]. Notably, the stability of circulating miRNAs in blood presents a significant opportunity for their use as minimally invasive biomarkers for diagnosing, predicting, and monitoring cardiovascular conditions, such as myocardial infarction, heart failure, atrial fibrillation, ventricular tachycardia, and sudden cardiac death [5, 6].

Several studies have characterized miRNA expression in cardiac tissues across different developmental stages. For instance, miRNAs such as miR-21, miR-29a, miR-129, miR-210, miR-211, miR-320, miR-423, and let-7c are highly expressed in the fetal heart [7]. In contrast, in the adult heart, sequencing studies have identified a subset of miRNAs, including miR-1, miR-16, miR-27b, miR-30d, miR-126, miR-133, miR-143, miR-208, and the let-7 family, that contribute to cardiac maintenance and disease pathogenesis [8, 9]. Furthermore, declining levels of circulating miRNAs, such as miR-18a, miR-27a, miR-30e, miR-26b, miR-199a, miR-106a, and miR-652, have been observed in heart failure patients [10]. Notably, reductions in miRNAs, including let-7i, miR-18b, miR-18a, miR-223, miR-301a, miR-652, and miR-423, have been associated with increased mortality risk within 180 days following acute heart failure admission [11]. Additionally, circulating miRNAs have been implicated in coronary artery disease, elevating the risk of sudden cardiac death (SCD). A study by Silverman et al. demonstrated that increased levels of miR-150, miR-299, and miR-301 were associated with a significantly higher SCD risk. Patients with elevated levels of these miRNAs exhibited a 4.8-fold increase in SCD risk (95% CI: 1.59–14.51; $p = 0.006$) [6].

Atrial fibrillation (AF) is the most prevalent cardiac arrhythmia, particularly among elderly populations, and often results from a combination of structural and electrical remodeling [12]. Early studies demonstrated a significant reduction in miR-1 levels (~86%) in atrial tissues from AF patients, suggesting a potential role in regulating inward-rectifier potassium currents (I_{K1}) [13]. Similarly, Lu et al. [14] reported that miR-328 overexpression increased AF susceptibility, whereas its knockdown reduced vulnerability in animal models. Additionally, miR-223 and miR-664 were elevated in atrial samples from AF patients, though miR-1 remained unchanged [14]. miR-29, which targets mRNAs encoding fibrosis-associated proteins, has been implicated in cardiac fibrosis and apoptosis, further contributing to AF development [15–18].

Emerging evidence suggests that specific miRNAs may serve as potential biomarkers for predicting postoperative AF (POAF). Elevated serum levels of miR-483 have been associated with increased POAF risk [19], while circulating miR-23a and miR-26a may contribute to AF pathophysiology [20]. Moreover, miR-328 has been linked to atrial remodeling by targeting genes involved in calcium channel regulation, including CACNA1C and CACNB2, which encode L-type Ca^{2+} channel subunits [14, 21, 22]. Ling et al. [23] identified miR-499 as significantly upregulated in AF patients, suggesting its role in electrical remodeling by modulating small-conductance Ca^{2+}-activated K^{+} channels. Additionally, miR-150 levels were found to be significantly reduced (3.2-fold in platelets and 1.5-fold in serum) in AF patients compared to disease-free controls [24].

Despite promising findings, miRNAs have yet to surpass traditional biomarkers, such as cardiac troponins, in acute myocardial infarction diagnosis. Traditional cardiovascular risk prediction models primarily rely on clinical variables and imaging data, yet they often fail to capture the molecular intricacies of disease progression. Integrating miRNA profiling with bioinformatics tools and machine learning algorithms offers a novel approach to enhancing predictive accuracy and identifying patient-specific risk factors [25].

2 Materials

This section outlines the essential materials required for miRNA extraction [26], quantification [27], bioinformatics analysis, and machine learning-based prediction models for cardiovascular event risk assessment. An overview of the protocol is illustrated in Fig. 1. The essential materials and tools required for each step of the miRNA-based biomarker workflow, along with their specific purposes, are summarized in Table 1.

2.1 Sample Collection

Proper sample collection is critical for maintaining RNA integrity and preventing contamination.

1. Serum collection tubes—Tubes without anticoagulants are used to collect whole blood for serum isolation.
2. Centrifuge—A centrifuge capable of operating at 1500 × *g* (for initial separation) and 12,000 × *g* (for debris removal) is required.
3. RNase-free pipette tips and microcentrifuge tubes—Essential for preventing RNA degradation during processing.

2.2 miRNA Extraction Kits

To ensure high-yield and high-purity RNA extraction, the following reagents are commonly used:

1. miRNeasy Serum/Plasma Kit (Qiagen)—Provides a silica membrane-based purification system optimized for miRNA isolation.
2. TRIzol LS Reagent (Thermo Fisher Scientific)—A phenol-based reagent widely used for RNA extraction from serum and plasma.

A

B

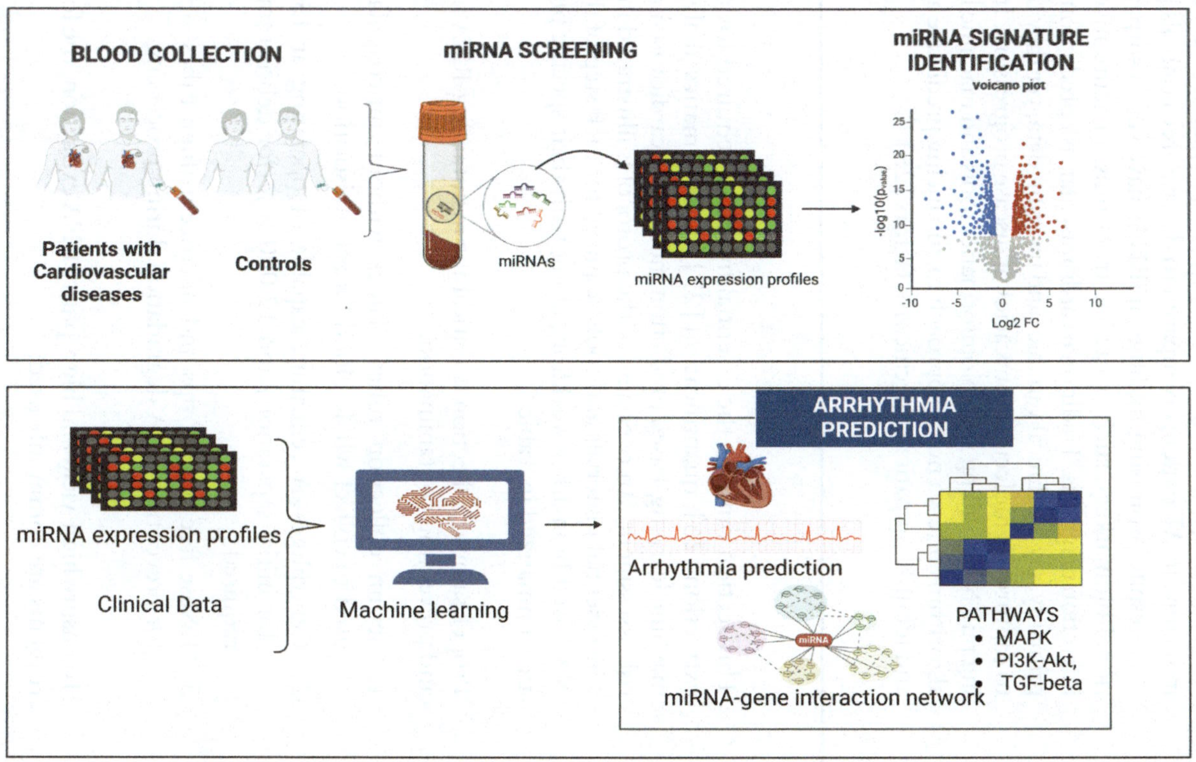

Fig. 1 Overview of the protocol. (**A**) Recruitment of participants and extraction of miRNA expression profiles from serum, followed by miRNA sequencing to identify an miRNA signature that predicts arrhythmia. (**B**) Integration of miRNA expression profiles and clinical data into a modeling workflow to identify high-risk populations and diagnostic interventions

Table 1
Summary of materials, tools, and their purpose in the miRNA-based cardiovascular biomarker protocol

Category	Materials and tools	Purpose
Sample collection	Serum collection tubes, centrifuge	Isolate serum for miRNA extraction
miRNA extraction	miRNeasy Kit, TRIzol LS Reagent	Extract miRNAs from serum
Quality control	Agilent Bioanalyzer, NanoDrop	Assess RNA integrity and purity
Quantification	TaqMan assays, NGS platforms	miRNA expression profiling
Bioinformatics	DESeq2, edgeR, scikit-learn	Differential expression and machine learning
Pathway analysis	KEGG, Reactome, DAVID	Functional analysis of miRNAs

2.3 Quality Control Tools

RNA integrity and concentration must be assessed before downstream applications:

1. Agilent 2100 Bioanalyzer—A microfluidics-based system that provides RNA integrity numbers (RINs) to assess sample quality.
2. NanoDrop spectrophotometer—Measures RNA purity using absorbance ratios (A260/A280 and A260/A230).

2.4 Quantification Platforms

To profile miRNA expression, the following techniques are used:

1. TaqMan Advanced miRNA Assays (Applied Biosystems)—A qRT-PCR-based approach for miRNA quantification.
2. Next-generation sequencing (NGS) platforms (Illumina MiSeq, NovaSeq)—Enable high-throughput miRNA sequencing for biomarker discovery.

2.5 Bioinformatics Tools

Computational analysis is necessary for miRNA expression analysis, target prediction, and pathway enrichment:

1. R-based analysis (Bioconductor packages: DESeq2 [28], edgeR [29], limma [30])—Libraries for differential expression analysis and normalization.
2. Python-based analysis (pandas [31], NumPy [32], scikit-learn [33], XGBoost [34])—Machine learning libraries for feature selection and predictive modeling.
3. miRNA databases (miRbase [35], TargetScan [36], miRTarBase [37])—Provide miRNA–gene interaction predictions.
4. Pathway analysis tools (Kyoto Encyclopedia of Genes and Genomes (KEGG) [38], Reactome [39], DAVID [40])—Identify biological pathways associated with predicted miRNA targets.

3 Methods

3.1 miRNA Extraction and Quantification

Serum Preparation

1. Collect 5 mL of venous blood in serum collection tubes.
2. Allow the blood to clot at room temperature for 30 min.
3. Centrifuge at 1500 × *g* for 10 min at 4°C to separate the serum.
4. Transfer the supernatant into RNase-free tubes and centrifuge at 12,000 × *g* for 10 min to remove cellular debris.
5. Aliquot 200 μL portions and store them at −80°C until RNA extraction.

RNA Extraction

1. Thaw serum on ice and mix 200 μL with 1 mL of TRIzol LS Reagent.
2. Vortex for 30 s and incubate at room temperature for 5 min.
3. Add 200 μL chloroform, shake vigorously for 15 s, and incubate for 3 min.
4. Centrifuge at 12,000 × *g* for 15 min at 4°C and transfer the aqueous phase to a fresh tube.
5. Precipitate RNA using isopropanol, wash with 75% ethanol, and dissolve in 14 μL RNase-free water.

Quality Control

1. Assess RNA integrity using the Agilent Bioanalyzer; the RNA integrity number (RIN) should be >7.
2. Measure RNA purity using the NanoDrop spectrophotometer (A260/A280 ratio between 1.8 and 2.0).

Quantification

1. For qRT-PCR, use TaqMan Advanced miRNA Assays following the manufacturer's protocol.
2. For NGS, prepare miRNA libraries using the NEBNext Multiplex Small RNA Library Prep Kit and sequence on an Illumina platform (minimum depth of ten million reads per sample).

3.2 Bioinformatics Pipeline for miRNA Analysis

Data Preprocessing

1. Import raw count data into R using "read.csv()."
2. Normalize using Trimmed Mean of M-values (TMM) method (edgeR [29]) or variance stabilizing transformation (VST) (DESeq2 [28]) or filter out low-expressed miRNAs (counts per million (CPM) <1 in at least 50% of samples).

Differential Expression Analysis

1. Identify differentially expressed miRNAs using DESeq2 [26], applying Benjamini–Hochberg correction for multiple testing. Consider miRNAs with: $|\log_2 \text{fold change}| > 1$ or false discovery rate (FDR) < 0.05.
2. Study-specific approach: miRNA expression profiles from AF/POAF patients and controls were analyzed using DESeq2. A Wald test was used to determine fold changes and significance, with an FDR-adjusted threshold of $q < 0.05$.

Target Prediction

1. Predict miRNA target genes using TargetScan [36], miRDB [41], and/or miRTarBase [37].
2. To enhance prediction accuracy, only gene targets present in at least two databases were considered. Identify POAF-associated targets using an intersection approach [42].

Pathway Enrichment Analysis

1. Perform KEGG pathway enrichment analysis using the "clusterProfiler" package in R [43].
2. Identify significantly enriched pathways with adjusted p-values <0.05.
3. Identify miRNA–disease association using HMDD v4.0 [44] and miRNet [45].

3.3 Machine Learning for Cardiovascular Event Prediction

Feature Selection

1. Use Least Absolute Shrinkage and Selection Operator (LASSO) regression [46] to identify key miRNAs associated with cardiovascular events.
2. Apply Recursive Feature Elimination (RFE) to refine feature selection [47].

Model Development

1. Split data into training and test/validation sets.
2. Train classification models using Random Forest [48], XGBoost [34], and Support Vector Machines (SVMs) [49].
3. Optimize hyperparameters using grid search with cross-validation [50].

Model Validation

1. Perform fivefold or tenfold cross-validation to assess model performance.
2. Evaluate predictive accuracy using receiver operating characteristic (ROC) curves and area under the curve (AUC).
3. Report classification metrics, including accuracy, sensitivity, specificity, precision, recall, and F1-score.

3.4 Results Interpretation

The effectiveness of this protocol was demonstrated in our previous investigation [42], where we applied it to identify miRNAs predictive of POAF. Here, we summarize key findings to illustrate the kind of results that can be obtained using this workflow, focusing on miRNA selection, machine learning model performance, pathway analysis, and disease associations.

Identification of a POAF-miRNA Signature

Using correlation-based feature selection [51], we identified a panel of 10 miRNAs from an initial set of 84 candidates after removing highly correlated miRNAs ($R < 0.80$). These miRNAs demonstrated significant differential expression between POAF patients and controls, suggesting their potential as biomarkers. The top ten POAF-miRNAs identified including hsa-miR-19a-3p, hsa-miR-19b-3p, hsa-miR-184, hsa-miR-200a-3p, hsa-let-7a-5p, hsa-miR-124-3p, hsa-miR-423-5p, hsa-miR-96-5p, hsa-miR-100-5p, and hsa-miR-17-5p. These miRNAs were significantly associated with atrial remodeling and fibrosis, key contributors to POAF pathogenesis [42].

Performance of Machine Learning Models in POAF Prediction

To assess the predictive utility of the POAF-miRNA signature, we applied four machine learning models—Random Forest [48], *k*-nearest neighbor (KNN) [52], XGBoost [34], and Support Vector Machine (SVM) [49]—to classify POAF cases and controls using a 70:30 train-test split.

Machine learning model performance metrics from our POAF study [42] is as follows:

1. Random Forest achieved perfect accuracy (AUC = 1.00) on training data, but its performance dropped to 80% on test data, suggesting slight overfitting.
2. KNN maintained stable performance across both datasets, achieving a test AUC of 0.77 with high specificity.
3. XGBoost demonstrated strong generalization, with an AUC of 0.83 in testing, making it one of the most promising models.
4. SVM had the weakest predictive power, with an AUC of 0.50, indicating that it may not be optimal for miRNA-based POAF classification.

These results highlight the strength of ensemble-based models (Random Forest, XGBoost) for miRNA-based cardiovascular risk prediction.

Pathway Enrichment Analysis of POAF-miRNAs

To understand the biological relevance of the POAF-miRNA signature, we conducted KEGG pathway enrichment analysis using the clusterProfiler package in R [43]. The top enriched pathways reflect key mechanisms underlying POAF pathogenesis, including fibrosis, inflammation, and ion channel regulation (Table 2).

Table 2
Top five enriched KEGG pathways associated with the POAF-miRNA signature

Pathway	Enriched miRNAs	*p*-value (adjusted)
TGF-beta signaling	hsa-miR-200a-3p, hsa-miR-17-5p	3.2e-4
MAPK signaling	hsa-miR-19a-3p, hsa-miR-19b-3p	1.6e-3
PI3K-Akt pathway	hsa-miR-184, hsa-let-7a-5p	2.1e-3
Calcium signaling	hsa-miR-124-3p, hsa-miR-423-5p	4.7e-3
Cardiac fibrosis regulation	hsa-miR-100-5p, hsa-miR-96-5p	7.8e-3

1. TGF-beta signaling, the most significantly enriched pathway, plays a crucial role in fibrosis and atrial remodeling, which are central to AF development [53].
2. MAPK and PI3K-Akt signaling pathways contribute to hypertrophic remodeling and cellular stress responses, both implicated in cardiovascular disease [54, 55].
3. Calcium signaling alterations are associated with arrhythmogenesis and AF progression [56].

Disease Associations of POAF-miRNA Signature

Beyond cardiovascular relevance, the identified miRNAs were significantly enriched in multiple disease pathways, demonstrating their broader biological role. We utilized miRNA-disease association information from HMDD v4.0 [44] and miRNet [45].

1. POAF-miRNA signature demonstrated strong associations with cardiovascular diseases, particularly in acute myocardial infarction and hypertrophic cardiomyopathy, as illustrated in Fig. 2.
2. Several miRNAs (hsa-let-7a-5p, hsa-miR-96-5p, hsa-miR-124-3p, and hsa-miR-17-5p) were linked to multiple diseases, indicating their broad biological impact (Table 3).
3. Most disease associations were cancer-related, highlighting potential shared molecular mechanisms between POAF and oncogenic pathways.

The integration of miRNA profiling and machine learning presents a novel approach for cardiovascular risk prediction, offering insights into molecular alterations that precede clinical symptoms. The findings from this study reinforce the value of miRNA-based biomarkers in disease diagnostics and risk stratification.

Clinical Implications and Challenges

1. Early detection and personalized medicine: miRNA biomarkers can enable early intervention before clinical symptoms appear, allowing for personalized treatment strategies.

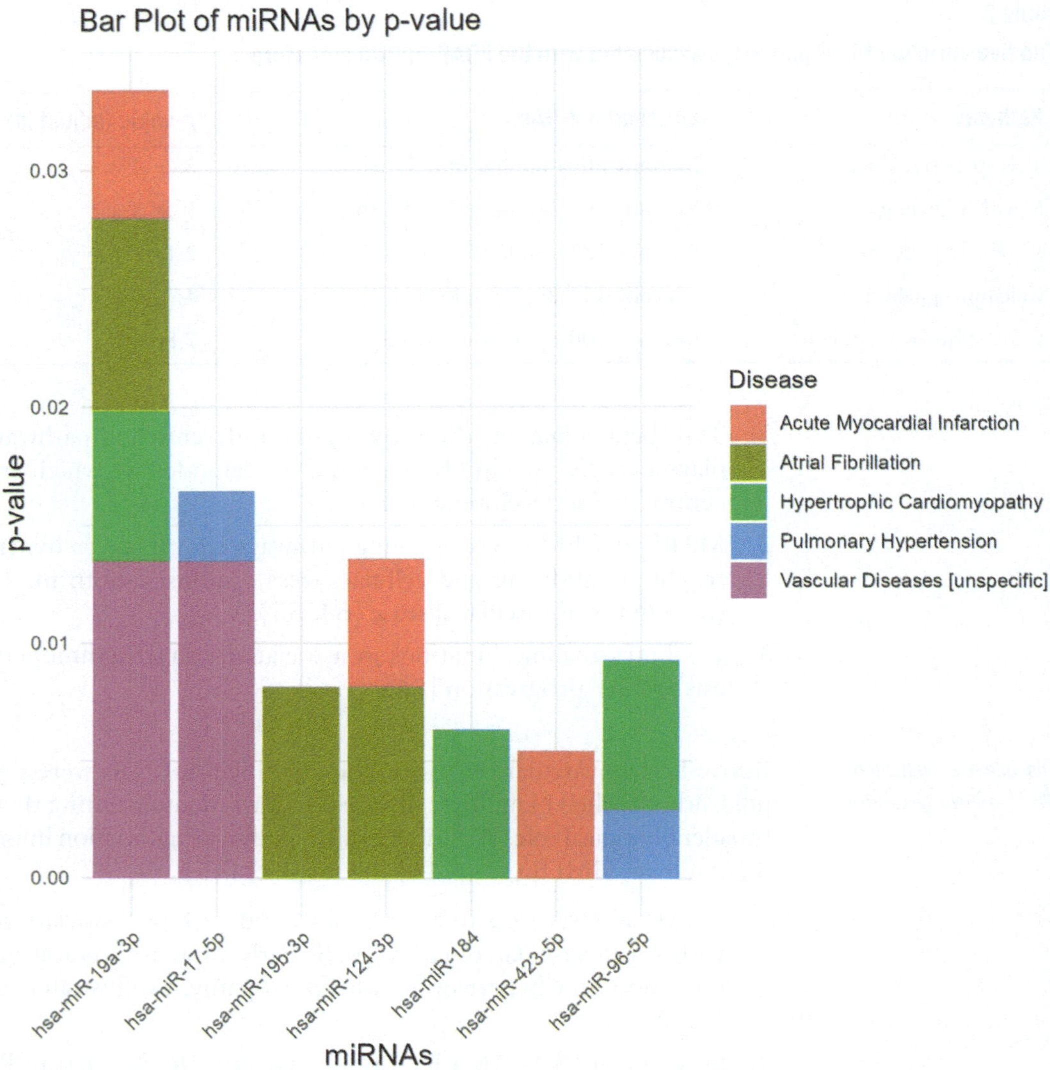

Fig. 2 Bar plot showing POAF-associated miRNAs and their involvement in cardiovascular diseases

2. Reproducibility and standardization: Consistent extraction and quantification protocols across laboratories are critical for reproducibility.
3. Differences in RNA isolation methods and data normalization approaches can introduce variability.
4. Patient heterogeneity: Age, sex, comorbidities, and genetic background may influence miRNA expression, necessitating large-scale, multicenter validation studies [57, 58].

Future Directions: Multi-omics Integration

To further enhance predictive accuracy and biological interpretation, future research should focus on:

Table 3
Top ten non-cardiovascular diseases linked to POAF-miRNA signature ($p < 0.001$)

Disease	Significant miRNAs
Vulvar carcinoma	hsa-miR-200a-3p, hsa-let-7a-5p
Multiple sclerosis	hsa-miR-19a-3p, hsa-miR-19b-3p
Retinoblastoma	hsa-miR-184, hsa-miR-100-5p
Kaposi's sarcoma	hsa-miR-96-5p, hsa-miR-423-5p
Medulloblastoma	hsa-miR-17-5p, hsa-miR-124-3p
Chronic kidney disease	hsa-let-7a-5p, hsa-miR-184
Macular degeneration	hsa-miR-100-5p, hsa-miR-423-5p
B-cell leukemia	hsa-miR-96-5p, hsa-miR-200a-3p
Crohn's disease	hsa-miR-17-5p, hsa-miR-19a-3p
Myeloid leukemia	hsa-miR-19b-3p, hsa-miR-124-3p

1. Multi-omics data integration: Combining miRNA data with proteomics, genomics, and metabolomics can improve risk prediction models.
2. Advanced machine learning techniques: Exploring deep learning approaches could refine miRNA-based classifiers.
3. Clinical translation: Efforts should be directed toward integrating miRNA-based diagnostics into routine clinical workflows, improving patient outcomes through precision medicine.

Conflict of Interest

The authors have no conflicts of interest to declare that are relevant to the content of this chapter.

References

1. Rüegger S, Großhans H (2012) MicroRNA turnover: when, how, and why. Trends Biochem Sci 37(10):436–446. https://doi.org/10.1016/j.tibs.2012.07.002
2. Condorelli G, Latronico MV, Cavarretta E (2014) microRNAs in cardiovascular diseases: current knowledge and the road ahead. J Am Coll Cardiol 63(21):2177–2187. https://doi.org/10.1016/j.jacc.2014.01.050
3. Creemers EE, Tijsen AJ, Pinto YM (2012) Circulating microRNAs: novel biomarkers and extracellular communicators in cardiovascular disease. Circ Res 110(3):483–495. https://doi.org/10.1161/circresaha.111.247452
4. van Rooij E, Olson EN (2012) MicroRNA therapeutics for cardiovascular disease: opportunities and obstacles. Nat Rev Drug Discov 11(11):860–872. https://doi.org/10.1038/nrd3864
5. Glinge C, Clauss S, Boddum K, Jabbari R, Jabbari J, Risgaard B, Tomsits P, Hildebrand B, Kääb S, Wakili R, Jespersen T, Tfelt-Hansen J (2017) Stability of circulating blood-based microRNAs—pre-analytic methodological

considerations. PLoS One 12(2):e0167969. https://doi.org/10.1371/journal.pone.0167969
6. Silverman MG, Yeri A, Moorthy MV, Camacho Garcia F, Chatterjee NA, Glinge CSA, Tfelt-Hansen J, Salvador AM, Pico AR, Shah R (2020) Circulating miRNAs and risk of sudden death in patients with coronary heart disease. Clin Electrophysiol 6(1):70–79
7. Thum T, Galuppo P, Wolf C, Fiedler J, Kneitz S, van Laake LW, Doevendans PA, Mummery CL, Borlak J, Haverich A, Gross C, Engelhardt S, Ertl G, Bauersachs J (2007) MicroRNAs in the human heart: a clue to fetal gene reprogramming in heart failure. Circulation 116(3):258–267. https://doi.org/10.1161/circulationaha.107.687947
8. Landgraf P, Rusu M, Sheridan R, Sewer A, Iovino N, Aravin A, Pfeffer S, Rice A, Kamphorst AO, Landthaler M, Lin C, Socci ND, Hermida L, Fulci V, Chiaretti S, Foà R, Schliwka J, Fuchs U, Novosel A, Müller RU, Schermer B, Bissels U, Inman J, Phan Q, Chien M, Weir DB, Choksi R, De Vita G, Frezzetti D, Trompeter HI, Hornung V, Teng G, Hartmann G, Palkovits M, Di Lauro R, Wernet P, Macino G, Rogler CE, Nagle JW, Ju J, Papavasiliou FN, Benzing T, Lichter P, Tam W, Brownstein MJ, Bosio A, Borkhardt A, Russo JJ, Sander C, Zavolan M, Tuschl T (2007) A mammalian microRNA expression atlas based on small RNA library sequencing. Cell 129(7):1401–1414. https://doi.org/10.1016/j.cell.2007.04.040
9. Thum T, Catalucci D, Bauersachs J (2008) MicroRNAs: novel regulators in cardiac development and disease. Cardiovasc Res 79(4):562–570. https://doi.org/10.1093/cvr/cvn137
10. Vegter EL, Ovchinnikova ES, van Veldhuisen DJ, Jaarsma T, Berezikov E, van der Meer P, Voors AA (2017) Low circulating microRNA levels in heart failure patients are associated with atherosclerotic disease and cardiovascular-related rehospitalizations. Clin Res Cardiol 106(8):598–609. https://doi.org/10.1007/s00392-017-1096-z
11. Ovchinnikova ES, Schmitter D, Vegter EL, Ter Maaten JM, Valente MA, Liu LC, van der Harst P, Pinto YM, de Boer RA, Meyer S, Teerlink JR, O'Connor CM, Metra M, Davison BA, Bloomfield DM, Cotter G, Cleland JG, Mebazaa A, Laribi S, Givertz MM, Ponikowski P, van der Meer P, van Veldhuisen DJ, Voors AA, Berezikov E (2016) Signature of circulating microRNAs in patients with acute heart failure. Eur J Heart Fail 18(4):414–423. https://doi.org/10.1002/ejhf.332
12. Santulli G, Iaccarino G, De Luca N, Trimarco B, Condorelli G (2014) Atrial fibrillation and microRNAs. Front Physiol 5:15. https://doi.org/10.3389/fphys.2014.00015
13. Girmatsion Z, Biliczki P, Bonauer A, Wimmer-Greinecker G, Scherer M, Moritz A, Bukowska A, Goette A, Nattel S, Hohnloser SH, Ehrlich JR (2009) Changes in microRNA-1 expression and IK1 up-regulation in human atrial fibrillation. Heart Rhythm 6(12):1802–1809. https://doi.org/10.1016/j.hrthm.2009.08.035
14. Lu Y, Zhang Y, Wang N, Pan Z, Gao X, Zhang F, Zhang Y, Shan H, Luo X, Bai Y, Sun L, Song W, Xu C, Wang Z, Yang B (2010) MicroRNA-328 contributes to adverse electrical remodeling in atrial fibrillation. Circulation 122(23):2378–2387. https://doi.org/10.1161/circulationaha.110.958967
15. Dawson K, Wakili R, Ordög B, Clauss S, Chen Y, Iwasaki Y, Voigt N, Qi XY, Sinner MF, Dobrev D, Kääb S, Nattel S (2013) MicroRNA29: a mechanistic contributor and potential biomarker in atrial fibrillation. Circulation 127(14):1466–1475. https://doi.org/10.1161/circulationaha.112.001207
16. Hale CS, Levis WR (2013) MicroRNA-29 and an integrated understanding of atrial fibrillation. J Drugs Dermatol 12(10):1083
17. Cushing L, Kuang PP, Qian J, Shao F, Wu J, Little F, Thannickal VJ, Cardoso WV, Lü J (2011) miR-29 is a major regulator of genes associated with pulmonary fibrosis. Am J Respir Cell Mol Biol 45(2):287–294. https://doi.org/10.1165/rcmb.2010-0323OC
18. Oliveira-Carvalho V, Carvalho VO, Bocchi EA (2013) The emerging role of miR-208a in the heart. DNA Cell Biol 32(1):8–12. https://doi.org/10.1089/dna.2012.1787
19. Harling L, Lambert J, Ashrafian H, Darzi A, Gooderham NJ, Athanasiou T (2017) Elevated serum microRNA 483-5p levels may predict patients at risk of post-operative atrial fibrillation. Eur J Cardiothorac Surg 51(1):73–78. https://doi.org/10.1093/ejcts/ezw245
20. Feldman A, Moreira DAR, Gun C, Wang HTL, Hirata MH, de Freitas Germano J, Leite GGS, Farsky P (2017) Analysis of circulating miR-1, miR-23a, and miR-26a in atrial fibrillation patients undergoing coronary bypass artery grafting surgery. Ann Hum Genet 81(3):99–105
21. Li C, Li X, Gao X, Zhang R, Zhang Y, Liang H, Xu C, Du W, Zhang Y, Liu X, Ma N, Xu Z, Wang L, Chen X, Lu Y, Ju J, Yang B, Shan H (2014) MicroRNA-328 as a regulator of cardiac hypertrophy. Int J Cardiol 173(2):268–276. https://doi.org/10.1016/j.ijcard.2014.02.035
22. Lu Y, Hou S, Huang D, Luo X, Zhang J, Chen J, Xu W (2015) Expression profile analysis of circulating microRNAs and their effects on ion

channels in Chinese atrial fibrillation patients. Int J Clin Exp Med 8(1):845–853
23. Ling TY, Wang XL, Chai Q, Lau TW, Koestler CM, Park SJ, Daly RC, Greason KL, Jen J, Wu LQ, Shen WF, Shen WK, Cha YM, Lee HC (2013) Regulation of the SK3 channel by microRNA-499—potential role in atrial fibrillation. Heart Rhythm 10(7):1001–1009. https://doi.org/10.1016/j.hrthm.2013.03.005
24. Goren Y, Meiri E, Hogan C, Mitchell H, Lebanony D, Salman N, Schliamser JE, Amir O (2014) Relation of reduced expression of MiR-150 in platelets to atrial fibrillation in patients with chronic systolic heart failure. Am J Cardiol 113(6):976–981. https://doi.org/10.1016/j.amjcard.2013.11.060
25. Dinesh KG, Arumugaraj K, Santhosh KD, Mareeswari V (2018) Prediction of cardiovascular disease using machine learning algorithms. IEEE, pp 1–7
26. Li Y, Kowdley KV (2012) Method for microRNA isolation from clinical serum samples. Anal Biochem 431(1):69–75. https://doi.org/10.1016/j.ab.2012.09.007
27. Wright K, de Silva K, Purdie AC, Plain KM (2020) Comparison of methods for miRNA isolation and quantification from ovine plasma. Sci Rep 10(1):825. https://doi.org/10.1038/s41598-020-57659-7
28. Love MI, Huber W, Anders S (2014) Moderated estimation of fold change and dispersion for RNA-seq data with DESeq2. Genome Biol 15:1–21
29. Robinson MD, McCarthy DJ, Smyth GK (2010) edgeR: a Bioconductor package for differential expression analysis of digital gene expression data. Bioinformatics 26(1):139–140
30. Smyth GK (2005) Limma: linear models for microarray data. Bioinformatics and computational biology solutions using R and Bioconductor. Springer, 397–420
31. McKinney W (2011) pandas: a foundational Python library for data analysis and statistics. Python for high performance and scientific computing 14(9):1–9
32. Harris CR, Millman KJ, Van Der Walt SJ, Gommers R, Virtanen P, Cournapeau D, Wieser E, Taylor J, Berg S, Smith NJ (2020) Array programming with NumPy. Nature 585(7825):357–362
33. Bisong E (2019) Introduction to Scikit-learn. In: Building machine learning and deep learning models on Google Cloud Platform: a comprehensive guide for beginners. Springer, pp 215–229
34. Chen T, Guestrin C (2016) Xgboost: a scalable tree boosting system. pp 785–794
35. Kozomara A, Birgaoanu M, Griffiths-Jones S (2019) miRBase: from microRNA sequences to function. Nucleic Acids Res 47(D1):D155–D162
36. McGeary SE, Lin KS, Shi CY, Pham TM, Bisaria N, Kelley GM, Bartel DP (2019) The biochemical basis of microRNA targeting efficacy. Science 366 (6472). pp 1741-1754 https://doi.org/10.1126/science.aav1741
37. Cui S, Yu S, Huang HY, Lin YC, Huang Y, Zhang B, Xiao J, Zuo H, Wang J, Li Z, Li G, Ma J, Chen B, Zhang H, Fu J, Wang L, Huang HD (2025) miRTarBase 2025: updates to the collection of experimentally validated microRNA-target interactions. Nucleic Acids Res 53(D1):D147–D156. https://doi.org/10.1093/nar/gkae1072
38. Kanehisa M (2002) The KEGG database. Wiley Online Library, pp 91–103
39. Fabregat A, Jupe S, Matthews L, Sidiropoulos K, Gillespie M, Garapati P, Haw R, Jassal B, Korninger F, May B (2018) The reactome pathway knowledgebase. Nucleic Acids Res 46(D1):D649–D655
40. Dennis G, Sherman BT, Hosack DA, Yang J, Gao W, Lane HC, Lempicki RA (2003) DAVID: database for annotation, visualization, and integrated discovery. Genome Biol 4:1–11
41. Chen Y, Wang X (2020) miRDB: an online database for prediction of functional microRNA targets. Nucleic Acids Res 48(D1):D127–D131
42. Yerukala Sathipati S, Carter T, Soodi D, Somto N, Shukla SK, Petronovich J, Ingrid G, Braxton J, Sharma P. MicroRNA signature predicts post operative atrial fibrillation after coronary artery bypass grafting. Sci Rep. 2025 May 28;15(1):18658. https://doi.org/10.1038/s41598-025-03042-3. PMID: 40436930; PMCID: PMC12119944.
43. Wu T, Hu E, Xu S, Chen M, Guo P, Dai Z, Feng T, Zhou L, Tang W, Zhan LI (2021) clusterProfiler 4.0: a universal enrichment tool for interpreting omics data. Innovation 2(3). pp 100141-100141
44. Cui C, Zhong B, Fan R, Cui Q (2024) HMDD v4. 0: a database for experimentally supported human microRNA-disease associations. Nucleic Acids Res 52(D1):D1327–D1332
45. Chang L, Zhou G, Soufan O, Xia J (2020) miRNet 2.0: network-based visual analytics for miRNA functional analysis and systems biology. Nucleic Acids Res 48(W1):W244–W251
46. Ranstam J, Cook JA (2018) LASSO regression. Br J Surg 105(10):1348–1348
47. Darst BF, Malecki KC, Engelman CD (2018) Using recursive feature elimination in random forest to account for correlated variables in high dimensional data. BMC Genet 19:1–6

48. Biau G, Scornet E (2016) A random forest guided tour. Test 25:197–227
49. Steinwart I, Christmann A (2008) Support vector machines. Springer Science & Business Media
50. Bergstra J, Bengio Y (2012) Random search for hyper-parameter optimization. J Mach Learn Res 13:2
51. Hall MA (1999) Correlation-based feature selection for machine learning. PhD thesis, University of Waikato, Hamilton, New Zealand
52. Peterson LE (2009) K-nearest neighbor. Scholarpedia 4(2):1883
53. Gramley F, Lorenzen J, Koellensperger E, Kettering K, Weiss C, Munzel T (2010) Atrial fibrosis and atrial fibrillation: the role of the TGF-β1 signaling pathway. Int J Cardiol 143(3):405–413
54. Qin W, Cao L, Massey IY (2021) Role of PI3K/Akt signaling pathway in cardiac fibrosis. Mol Cell Biochem 476(11):4045–4059
55. Takano APC, Senger N, Barreto-Chaves MLM (2020) The endocrinological component and signaling pathways associated to cardiac hypertrophy. Mol Cell Endocrinol 518:110972
56. Landstrom AP, Dobrev D, Wehrens XHT (2017) Calcium signaling and cardiac arrhythmias. Circ Res 120(12):1969–1993
57. Felekkis K, Papaneophytou C (2020) Challenges in using circulating micro-RNAs as biomarkers for cardiovascular diseases. Int J Mol Sci 21(2). pp 561–564. https://doi.org/10.3390/ijms21020561
58. Siasos G, Bletsa E, Stampouloglou PK, Oikonomou E, Tsigkou V, Paschou SA, Vlasis K, Marinos G, Vavuranakis M, Stefanadis C, Tousoulis D (2020) MicroRNAs in cardiovascular disease. Hellenic J Cardiol 61(3):165–173. https://doi.org/10.1016/j.hjc.2020.03.003

Chapter 9

Large Language Models for Non-Coding RNA Biomarker Discovery in Breast Cancer

Tamizhini Loganathan

Abstract

Breast cancer (BC) remains a leading cause of cancer-related mortality globally, driven by its molecular heterogeneity and complex tumor biology. Early and accurate detection is critical for improving patient survival and guiding targeted therapies. Noncoding RNAs (ncRNAs), particularly circular RNAs (circRNAs), small nucleolar RNAs (snoRNAs), and PIWI-interacting RNAs (piRNAs), have emerged as key regulators in cancer progression and as potential biomarkers. However, the sheer volume of omics data and literature poses challenges in extracting actionable insights. Recent advances in large language models (LLMs) offer new opportunities to accelerate biomarker discovery through semantic reasoning, knowledge integration, and pattern recognition. This chapter explores the integration of LLMs with ncRNA biology, focusing on circRNAs, snoRNAs, and piRNAs in BC, and proposes a computational framework for biomarker identification.

Keywords BC, LLM, ncRNA, Biomarker

1 Introduction

Breast cancer (BC) remains a leading cause of cancer-related deaths among women, and its clinical management is complicated by the biological diversity of its subtypes, including Luminal A, Luminal B, HER2-enriched, and triple-negative breast cancer (TNBC) [1]. Each subtype is characterized by distinct molecular features, treatment responses, and prognostic outcomes, highlighting the urgent need for precise biomarkers that can support early diagnosis, stratification of patients, and personalized therapies [2]. Conventional biomarkers, such as hormone receptors and HER2 status, provide valuable information but are insufficient to fully capture the complexity of tumor heterogeneity [3]. Therefore, growing attention has turned to noncoding RNAs (ncRNAs), which provide a diverse yet underexplored reservoir of molecular insights [4].

Circular RNAs (circRNAs), for instance, have attracted attention due to their covalently closed loop structures, which render

Y-h Taguchi (ed.), *AI/ML-Driven Gene Analysis*, Methods in Molecular Biology, vol. 3037,
https://doi.org/10.1007/978-1-0716-5284-8_9,

them resistant to exonuclease degradation, making them highly stable in tissues and biofluids such as plasma and saliva [5, 6]. They can function as microRNA sponges, regulators of transcription, or interactors with RNA-binding proteins, thereby influencing key oncogenic pathways in BC [7, 8]. Similarly, small nucleolar RNAs (snoRNAs) are emerging as regulators of ribosome biogenesis and post-transcriptional RNA modifications, processes that are frequently hijacked during malignant transformation [9]. Dysregulated snoRNA expression has been linked to tumor proliferation and metastasis, underscoring their potential as both diagnostic and therapeutic biomarkers [10]. In addition, PIWI-interacting RNAs (piRNAs), once thought to be restricted to germline cells, are now recognized for their role in maintaining genome integrity and modulating epigenetic landscapes in somatic cancers, including BC [11, 12].

The discovery and validation of such ncRNA biomarkers, however, pose significant challenges due to the complexity of multiomics data and the vast, unstructured biomedical literature [13]. Standard bioinformatics pipelines often fall short in integrating diverse data modalities, functional annotations, and experimental findings into cohesive insights [14]. This is where large language models (LLMs) offer transformative potential. Trained on large-scale biomedical corpora, LLMs can efficiently mine unstructured literature, extract context-specific biomarker associations, and even propose mechanistic hypotheses by linking molecular functions to clinical outcomes [15]. Unlike rule-based text-mining systems, LLMs capture nuanced relationships and emerging concepts, which are critical in a rapidly evolving field like cancer biology [15].

By combining the high-throughput nature of omics data with the knowledge-driven reasoning capabilities of LLMs, researchers can accelerate the discovery of clinically actionable ncRNAs in BC [13–15]. These AI-powered approaches enable more accurate biomarker prioritization, guide experimental validation, and facilitate the design of personalized therapeutic strategies [14, 15]. Ultimately, the integration of ncRNA biology with LLM-based analytics holds the promise of improving BC prognosis, enhancing precision oncology, and reducing disease burden worldwide [15].

2 Circular RNA, snoRNA, and piRNA in BC

2.1 Circular RNAs (circRNAs) in BC

Circular RNAs (circRNAs) are a special class of endogenous noncoding RNAs characterized by a covalently closed loop structure generated through back-splicing events. This circular configuration makes them resistant to exonuclease-mediated degradation, leading to greater stability than linear RNAs. CircRNAs are often cell-type and tissue-specific, which adds to their potential as precise biomarkers [16, 17].

In BC, circRNAs regulate oncogenesis and tumor progression through multiple mechanisms:miRNA sponging: many circRNAs act as competing endogenous RNAs (ceRNAs), binding and sequestering microRNAs, thereby preventing them from repressing their target mRNAs. For example, circRNA circHIPK3 has been implicated in regulating BC proliferation and metastasis [7, 18, 19]. Interaction with proteins: some circRNAs bind to RNA-binding proteins (RBPs) and modulate their function, influencing signaling pathways relevant to tumor progression [20]. Regulation of transcription/translation: certain circRNAs can affect parental gene transcription, and a few have even been shown to encode small peptides with functional roles [20].

Clinically, circRNAs are detectable in serum, plasma, and exosomes, making them minimally invasive biomarkers for early diagnosis and disease monitoring. Dysregulated circRNAs have been correlated with BC subtype specificity, tumor grade, and treatment response, highlighting their potential as therapeutic targets [20].

2.2 Small Nucleolar RNAs (snoRNAs) in BC

Small nucleolar RNAs (snoRNAs) are a conserved class of ncRNAs primarily localized in the nucleolus, where they guide chemical modifications of other RNAs, such as 2′-O-methylation and pseudouridylation of ribosomal RNAs (rRNAs) and small nuclear RNAs (snRNAs). Traditionally considered housekeeping molecules, snoRNAs are now recognized as dynamic regulators of cancer biology [21].

In BC, dysregulation of snoRNAs influences several cancer hallmarks. Oncogenic snoRNAs: overexpression of certain snoRNAs enhances ribosome biogenesis and protein translation, supporting the metabolic demands of proliferating cancer cells. Tumor suppressor snoRNAs: Some snoRNAs, when downregulated, impair normal RNA modification processes, leading to uncontrolled signaling cascades and tumorigenesis [REF]. Chemoresistance: abnormal snoRNA expression has been linked to resistance against commonly used chemotherapeutic drugs, such as tamoxifen in hormone receptor-positive BC [22].

Clinically, snoRNAs serve as prognostic biomarkers, as altered expression patterns correlate with tumor stage, aggressiveness, and patient survival outcomes. Their stability and detectability in patient biofluids make them candidates for liquid biopsy-based diagnostics [23].

2.3 PIWI-Interacting RNAs (piRNAs) in BC

PIWI-interacting RNAs (piRNAs) are a distinct class of small ncRNAs, typically 24–31 nucleotides in length, that interact with PIWI proteins, a subfamily of Argonaute proteins. Originally identified in germline cells for their role in silencing transposable elements, piRNAs are now known to function in somatic cells, including cancer cells [24].

In BC, piRNAs contribute to tumor progression and therapy resistance via multiple mechanisms: epigenetic regulation: piRNAs influence DNA methylation and histone modifications, thereby

Table 1
Mechanism of ncRNA (circRNA, snoRNA, and piRNA) and its clinical potential

ncRNA type	Biological role	Dysregulation in BC	Clinical potential
circRNAs	Act as miRNA sponges, regulate transcription, interact with RNA-binding proteins.	Overexpressed or downregulated depending on subtype (e.g., TNBC, Luminal B).	Diagnostic biomarkers (detectable in plasma), subtype classification, therapy targets.
snoRNAs	Guide rRNA modifications (2'-O-methylation, pseudouridylation), regulate ribosome biogenesis.	Altered snoRNA expression linked to tumor growth, metastasis, and chemoresistance.	Prognostic biomarkers, predictors of treatment response.
piRNAs	Maintain genome stability, regulate epigenetic modifications, silence transposons.	Abnormal expression contributes to tumor initiation, EMT, and therapy resistance.	Epigenetic biomarkers, potential therapeutic targets.

reprogramming gene expression patterns relevant to oncogenesis [25]. Transposon silencing: by repressing mobile genetic elements, piRNAs maintain genomic stability. Dysregulation of piRNAs can compromise this safeguard, leading to genomic instability, and malignant transformation [26]. Pathway modulation: specific piRNAs modulate signaling pathways such as PI3K/AKT, Wnt/β-catenin, and EMT-related cascades, thereby promoting invasion, metastasis, and stemness in BC cells [26].

Clinically, piRNAs represent a novel class of biomarkers for early detection and subtype classification, given their tissue-specific expression patterns. Their dual roles acting either as oncogenic drivers or tumor suppressors depending on context make them attractive, yet complex, therapeutic targets.

Together, circRNAs, snoRNAs, and piRNAs form an emerging landscape of regulatory ncRNAs in BC. Their stability, specificity, and regulatory versatility underscore their promise as diagnostic, prognostic, and therapeutic biomarkers. The simplified table of circRNA, snoRNA, piRNA in BC (Table 1). The detail information of ncRNA were mentioned in the Fig. 1.

3 Role of Large Language Models in Biomarker Discovery

Large language models (LLMs) are transforming the landscape of biomarker discovery by addressing some of the biggest challenges in cancer research, particularly the complexity of integrating vast amounts of biological data with unstructured biomedical literature [27]. Traditional approaches to biomarker identification often rely

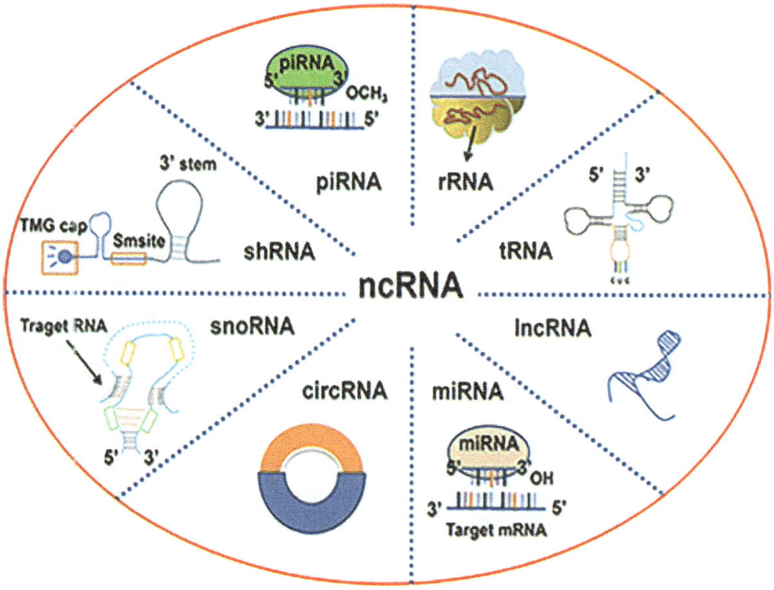

Fig. 1 The different types of ncRNA representations

on structured databases or manual literature review, which can be time-consuming and incomplete given the exponential growth of scientific publications. LLMs, trained on large-scale biomedical corpora, are uniquely equipped to process unstructured text and extract meaningful relationships between genes, noncoding RNAs, proteins, signaling pathways, and disease phenotypes [28]. This allows them to uncover novel associations, such as the role of specific circRNAs, snoRNAs, or piRNAs in BC progression.

One of the greatest strengths of LLMs is their ability to integrate and contextualize multiomics data. High-throughput platforms like RNA-seq and proteomics generate massive datasets, but interpreting these in relation to clinical outcomes requires connecting them with existing biological knowledge [29]. LLMs can assist by linking expression profiles of potential biomarkers with relevant functional annotations, pathways, and survival analyses documented in the literature. For example, when applied to BC datasets, LLMs can help prioritize candidate ncRNAs that correlate with tumor subtype, prognosis, or therapy resistance, accelerating the process of narrowing down targets for experimental validation [30, 31].

In addition to mining and integration, LLMs contribute to knowledge-driven hypothesis generation. Unlike conventional bioinformatics pipelines that primarily analyze patterns, LLMs can infer potential mechanisms by drawing connections across different domains of knowledge [29]. These AI-assisted insights open up new avenues for experimental exploration, making LLMs valuable partners in hypothesis-driven research [29].

Ultimately, the application of LLMs in biomarker discovery supports the advancement of precision oncology. By integrating patient-specific omics profiles with the broader body of biomedical evidence, LLMs can help identify ncRNAs or other biomarkers that are most relevant for individualized treatment strategies [32]. In BC, this could mean distinguishing molecular signatures between subtypes such as Luminal A and Triple-Negative BC, or predicting which patients are likely to respond to targeted therapies. As clinical decision-support tools, LLMs hold the promise of making biomarker discovery more efficient, scalable, and clinically actionable, thereby bridging the gap between molecular research and patient care [32].

4 LLM-Based Framework for ncRNA Biomarker Discovery

4.1 Data Sources

Biomarker discovery relies greatly on the breadth and quality of data sources, and in the case of ncRNAs, this requires drawing from both structured repositories and unstructured biomedical literature [33]. Mining biomedical literature such as PubMed, PMC, and clinical trial databases provides access to up-to-date insights into ncRNAs, including their expression patterns, disease associations, and experimental findings [34]. For example, miR-21 is frequently reported as a driver of cancer progression, while miR-122 is often cited as a biomarker for liver disease. Large language models can accelerate this process by scanning thousands of publications in minutes, extracting relevant findings that would otherwise take years to curate manually [33]. Complementing this, curated repositories such as circRNAs, circBase [35] offers foundational sequence and annotation data across species, while circAtlas integrates large-scale RNA-seq datasets to present tissue-specific expression profiles. Databases such as Circ2Disease [36] and CSCD [37] focus on experimentally validated circRNA–disease associations, particularly in cancer contexts. For snoRNAs, snoDB [38] compile sequence information, expression profiles, and functional details, whereas snOPY [39] provides insights into snoRNA–target interactions and RNA modification sites, all of which are integrated within RNAcentral for unified access [40]. piRNA research is supported by resources like piRBase [41] and piRNABank [42], which catalog piRNA sequences, genomic locations, and clusters, while piRNAclusterDB highlights their genomic organization and conservation. Furthermore, piRDisease links piRNAs to experimentally validated disease associations, offering direct translational relevance [43]. Together, these repositories complement broader databases such as TCGA [44] and GTEx [45], enabling a multilayered and clinically informed view of ncRNAs across biological and disease contexts. There are many databases represented for ncRNA [46].

Beyond individual databases, multiomics integration provides a comprehensive view of ncRNA function: transcriptomics (RNA-seq, scRNA-seq) captures expression across tissues and conditions, proteomics reflects changes in protein abundance, epigenomics highlights roles in chromatin remodeling and DNA methylation, and metabolomics reveals downstream phenotypic consequences of ncRNA regulation [47]. Clinical datasets further establish biomarker relevance by linking ncRNA profiles with patient outcomes such as overall survival, progression-free survival, treatment response, disease stage, and histopathology. Once acquired, these heterogeneous data require preprocessing to ensure reliability and integration. Text preprocessing resolves inconsistencies in biomedical terminology (e.g., miR-21 vs. hsa-miR-21) through entity normalization, while data harmonization maps disparate database identifiers to common standards such as HGNC and Ensembl [48, 49]. Expression data are standardized using normalization methods such as TPM, RPKM, or DESeq2, and batch effects introduced by technical differences across cohorts are corrected with tools like ComBat. The outcome of these steps is a unified, high-quality dataset that provides a robust foundation for reliable downstream knowledge modeling [50].

4.2 Knowledge Representation

Noncoding RNA biomarker discovery requires integration of diverse biological information into a holistic framework, and knowledge graphs (KGs) provide a powerful way to achieve this by representing entities and their relationships. In such a graph, nodes correspond to key entities such as ncRNAs, genes, proteins, diseases, pathways, drugs, and phenotypes, while edges capture relationships including regulatory interactions (e.g., ncRNA → regulates → gene), disease associations (ncRNA → associated with → disease), and pathway modulation (ncRNA → modulates → signaling pathway). Each edge can be assigned weights based on evidence confidence, while node attributes may encode expression levels, tissue specificity, or validation status, enabling multidimensional analysis (e.g., the interaction miR-34a → inhibits → BCL2 → associated with → apoptosis in cancer) [51]. This illustrates how KGs capture biological processes beyond simple pairwise links, reflecting layered mechanistic insights. However, traditional KGs are often constrained by incomplete or sparse data, a limitation that can be addressed through semantic enrichment with large language models (LLMs). Biomedical LLMs such as BioBERT [52], PubMedGPT [53], and BioGPT [54] generate embeddings that provide contextual vector representations for ncRNAs, diseases, and pathways, supporting prediction of missing links by inferring associations from frequent comentions in the literature. These embeddings further allow clustering of functionally related ncRNAs or disease groups, revealing novel biomarker candidates. The outcome is a semantically enriched knowledge graph that integrates curated databases with contextual knowledge from biomedical literature, enabling deeper reasoning and discovery in ncRNA biology [55].

4.3 LLM-Powered Modules

Large Language Models (LLMs) are increasingly being applied to biomedical research, offering powerful tools for automating knowledge extraction, generating new hypotheses, integrating complex datasets, and prioritizing biomarkers. One important application is information extraction, where LLMs enable the large-scale identification and structuring of insights from scientific literature. Through tasks such as named entity recognition (NER), LLMs can detect mentions of ncRNAs, genes, and diseases in text. Relation extraction extends this by uncovering functional or associative links, e.g., recognizing that "miR-155 suppresses SOCS1 and promotes lymphoma." Summarization further condenses multi-page research findings into concise, structured knowledge entries. For instance, an extracted insight could be represented as: entity: miR-155; relation: downregulates; target: SOCS1; disease: lymphoma [56].

Beyond extraction, LLMs also enable hypothesis generation, moving from descriptive analysis to predictive discovery. Unlike conventional data-mining methods, LLMs can generate novel biological hypotheses by leveraging prompt engineering and contextual reasoning. For example, when prompted with known miRNAs involved in breast cancer metastasis, an LLM might propose additional candidates by analyzing pathway similarities. It can also suggest context-specific mechanisms, such as proposing miR-200 as a potential biomarker for epithelial–mesenchymal transition (EMT). Furthermore, LLMs support counterfactual analysis, where hypothetical scenarios can be tested such as predicting the biological consequences of silencing miR-21 in hepatocellular carcinoma [57].

Another major contribution of LLMs lies in multiomics integration, where they assist in connecting ncRNA function with broader biological networks. By correlating across different omics layers, LLMs can link ncRNA dysregulation to downstream protein or metabolite changes. Moreover, they can highlight patterns, including clusters of coexpressed ncRNAs across tissue types, which may suggest shared regulatory functions or disease associations [58].

Finally, LLMs aid in biomarker prioritization, a crucial step in identifying clinically relevant candidates among many possibilities. They can rank biomarkers by evaluating multiple dimensions: statistical robustness (whether findings are reproducible across datasets), biological plausibility (consistency with known pathways and molecular mechanisms), clinical utility (correlation with survival, treatment response, or disease progression), and literature support (weighted by the number and quality of supporting studies). Importantly, LLMs can generate explainable reports that summarize these factors for each candidate. This systematic approach accelerates the translation of molecular discoveries into clinically actionable insights [58].

4.4 Validation and Feedback

Validation is a critical step in ensuring that predictions made by large language models (LLMs) and computational pipelines are reliable and biologically meaningful. One important layer of this process is in silico validation, where predictions are tested computationally against independent datasets and established standards. For example, cross-validation can be performed by comparing results across different cohorts, such as The Cancer Genome Atlas (TCGA) and the Genotype-Tissue Expression (GTEx) project, to confirm that findings are consistent across populations. Additionally, network robustness tests can be applied to examine whether predicted interactions between ncRNAs, genes, and proteins remain stable under varying conditions or perturbations in the data. Predictions can also be benchmarked against gold-standard biomarkers to ensure that the model can replicate established findings before new candidates are considered credible [59, 60].

Following computational checks, experimental validation is essential to confirm predictions in a biological setting. This begins with expression validation, where methods such as quantitative PCR (qPCR), RNA fluorescence in situ hybridization (RNA-FISH), or RNA sequencing (RNA-seq) are used to measure and confirm the presence and dysregulation of candidate ncRNAs [61]. Functional assays provide further insight by testing whether manipulating these molecules has measurable biological effects—for instance, siRNA knockdown or CRISPR-Cas9 knockout experiments can reveal whether silencing a predicted ncRNA alters cell proliferation, migration, or apoptosis. To establish clinical or therapeutic relevance, animal models may also be employed, allowing researchers to validate whether ncRNA perturbations influence disease progression or treatment response in vivo [62].

Finally, expert curation provides the human oversight needed to refine and contextualize LLM-generated predictions. Domain experts assess the biological plausibility of proposed interactions, ensuring that predictions align with known molecular mechanisms or disease processes. They also play a key role in eliminating false positives, such as spurious associations arising from irrelevant or misinterpreted literature mentions. Importantly, this expert feedback contributes to a continuous improvement cycle: corrected and validated outputs are reintroduced into the LLM pipeline, enabling iterative retraining, and refinement of the model. This feedback loop strengthens predictive accuracy over time, ensuring that the integration of artificial intelligence into biomedical research produces results that are not only computationally sound but also biologically and clinically meaningful [63, 64]. The detail framework of LLM-based biomarker discovery pipeline were mentioned in the Fig. 2.

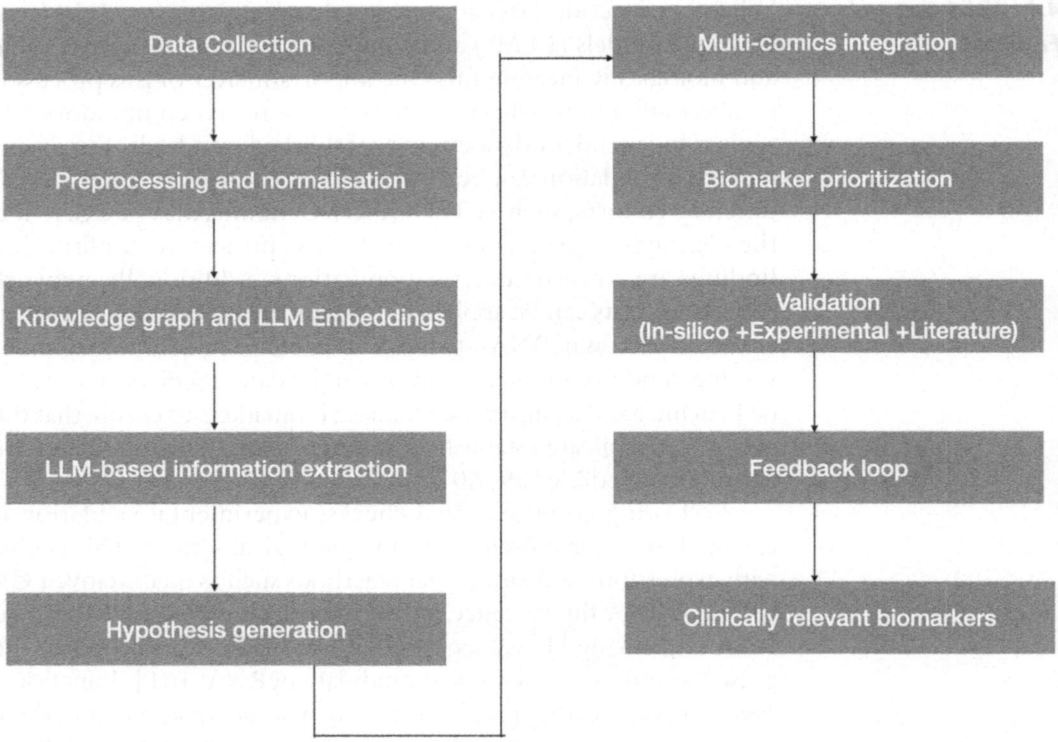

Fig. 2 Workflow of LLM-based biomarker discovery pipeline

5 Advantages of LLM-Based Approach

LLMs bring several key advantages to biomedical research, making them powerful tools for handling the complexity of biological data and literature. They are highly scalable, capable of rapidly processing millions of scientific papers, clinical records, and omics datasets in a fraction of the time, it would take human experts, allowing researchers to keep pace with the ever-growing volume of biomedical information. They are also integrative, combining insights from both structured sources such as genomic databases, protein interaction maps, and clinical trial results and unstructured sources, including journal articles, preprints, and patient notes. This integrative ability enables LLMs to connect diverse layers of information that traditional methods often analyze in isolation. Another major strength is their context-aware reasoning, which allows them to capture subtle relationships across pathways, cell types, and diseases; e.g., they can identify when the same ncRNA plays different roles depending on tissue type or disease state. Importantly, LLMs are also explainable, producing human-readable justifications that clarify why a certain relationship, pathway, or biomarker was prioritized, thus increasing transparency and trust among researchers and clinicians. Finally, they accelerate discovery by reducing the time required for manual curation and synthesis tasks that once spanned years can now be condensed into weeks thereby speeding up the generation of testable hypotheses and the translation of basic research into clinical applications.

6 Future Directions

The future of LLM applications in biomedicine is shaped by several promising directions that expand their utility and impact. One major advancement lies in the development of multimodal LLMs, which can integrate diverse data types such as omics datasets, clinical text, and medical imaging, thereby providing a more comprehensive understanding of disease mechanisms. Another important application is the creation of interactive clinical assistants, where LLM-powered tools can help clinicians interpret biomarker data in real time, offering clear explanations of molecular findings and their potential clinical significance. These systems can be further improved through active learning, a process in which expert feedback is continuously incorporated to refine predictions, correct errors, and enhance model accuracy over time. LLMs also enable cross-disease biomarker discovery, identifying ncRNAs, and other molecular signatures that play roles across multiple cancers or disease types, thereby uncovering shared pathways and broad therapeutic opportunities. Finally, these models pave the way for personalized medicine, where patient-specific omics profiles can be analyzed to predict individualized biomarkers and treatment responses. By tailoring insights to each patient's unique molecular landscape, LLMs hold the potential to guide precision diagnostics and therapies, ultimately transforming clinical care.

7 Conclusion

The integration of LLMs into ncRNA biomarker discovery pipelines represents a paradigm shift. By combining large-scale text mining, knowledge graph construction, and multiomics integration with validation and expert oversight, this framework enables rapid, explainable, and clinically relevant biomarker discovery. In the long term, such systems could become cornerstones of precision medicine, providing personalized diagnostic and prognostic tools.

Acknowledgments

The author would like to take this opportunity to thank the management of Vellore Institute of Technology (VIT), Vellore, India, for providing the necessary facilities and encouragement to carry out this work.

Data Availability The current study data are available in the main manuscript files.

Funding No funding agency was involved in the present study.
Author Contribution

Tamizhini Loganathan was integral to the study's design, data collection, and experimentation. She acquired, analyzed, and interpreted the results. She also drafted the manuscript and supervised the entire study and involvement spanned the study's design, data acquisition, analysis, and interpretation, as well as critically reviewing the manuscript. The author also contributed to editing and approved the final version of the article.

Competing Interests The authors have no conflicts of interest to declare that are relevant to the content of this chapter.

References

1. Xiong X, Zheng LW, Ding Y, Chen YF, Cai YW, Wang LP et al (2025) Breast cancer: pathogenesis and treatments. Signal Transduct Targeted Ther 10(1):49. https://www.nature.com/articles/s41392-024-02108-4
2. Yersal O, Barutca S (2014) Biological subtypes of breast cancer: prognostic and therapeutic implications. World J Clin Oncol 5(3):412
3. Gu TQ, Xiao YL, Shao ZM (2024) Intratumor heterogeneity in breast cancer: tracing its origins and translating findings into clinical practice. Precis Med Eng 1(1):100006
4. Diamantopoulos MA, Tsiakanikas P, Scorilas A (2018) Non-coding RNAs: the riddle of the transcriptome and their perspectives in cancer. Ann Transl Med 6(12):241–241. https://www.ncbi.nlm.nih.gov/pmc/articles/PMC6046292/ [Internet] Jun [cited 2019 Nov 1]
5. Pu J, Yan X, Zhang H (2024) The potential of circular RNAs as biomarkers and therapeutic targets for gastric cancer: a comprehensive review. J Adv Res 75:311
6. Zhang Y, Wang Y, Su X, Wang P, Lin W (2021) The value of circulating circular rna in cancer diagnosis, monitoring, prognosis, and guiding treatment. Front Oncol 11:736546
7. Zhu J, Li Q, Wu Z, Xu W, Jiang R (2024) Circular RNA-mediated miRNA sponge & RNA binding protein in biological modulation of breast cancer. Noncoding RNA Res 9(1):262–276
8. Ma B, Wang S, Wu W, Shan P, Chen Y, Meng J et al (2023) Mechanisms of circRNA/lncRNA-miRNA interactions and applications in disease and drug research. Biomed Pharmacother 162:114672. https://www.sciencedirect.com/science/article/pii/S0753332223004602 [Internet]
9. Li Y, Chen X, Xiao S, Wang H, Li B, Zhang M et al (2025) Unlocking the life code: a review of SnoRNA functional diversity and disease relevance. Cell Commun Signal 23(1):266
10. Wang Y, Fu M, Zheng Z, Feng J, Zhang C (2025) Small nucleolar RNAs: biological functions and diseases. MedComm 6(7):e70257. https://pmc.ncbi.nlm.nih.gov/articles/PMC12205218/
11. Pratap PD, Raza ST, Ahmad S, Rajput M (2025) From biogenesis to biomarkers: the role of piRNAs and PIWI proteins in cervical cancer and beyond. Egypt J Med Hum Genet 26(1):101
12. Wu X, Pan Y, Fang Y, Zhang J, Xie M, Yang F et al (2020) The biogenesis and functions of piRNAs in human diseases. Mol Ther Nucleic Acids 21:108–120
13. Wolde T, Bhardwaj V, Pandey V (2025) Current bioinformatics tools in precision oncology. MedComm 6(7):e70243
14. Davis-Turak J, Courtney SM, Hazard ES, Glen WB, da Silveira WA, Wesselman T et al (2017) Genomics pipelines and data integration: challenges and opportunities in the research setting. Expert Rev Mol Diagn 17(3):225–237
15. Lu J, Choi K, Maksim E, Jogarao G, Goswami S, Liu Q et al (2025) Large language models and their applications in drug discovery and development: a primer. Clin Transl Sci 18(4):e70205. https://pmc.ncbi.nlm.nih.gov/articles/PMC11984503/
16. Santer L, Bär C, Thum T (2019) Circular RNAs: a novel class of functional RNA molecules with a therapeutic perspective. Mol Ther 27(8):1350–1363
17. Sharma AR, Bhattacharya M, Bhakta S, Saha A, Lee SS, Chakraborty C (2021) Recent research

progress on circular RNAs: biogenesis, properties, functions, and therapeutic potential. Mol Ther Nucleic Acids 25:355–371. https://www.sciencedirect.com/science/article/pii/S2162253121001402 #bib1 [Internet] Sep 3 [cited 2022 Mar 18]
18. Bahadoran E, Mohammadi D, Jalilvand M, Moghbelinejad S (2025) Evaluation of CircHIPK3 biomarker potential in breast cancer. Pract Lab Med 45:e00470. https://pmc.ncbi.nlm.nih.gov/articles/PMC11984561/ [Internet] Jul [cited 2025 Oct 2]
19. Huang Y, Zhang C, Xiong J, Ren H (2020) Emerging important roles of circRNAs in human cancer and other diseases. Genes Dis 8(4):412
20. Huang A, Zheng H, Wu Z, Chen M, Huang Y (2020) Circular RNA-protein interactions: functions, mechanisms, and identification. Theranostics 10(8):3503–3517
21. van der Werf J, Chin C, Fleming N (2021) SnoRNA in cancer progression, metastasis and immunotherapy response. Biology 10(8):809
22. Hu X, Cui W, Liu M, Zhang F, Zhao Y, Zhang M et al (2024) SnoRNAs: the promising targets for anti-tumor therapy. J Pharm Anal 14(11):101064. https://www.sciencedirect.com/science/article/pii/S2095177924001618 [Internet]
23. Gao L, Fan J, He J, Che X, Wang X, Han C (2024) Small nucleolar RNAs as diagnostic and prognostic biomarkers in cancer: a systematic review and meta-analysis. Technol Cancer Res Treat 23:15330338241245939. https://pmc.ncbi.nlm.nih.gov/articles/PMC11102679/
24. Iwasaki YW, Siomi MC, Siomi H (2015) PIWI-interacting RNA: its biogenesis and functions. Annu Rev Biochem 84(1):405–433
25. Jia DD, Jiang H, Zhang YF, Zhang Y, Qian LL, Zhang YF (2022) The regulatory function of piRNA/PIWI complex in cancer and other human diseases: the role of DNA methylation. Int J Biol Sci 18(8):3358–3373. https://ijbs.com/v18p3358.htm [Internet] May 9 [cited 2022 Nov 28]
26. Halic M, Moazed D (2009) Transposon silencing by piRNAs. Cell 138(6):1058–1060
27. Sarumi OA, Heider D (2024) Large language models and their applications in bioinformatics. Comput Struct Biotechnol J 23:3498–3505
28. Chen Z, Liu R, Huang S, Guo Y, Ren Y (2025) A survey of large-scale deep learning models in medicine and healthcare. Comput Model Eng Sci 144(1):37–81. https://www.sciencedirect.com/org/science/article/pii/S1526149225002206 [Internet] [cited 2025 Oct 3]
29. Liu J, Yang M, Yu Y, Xu H, Li K, Zhou X (2024) Large language models in bioinformatics: applications and perspectives. Preprint at https://arxiv.org/abs/2401.04155. https://pmc.ncbi.nlm.nih.gov/articles/PMC10802675/
30. Elsborg J, Salvatore M (2023) Using LLMs and explainable ML to analyze biomarkers at single-cell level for improved understanding of diseases. Biomolecules 13(10):1516–1516
31. Pallumeera M, Giang JC, Singh R, Pracha NS, Makary MS (2025) Evolving and novel applications of artificial intelligence in cancer imaging. Cancers 17(9):1510. https://www.mdpi.com/2072-6694/17/9/1510 [Internet]
32. Alum EU (2025) AI-driven biomarker discovery: enhancing precision in cancer diagnosis and prognosis. Discov Oncol 16(1):313
33. Arango-Argoty G, Bikiel DE, Sun GJ, Kipkogei E, Smith KM, Pro SC et al (2025) AI-driven predictive biomarker discovery with contrastive learning to improve clinical trial outcomes. Cancer Cell 43(5):875. https://www.cell.com/cancer-cell/fulltext/S1535-6108(25)00130-8
34. Fan J (2022) Literature mining of disease associated noncoding RNA in the omics era. Molecules 27(15):4710
35. Glažar P, Papavasileiou P, Rajewsky N (2014) circBase: a database for circular RNAs. RNA 20(11):1666–1670
36. Yao D, Zhang L, Zheng M, Sun X, Lu Y, Liu P (2018) Circ2Disease: a manually curated database of experimentally validated circRNAs in human disease. Sci Rep 8(1):11018
37. Xia S, Feng J, Chen K, Ma Y, Gong J, Cai F et al (2018) CSCD: a database for cancer-specific circular RNAs. Nucleic Acids Res 46(D1):D925–D929. https://academic.oup.com/nar/article/46/D1/D925/4259027 [Internet] Jan 4 [cited 2021 May 18]
38. Xie J, Zhang M, Zhou T, Hua X, Tang L, Wu W (2006) Sno/scaRNAbase: a curated database for small nucleolar RNAs and cajal body-specific RNAs. Nucleic Acids Res 35:D183–D187
39. Yoshihama M, Nakao A, Kenmochi N (2013) snOPY: a small nucleolar RNA orthological gene database. BMC Res Notes 6(1):426
40. Sweeney BA, Petrov AI, Burkov B, Finn RD, Bateman A, Szymanski M et al (2018) RNAcentral: a hub of information for non-coding RNA sequences. Nucleic Acids Res 47(D1):D221–D229
41. Wang J, Shi Y, Zhou H, Zhang P, Song T, Ying Z et al (2021) piRBase: integrating piRNA annotation in all aspects. Nucleic Acids Res 50(D1):D265–D272
42. Sai Lakshmi S, Agrawal S (2007) piRNABank: a web resource on classified and clustered Piwi-interacting RNAs. Nucleic Acids Res 36(suppl_1):D173–D177
43. Muhammad A, Waheed R, Khan NA, Jiang H, Song X (2019) piRDisease v1.0: a manually curated database for piRNA associated diseases. Database (oxford) 2019:baz052. https://pubmed.ncbi.nlm.nih.gov/31267133/ [Internet] Jan;2019:baz052

44. Tomczak K, Czerwińska P, Wiznerowicz M (2015) Review the cancer genome Atlas (TCGA): an immeasurable source of knowledge. Współcz Onkol 1A(19):68–77. https://www.ncbi.nlm.nih.gov/pmc/articles/PMC4322527/ [Internet]
45. Lonsdale J, Thomas J, Salvatore M, Phillips R, Lo E, Shad S et al (2013) The genotype-tissue expression (GTEx) project. Nat Genet 45(6):580–585
46. Loganathan T, Doss CGP (2023) Non-coding RNAs in human health and disease: potential function as biomarkers and therapeutic targets. Funct Integr Genomics 23(1):33
47. O'Connor LM, O'Connor BA, Lim SB, Zeng J, Lo CH (2023) Integrative multi-omics and systems bioinformatics in translational neuroscience: a data mining perspective. J Pharm Anal 13(8):836–850. https://www.sciencedirect.com/science/article/pii/S2095177923001235?via%3Dihub [Internet]
48. Liu Y, Chen J, Yang D, Liu C, Tang C, Cai S et al (2025) Machine learning combined with multi-omics to identify immune-related LncRNA signature as biomarkers for predicting breast cancer prognosis. Sci Rep 15(1):23863. https://pmc.ncbi.nlm.nih.gov/articles/PMC12227569/
49. de Gonzalo-Calvo D, Karaduzovic-Hadziabdic K, Dalgaard LT, Dieterich C, Perez-Pons M, Artemis H et al (2024) Machine learning for catalysing the integration of noncoding RNA in research and clinical practice. EBioMedicine 106:105247–105247. https://www.thelancet.com/journals/ebiom/article/PIIS2352-3964(24)00283-4/fulltext [Internet] Jul 18 [cited 2025 Apr 5]
50. Abbas-Aghababazadeh F, Li Q, Fridley BL (2018) Comparison of normalization approaches for gene expression studies completed with high-throughput sequencing. PLOS ONE 13(10):e0206312
51. Cavalleri E, Cabri A, Soto-Gomez M, Bonfitto S, Perlasca P, Gliozzo J et al (2024) An ontology-based knowledge graph for representing interactions involving RNA molecules. Sci Data 11(1):906. https://pmc.ncbi.nlm.nih.gov/articles/PMC11341713/
52. Lee J, Yoon W, Kim S, Kim D, Kim S, So CH et al (2019) BioBERT: a pre-trained biomedical language representation model for biomedical text mining. Bioinformatics 36(4):1234. https://academic.oup.com/bioinformatics/advance-article/. https://doi.org/10.1093/bioinformatics/btz682/5566506
53. Mackenzie E, Cheng R, Zhang P (2025) GPT meets PubMed: a novel approach to literature review using a large language model to crowdsource migraine medication reviews. BMC Neurol 25(1):69
54. Luo R, Sun L, Xia Y, Qin T, Zhang S, Poon H et al (2022) BioGPT: generative pre-trained transformer for biomedical text generation and mining. Brief Bioinform 23(6):bbac409
55. J.Harry C, Putman T, Schaper K, Unni D, Hegde H, Callahan TJ et al (2023) KG-Hub–building and exchanging biological knowledge graphs. Bioinformatics 39(7):btad418
56. Cao Z, Keloth VK, Xie Q, Qian L, Liu Y, Wang Y et al (2025) The development landscape of large language models for biomedical applications. Annu Rev Biomed Data Sci 8(1):251–274. https://pmc.ncbi.nlm.nih.gov/articles/PMC12372014/ [Internet] Aug 11 [cited 2025 Oct 5]
57. Zhou Y, Liu H, Srivastava T, Mei H, Tan C (2024) Hypothesis generation with large language models. Proceedings of the 1st Workshop on NLP for Science (NLP4Science). pp 117–139. https://www.semanticscholar.org/paper/Hypothesis-Generation-with-Large-Language-Models-Zhou-Liu/975b23dd7f82ea53ccf9a0c6a5d65368fb19c3d8
58. Lin A, Ye J, Qi C, Zhu L, Mou W, Gan W et al (2025) Bridging artificial intelligence and biological sciences: a comprehensive review of large language models in bioinformatics. Brief Bioinform 26(4):bbaf357. https://pmc.ncbi.nlm.nih.gov/articles/PMC12289552/
59. Cheligeer K, Wu G, Laws A, Quan ML, Li A, Brisson AM et al (2024) Validation of large language models for detecting pathologic complete response in breast cancer using population-based pathology reports. BMC Med Inform Decis Mak 24(1):283
60. Bzdok D, Thieme A, Oleksiy L, Wren P, Ray T, Reddy S (2024) Data science opportunities of large language models for neuroscience and biomedicine. Neuron 112(5):698–717
61. Dymond JS (2013) Explanatory chapter: quantitative PCR. Methods Enzymol 529:279–289. https://pubmed.ncbi.nlm.nih.gov/24011054/ [Internet]
62. Mukherjee P, Roy S, Ghosh D, Nandi SK (2022) Role of animal models in biomedical research: a review. Lab Anim Res 38(1):18. https://pmc.ncbi.nlm.nih.gov/articles/PMC9247923/
63. Huang J, Xu Y, Wang Q, Wang QC, Liang X, Wang F et al (2025) Foundation models and intelligent decision-making: progress, challenges, and perspectives. Innovation 6:100948. https://www.cell.com/the-innovation/fulltext/S2666-6758(25)00151-1
64. Androulakis IP, Cucurull-Sanchez L, Kondic A, Mehta K, Pichardo C, Pryor M et al (2025) The dawn of a new era: can machine learning and large language models reshape QSP modeling? J Pharmacokinet Pharmacodyn 52(4):36

Check for updates

Chapter 10

Comprehensive Guide to Gene Expression Analysis from Bulk and Single-Nucleus Transcriptomes

S. Akila Parvathy Dharshini, Y-h Taguchi and M. Michael Gromiha

Abstract

RNA sequencing is a revolutionary technique for studying gene expression, providing a global transcriptome landscape that helps us understand disease-associated patterns. To gain insights into cellular heterogeneity, the advancement of single-nucleus RNA sequencing (snRNA-seq) has emerged as a powerful tool for analyzing gene expression at the single-cell level. The data generated by these techniques are massive, and handling such large datasets requires knowledge of big data analysis and machine learning methods to effectively manage and interpret the data. In this chapter, we cover quality control, normalization, sparse data handling, and transcript quantification for both bulk and snRNA-seq, along with strategies to address challenges such as multi-mapped reads and batch effects. Additionally, we examine how artificial intelligence and machine learning techniques can improve data processing and disease-associated pattern recognition. By comparing different methodologies, we highlight the strengths and limitations of both approaches and provide guidance on selecting the most appropriate strategy based on specific research objectives.

Keywords Single-nucleus RNA sequencing, Bulk RNA sequencing, Cellular heterogeneity, Data handling, Batch effects

1 Introduction

Differential gene expression analysis plays a crucial role in understanding disease-associated pathways. Traditionally, microarray technology was widely used for gene expression studies. However, advancements in next-generation sequencing (NGS) have transformed the field, allowing researchers to analyze gene and transcript expression at single-cell and spatial resolution [1–3]. Studying mutations through RNA sequencing provides insights into low-frequency mutations and splice variants, which can affect isoform expression and overall gene regulation [4].

Y-h Taguchi (ed.), *AI/ML-Driven Gene Analysis*, Methods in Molecular Biology, vol. 3037,
https://doi.org/10.1007/978-1-0716-5284-8_10,

The integration of artificial intelligence (AI) and machine learning (ML) has revolutionized gene expression analysis by enabling automated data processing, pattern recognition, and cell–cell interaction analysis [5]. These techniques enhance our ability to identify key biomarkers, classify cell types, and extract hidden biological insights from large-scale datasets.

Emerging AI-driven approaches now aim to integrate multi-omics data, including genomics, transcriptomics, and proteomics, to create a comprehensive cellular landscape. This holistic view not only improves disease modeling but also paves the way for precision medicine by identifying novel therapeutic targets and personalized treatment strategies. In this chapter, we are going to discuss about the best practices to perform gene expression analysis from bulk and single-cell data, and Fig. 1 illustrates the flowchart for gene expression analysis.

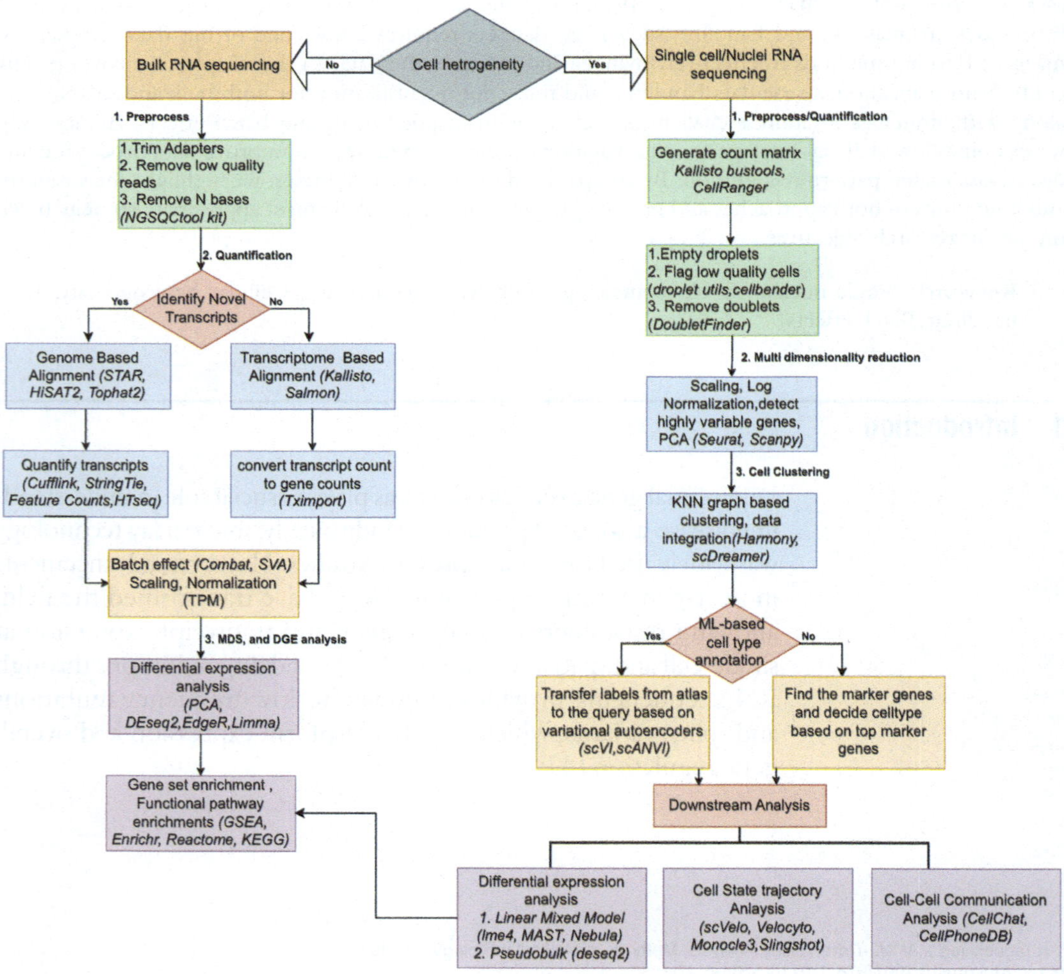

Fig. 1 Flowchart for gene expression analysis from bulk and single nuclei data

2 Bulk RNA-seq–Based Gene Expression Analysis

Bulk RNA sequencing (bulk RNA-seq) is a widely used technique for measuring gene expression across a mixture of cells within a tissue sample. It captures the average gene expression profile of all cells in the sample, making it useful for identifying global transcriptional changes between different conditions, such as healthy versus diseased tissue. Bulk RNA-seq treats the tissue as a homogeneous mixture, similar to blending different fruits into a smoothie. This means that while it effectively detects overall gene expression differences, it cannot distinguish expression changes occurring in specific cell populations. Despite this limitation, bulk RNA-seq remains a powerful tool for studying gene regulation, disease mechanisms, and pathway alterations, especially when combined with computational deconvolution methods to infer contributions from different cell types [6].

2.1 Preprocessing of Bulk RNA-seq Data

The first step in preprocessing bulk RNA sequencing (RNA-seq) data is removing adapter contamination and filtering out low-quality reads based on Phred quality scores. Tools such as the NGS QC Toolkit [7] and Cutadapt are commonly used for this purpose. After cleaning the data, it can be aligned to a reference genome or transcriptome using splice-aware alignment tools such as STAR [8]. Genome-based alignment can be enhanced by providing known splice junctions as a BED file, which allows for accurate recognition of exon–exon boundaries. Appropriate BED files can be downloaded from Ensembl. Alternatively, a faster approach involves mapping the reads directly to a reference transcriptome using tools such as Kallisto [9] or Salmon [10]. The choice between genome- or transcriptome-based alignment depends on the research objectives. For studies focused on discovering novel splice junctions or alternative splicing isoforms, genome-based alignment is preferable. However, if the goal is to efficiently quantify known transcripts, transcriptome-based alignment may be more suitable.

2.2 Quantification of Transcripts

After performing genome-based alignment, transcript quantification can be carried out using tools such as Cufflinks [11] or StringTie [12], which assign transcripts based on alignment data. Alternatively, count-based methods like HTSeq [13] or featureCounts [14] can be used to count the number of reads mapped to each gene. These tools provide accurate and consistent gene-level expression data, which are essential for downstream analysis.

2.3 Normalization

Transcript expression data often need to be normalized to account for technical biases, such as sequencing depth and gene length. For example, if one gene has multiple transcript variants, it may appear to have higher expression simply because it spans more nucleotides, which could result in more reads being mapped to it. Similarly, if one sample has more total reads than another, it could skew the expression levels. One common normalization method is transcripts per million (TPM), which adjusts for both the gene length and the total read count per sample. TPM normalization is advantageous because it allows for easy comparison of gene expression between samples, making it especially useful when analyzing datasets with different sequencing depths or comparing multiple conditions. However, TPM normalization assumes that the overall transcript pool in each sample is similar, which may not always be the case.

2.4 Handling Multi-mapped Reads

In RNA-seq analysis, multi-mapped reads (reads that align to multiple locations in the genome) can present challenges. Traditional methods often either randomly assign these reads or discard them, which can lead to biases or loss of valuable information. To address this, more advanced techniques, such as read weighting or specialized alignment tools, can be used to handle multi-mapped reads more effectively. Additionally, by filtering reads based on mapping quality, it is possible to exclude multi-mapped reads; however, this approach may also result in the loss of important data by only considering uniquely mapped reads. These strategies help ensure that the contributions of multi-mapped reads are properly accounted for minimizing potential biases in downstream analysis.

2.5 Batch Effect and Correction

Batch effects can arise from technical variations between samples, often due to differences in sequencing runs, sample preparation, or other experimental factors. These effects can introduce systematic biases that obscure true biological differences. To correct for batch effects, several methods, such as ComBat [15] or other empirical Bayes approaches, can be used. These methods help to adjust for these unwanted variations, ensuring that the observed differences in gene expression are primarily biological rather than technical.

2.6 Differential Gene Expression (DEG) Analysis

The final step in RNA-seq analysis is to perform differential gene expression (DEG) analysis to identify genes that show statistically significant differences in expression between conditions, such as disease versus control. A crucial initial step in DEG analysis is filtering out genes with low counts across all samples. These genes typically show low variance and are unlikely to be biologically relevant, so removing them improves the accuracy and efficiency of downstream analysis. After filtering, the next step is to visualize the data using principal component analysis (PCA). This technique helps to reduce the dimensionality of the data and typically reveals a clear separation between conditions, with control samples clustering together and disease samples forming their own group. This visualization provides insight into how well the samples are distinguished based on gene expression and helps assess potential outliers.

Next, transcript-level quantification is converted to gene-level abundance using tools such as tximport, which aggregates transcript counts based on a transcript-to-gene mapping file. After obtaining gene abundance, DEG analysis is performed using tools such as DESeq2 [16] or edgeR [17]. Gene dispersion is calculated to assess variance, guiding the construction of a model. A design matrix is created to account for batch effects and separate fixed effects (e.g., experimental condition) from random effects (e.g., individual subject). Following this, DEG analysis calculates the fold change for each gene, identifying those that are differentially expressed, with a typical threshold of log2 fold change ≥ 1.5. Statistical tests are applied to calculate FDR-adjusted *p*-values using Benjamini–Hochberg correction, ensuring statistical validity and reducing the likelihood of false positives. Once DEGs are identified, additional analyses, such as gene set enrichment analysis (GSEA) [18], can be performed to investigate the biological relevance of the DEGs. Pathway enrichment analysis through resources such as Gene Ontology, KEGG or Reactome helps identify key biological processes and pathways that are enriched in the DEGs, providing further insights into disease mechanisms. Furthermore, performing a correlation analysis across samples helps assess the relationship between conditions, confirming whether control and disease samples cluster as expected. Adequate biological replicates are crucial for ensuring that the DEG analysis yields reliable and reproducible results. This comprehensive pipeline enables robust identification of DEGs, providing key insights for further biological interpretation and functional analysis.

3 Single-Cell/Single-Nucleus–Based Gene Expression Analysis

Single-nucleus RNA sequencing (snRNA-seq) offers a powerful advantage in studying gene expression at the single-cell level, particularly for tissues that are challenging to dissociate or for studying rare cell types within complex tissues. Unlike traditional bulk RNA-seq, which provides an averaged gene expression profile from a mixture of cells, snRNA-seq captures the gene expression of individual nuclei, allowing for a more detailed and nuanced understanding of cellular diversity and tissue organization. This technique is particularly useful in studying brain tissue, tumors, or other densely packed tissues where it is difficult to isolate individual cells.

However, single-nucleus data often present unique challenges, including higher noise levels, gene dropouts, and sparsity due to the limited amount of RNA captured from each nucleus/cell. These issues make data processing and interpretation more complex, and thus, the need for advanced computational tools becomes critical. Artificial intelligence (AI) and machine learning (ML) techniques are increasingly essential in processing large-scale single-nucleus datasets. AI can help in improving data quality through advanced imputation methods, identifying rare or low-abundance cell populations, and deciphering complex patterns of gene expression. Here, we discuss the best practices for analyzing single-cell/nucleus data.

3.1 Preprocessing

The first step in preprocessing single-cell RNA sequencing (scRNA-seq) data is to generate a count matrix for each sample. This can be done using tools such as Cell Ranger or Kallisto-Bustools [9], both of which rely on a reference transcriptome index (pre-mRNA or mRNA) for alignment. The resulting count matrix is typically organized with cells (m) as rows and genes or transcripts (n) as columns, representing the expression levels of each gene across all individual cells.

Once the transcript counts are obtained, it is essential to preprocess the data by filtering out low-quality cells, ambient RNA, and empty droplets. Tools such as DropletUtils [19] or the CellBender pipeline can assist in identifying and removing these unwanted components. One common filtering step involves removing cells with high mitochondrial gene content, which can be indicative of poor-quality or stressed cells. A typical threshold for mitochondrial gene content is 5%, although this can vary depending on the dataset and experimental conditions.

Another critical step is identifying and removing low-count genes, as well as setting the appropriate threshold for unique molecular identifiers (UMIs). This is often done by analyzing the knee and inflection points in the elbow plot generated by DropletUtils, which provides insights into the UMI distribution and helps determine a cutoff value for filtering out low-quality cells.

Additionally, doublets—instances where two droplets contain the RNA from two separate cells—can sometimes appear in the data. These doublets can skew analysis and need to be identified and removed. The DoubletFinder algorithm [20] is commonly used to detect doublets, which typically exhibit higher UMI counts compared to single cells. By applying the DoubletFinder tool, you can effectively exclude doublet cells from the dataset.

All of these preprocessing steps must be performed for each sample individually to ensure that low-quality cells, ambient RNA, and doublets are properly removed. This ensures a high-quality dataset, setting the foundation for accurate downstream analysis.

3.2 Scaling, Normalization, and PCA

In single-cell RNA sequencing analysis, preprocessing steps such as normalization, scaling, and dimensionality reduction are primarily handled by pipelines such as Scanpy and Seurat. After preprocessing, the data are typically log-normalized and scaled to ensure comparability across cells, as both Scanpy [21] and Seurat [22] offer built-in methods for log-transformation and normalization. This step is important for ensuring that genes with high expression levels do not dominate the analysis. Once the data are normalized, highly variable genes (HVGs) are identified. HVGs are those that show greater variation across cells and are typically selected for dimensionality reduction methods such as principal component analysis (PCA). Identifying HVGs is essential for reducing noise and focusing on genes that are more likely to drive biological variation in the dataset.

Following the identification of HVGs, PCA is applied to reduce the dimensionality of the data, capturing the most important features while reducing the number of dimensions. This step is common in both Scanpy and Seurat pipelines and is crucial for exploring the structure of the data in a lower dimensional space. After PCA, *k*-nearest neighbors (KNN) clustering is applied to generate a neighborhood graph. The number of neighbors (*k*) can be adjusted depending on the dataset's characteristics. For global structure capture, a higher *k* value (e.g., $k = 30$) is used, while for focusing on local structures, a lower *k* value (e.g., $k = 10$) is preferred. Scanpy and Seurat typically default to values between $k = 15$ and $k = 20$, but optimizing the *k* value can improve the quality of clustering based on the data.

3.3 Integration and Leiden Clustering

In single-cell RNA sequencing analysis, batch effects can occur when data are generated across different conditions, times, or experimental setups. For example, if RNA-seq samples are collected on five different days, the data may show clustering based on the sequencing date rather than the biological signal, which is the primary focus. To overcome this issue, data integration methods such as Harmony [23] and scDREAMER [24] algorithms can be used to align data from different batches into a common space, ensuring that biological variations are preserved while mitigating batch effects.

Once batch effects are corrected, clustering can be performed using algorithms such as Leiden, which builds a graph based on *k*-nearest neighbors (KNN). Leiden clustering works by partitioning the data into communities or clusters based on their proximity to each other in the high-dimensional space. To achieve meaningful and biologically relevant clustering, it is crucial to determine the appropriate clustering resolution. This can be done by evaluating clustering quality using metrics such as the silhouette score or the adjusted Rand index (ARI), which measure the coherence and reproducibility of clusters. If the resolution is set too high, the analysis may generate too many clusters that are biologically irrelevant, whereas setting it too low could group distinct cell types together. In cases where standard Leiden clustering does not fully capture the biological diversity, further refinements can be made by utilizing additional tools, such as the scTree method, which helps improve the clustering process. scTree [25] builds hierarchical trees from clusters, allowing users to visualize the relationships between different clusters more effectively. This method can be particularly useful for resolving nested or hierarchical relationships between clusters. t-SNE and UMAP can be used to visualize and validate clusters.

3.4 Cell Type Annotation

Once clusters are identified, the next critical step is to assign cell types to each cluster. Accurate annotation of cell types is essential for understanding the biological meaning behind each cluster. This can be achieved by using known marker genes specific to each cell type. For instance, in brain tissue, clusters can be annotated to represent excitatory neurons, inhibitory neurons, astrocytes, microglia, oligodendrocytes, oligodendrocyte precursor cells (OPCs), endothelial cells, and vascular-like mural cells (VLMCs), among others. These marker genes serve as reliable indicators of cell identity and help map the clusters to the corresponding cell types.

Machine learning-based tools such as SingleR [26] and CellTypist [27] are commonly used to facilitate the annotation process. These tools use canonical gene sets to automatically assign cell types to clusters, often relying on well-established marker gene signatures. While these tools are effective, their accuracy depends on the comprehensiveness and specificity of the marker gene sets used.

For more sophisticated and nuanced annotations, advanced machine learning models such as scVI [28] and scANVI can be employed. These tools predict cell types by not only using marker gene sets but also by considering latent biological factors that may be overlooked by traditional methods. scVI and scANVI leverage probabilistic models to capture complex patterns of gene expression, allowing for more accurate cell type predictions, especially when working with highly heterogeneous data.

Furthermore, integrating external reference datasets for cell type annotation can improve the resolution of the annotations. These references may include cell type–specific RNA-seq data, single-cell atlases, or transcriptomic databases. By mapping the clusters to these well-characterized reference datasets, one can achieve better confidence in the cell type predictions.

Finally, it is important to note that manual curation or expert knowledge is sometimes needed, especially in the case of novel or rare cell types that may not be fully represented in the current reference datasets. In such cases, researchers may need to manually inspect marker gene expression patterns, use additional data types (such as proteomics or spatial transcriptomics), or integrate with other experimental approaches to confirm cell type identities.

In summary, accurate cell type annotation is essential for interpreting scRNA-seq data. Using a combination of known marker genes, machine learning tools, and reference datasets can significantly improve the reliability and biological relevance of cell type identification. However, in some instances, manual validation and expert input may still be necessary to ensure accurate interpretation, especially for less characterized or novel cell populations.

3.5 Differential Expression Analysis from Single-Cell Data

The next critical step is identifying differential expression (DE) patterns between conditions, such as disease versus normal. The first step in DE analysis is filtering out genes with low expression. To avoid noise from genes with minimal expression, it is important to retain only those genes that are present in at least 15% of the cells across the dataset.

In the next step, a reference factor should be defined to control for potential confounders that could affect the results. For instance, biological variables such as age, sex, and RNA sequencing depth may introduce biases. For example, differential expression patterns can sometimes be influenced by higher RNA transcript counts in one group, and not the condition being studied. Therefore, it is necessary to include such factors as fixed effects in the model to ensure that the DEGs detected are not driven by confounding variables.

The subject (individual) is typically considered as a random effect, which helps account for variation between subjects, ensuring that the differential expression is truly reflective of the conditions being compared (such as disease vs. normal), and not skewed by individual differences such as age or sex. This approach allows for more accurate identification of DEGs by minimizing the influence of confounding factors.

For DEG analysis, linear mixed models (LMMs) are widely used, where both fixed and random effects can be specified. Implementing rigorous statistical tests, such as MAST [29], or lme4 [30], is essential to identify statistically significant genes. To further control for multiple testing, false discovery rate (FDR) correction methods (e.g., Benjamini–Hochberg correction) should be applied to ensure the validity of the results.

In addition to these methods, pseudobulking is an effective approach, particularly when dealing with single-cell RNA-seq data, which often suffers from low sample sizes and gene dropouts. Pseudobulking involves aggregating counts from individual cells within each sample to create bulk-like profiles that can be used to perform DEG analysis. This method can be implemented using tools such as pyDESeq2 [31], which combines single-cell RNA-seq data into "pseudo-bulk" samples, reducing the impact of pseudoreplication and enabling more robust DEG analysis.

In summary, the use of linear mixed models, appropriate control for confounding variables, pseudobulking, and rigorous statistical testing are essential for robust differential expression analysis in bulk or single-cell RNA-seq data. These strategies ensure that the identified DEGs reflect true biological differences and are not confounded by other factors. Once DEGs are identified, performing gene set enrichment analysis (GSEA) can help identify enriched pathways or biological processes. Kyoto Encyclopedia of Genes and Genomes (KEGG) and Reactome are widely used databases to assess pathway enrichment. This additional analysis can provide deeper insights into the underlying biological mechanisms involved in the observed differential expression patterns.

3.6 Pseudotime Analysis

To explore cell states and their trajectories, tools such as Monocle3 [32], scVelo [33], and Slingshot [34] are used to order cells based on pseudotime, allowing us to track how cells transition between different states. For example, in a study of microglial cells in the brain, we might examine how these cells move from a resting to an activated state in response to injury or inflammation. By applying Monocle3 or scVelo, we can generate a pseudotime trajectory that shows how microglial cells progressively transition from a resting state to an intermediate activation state, and finally to a fully activated state. Using pseudotime gradient analysis (PAGA), we can further identify key transition points, highlighting specific molecular changes or markers associated with these states. This approach is crucial for understanding dynamic cell behavior in response to environmental signals, providing insights into transient cell states and their roles in processes such as neuroinflammation.

3.7 Cell–Cell Communication Analysis

To analyze cell–cell communication, tools such as CellChat [35] and CellphoneDB [36] are commonly used to explore interactions between different cell subtypes. Communication networks are constructed to compare the interactions both within individual cell subtypes and across different subtypes. To ensure accuracy, the average expression ("trimean") of genes encoding ligands and receptors is calculated for each cell subtype using a curated interaction database. To address variations in the number of nuclei present in each subtype, the communication probability is computed while factoring in the population size of each subtype (population size = "True"). This approach helps minimize bias from more abundant cell types, which might show a higher number of interactions compared to rarer ones. Furthermore, communications involving cell types with fewer than ten nuclei are filtered out (min_cells = 10), ensuring that only robust interactions are considered. For identifying statistically significant ligand–receptor pairs that are either enriched or underrepresented, differential interaction testing is applied with default thresholds. These practices provide a comprehensive and unbiased view of the dynamic communication networks between cell subtypes, offering valuable insights into cellular behaviors and their roles in biological processes and diseases.

In conclusion, it is mandatory to perform necessary quality checks before doing any downstream analysis and account for normalization and correct for batch effect, which helps to pick up the true biological variation other than noise. In single-cell data, careful interpretation of clusters and their resolution is important, which may affect the associated pathway and functional analysis. By adhering to these best practices and leveraging the latest computational methods, researchers can ensure high-quality and reproducible results that contribute to our understanding of gene expression, cell behavior, and disease mechanisms.

Acknowledgments

The authors would like to thank the Department of Biotechnology, Indian Institute of Technology Madras for infrastructure facilities. S. Akila Parvathy Dharshini thanks the Ministry of Human Resource Development (MHRD), India for providing a research fellowship.

Conflict of Interest The authors have no conflicts of interest to declare that are relevant to the content of this chapter.

References

1. Li X, Wang C-Y (2021) From bulk, single-cell to spatial RNA sequencing. Int J Oral Sci 13(1):36. https://doi.org/10.1038/s41368-021-00146-0
2. Piwecka M, Rajewsky N, Rybak-Wolf A (2023) Single-cell and spatial transcriptomics: deciphering brain complexity in health and disease. Nat Rev Neurol 19(6):346–362. https://doi.org/10.1038/s41582-023-00809-y
3. Grindberg RV, Yee-Greenbaum JL, Mcconnell MJ, Novotny M, O'Shaughnessy AL, Lambert GM et al (2013) RNA-sequencing from single nuclei. Proc Natl Acad Sci 110(49):19802–19807. https://doi.org/10.1073/pnas.1319700110
4. Townsend SE, Westfall JJ, Navarro JB, Koboldt DC, Mardis ER, Miller KE et al (2023) Single-nuclei transcriptomics enable detection of somatic variants in patient brain tissue. Sci Rep 13(1):527. https://doi.org/10.1038/s41598-023-27700-6
5. Armingol E, Officer A, Harismendy O, Lewis NE (2021) Deciphering cell–cell interactions and communication from gene expression. Nat Rev Genet 22(2):71–88. https://doi.org/10.1038/s41576-020-00292-x
6. Nguyen H, Nguyen H, Tran D, Draghici S, Nguyen T (2024) Fourteen years of cellular deconvolution: methodology, applications, technical evaluation and outstanding challenges. Nucleic Acids Res 52(9):4761–4783. https://doi.org/10.1093/nar/gkae267
7. Dai M, Thompson RC, Maher C, Contreras-Galindo R, Kaplan MH, Markovitz DM et al (2010) NGSQC: cross-platform quality analysis pipeline for deep sequencing data. BMC Genomics 11(Suppl 4):S7. https://doi.org/10.1186/1471-2164-11-S4-S7
8. Dobin A, Davis CA, Schlesinger F, Drenkow J, Zaleski C, Jha S, Batut P et al (2013) STAR: ultrafast universal RNA-seq aligner. Bioinformatics 29(1):15–21
9. Melsted P, Booeshaghi AS, Liu L, Gao F, Lu L, Min KHJ et al (2021) Modular, efficient and constant-memory single-cell RNA-seq preprocessing. Nat Biotechnol 39(7):813–818. https://doi.org/10.1038/s41587-021-00870-2
10. Patro R, Duggal G, Love MI, Irizarry RA, Kingsford C (2017) Salmon provides fast and bias-aware quantification of transcript expression. Nat Methods 14(4):417–419. https://doi.org/10.1038/nmeth.4197
11. Trapnell C, Roberts A, Goff L, Pertea G, Kim D, Kelley DR et al (2012) Differential gene and transcript expression analysis of RNA-seq experiments with TopHat and Cufflinks. Nat Protoc 7(3):562–578. https://doi.org/10.1038/nprot.2012.016
12. Pertea M, Pertea GM, Antonescu CM, Chang T-C, Mendell JT, Salzberg SL (2015) StringTie enables improved reconstruction of a transcriptome from RNA-seq reads. Nat Biotechnol 33(3):290–295. https://doi.org/10.1038/nbt.3122
13. Anders S, Pyl PT, Huber W (2015) HTSeq—a Python framework to work with high-throughput sequencing data. Bioinformatics 31(2):166–169. https://doi.org/10.1093/bioinformatics/btu638
14. Liao Y, Smyth GK, Shi W (2014) featureCounts: an efficient general purpose program for assigning sequence reads to genomic features. Bioinformatics 30(7):923–930. https://doi.org/10.1093/bioinformatics/btt656
15. Zhang Y, Parmigiani G, Johnson WE (2020) ComBat-seq: batch effect adjustment for RNA-seq count data. NAR Genom Bioinform 2(3):lqaa078. https://doi.org/10.1093/nargab/lqaa078.
16. Love MI, Huber W, Anders S (2014) Moderated estimation of fold change and dispersion for RNA-seq data with DESeq2. Genome Biol 15(12):550. https://doi.org/10.1186/s13059-014-0550-8

17. Robinson MD, Mccarthy DJ, Smyth GK (2010) edgeR: a Bioconductor package for differential expression analysis of digital gene expression data. Bioinformatics 26(1):139–140. https://doi.org/10.1093/bioinformatics/btp616
18. Fang Z, Liu X, Peltz G (2023) GSEApy: a comprehensive package for performing gene set enrichment analysis in Python. Bioinformatics 39(1):btac757. https://doi.org/10.1093/bioinformatics/btac757.
19. Lun ATL, Riesenfeld S, Andrews T, Dao TP, Gomes T, Marioni JC et al (2019) EmptyDrops: distinguishing cells from empty droplets in droplet-based single-cell RNA sequencing data. Genome Biol 20(1):63. https://doi.org/10.1186/s13059-019-1662-y
20. McGinnis CS, Murrow LM, Gartner ZJ (2019) DoubletFinder: doublet detection in single-cell RNA sequencing data using artificial nearest neighbors. Cell Syst 8(4):329–337.e4. https://doi.org/10.1016/j.cels.2019.03.003
21. Wolf FA, Angerer P, Theis FJ (2018) SCANPY: large-scale single-cell gene expression data analysis. Genome Biol 19(1):15. https://doi.org/10.1186/s13059-017-1382-0
22. Butler A, Hoffman P, Smibert P, Papalexi E, Satija R (2018) Integrating single-cell transcriptomic data across different conditions, technologies, and species. Nat Biotechnol 36(5):411–420. https://doi.org/10.1038/nbt.4096
23. Korsunsky I, Millard N, Fan J, Slowikowski K, Zhang F, Wei K et al (2019) Fast, sensitive and accurate integration of single-cell data with Harmony. Nat Methods 16(12):1289–1296. https://doi.org/10.1038/s41592-019-0619-0
24. Shree A, Pavan MK, Zafar H (2023) scDREAMER for atlas-level integration of single-cell datasets using deep generative model paired with adversarial classifier. Nat Commun 14(1):7781. https://doi.org/10.1038/s41467-023-43590-8
25. Paez J, Wendt M, Lanman N (2020) scTree: an R package to generate antibody-compatible classifiers from single-cell sequencing data. J Open Source Softw 5(48):2061. https://doi.org/10.21105/joss.02061
26. Aran D, Looney AP, Liu L, Wu E, Fong V, Hsu A et al (2019) Reference-based analysis of lung single-cell sequencing reveals a transitional profibrotic macrophage. Nat Immunol 20(2):163–172. https://doi.org/10.1038/s41590-018-0276-y
27. Domínguez Conde C, Xu C, Jarvis LB, Rainbow DB, Wells SB, Gomes T et al (2022) Cross-tissue immune cell analysis reveals tissue-specific features in humans. Science 376 (6594):eabl5197. https://doi.org/10.1126/science.abl5197
28. Xu C, Lopez R, Mehlman E, Regier J, Jordan MI, Yosef N (2021) Probabilistic harmonization and annotation of single-cell transcriptomics data with deep generative models. Mol Syst Biol 17(1):e9620. https://doi.org/10.15252/msb.20209620
29. Finak G, McDavid A, Yajima M, Deng J, Gersuk V, Shalek AK et al (2015) MAST: a flexible statistical framework for assessing transcriptional changes and characterizing heterogeneity in single-cell RNA sequencing data. Genome Biol 16:278. https://doi.org/10.1186/s13059-015-0844-5
30. Luke SG (2017) Evaluating significance in linear mixed-effects models in R. Behav Res Methods 49(4):1494–1502. https://doi.org/10.3758/s13428-016-0809-y
31. Muzellec B, Teleńczuk M, Cabeli V, Andreux M (2023) PyDESeq2: a python package for bulk RNA-seq differential expression analysis. Bioinformatics 39(9):btad547. https://doi.org/10.1093/bioinformatics/btad547
32. Cao J, Spielmann M, Qiu X, Huang X, Ibrahim DM, Hill AJ et al (2019) The single-cell transcriptional landscape of mammalian organogenesis. Nature 566(7745):496–502. https://doi.org/10.1038/s41586-019-0969-x
33. Bergen V, Lange M, Peidli S, Wolf FA, Theis FJ (2020) Generalizing RNA velocity to transient cell states through dynamical modeling. Nat Biotechnol 38(12):1408–1414. https://doi.org/10.1038/s41587-020-0591-3
34. Street K, Risso D, Fletcher RB, Das D, Ngai J, Yosef N et al (2018) Slingshot: cell lineage and pseudotime inference for single-cell transcriptomics. BMC Genomics 19(1):477. https://doi.org/10.1186/s12864-018-4772-0
35. Jin S, Guerrero-Juarez CF, Zhang L, Chang I, Ramos R, Kuan CH et al (2021) Inference and analysis of cell-cell communication using CellChat. Nat Commun 12(1):1088. https://doi.org/10.1038/s41467-021-21246-9
36. Efremova M, Vento-Tormo M, Teichmann SA, Vento-Tormo R (2020) CellPhoneDB: inferring cell–cell communication from combined expression of multi-subunit ligand–receptor complexes. Nat Protoc 15(4):1484–1506. https://doi.org/10.1038/s41596-020-0292-x

Chapter 11

RNA Structure and Its Function

Shunsuke Sumi, Fumiya Ito, Ruiqi Xu, Hirohide Saito and Risa Karakida Kawaguchi

Abstract

RNA molecules were once regarded merely as intermediates in the transmission of genetic information from DNA, but are now emerging as key players in complex cellular regulation. Driven by the recent discovery of diverse functions of non-coding and coding RNAs, a deep understanding of RNA structure, and ultimately their interaction has become essential for both basic and applied research in RNA biology, including drug discovery efforts targeting RNA. However, its inherent structural instability and variability have made experimental analyses, such as X-ray crystallography and NMR, challenging and often inadequate. For this reason, continuous efforts have been devoted to advancing computational structure prediction. With growing attention to the role of RNA as a signaling molecule, a vast amount of functional RNA sequence and structure data has been accumulated so that it makes it feasible to apply machine learning (ML) and artificial intelligence (AI) technologies to further enhance the power of computational structure analysis in a data-driven manner. In this section, we introduce current gold-standard RNA structure prediction approaches and cutting-edge ML methods that can contribute to inferring RNA functions. We first describe the basics of RNA structure classification and diverse non-coding functional RNAs identified so far. Next, the example use cases of several RNA analysis tools, including computational prediction with the aid of structure probing methods, are provided. Finally, we introduce software protocols for generating RNA family sequences using a novel methodology called *RfamGen*, enabling readers to explore how cutting-edge ML can be leveraged for not only structure prediction but also the design of artificial RNA sequences to engineer novel RNA functions.

Keywords RNA secondary structure, RNA tertiary structure, Cross-linking and immunoprecipitation (CLIP), RNA binding protein (RBP), RNA family, Variational autoencoder

1 Introduction

1.1 RNA: From the Origin of Life to a Master Regulator of the Cell

RNA is a nucleotide sequence that consists of Adenosine (A), Cytosine (C), Guanosine (G), and Uridine (U) triphosphates. Once, RNA was merely treated as an information messenger from DNA, which consists of deoxy (d-) A, C, G, and Thymidine (T) or 5-methyluridine triphosphates. It is just slightly different in a chemical structure yet represents a significantly more stable form. One of the major functional differences of RNA

Y-h Taguchi (ed.), *AI/ML-Driven Gene Analysis*, Methods in Molecular Biology, vol. 3037,
https://doi.org/10.1007/978-1-0716-5284-8_11,

from DNA is the wide diversity of their interaction repertoire for the reaction, such as proteins, metabolites, and ligands, including ions, to be involved in the essential biological reactions. For example, coding pre-mRNAs are made mature into mRNAs after cutting out intronic regions and pasting exons by the spliceosome, which consists of five small nuclear RNAs (U1, U2, U4, U5, and U6). In another example, mRNAs are translated into proteins through the ribosome, whose components are four rRNAs and 80 ribosomal proteins (in the range of 78-88 depending on the definition) in eukaryotes [1]. These untranslated RNAs, termed non-coding RNAs (ncRNAs), exhibit significant evolutionary conservation at both sequence and structural levels [2]. Taken together, the existence of the inevitable interplay between RNA structure and function has long been suggested.

1.2 MicroRNA: A Tiny RNA Fragment Whose Sequence and Structure Are Essential to Control Transcriptome

An increasing number of novel ncRNAs have been identified along with the discovery of novel regulatory functions [3]. microRNA (miRNA)——for which the 2024 Nobel prize in physiology or medicine was awarded——is one of the prominent examples. A tiny fragment of 22nt length from a gene lin-4 was the first miRNA identified. Assisted by Argonaute family proteins, this miRNA negatively regulates another gene lin-14 via RNA-RNA binding [4, 5]. While miRNAs recognize the target RNAs by antisense complementary sequences mostly in 3′ untranslated regions (UTR), the interaction between RNA and protein is mainly intermediated by their structures. For instance, miRNAs are derived from pri-miRNAs that have a hairpin-like structure, following cleavage by Drosha and Dicer, then loaded onto Argonaute, which are eventually recruited to the complement mRNA region. As of 2025, miRBase provides the list of miRNAs, where 2,654 out of 38,589 entries are registered as human miRNAs [6]. Preferable sequence features for miRNAs were reported [7]; however, Drosha and Dicer identify miRNAs primarily through their structural features rather than sequence. RNA secondary structure, or whether each region forms internal base pairs or being single-stranded, plays an indispensable role to determine a way of RNA's binding. Thanks to such binding machinery, the RNA Binding Proteins (RBPs) essential for miRNA maturation are capable of engaging with miRNAs exhibiting a wide range of sequence diversity. It is strikingly different from a binding manner of DNA, which relies on DNA motifs and chromatin structure. Understanding the structures of RNAs is, therefore, a significant step for unveiling their interaction network [8].

1.3 RNA Structure Analysis Reveals the Functional Roles of ncRNAs

Here, we describe clear and straightforward guidelines for an RNA biologist and novice bioinformatician to analyze the function of RNA, mainly focusing on structure prediction and motif analysis. With a focus on usability and feasibility, we picked up three platforms, ViennaRNA [9], Rtools [10], and RNA workbench Galaxy server [11], to carry out gold-standard RNA structure prediction analysis.

Additionally, we provide example use cases of several RNA analysis tools, including the structure prediction, referring to the sequencing data of structure probing methods using RNAframework [12]. Beyond these structure prediction approaches, ML and AI methodologies can provide insights into the potential functions of individual RNA molecules and their interacting partners. We introduce a protocol for generating RNA family sequences using a novel methodology called RfamGen [13], enabling readers to explore how cutting-edge ML can be leveraged not only for structure prediction but also for designing new sequences to engineer novel RNA functions.

2 Materials

2.1 Structure Nomenclature and Notation for Representing Diverse RNA 2D and 3D Structures

To investigate the relationship between RNA structure and function, there are two categories of RNA structure: secondary structure (2D) and tertiary structure (3D). Several community-wide competitions have been held to benchmark the prediction accuracy of 2D [14–16] and 3D structure tools [17, 18]. A widely applied approach for RNA 2D and 3D structure prediction can be classified into physics-based and ML-based approaches (Fig. 1). Specifically, the thermodynamic energy model, called Nearest Neighbor (NN) models, is one of the established physics-based models for RNA secondary structure prediction. For RNA 3D structure prediction, molecular dynamics simulations and Monte Carlo sampling methods are adopted to the high-performance physics-based models. Recently, it is rarely possible to classify the methods into these two categories because cutting-edge methods tend to integrate multiple methodologies forming hybrid frameworks to leverage the strengths of each. In addition, some tools apply the data-based refinement step to integrate external structure data, such as RNA probing data for 2D and template structure library from Protein Data Bank (PDB) for 3D structures. The previous

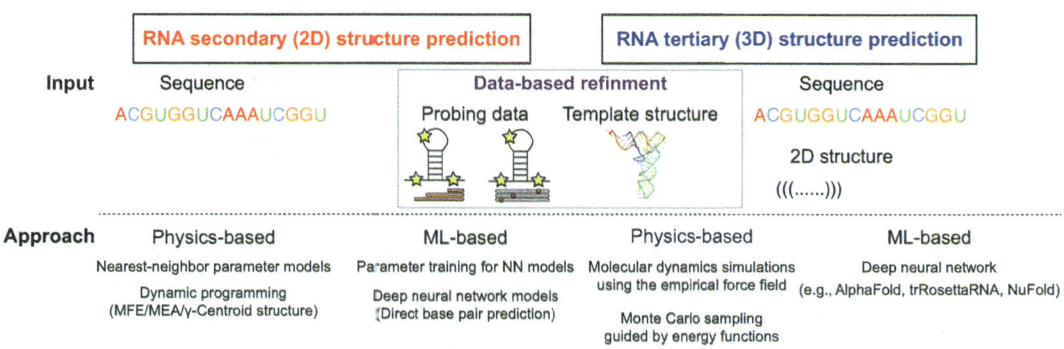

Fig. 1 Classification of RNA secondary (2D) and tertiary (3D) structure prediction

reviews provide valuable insights for readers who wish to learn the advantages of different approaches [19–21].

While an accurate 3D structure prediction is highly demanded for studying RNA functions, the overall prediction accuracy is still insufficient for precise de novo structure prediction at a practical level. Even cutting-edge folding methods fail to obtain a comparable accuracy of RNA and RNA-protein complex 3D structures to protein and protein-protein complexes (e.g., prediction assessment for CASP 16 [22]). To overcome that problem, instead, RNA secondary structure has been widely used for RNA functional analysis. RNA secondary structure mainly consists of base pairs between complementary bases (A-U and C-G, called canonical pairs) and wobble pairs (G-U). They make an RNA structure stable enough to influence its 3D structure so that a prediction of RNA 3D structure often exploits the results of RNA secondary structure prediction tools and sequence covariation [23, 24] At a closer look into the molecular structure of RNA, the interaction can take place in three possible angular configurations: Watson-Crick, Hoogsteen, and Sugar edges (Fig. 2A). To be more specific, according to the LW classification [25], RNA bases can interact through three distinct edges in either cis or trans orientations, resulting in a total of twelve possible base-pairing geometries. These various interaction patterns are observed in rRNA secondary structure to form the complex [26]. In RNA secondary structure prediction, however, prediction models and training datasets are mainly designed to predict Watson-Click and Wobble base pairs for their strong contribution to the structure stability [27].

RNA secondary structures of Watson-Click and Wobble base pairs can be represented by dot and bracket notation (Fig. 2B). Dots represent loop bases, and brackets do one of the base pairs. Nested

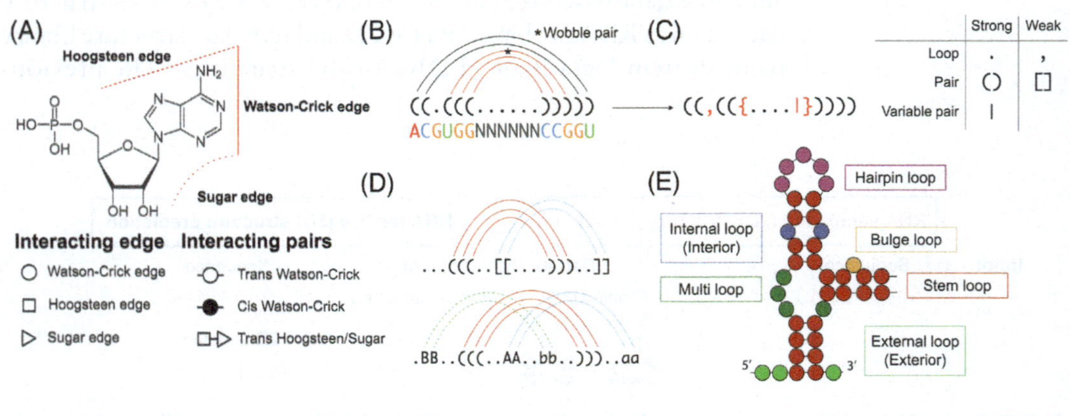

Fig. 2 (**A**) RNA base pairing via three different edges. (**B**) Dot-bracket notation of pseudoknot-free RNA secondary structure. (**C**) Pseudo dot bracket notation example, where strong loop and pair bases are defined to have a probability >2/3 in ViennaRNA [9]. (**D**) Extended dot-bracket notations for the secondary structure with pseudoknots. (**E**) Major loop motifs depicted in an example RNA structure. External, Stem, Internal, Hairpin, Bulge, and Multi loops are shown in light green, red, blue, pink, orange, and dark green

base pairs are parsed such that the leftmost opening bracket "(" is paired with the rightmost closing bracket ")" in this notation. In order to represent more complex structure information, some extended notations are used, such as pseudo dot-bracket notation to represent strong and weak structure motifs and extended dot-bracket notation to include additional non-nested base pairs (Fig. 2C, D). Although not introduced here, another notation, Washington University Secondary Structure (WUSS) notation is popular to encode the structure information in consensus secondary structures [28]. By the combination of base pairs and loop bases, loop bases can be decomposed into 6 loop motifs: External, Stem, Internal, Hairpin, Bulge, and Multi loops (Fig. 2E). Multi loops are also called Junctions with the information on how many stems exist (two-stem, three-stem, and four-stem junctions). The previous high-throughput experimental studies have revealed each motif is recognized by RBPs in a different way, suggesting high-context-dependent RNA binding mechanisms exist [29, 30]. Beyond the nested base pairs, pseudoknots, or base pairs crossing over between a loop region and outside that loop, are observed in the secondary structures of functional RNAs [31]. Using an extended dot-bracket notation to include pseudoknot structures in an unambiguous way, extra parentheses or upper and lower alphabets are utilized to indicate each pseudoknot pair (the example usage is shown in Fig. 2D). While pseudoknots are classified into one of the topologies of RNA secondary structure, exploring pseudoknot structures will increase the complexity of structures and computational time exhaustively. For that reason, many structure prediction tools ignore pseudoknots except for a few pseudoknot-oriented tools [32], but they are invaluable elements to determine RNA 3D structure at the same time.

In Fig. 3, several example RNA structures are presented from both two-dimensional and three-dimensional perspectives. Figure 3A is one of the examples of a kissing loop structure, which consists of pseudoknot pairing between two hairpins. Pseudoknot motifs are widely involved in viral infection processes, and the initialization of HIV-1 genomic RNA dimerization occurs through the formation of kissing loop interactions [33]. A kink-turn loop is another example of the 3D structural motif, which includes a specific secondary structure. As a kink-turn motif of *Haroarculamarismortui* Kt-7, the large ribosomal unit contains the combination of Watson–Crick and Hoogsteen/Sugar base pairs, and the exposed bulge loop can be recognized by L7Ae protein to inhibit translation [34, 35] (Fig. 3B). tRNAs are known as the example of coaxial stacking because the interaction between acceptor stem and T loop is one of the keys to form L-shape 3D structure from a cloverleaf-like secondary structure (Fig. 3C). Furthermore, in addition to those, other well-defined tertiary structural motifs have been identified, such as hairpin loop-bulge contact including A-minor motif between GNRA tetraloop (3-mer hairpin) and other loop bases [36], intramolecular or intermolecular parallel

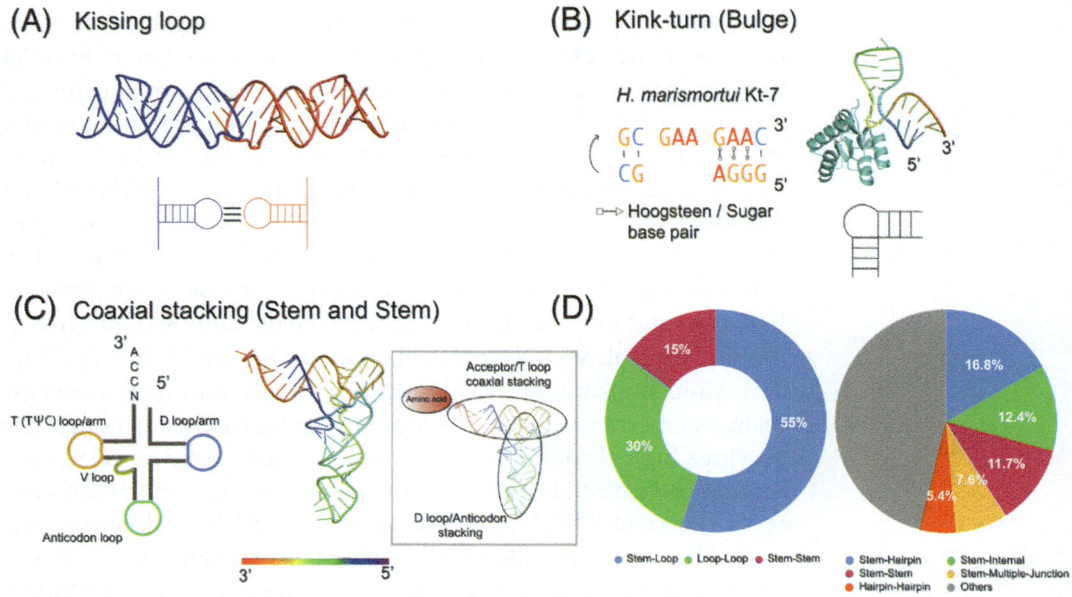

Fig. 3 (**A–C**) 3D and 2D structures of canonical RNA structure motifs (PDB ID is 2D1B, 4BW0, and 6TNA, respectively). (**A**) Kissing loop at HIV-1 genome dimerization initiation sites. (**B**) Kink-turn found in helix 7 (Kt-7) of *Haloarcula marismortui* 23S rRNA bound by *Archaeoglobus fulgidus* L7Ae protein. (**C**) *Saccharomyces cerevisiae* phenylalanine tRNA. (**D**) Long-range tertiary interactions and the associated RNA secondary-structure elements identified in non-redundant RNA 3D structures reported by Bohdan et al. [39]

G-quadruplex [37], or triplex structures [38]. According to the comprehensive survey by Bohdan et al, the dominant categories of long-range tertiary interactions in RNA 3D structures are stem-loop (55%), loop-loop (30%), and stem-stem (15%) [39] (Fig. 3D). In terms of secondary-structure motif pairs, different frequencies are observed among RNA motif elements; the most frequent interactions are stem-hairpin, stem-internal, stem-stem, stem-multiple-junction, and hairpin-hairpin. In this way, the diversity of interactions underlying RNA 3D structures is closely linked to the presence of secondary structure motifs. Consequently, improving the accuracy of both secondary and tertiary structure prediction remains a central goal in RNA functional analysis.

2.2 Secondary Structure of Non-Coding RNAs

RNA secondary structure prediction has been widely performed for ncRNAs to discover the evolutionarily conserved functional structures. Although we still do not have a complete guide for ncRNAs, 24 classes of ncRNAs have been officially accepted since 2017 by the International Nucleotide Sequence Database Collaboration (INSDC) (Table 1). The list includes housekeeping or classical ncRNAs (e.g., rRNAs, tRNAs, snRNAs, snoRNAs, and telomerase-associated RNAs); structural ncRNAs involved in fundamental cellular processes (e.g., scRNA, SRP RNA, vault RNA, and Y RNA); ribozymes; short regulatory ncRNAs (e.g., miRNAs, siRNAs, piRNAs, rasiRNAs, and

Table 1
List of ncRNA classes defined by the INSDC submission guideline from [40]

ncRNA	Abstract	Sequence ontology	Classification
antisense_RNA		SO:000064	Regulatory
autocatalytically_spliced_intron	self-splicing intron.self-splicing intron	SO:0000588	Ribozyme
ribozyme		SO:0000374	Ribozyme
hammerhead_ribozyme		SO:0000380	Ribozyme
lncRNA	long non-coding RNA	SO:0001877	Long, structural, and unknown
RNase_P_RNA	RNA component of Ribonuclease P	SO:0000386	Ribozyme
RNase_MRP_RNA	RNA component of Ribonuclease MRP	SO:0000385	Enzymatic
telomerase_RNA	RNA component of telomerase	SO:0000390	Classic
guide_RNA	short 3′-uridylated RNA that forms a duplex with edited mRNA	SO:0000602	Others
sgRNA	Single-guide RNA	SO:0001998	Others
rasiRNA	Repeat-associated small interfering RNA	SO:0000454	Regulatory
scRNA	Small cytoplasmic RNA	SO:0000013	Structural
scaRNA	A ncRNA specific to the Cajal body	SO:0002095	Enzymatic
siRNA	small interfering RNA	SO:0000646	Regulatory
pre-miRNA	pre-micro RNA	SO:0001244	Regulatory
miRNA	micro RNA	SO:0000276	Regulatory
piRNA	PIWI-interacting RNA	SO:0001035	Regulatory
snoRNA	small nucleolar RNA	SO:0000275	Classic
snRNA	small nuclear RNA	SO:0000274	Classic
SRP_RNA	RNA component of signal recognition particle RNP	SO:0000590	Structural
vault_RNA	RNA component of the vault RNP	SO:0000404	Structural
Y_RNA	RNA component of the Ro RNP	SO:0000404	Structural
circRNA	circular RNA from backspliced exons or intron	SO:0000405	Regulatory
other	ncRNA_class not included in any other term	SO:0002291	Others

antisense RNAs); and long ncRNAs (lncRNAs), which encompass both structural and functionally uncharacterized transcripts.

The inherent functions of RNA itself have gained attention after an intronic region was discovered from the hint of unexpected length of mature mRNA in 1977 [3]. Then, Sanger sequencing technology enabled RNA biologists to identify unknown RNA fragments more easily. The first discovery of miRNAs was in 1993, followed by the foundational study of siRNA and RNAi in 1998 [41]. Currently, small regulatory RNAs, particularly miRNAs, are widely acknowledged to play crucial roles across diverse biological pathways in mammalian cells, such as stem cell [42], cell death [43], cancer [44], or innate immune response [45]. Due to the diversity of their target transcripts and easy control of their expression, miRNAs have been actively applied to cellular engineering, such as RNAi for gene knockdown [46] or miRNA switch for miRNA-responsive cell purification system [47].

On the other hand, functional assays, including structural motif search, are still ongoing for lncRNAs. Subsequent to the discovery of small regulatory RNAs, a wide variety of ncRNAs of different lengths have been identified. For example, several long regulatory RNAs, meiRNA, hsrω, roX1 and roX2, and H19 and XIST are well known for their important roles across diverse species, tissues, and conditions [48]. By comprehensive RNA sequencing analysis, pervasive expression of lncRNAs is now generally accepted, as an enormous number of human lncRNAs have been registered in public databases, such as 15,767 lncRNAs in GENCODE Release 25 [49] or 96,308 lncRNA genes in NONCODEV5 [50]. Due to the weak constraint for their function and structure, lncRNAs are known to have evolved rapidly in general, which makes it difficult to find a common sequential or structural motif for annotation.

Nevertheless, several cases have already demonstrated that RNA structure can directly contribute to lncRNA function. COOLAIR is the lncRNA that regulates FLC transcription and flowering time in *Arabidopsis thaliana*. Recently, their in vivo structure was directly determined by the single-molecule-based RNA structure profiling method for a systematic characterization of the COOLAIR transcript isoforms [51]. Interestingly, an increase in large bulges and adjacent helices enhances COOLAIR–FLC chromatin association, thereby accelerating flowering potentially. Their finding suggests that lncRNA conformational changes may play a functional role in plant environmental responses. While this is a particularly notable and successful example, many lncRNAs are known to have conserved co-expression patterns, cell-type specificity, and partially conserved regions within the sequences [52, 53], where core secondary structure motifs are predicted based on lncRNA consensus sequences and their functionality has been actively investigated. Furthermore, high-throughput perturbation techniques using antisense oligonucleotides and CRISPRi have opened the door to experimental lncRNA annotation [54, 55].

These studies have begun to reveal cell-type-specific regulatory mechanisms of lncRNAs and demonstrate that loss of lncRNA function can markedly affect cell growth in a cell-type-dependent manner.

Among diverse ncRNA classes, certain ones exhibit a strong enrichment of repetitive sequences, making the estimated number of ncRNA transcripts ambiguous when using short-read sequencing. However, long-read sequencing technologies developed by Oxford Nanopore Technologies (ONT) and Pacific Biosciences (PacBio), which have recently emerged, are expected to drive major innovations in ncRNA research. For instance, telomere-to-telomere (T2T) genome assemblies constructed by taking advantage of both long-read sequencing platforms have resolved most of the gaps in repetitive regions of the human reference genome [56]. Differences in the numbers of ncRNA genes annotated in RefSeq between the GRCh38 (reference constructed by short-read sequencing) and T2T CHM13 genome assemblies are summarized in Fig. 4, where two different algorithms LiftOff [56] and LiftOn [57] are applied. Most ncRNA classes show an increased number of transcripts in T2T CHM13 compared with GRCh38, except for two classes: snoRNA and ncRNA. Notably, the increase in rRNA is particularly drastic, and the number of Y RNA genes has also risen from four to seven. In fact,

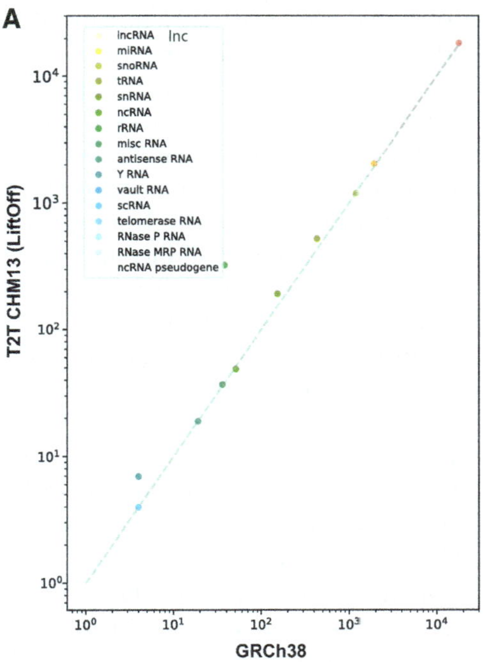

B

	GRCh38	T2T CHM13	
Non-coding RNA class	LiftOff	LiftOff	LiftOn
lncRNA	17793	18389	18723
miRNA	1914	2047	2383
snoRNA	1195	1188	1187
tRNA	431	522	548
snRNA	153	192	192
ncRNA	51	49	49
rRNA	38	325	-
misc RNA	36	37	44
antisense RNA	19	19	19
Y RNA	4	7	7
vault RNA	4	4	4
scRNA	4	4	4
telomerase RNA	1	1	1
RNase P RNA	1	1	1
RNase MRP RNA	1	1	1
ncRNA pseudogene	1	1	-

Fig. 4 (**A**) and (**B**) Difference in the number of ncRNA genes mapped on GRCh38 and T2T CHM13. (**A**) Gene count comparison between GRCh38 and T2T CHM13 v2 using the LiftOff program. (**B**) Gene count summary for GRCh38 and T2T CHM13 v2 with Refseq annotation release 110 using LiftOff [60] and T2T CHM13 with Refseq release 220 using the LiftOn program [61]. Each data point is obtained from the statistics from [62] and [63]

only four Y RNA genes—collectively referred to as hY genes—are characterized in the human genome. They are all localized within a single chromosomal locus on chr7q36 [57] and have been implicated in cancer proliferation. However, nearly 1,000 hY pseudogenes are scattered across all chromosomes [58]. In the T2T annotated gene list, three additional hY-like genes appear on chr12, 14, and 20, identified by the LiftOff program with a threshold of >95% sequence identity, whereas their concrete functions still remain unclear. On the other hand, rRNAs are a representative example of highly repetitive genes and are not well annotated in GRCh38 main chromosomes. Among different rRNA genes, RNA5S is the only rDNA encoded on chr1, and other rRNA components are produced from RNA45S genes located in nucleolar organizer regions (NORs) on chr13, 14, 15, 21, and 22 [59]. Their copy numbers vary widely among individuals, ranging from 1–3 to more than 140 per NOR [61]. The sequence diversity of rDNAs has thus inevitably been overlooked in many sequencing analyses. In the T2T genome, 99 RNA5S are found on chr1, and 226 non-overlapped rDNA regions are detected in other chromosomes, in total 325 rDNA copies. Accumulating accurate libraries of polymorphic high-copy-number sequences, such as rRNAs, will help elucidate conformational diversity and its relationship to function, not only in the coding transcript isoforms but also in human polymorphic ncRNAs.

2.3 Secondary Structure of Coding RNAs

Even in coding RNAs, various RNA secondary structure motifs are known to be functional and associated with diverse biological regulations of mRNAs, including splicing and editing, transport and localization, translation, and stability [64–66]. However, the prediction of global structure is not practical for coding RNAs because of limited prediction accuracy and the heavy computational cost for long sequences [67]. Instead, analyses of relatively longer RNA sequences often focus on local structural accessibility and specific motif distribution rather than global structure prediction [68, 69]. By investigating secondary structure motifs enriched in the groups of RNAs that are under post-transcriptional regulation, key regulatory motifs have been also identified [70], many of which overlap with RBP binding sites [71]. Therefore, combining structure prediction methods with experimental data from Cross-Linking Immunoprecipitation (CLIP)-seq and complementary approaches provides a robust framework for elucidating the mechanisms of post-transcriptional regulation mediated by RNA structure [72, 73]. ML models trained for CLIP data have demonstrated the importance of both primary and secondary structures for RNA-RBP interactions [74, 75]. Furthermore, cutting-edge deep generative models for designing mRNAs with enhanced translation and stability have also revealed that they can automatically recapitulate structural tendencies of efficient RNAs, such as high accessibility in the 5′UTR and stronger structural constraints in the CDS.

Collectively, these studies pave the way for a more comprehensive understanding of post-transcriptional regulation mediated by RNA secondary structure through the integration of structural prediction and high-throughput experiments, leveraging the power of ML and AI.

3 Methods

In this chapter, we introduce different approaches to explore the function of RNAs through their conformational characteristics. To cover a wide variety of RNA functional analysis, we pick up three different structure analyses: (1) RNA secondary structure prediction from the sequence, (2) RNA secondary structure prediction by the sequence and structure probing data, and (3) de novo RNA design for desired structural folding as an example of a deep learning-based AI application for cell engineering.

3.1 RNA Structure Prediction From the Sequence

As a sample sequence, we used a *Homosapiens* tRNA-His sequence and its reference structure for single-molecule structure prediction (RNAcentral ID is URS000001FD4B_9606 [76]). For RNA-RNA interaction, a miRNA-lncRNA interaction between hsa-miR-873-5p and *H. sapiens* growth arrest specific 5 (GAS5) transcript variant 1 was predicted and visualized [77].

ViennaRNA

ViennaRNA [9] is one of the most widely used integrated platforms for RNA secondary structure analyses. In addition to traditional installation of the source code, it now supports Conda and pip interfaces to simplify the setup process. Moreover, their web server includes more than 20 ready-to-use online services for RNA structure studies. For predicting secondary structures from nucleotide sequences, **RNAfold** [78] is undoubtedly the first choice due to its high feasibility. A simple command is sufficient to predict the minimum free energy (MFE) structure, which represents the most thermodynamically stable conformation among all possible structures (Fig. 5A).

```
RNAfold < tRNA.fa
>tRNA
GUAAAUAUAGUUUAACCAAAACAUCAGAUUGUGAAUCUGACAACA-
GAGGCUUAUGGCCCCUUAUUUACC
(((((((..((((.....)))).(((((((...))))))).....((.((((...
)))).))))))))). (-12.60)
```

Then, it is also important to examine the MEA (maximum expected accuracy) and γ-centroid structures as follows, since the MFE structure may represent only one of many possible conformations and can sometimes have an extremely low probability. These alternative representations provide more reliable insights about the conformational ensemble in vivo rather than focusing solely on the single structure.

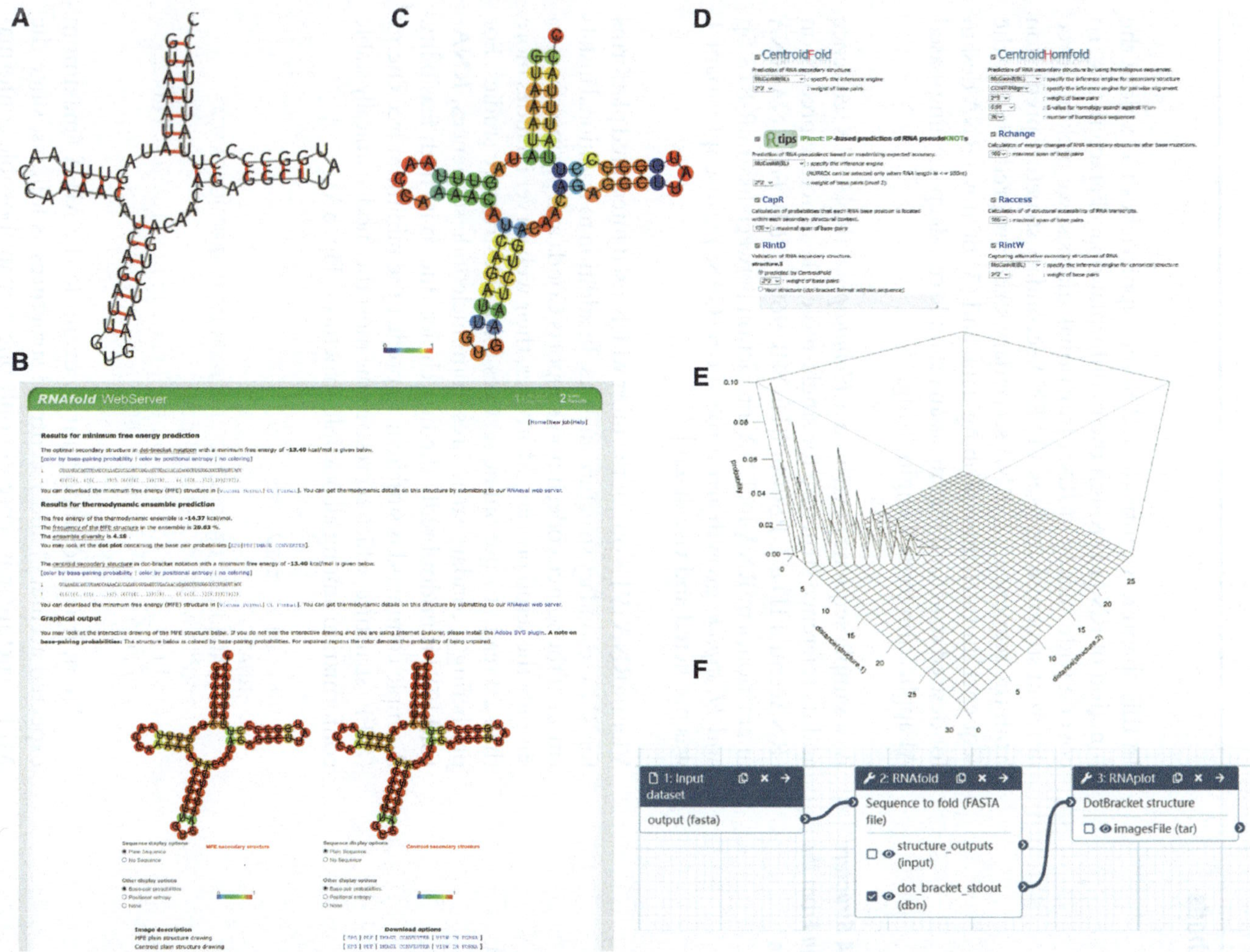

Fig. 5 RNA secondary structure prediction of human tRNA-His. (**A**) Predicted secondary structure by RNAfold. (**B**) RNAfold output visualized on the RNAfold web server. (**C**) Predicted γ-centroid structure by Rtools. (**D**) Screenshot of the Rtools interface. (**E**) RintD output comparing two structures. (**F**) Galaxy RNA workbench graphical user interface

```
RNAfold -MEA -d2 -p
CGACGUAGAUGCUAGCUGACUCGAUGC
(((.((((.......)).)))))....
minimum free energy = -1.90 kcal/mol
(((.((((.......))},})))....
free energy of ensemble = -2.86 kcal/mol
(((.(.((.......))..)))).... { 0.80 d=2.81}
(((.((((.......))).)))).... { -1.90 MEA=22.32}
frequency of mfe structure in ensemble 0.20997;
ensemble diversity 4.19
```

Using RNAfold webserver (http://rna.tbi.univie.ac.at//cgi-bin/RNAWebSuite/RNAfold.cgi), both the MFE and centroid structures can be visualized with color schemes indicating base pair probabilities (Fig. 5B, C). In addition, a mountain plot is provided to examine positional entropy, allowing users to assess the structural variability. To take advantage of recent ML developments, you can switch energy parameter models from a traditional thermodynamic-based model to a data-driven optimized one.

Rtools

Rtools [10] is another integrative platform to analyze the structural characteristics of RNA from multiple perspectives (http://rtools.cbrc.jp/). In this platform, highly accessible regions and potential pseudoknot regions are predicted and visualized by **Raccess** [79], **CentroidFold,** and **IPknot** [80, 81], respectively (Fig. 5D). Moreover, **RintD** and **RintW** results enable us to validate the reliability of predicted structures and explore the stable alternative structures, by comparing CentroidFold and RNAfold-based predictions (Fig. 5E), and potential alternative structures by decomposing the base pairing probability matrix. You can install each method locally for more detailed analysis as well.

Galaxy RNA Workbench

Galaxy is an open-source web-based platform for bioinformatics, freely accessible and licensed for both academic and commercial use. The Galaxy RNA workbench provides a collection of tools for RNA secondary structure analysis [11]. The latest release, **RNA Galaxy workbench 2** (https://rna.usegalaxy.eu/), offers a user-friendly interface via the European Galaxy server. For users familiar with Docker, the entire workbench can also be run locally using the provided Docker image. Within this platform, eight tools dedicated to RNA structure prediction and analysis are available, along with essential utilities for RNA-seq data processing, annotation, and interactome analysis. A distinctive feature of Galaxy is its interpretable workflow interface, which allows users to intuitively connect the input and output of different tools (Fig. 5F). In the example shown, an input FASTA file uploaded to the server is processed sequentially by RNAfold and RNAplot, as demonstrated in Sect. 1.1. This platform is helpful for integrating transcriptomic and structural analysis aiming at functional RNA annotation.

IntaRNA

Beyond single-molecule structure prediction, predicting RNA-RNA complex structures is crucial for understanding the functions and interactions of RNA molecules. For RNA-RNA interaction analysis, two major strategies are possible: one jointly folds two interacting molecules to obtain a common secondary structure [82], while the other models the interaction free energy as the summation of the opening and hybridization energies of the interacting regions [83]. In ViennaRNA, for instance, **RNAcofold** implements the former [84], whereas **RNAup** employs the latter approach [85]. Because its primary application is to identify interaction sites between a long target RNA and a short query RNA, **IntaRNA** employs the second strategy but with some heuristics to make the runtime much shorter, such as seed-and-extend search features and sparsification for the extended hybridization energy matrix. Rtools, on the other hand, provides a link to access **Rtips** [86], where fast RNA–RNA interaction analysis can be performed by a different approach, integer programming, using **RactIP** [87].

IntaRNA web server is provided as part of the Freiburg RNA tools (https://rna.informatik.uni-freiburg.de/IntaRNA/). By providing a short RNA sequence (e.g., bacterial sRNAs or eukaryotic miRNAs) as a query and long RNA sequences (e.g., mRNAs) as a target, IntaRNA evaluates RNA-RNA interactions between each query-target pair (Fig. 6). Position-wise minimal energy profiles can serve as valuable clues for exploring potential sequence-wide RNA-RNA affinities avoiding the stable internal base pairs, particularly in cases where multiple distant regions may interact with another RNA. For researchers interested in specific types of RNA-RNA interactions, precomputed databases such as **TargetScan** (miRNA and mRNA interaction) [88] and **LncRRIsearch** (lncRNAs and mRNA) [89] are also available.

3.2 RNA Structure Prediction with Structure Probing Data

As previously discussed, in silico structure prediction is a powerful approach for RNA functional analysis, whereas its results can sometimes show large discrepancies from in vivo folding due to RNA modifications, interference by other molecules, or inaccuracies in folding models. These limitations have prompted researchers to apply additional data-driven refinement steps to achieve more accurate structure prediction. This is particularly critical for RNA species that are heavily modified in vivo. For example, the secondary structure prediction of deprotenized 16S rRNA from *Escherichia coli* was dramatically improved from 46.2% positive predictive value (PPV) using a purely thermodynamic model to 95.1% when guided by structure probing data [90]. However, applying structure probing analysis to a pool of folding RNAs rather than to a purified RNA species increases the data sparseness and stochastic detection of reaction events, thereby amplifying the inherent noise in the obtained data. For that reason, balancing experimental and predicted base pairing probabilities in a supervised way is essential for reliable structure determination. Here,

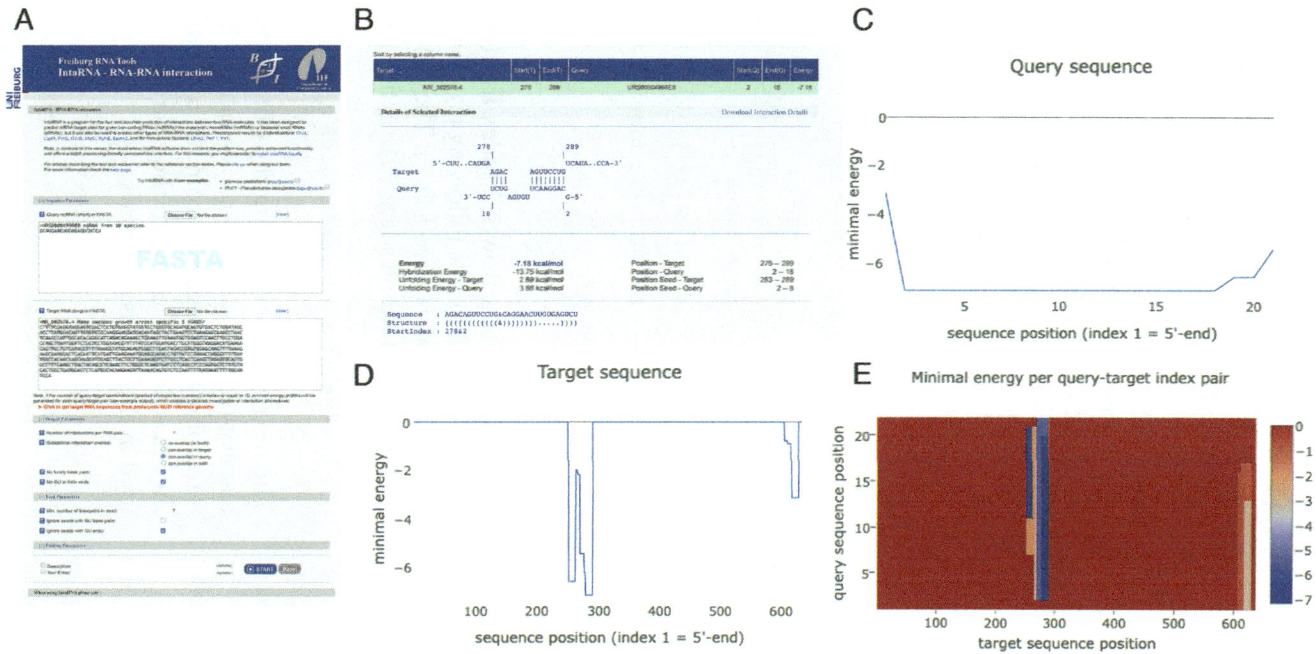

Fig. 6 IntaRNA interface and results. (**A**) Screenshot of the IntaRNA interface. (**B**) Example text output of a predicted interaction. (**C** and **D**) Minimal interaction energies of the query (**C**) and target (**D**) sequences. (**E**) Two-dimensional minimal energy landscape of the query and target sequences

we introduce a straightforward, manual protocol for data processing and structure prediction assisted by structure probing data, using **RNAFramework** [12].

Set-Up: Reference and Index Construction

RNAframework has been developed for rapid and interpretable analysis of general structure probing data, as well as for high-throughput mapping of post-transcriptional modifications. In the setup process, the reference RNA sequences to be mapped are prepared in FASTA format. For mutational profiling (MaP) approaches, including SHAPE-Map [91] and DMS-Map [92], untreated samples may not always be necessary.

In this example, we analyze SHAPE-MaP data for SreA RNA in the Sequence Read Archive (SRA) database, whose SRA ID is SRR30153238 for DMSO-treated (untreated) and SRR30153239 for 1-methyl-7-nitroisatoic anhydride (1m7)-treated (treated) samples [93]. The example starting directory structure is as follows:

```
.
├── index
├── input
│   ├── SreA.fasta
│   ├── SRR30153238.fastq # untreated sample
│   └── SRR30153239.fastq # treated sample
└── output
```

Next, create a Bowtie2 index from the reference FASTA file. This is required for the following processing step since Bowtie2 will be used internally (`-bowtie2`). The following command generates the Bowtie2 index files (e.g., `.bt2` files) in the `index/` directory:

```
bowtie2-build input/SreA.fasta index/SreA
```

Processing: Read-Count Normalization and Computation of Reactivity Scores

The next step is processing the obtained FASTQ files to compute reactivity scores using `rf-map` command. The key task in this process is to compare the signals from the treated and untreated reads after they have been mapped to the reference sequences. The command used in this step is as follows

```
rf-map -b2 -bi index/SreA input/SRR30153238.fastq
input/SRR30153239.fastq -ow -o output/rf-map
```

where the output directory is specified with the -o option. This will produce BAM files (`SRR30153239.bam` and `SRR30153238.bam`) and their respective index files (`SRR30153239.bam.bai` and `SRR30153238.bam.bai`) in the `output/rf-map/` folder.

Next, count the mutation frequencies at each position of the reference sequence for both the untreated and treated samples. Adding the -m option generates mutation frequencies. The reference file is specified with the -f option.

For untreated samples, the commands used are as follows.

```
rf-count -m -f input/SreA.fasta output/rf-map/
SRR30153238.bam -ow -o output/rf-count/
rf-count_SRR30153238
```

For treated samples, the commands are as follows.

```
rf-count -m -f input/SreA.fasta output/rf-map/
SRR30153239.bam -ow -o output/rf-count/
rf-count_SRR30153239
```

Each run outputs a .rc file containing mutation and coverage information, along with an accompanying index.rci file that stores reference index data. Subsequently, all .rc files are integrated to calculate per-base reactivity signals by comparing the mutation counts and read coverage between the treated and untreated sample. The resulting raw signal is then normalized using several customized normalization schemes, which can be specified with the -nm option.

```
rf-norm -sm 3 -nm 3 \
       -u output/rf-count/rf-count_SRR30153238/
SRR30153238.rc \
       -t output/rf-count/rf-count_SRR30153239/
SRR30153239.rc \
       -i output/rf-count/rf-count_SRR30153239/
index.rci \
       -ow -o output/rf-norm
```

Prediction: RNA Secondary-Structure Modeling Assisted by Reactivity Data

As mentioned in the beginning of Sect. 2.1, leveraging the computational structure prediction and experimentally observed data is a key to fully exploiting structure probing data. In RNAframework, this integration is achieved through three main steps. First, base pairs predicted with extremely high confidence (>99%) are retained as hard constraints for Step 3. Then, MFE structure prediction is performed with soft constraints incorporating the probing reactivity scores. Base pairs with moderate confidence (>50%) are also retained and carried forward to the next step. In that step, their pairing probabilities that are averaged across all windows in which they appear are used to select for further analysis. In the final step, pseudoknots are identified using the same algorithmic approach implemented in ShapeKnots [94]. Predicted pseudoknotted base-pairs are defined as a hit only if they appear in more than 50% of sliding windows and do not conflict with the base pairs predicted at the moderate-confidence threshold in the previous step.

The command to use rf-fold is as follows (Fig. 7).

```
rf-fold -g -w -pk -ow output/rf-norm -o output/
rf-fold
```

The final directory structure is as follows.

```
.
├── index
│   ├── SreA.1.bt2
│   ├── SreA.2.bt2
│   ├── SreA.3.bt2
│   ├── SreA.4.bt2
│   ├── SreA.rev.1.bt2
│   └── SreA.rev.2.bt2
├── input
│   ├── SreA.fasta
│   ├── SRR30153238.fastq
│   └── SRR30153239.fastq
└── output
    ├── rf-count
    │   ├── rf-count_SRR30153238
    │   │   ├── index.rci
    │   │   └── SRR30153238.rc
    │   └── rf-count_SRR30153239
    │       ├── index.rci
    │       └── SRR30153239.rc
    ├── rf-fold
    │   ├── images
    │   │   └── SreA.svg
    │   └── structures
    │       └── SreA.db
    ├── rf-map
    │   ├── SRR30153238.bam
    │   ├── SRR30153238.bam.bai
    │   ├── SRR30153239.bam
    │   └── SRR30153239.bam.bai
        └── rf-norm
            └── SreA.xml
```

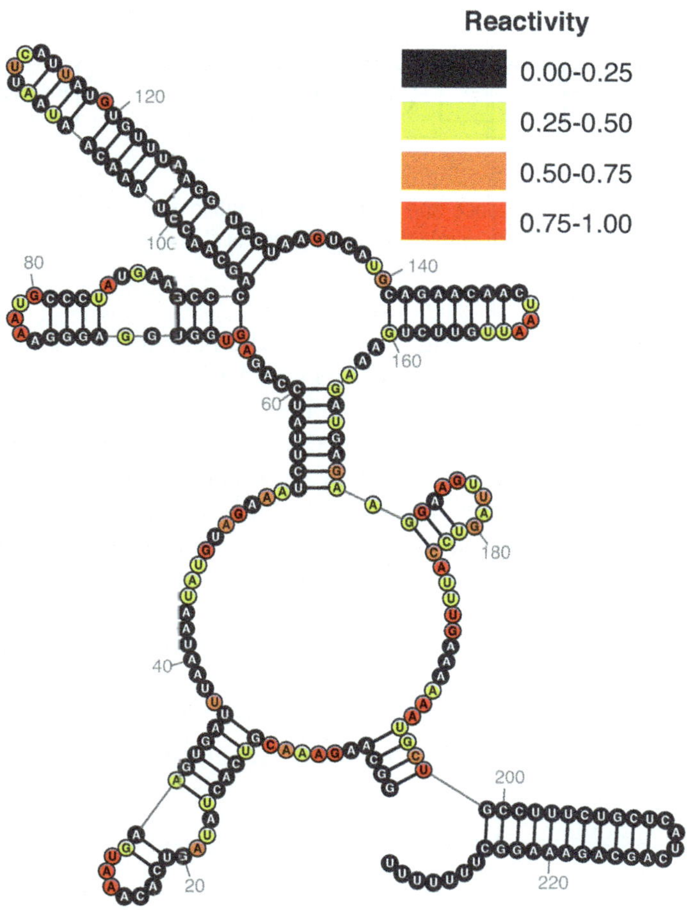

Fig. 7 The final predicted RNA secondary structure guided by SHAPE reactivity scores, visualized with RNACanvas [95]

3.3 Sequence Generation by RfamGen

RNA design is a rapidly developing area that aims to generate novel RNA sequences with desired secondary or tertiary structures, catalytic activities, or binding properties. Traditionally, RNA inverse folding methods have been used to identify sequences compatible with a given target structure through thermodynamic optimization or heuristic search. However, these conventional approaches often struggle to capture subtle covariation patterns or sequence–structure constraints encoded in RNA families. RNA family is a concept to summarize sequences with shared motifs and functions. Representative examples of RNA families are tRNA, ribosome, ribozymes, and so on. So far, over 4,000 RNA families have been reported in the Rfam database [28]. In this final section, we show an example protocol to generate or design RNA sequences, focusing on RNA family. **RfamGen** is one of the earliest methods for RNA design by ML [13], utilizing a variationalautoencoder (VAE) to generate new RNA sequences while training to mimic the training

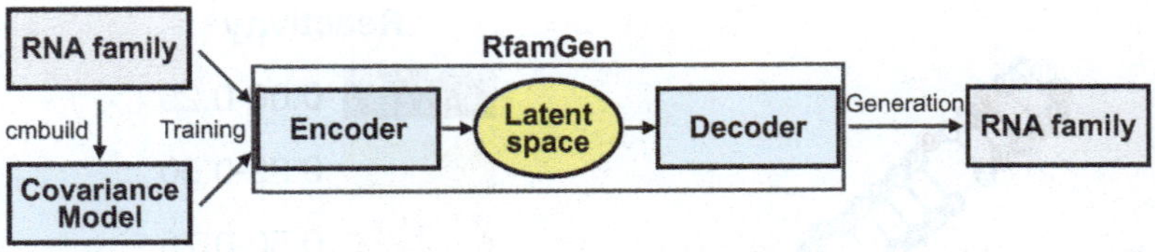

Fig. 8 Architecture of RfamGen. Sequence and structure information are used to train RfamGen through a covariance model. RfamGen is trained to mimic training data and is able to generate new sequences similar to training sequences

sequences (Fig. 8). One of the benefits of RfamGen is integration of the covariance model with VAE. Covariance model is a statistical model describing sequence and structure conservation of an RNA family by a tree-based Markov Model called stochastic context-free grammar [96, 97]. The covariance model has been used to identify RNA family sequences, but it has been rarely used to generate new functional sequences. RfamGen enhanced the generative capacity by information of sequence and structure through the covariance model.

Set Up the Environment

The environment of RfamGen is easy to build by using conda or mamba.

Here is an example code for set

```
git clone https://github.com/Shunsuke-1994/rfamgen.
git
cd rfamgen
mamba install -f requirements_rfamgen.yaml
mamba activate rfamgen
```

Convert a Stockholm File to a Covariance Model File

Another distinctive feature of RfamGen is to use the covariance model as a sequence- and structure-aware template of generation. The covariance model is constructed from a multiple sequence alignment (MSA) and its consensus structure by `cmbuild` of **Infernal** [98]. In this example, we use pistol ribozymes [99] in the ZashaWeinberg database (https://bitbucket.org/zashaw/zashaweinbergdata/src/master/ts/pistol.sto) for training of RfamGen.

```
git clone https://bitbucket.org/zashaw/
zashaweinbergdata.git
cd zashaweinbergdata/ts/
```

In the Stockholm-formatted file (`pistol.sto`), there is a structural annotation in the last line (the "#=GC SS_cons" line) as follows:

```
tail -n3 zashaweinbergdata/ts/pistol.sto
GSLNARP_GFPJP1N02HP-
7RG/65-131                          GGACGGCAG.AGCGU-
CC.CUAAAUA..GGCGU.UAAGCUCUG.CGCG.GGCGCC..............
.GACCACCG.................GGCGCC.GU.CGUU
#=GC SS_cons
          ««..AAA.AA.»».........««......
aaaaa.--.«««««««««««.........»»»»»»»»»»»....»»
//
```

When no secondary structure information is available, the consensus structure can be annotated in several ways, such as manual annotation, structure prediction, or experimental determinations by structure probing. For instance, **RNAalifold** [100] of ViennaRNA predicts a consensus structure from an MSA by integrating thermodynamics of RNA stability and evolutionary conservation. Optionally, RNAalifold is able to integrate structure probing data with `-shape` option. Here shows an example of structure estimation by RNAalifold.

```
RNAalifold -noPS -aln-
stk=zashaweinbergdata/ts/pistol_RNAalifold
zashaweinbergdata/ts/pistol.sto
# if you have structure probing data
RNAalifold -noPS -aln-
stk=zashaweinbergdata/ts/pistol_RNAalifold -shape
zashaweinbergdata/ts/test.shape zashaweinbergdata/
ts/pistol.sto


676 sequences; length of alignment 110.
>pistol
ACUCGUCUG_GGCGAGU_AUAAAUA__GUAAU_UAGGCCCAG_AGCG_
UCCCGGC___________
____GAUU_____________________GGCCGGGG_GU_UUAG
.....((((.(((.....................))))))).)....((((((((((.........
.........................))))))))))........ (-27.12 = -21.26
+ -5.86)
```

RNAalifold with the `-aln-stk=pistol_RNAalifold` option generates a new Stockholm file `pistol_RNAalifold.sto` with the predicted consensus structure as follows

```
tail -n4 zashaweinbergdata/ts/pistol_RNAalifold.stk
GSLNARP_GFPJP1N02HP7RG/65-131
     GGACGGCAG-AGCGUCC-
CUAAAUA-GGCGU-UAAGCUCUG-CGCG-
GGCGCC_____________________
GACCACCG____________________GGCGCC-GU-CGUU
#=GC RF
ACUCGUCUG_GGCGAGU_AUAAAUA__GUAAU_UAGGCCCAG_AGCG_
UCCCGGC_______________GAUU____________________
GGCCGGGG_GU_UUAG
#=GC SS_cons
.....((((.(((.....................))))))).)....((((((((((.........
...... ..................))))))))))........
//
```

A file of the covariance model (`.cm` file) of pistol ribozyme can be constructed by cmbuild command of Infernal follows:

```
cmbuild zashaweinbergdata/ts/pistol.cm
zashaweinbergdata/ts/pistol.sto
```

RfamGen learns one-hot encoded HDF5 datasets derived from Infernal traceback information aligned to the covariance model file. The repository of RfamGen provides scripts that wrap the required steps:

```
# (0. prepare fasta file using esl-reformat in
HMMER)
esl-reformat fasta zashaweinbergdata/ts/pistol.sto
>
zashaweinbergdata/ts/pistol.fasta


# 1. Align sequences to the CM
# this command generates a stockholm file with the
same basename
python scripts/run_cmalign.py \
        -fasta zashaweinbergdata/ts/pistol.fasta \
        -cmfile zashaweinbergdata/ts/pistol.cm \
        -cpu 4


# 2. Convert traceback to one-hot representation
python scripts/make_onehot_from_traceback.py \
        -traceback zashaweinbergdata/ts/pistol_
notrunc_traceback.txt.gz \
        -cmfile zashaweinbergdata/ts/pistol.cm


# 3. Split into train/validation/test sets
python scripts/split_onehot_train_valid_test.py \
        -i zashaweinbergdata/ts/pistol_notrunc_
traceback_onehot_cm.h5 \
        -train_ratio 0.7
```

Optionally, to reduce redundancy and prevent over-representation of similar sequences, sequence-specific weights can be generated (for training and validation data):

```
python scripts/generate_weight.py \
        -mode cm \
        -i zashaweinbergdata/ts/pistol_notrunc_
traceback_onehot_cm_train.h5 \
        -threshold 0.1 \
        -o zashaweinbergdata/ts/pistol_train_weight.
h5
```

Train the VAE Model

RfamGen utilizes the VAE architecture, which has the internal space representing the data, called latent space (Fig. 8). RfamGen is trained to approximate the data distribution in the latent space to a Gaussian distribution, while trained to recover the training sequences from the latent space. Training is initiated using `scripts/train.py`. The key parameters here are the latent-space dimension (`-z_dim`), learning rate, and β term for Kullback-Leibler Divergence regularization.

```
python scripts/train.py \
      -data_dir zashaweinbergdata/ts/ \
      -X_train pistol_notrunc_traceback_onehot_cm_
train.h5 \
      -w_train pistol_train_weight.h5 \
      -X_valid pistol_notrunc_traceback_onehot_cm_
valid.h5 \
      -w_valid pistol_valid_weight.h5 \
      -beta 1e-3 -epoch 200 -batch_size 8 -z_dim
16 \
      -learning_rate 1e-3 -use_early_stopping \
      -log -log_dir./outputs/pistol -save_ckpt -
ckpt_iter 5
```

This command trains the VAE and saves a config file of the model, intermediate checkpoints, and the final model under `./outputs/pistol/`.

Generate Sequences by RfamGen

After training, new RNA sequences similar to the training data can be generated by sampling from the learned latent space using a Gaussian distribution:

```
python scripts/sampling_from_gauss.py \
     -config./outputs/pistol/config.yaml \
     -ckpt./outputs/pistol/model_epoch23.pt \
     -cmfile zashaweinbergdata/ts/pistol.cm \
     -outfasta./outputs/pistol/pistol_generated.
fasta \
     -n_samples 1000
```

The resulting file `pistol_generated.fa` contains de novo RNA sequences that conform to the family covariance model while preserving learned covariation features.

```
head -n2 outputs/pistol/pistol_generated.fasta
>seq0
ACUCGAUCAGGCGAGUAUAAACAGGCAUUAGGCCUAGUGCGUCCGGGCUGU
AUUAACGGCCCGGGGUUGCA
```

By briefly checking on Rfam database [28], the generated sequence #0 is recognized as pistol ribozyme (Fig. 9A). Instead, you can use `cmsearch` or `cmalign` to quantify the pistol-ribozyme-likeliness.

Visualization with R2R

Next, we visualize the conservation of natural and generated pistol ribozymes with R2R [101]. Because R2R takes a Stockholm file as input, the generated sequences need to be aligned.

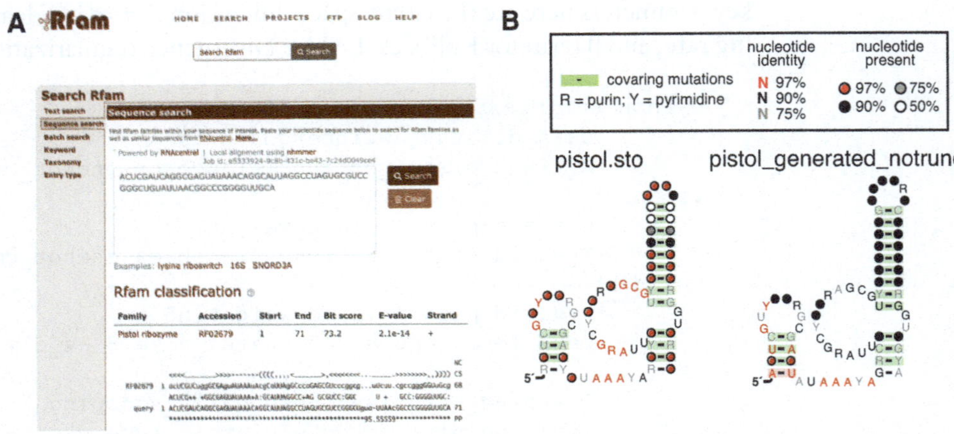

Fig. 9 (**A**) Rfam database interface and sequence search results. Screenshot of the Rfam database shows the generated sequence from RfamGen is recognized as a pistol ribozyme. (**B**) R2R visualization of the training (left) and generated (right) sequences. The annotations on the secondary structures reflect the conservation degrees of nucleotides and base pairs as shown in the box

```
python scripts/run_cmalign.py \
        -fasta outputs/pistol/pistol_generated.fa \
        -cmfile zashaweinbergdata/ts/pistol.cm -cpu 4
```

The environment of R2R can be set up as follows.

```
mamba create -n r2r && mamba activate r2r
mamba install -c bioconda r2r
mamba deactivate
```

Then, edit the PATH in the `scripts/r2r.py`

```
os.environ["PATH"] = "/path_to_mamba/envs/r2r/bin/
r2r"
```

Finally, this wrapper script of R2R generates the consensus diagrams (Fig. 9B).

```
# training sequences
python scripts/r2r.py \
        -i zashaweinbergdata/ts/pistol.sto \
        -o zashaweinbergdata/ts/pistol.r2r.pdf
# generated sequences
python scripts/r2r.py \
        -i outputs/pistol/pistol_generated_notrunc.
sto \
        -o outputs/pistol/pistol_generated_notrunc.
r2r.pdf
```

As shown in Fig. 9B, the generated sequences showed similar nucleotide and base pair conservation to the training sequences. Although some minor differences in nucleotide conservation can be observed, this may be improved by applying alternative sampling strategies rather than relying on the latent space because the underlying data distribution is not always well approximated by Gaussian. Besides, if you have any extra annotations (e.g., catalytic activity or sequence features) of the training sequences, you can get the sequences of interest based on sampling from the close coordinations of the target annotations in the latent space. Thereby, RfamGen can be used to engineer or design RNA family sequences with desired properties.

4 Notes

Currently, compared to a drastic improvement of protein 3D folding by AI-based technology, an accurate prediction of RNA 3D structure, or even RNA 3D motif prediction, is still challenging [102, 103]. Nevertheless, the importance of RNA 3D structure has grown rapidly due to the potential of RNA oligos for drug discovery and the development of a vaccine. The largest difference between RNA and protein 3D structure prediction is the number of available "correct" structures in the database [104]. As of 2025, around 2,000 entries are RNA-only structures, while those of protein-only are almost 202,000 in PDB. A new methodology for structure analysis, such as cryo-electron microscopy (EM) or atomic force microscope (AFM) [105, 106], will overcome the data sparsity and realize more practical RNA 3D structure prediction.

It is worth noting that most of the RNA structure analysis tools consider RNA is primarily composed of the base sequence ACGU. But in some limited biological conditions, other types of bases, such as inosine and xanthine triphosphates, have been observed to be incorporated into DNA and RNA as a rare base [107]. Since the current sequencing technology cannot capture those events without customizing an experimental protocol for targeting each rare base, their conformational influences are almost ignored for their potential impact [108–110]. Besides, a variety of modifications have been directly introduced to RNA bases, which may be endogenous or artificially created to reduce the immune reaction. Those changes potentially disrupt a local structure [111]. In fact, inosine bases are known to involve a wobble base pair (I-U, I-A, and I-C). To overcome the problem of in vivo modification and rare base inclusion, direct RNA sequencing technology is a promising technology as its base and modification detection accuracy has been improved [112].

Lastly, many generative modeling approaches other than RfamGen have recently been proposed. While RfamGen focuses on the MSA of structured RNAs, some frameworks are designed to be more flexible without demanding either an MSA or explicit RNA structural information. For example, GenerRNA is a framework that generates raw RNA sequences using a large language model based on GPT-2 [113]. However, generative modeling of RNA is still an emerging and immature technology that requires further improvement, and thus, continued efforts to combine careful experimental validation with in silico design are still needed.

Acknowledgments

SS is supported by JST ACT-X JPMJAX24L8 and JSPS KAKENHI Grant Number 24K23175. FI is supported by JSPS KAKENHI Grant Number 24KJ1491. HS and RKK were supported by JP24bm1323001. HS is supported by JST (CREST) Grant Number JPMJCR23B3 and Japan Agency for Medical Research and Development (AMED) Grant Numbers JP23bm1323001, JP23bm1223002, JP23bm1123040. RKK was supported by JST ACT-X JPMJAX24L5, JSPS KAKENHI Grant Number 23K14165, AMED Grant Number JP23bm1323001, and the iPS Cell Research Fund from the Center for iPS Cell Research and Application, Kyoto University.

Conflict of Interest The authors have no conflicts of interest to declare that are relevant to the content of this chapter.

References

1. Zhou X, Liao WJ, Liao JM, Liao P, Lu H (2015) Ribosomal proteins: functions beyond the ribosome. J Mol Cell Biol 7(2):92–104
2. Rivas E (2021) Evolutionary conservation of RNA sequence and structure. Wiley Interdiscip Rev: RNA 12(5):e1649
3. Mattick JS, Makunin IV (2006) Non-coding RNA. Hum Mol Genet 15(suppl_1):R17–R29
4. Wightman B, Ha I, Ruvkun G (1993) Posttranscriptional regulation of the heterochronic gene lin-14 by lin-4 mediates temporal pattern formation in C. elegans. Cell 75(5):855–862
5. Lee RC, Feinbaum RL, Ambros V (1993) The C. elegans heterochronic gene lin-4 encodes small RNAs with antisense complementarity to lin-14. Cell 75(5):843–854
6. Kozomara A, Birgaoanu M, Griffiths-Jones S (2019) miRBase: from microRNA sequences to function. Nucleic Acids Res 47(D1):D155–D162
7. Hu HY, Yan Z, Xu Y, Hu H, Menzel C, Zhou YH et al. (2009) Sequence features associated with microRNA strand selection in humans and flies. BMC Genomics 10: 413
8. Sato K, Hamada M (2023) Recent trends in RNA informatics: a review of machine learning and deep learning for RNA secondary structure prediction and RNA drug discovery. Brief Bioinform 24(4):bbad186
9. Lorenz R, Bernhart SH, Höner Zu Siederdissen C, Tafer H, Flamm C, Stadler PF et al. (2011) ViennaRNA Package 2.0. Algorithms Mol Biol 6:26. 24
10. Ono Y, Asai K (2023) Rtools: a web server for various secondary structural analyses on single RNA sequences. Methods Mol Biol 2586:1–14
11. Grüning BA, Fallmann J, Yusuf D, Will S, Erxleben A, Eggenhofer F et al. (2017) The RNA workbench: best practices for RNA and high-throughput sequencing bioinformatics in Galaxy. Nucleic Acids Res 45(W1):W560–W566
12. Incarnato D, Morandi E, Simon LM, Oliviero S (2018) RNA framework: an all-in-one toolkit for the analysis of RNA structures and post-transcriptional modifications. Nucleic Acids Res 46(16):e97
13. Sumi S, Hamada M, Saito H (2024) Deep generative design of RNA family sequences. Nat Methods 21(3):435–443
14. Wayment-Steele HK, Kladwang W, Strom AI, Lee J, Treuille A, Becka A et al. (2022) RNA secondary structure packages evaluated and improved by high-throughput experiments. Nat Methods 19(10):1234–1242

15. Zablocki LI, Bugnon LA, Gerard M, Di Persia L, Stegmayer G, Milone DH (2025) Comprehensive benchmarking of large language models for RNA secondary structure prediction. Brief Bioinform 26(2):bbaf137
16. Puton T, Kozlowski LP, Rother KM, Bujnicki JM (2014) CompaRNA: a server for continuous benchmarking of automated methods for RNA secondary structure prediction. Nucleic Acids Res 42(8):5403–5406
17. Bu F, Adam Y, Adamiak RW, Antczak M, de Aquino BRH, Badepally NG et al. (2025) RNA-puzzles round V: blind predictions of 23 RNA structures. Nat Methods 22(2):399–411
18. Kretsch RC, Hummer AM, He S, Yuan R, Zhang J, Karagianes T et al (2025) Assessment of nucleic acid structure prediction in CASP16. bioRxiv. 2025.05.06.652459
19. Zhang J, Fei Y, Sun L, Zhang QC (2022) Advances and opportunities in RNA structure experimental determination and computational modeling. Nat Methods 19(10):1193–1207
20. Cao X, Zhang Y, Ding Y, Wan Y (2024) Identification of RNA structures and their roles in RNA functions. Nat Rev Mol Cell Biol 25(10):784–801
21. Yang S, Pham NT, Li Z, Baik JY, Lee J, Zhai T et al (2025) Advances in RNA secondary structure prediction and RNA modifications: methods, data, and applications. arXiv. 2501.04056
22. Zhang J, Yuan R, Kryshtafovych A, Kretsch RC, Schaeffer RD, Zhou J et al (2025) Assessment of protein complex predictions in CASP16: are we making progress? bioRxiv. 2025.05.29.656875
23. Nithin C, Kmiecik S, Błaszczyk R, Nowicka J, Tuszyńska I (2024) Comparative analysis of RNA 3D structure prediction methods: towards enhanced modeling of RNA-ligand interactions. Nucleic Acids Res 52(13):7465–7486
24. Karan A, Rivas E (2025) All-at-once RNA folding with 3D motif prediction framed by evolutionary information. Nat Methods 22(10):2094–2106
25. Leontis NB, Stombaugh J, Westhof E (2002) The non-Watson-Crick base pairs and their associated isostericity matrices Nucleic Acids Res 30(16):3497–3531
26. Petrov AS, Bernier CR, Hershkovits E, Xue Y, Waterbury CC, Hsiao C et al. (2013) Secondary structure and domain architecture of the 23S and 5S rRNAs. Nucleic Acids Res 41(15):7522–7535
27. Danaee P, Rouches M, Wiley M, Deng D, Huang L, Hendrix D (2018) bpRNA: large-scale automated annotation and analysis of RNA secondary structure. Nucleic Acids Res 46(11):5381–5394
28. Ontiveros-Palacios N, Cooke E, Nawrocki EP, Triebel S, Marz M, Rivas E et al. (2025) Rfam 15: RNA families database in 2025. Nucleic Acids Res 53(D1):D258–D267
29. Dominguez D, Freese P, Alexis MS, Su A, Hochman M, Palden T et al. (2018) Sequence, structure, and context preferences of human RNA binding proteins. Mol Cell 70(5):854–867.e9
30. Fukunaga T, Ozaki H, Terai G, Asai K, Iwasaki W, Kiryu H (2014) CapR: revealing structural specificities of RNA-binding protein target recognition using CLIP-seq data. Genome Biol 15(1):R16
31. Brierley I, Pennell S, Gilbert RJC (2007) Viral RNA pseudoknots: versatile motifs in gene expression and replication. Nat Rev Microbiol 5(8):598–610
32. Sato K, Kato Y (2022) Prediction of RNA secondary structure including pseudoknots for long sequences. Brief Bioinform 23(1):bbab395
33. Baba S, Takahashi KI, Noguchi S, Takaku H, Koyanagi Y, Yamamoto N et al. (2005) Solution RNA structures of the HIV-1 dimerization initiation site in the kissing-loop and extended-duplex dimers. J Biochem 138(5):583–592
34. Huang L, Lilley DMJ (2016) The kink turn, a key architectural element in RNA structure. J Mol Biol 428(5 Pt A):790–801
35. Saito H, Kobayashi T, Hara T, Fujita Y, Hayashi K, Furushima R et al. (2010) Synthetic translational regulation by an L7Ae-kink-turn RNP switch. Nat Chem Biol 6(1):71–78
36. Correll CC, Swinger K (2003) Common and distinctive features of GNRA tetraloops based on a GUAA tetraloop structure at 1.4 A resolution. RNA 9(3):355–363
37. Varshney D, Spiegel J, Zyner K, Tannahill D, Balasubramanian S (2020) The regulation and functions of DNA and RNA G-quadruplexes. Nat Rev Mol Cell Biol 21(8):459–474
38. Vlieghe D, Van Meervelt L, Dautant A, Gallois B, Précigoux G, Kennard O (1996) Parallel and antiparallel (G.GC)2 triple helix fragments in a crystal structure. Science 273(5282):1702–1705
39. Bohdan DR, Voronina VV, Bujnicki JM, Baulin EF (2023) A comprehensive survey of long-range tertiary interactions and motifs in non-coding RNA structures. Nucleic Acids Res 51(16):8367–8382
40. International Nucleotide Sequence Database Collaboration (2017). https://www.insdc.org/submitting-standards/ncrna-vocabulary/ Accessed Oct 2025

41. Fire A, Xu S, Montgomery MK, Kostas SA, Driver SE, Mello CC (1998) Potent and specific genetic interference by double-stranded RNA in caenorhabditis elegans. Nature 391(6669):806–811
42. Phinney DG and Gallicano GI (2011) The emerging role of microRNAs in adult stem cells. In: Phinney D (ed) Adult stem cells. stem cell biology and regenerative medicine. Humana Press
43. Jovanovic M, Hengartner MO (2006) miRNAs and apoptosis: RNAs to die for. Oncogene 25(46):6176–6187
44. Peng Y, Croce CM (2016) The role of MicroRNAs in human cancer. Signal Transduct Target Ther 1(1):1–9
45. Takahashi T, Nakano Y, Onomoto K, Yoneyama M, Ui-Tei K (2020) LGP2 virus sensor enhances apoptosis by upregulating apoptosis regulatory genes through TRBP-bound miRNAs during viral infection. Nucleic Acids Res 48(3):1494–1507
46. Lam JKW, Chow MYT, Zhang Y, Leung SWS (2015) siRNA versus miRNA as therapeutics for gene silencing. Mol Ther Nucleic Acids 4(9):e252
47. Fujita Y, Hirosawa M, Hayashi K, Hatani T, Yoshida Y, Yamamoto T et al. (2022) A versatile and robust cell purification system with an RNA-only circuit composed of microRNA-responsive ON and OFF switches. Sci Adv 8(1):eabj1793
48. Mattick JS, Amaral PP, Carninci P, Carpenter S, Chang HY, Chen LL et al. (2023) Long non-coding RNAs: definitions, functions, challenges and recommendations. Nat Rev Mol Cell Biol 24(6):430–447
49. Mudge JM, Carbonell-Sala S, Diekhans M, Martinez JG, Hunt T, Jungreis I et al. (2025) GENCODE 2025: reference gene annotation for human and mouse. Nucleic Acids Res 53(D1):D966–D975
50. Fang S, Zhang L, Guo J, Niu Y, Wu Y, Li H et al. (2018) NONCODEV5: a comprehensive annotation database for long non-coding RNAs. Nucleic Acids Res 46(D1):D308–D314
51. Yang M, Zhu P, Cheema J, Bloomer R, Mikulski P, Liu Q et al. (2022) In vivo single-molecule analysis reveals COOLAIR RNA structural diversity. Nature 609(7926):394–399
52. Necsulea A, Soumillon M, Warnefors M, Liechti A, Daish T, Zeller U et al. (2014) The evolution of lncRNA repertoires and expression patterns in tetrapods. Nature 505(7485):635–640
53. Huang W, Xiong T, Zhao Y, Heng J, Han G, Wang P et al. (2024) Computational prediction and experimental validation identify functionally conserved lncRNAs from zebrafish to human. Nat Genet 56(1):124–135
54. Liu SJ, Horlbeck MA, Cho SW, Birk HS, Malatesta M, He D et al. (2017) CRISPRi-based genome-scale identification of functional long noncoding RNA loci in human cells. Science 355:eaah7111
55. Yip CW, Hon CC, Yasuzawa K, Sivaraman DM, Ramilowski JA, Shibayama Y et al. (2022) Antisense-oligonucleotide-mediated perturbation of long non-coding RNA reveals functional features in stem cells and across cell types. Cell Rep 41(13):111893
56. Nurk S, Koren S, Rhie A, Rautiainen M, Bzikadze AV, Mikheenko A et al. (2022) The complete sequence of a human genome. Science 376(6588):44–53
57. Campo A, Aliquò F, Velletri T, Campo S (2025) YRNAs: biosynthesis, structure, functions and involvment in cancer development. Discov Oncol 16(1):176
58. Gulìa C, Signore F, Gaffi M, Gigli S, Votino R, Nucciotti R et al. (2020) Y RNA: an overview of their role as potential biomarkers and molecular targets in human cancers. Cancers (Basel) 12(5):1238
59. Rothschild D, Susanto TT, Sui X, Spence JP, Rangan R, Genuth NR et al. (2024) Diversity of ribosomes at the level of rRNA variation associated with human health and disease. Cell Genom 4(9):100629
60. Shumate A, Salzberg SL (2021) Liftoff: accurate mapping of gene annotations. Bioinformatics 37(12):1639–1643
61. Chao KH, Heinz JM, Hoh C, Mao A, Shumate A, Pertea M et al. (2025) Combining DNA and protein alignments to improve genome annotation with LiftOn. Genome Res 35(2):311–325
62. T2T Annotation. https://ccb.jhu.edu/T2T.shtml. Accessed Oct 2025
63. LiftOn documentation. https://ccb.jhu.edu/lifton. Accessed Oct 2025
64. Mokrejs M, Masek T, Vopálensky V, Hlubucek P, Delbos P, Pospísek M (2010) IRESite–a tool for the examination of viral and cellular internal ribosome entry sites. Nucleic Acids Res 38(Database issue):D131–D136
65. Weickhmann AK, Keller H, Wurm JP, Strebitzer E, Juen MA, Kremser J et al. (2019) The structure of the SAM/SAH-binding riboswitch. Nucleic Acids Res 47(5):2654–2665
66. Hiller M, Pudimat R, Busch A, Backofen R (2006) Using RNA secondary structures to guide sequence motif finding towards single-stranded regions. Nucleic Acids Res 34(17):e117

67. Saunders SJ, Maticzka D, Möhl M, Gagnon JN, Brown CM, Backofen R (2012) Global or local? predicting secondary structure and accessibility in MRNAs. Nucleic Acids Res 40(12):5215–5226
68. Kawaguchi R, Kiryu H (2016) Parallel computation of genome-scale RNA secondary structure to detect structural constraints on human genome. BMC Bioinformatics 17(1):203
69. Waldl M, Spicher T, Lorenz R, Beckmann IK, Hofacker IL, Löhneysen SV et al. (2023) Local RNA folding revisited. J Bioinform Comput Biol 21(4):2350016
70. Rabani M, Kertesz M, Segal E (2008) Computational prediction of RNA structural motifs involved in posttranscriptional regulatory processes. Proc Natl Acad Sci U S A 105(39):14885–14890
71. Vaughn JN, Ellingson SR, Mignone F, von Arnim A (2012) Known and novel post-transcriptional regulatory sequences are conserved across plant families. RNA 18(3):368–384
72. Hafner M, Katsantoni M, Köster T, Marks J, Mukherjee J, Staiger D et al. (2021) CLIP and complementary methods. Nat Rev Methods Primers 1(1):1–23
73. Sasse A, Ray D, Laverty KU, Tam CL, Albu M, Zheng H et al (2025) A resource of RNA-binding protein motifs across eukaryotes reveals evolutionary dynamics and gene-regulatory function. Nat Biotechnol. https://doi.org/10.1038/s41587-025-02733-6
74. Miyake H, Kawaguchi RK, Kiryu H (2024) RNAelem: an algorithm for discovering sequence-structure motifs in RNA bound by RNA-binding proteins. Bioinform Adv 4(1):vbae144
75. Maticzka D, Lange SJ, Costa F, Backofen R (2014) GraphProt: modeling binding preferences of RNA-binding proteins. Genome Biol 15(1):R17
76. RNAcentral Consortium (2021) RNAcentral 2021: secondary structure integration, improved sequence search and new member databases. Nucleic Acids Res 49(D1):D212–D220
77. Chen L, Chen L, Zuo L, Gao Z, Shi Y, Yuan P et al. (2018) Short communication: long noncoding RNA GAS5 inhibits HIV-1 replication through interaction with miR-873. AIDS Res Hum Retroviruses 34(6):544–549
78. Hofacker IL, Fontana W, Stadler PF, Bonhoeffer LS, Tacker M, Schuster P (1994) Fast folding and comparison of RNA secondary structures. Monatsh Chem 125(2):167–188
79. Kiryu H, Terai G, Imamura O, Yoneyama H, Suzuki K, Asai K (2011) A detailed investigation of accessibilities around target sites of siRNAs and miRNAs. Bioinformatics 27(13):1788–1797
80. Sato K, Hamada M, Asai K, Mituyama T (2009) CENTROIDFOLD: a web server for RNA secondary structure prediction. Nucleic Acids Res 37(Web Server issue):W277–W280
81. Sato K, Kato Y, Hamada M, Akutsu T, Asai K (2011) IPknot: fast and accurate prediction of RNA secondary structures with pseudoknots using integer programming. Bioinformatics 27(13):i85–i93
82. Raden M, Ali SM, Alkhnbashi OS, Busch A, Costa F, Davis JA et al. (2018) Freiburg RNA tools: a central online resource for RNA-focused research and teaching. Nucleic Acids Res 46(W1):W25–W29
83. Busch A, Richter AS, Backofen R (2008) IntaRNA: efficient prediction of bacterial sRNA targets incorporating target site accessibility and seed regions. Bioinformatics 24(24):2849–2856
84. Bernhart SH, Tafer H, Mückstein U, Flamm C, Stadler PF, Hofacker IL (2006) Partition function and base pairing probabilities of RNA heterodimers. Algorithms Mol Biol 1(1):3
85. Mückstein U, Tafer H, Hackermüller J, Bernhart SH, Stadler PF, Hofacker IL (2006) Thermodynamics of RNA-RNA binding. Bioinformatics 22(10):1177–1182
86. Kato Y, Sato K, Asai K, Akutsu T (2012) Rtips: fast and accurate tools for RNA 2D structure prediction using integer programming. Nucleic Acids Res 40(Web Server issue):W29–W34
87. Kato Y, Sato K, Hamada M, Watanabe Y, Asai K, Akutsu T (2010) RactIP: fast and accurate prediction of RNA-RNA interaction using integer programming. Bioinformatics 26(18):i460–i466
88. Agarwal V, Bell GW, Nam JW, Bartel DP (2015) Predicting effective microRNA target sites in mammalian mRNAs. eLife 4:e05005
89. Fukunaga T, Iwakiri J, Ono Y, Hamada M (2019) LncRRIsearch: a web server for lncRNA-RNA interaction prediction integrated with tissue-specific expression and subcellular localization data. Front Genet 10:462
90. Deigan KE, Li TW, Mathews DH, Weeks KM (2009) Accurate SHAPE-directed RNA structure determination. Proc Natl Acad Sci U S A 106(1):97–102
91. Siegfried NA, Busan S, Rice GM, Nelson JAE, Weeks KM (2014) RNA motif discovery by SHAPE and mutational profiling (SHAPE-MaP). Nat Methods 11(9):959–965
92. Zubradt M, Gupta P, Persad S, Lambowitz AM, Weissman JS, Rouskin S (2017) DMS-MaPseq for genome-wide or targeted RNA

structure probing in vivo. Nat Methods 14(1):75–82
93. Hall I, O'Steen M, Gold S, Keane SC, Weidmann CA (2024) Template switching enables chemical probing of native RNA structures. RNA 31(1):113–125
94. Hajdin CE, Bellaousov S, Huggins W, Leonard CW, Mathews DH, Weeks KM (2013) Accurate SHAPE-directed RNA secondary structure modeling, including pseudoknots. Proc Natl Acad Sci U S A 110(14):5498–5503
95. Johnson PZ, Simon AE (2023) RNAcanvas: interactive drawing and exploration of nucleic acid structures. Nucleic Acids Res 51(W1):W501–W508
96. Eddy SR, Durbin R (1994) RNA sequence analysis using covariance models. Nucleic Acids Res 22(11):2079–2088
97. Sakakibara Y, Brown M, Underwood RC, Mian S, and Haussler D (1994) Stochastic context-free grammars for modeling RNA. Proceedings of the Twenty-Seventh Hawaii international conference on system sciences, IEEE, pp 284–293
98. Nawrocki EP, Eddy SR (2013) Infernal 1.1: 100-fold faster RNA homology searches. Bioinformatics 29(22):2933–2935
99. Weinberg Z, Kim PB, Chen TH, Li S, Harris KA, Lünse CE et al. (2015) New classes of self-cleaving ribozymes revealed by comparative genomics analysis. Nat Chem Biol 11(8):606–610
100. Bernhart SH, Hofacker IL, Will S, Gruber AR, Stadler PF (2008) RNAalifold: improved consensus structure prediction for RNA alignments. BMC Bioinformatics 9: 474
101. Weinberg Z, Breaker RR (2011) R2R–software to speed the depiction of aesthetic consensus RNA secondary structures. BMC Bioinformatics 12: 3
102. Wang W, Feng C, Han R, Wang Z, Ye L, Du Z et al. (2023) trRosettaRNA: automated prediction of RNA 3D structure with transformer network. Nat Commun 14(1):7266
103. Parlea LG, Sweeney BA, Hosseini-Asanjan M, Zirbel CL, Leontis NB (2016) The RNA 3D Motif Atlas: computational methods for extraction, organization and evaluation of RNA motifs. Methods 103:99–119
104. Kawaguchi RK, Iwakiri J (2023) Preface. RNA structure prediction. Springer Nature
105. Ma H, Jia X, Zhang K, Su Z (2022) Cryo-EM advances in RNA structure determination. Signal Transduct Target Ther 7(1):58
106. Ding J, Lee YT, Bhandari Y, Schwieters CD, Fan L, Yu P et al. (2023) Visualizing RNA conformational and architectural heterogeneity in solution. Nat Commun 14(1):714
107. Pang B, McFaline JL, Burgis NE, Dong M, Taghizadeh K, Sullivan MR et al. (2012) Defects in purine nucleotide metabolism lead to substantial incorporation of xanthine and hypoxanthine into DNA and RNA. Proc Natl Acad Sci U S A 109(7):2319–2324
108. Mair S, Erharter K, Renard E, Brillet K, Brunner M, Lusser A et al. (2022) Towards a comprehensive understanding of RNA deamination: synthesis and properties of xanthosine-modified RNA. Nucleic Acids Res 50(11):6038–6051
109. Mendoza HG, Beal PA (2024) Structural and functional effects of inosine modification in mRNA. RNA 30(5):512–520
110. Sakuraba S, Iwakiri J, Hamada M, Kameda T, Tsuji G, Kimura Y et al. (2020) Free-energy calculation of ribonucleic inosines and its application to nearest-neighbor parameters. J Chem Theory Comput 16(9):5923–5935
111. Spitale RC, Flynn RA, Zhang QC, Crisalli P, Lee B, Jung JW et al. (2015) Structural imprints in vivo decode RNA regulatory mechanisms. Nature 519(7544):486–490
112. Garalde DR, Snell EA, Jachimowicz D, Sipos B, Lloyd JH, Bruce M et al. (2018) Highly parallel direct RNA sequencing on an array of nanopores. Nat Methods 15(3):201–206
113. Zhao Y, Oono K, Takizawa H, Kotera M (2024) GenerRNA: a generative pre-trained language model for de novo RNA design. PLoS One 19(10):e0310814

Check for updates

Chapter 12

AI/ML-Driven Gene Analysis: New Perspectives on Variant Calling in Normal Human Tissue Using scRNA-seq Data

Satoshi Oota

Abstract

Advances in artificial intelligence (AI) and machine learning (ML) have rapidly transformed bioinformatics, offering new solutions for data-intensive challenges in genomics. In this chapter, we introduce a practical protocol that contrasts a conventional variant-calling approach with a modern AI/ML-based method using single-cell RNA sequencing (scRNA-seq) data. Focusing on somatic variant detection in a normal human tissue, we explore the characteristics of variant calls—including variant types, read depth, and variant allele frequency (VAF)—and address technical challenges such as alignment artifacts near splice junctions and noise in RNA-seq data. We demonstrate that AI-based methods, such as DeepVariant, provide enhanced accuracy and confidence in genotype prediction compared to rule-based tools such as RNA-Mutect2. By outlining comparative workflows and analysis outputs, this chapter highlights the growing potential of AI/ML in improving variant discovery and interpretation in transcriptomic data, particularly in contexts lacking matched-normal controls.

Keywords Artificial intelligence (AI), Machine learning (ML), Single-cell RNA sequencing (scRNA-seq), Variant calling, Somatic variants, DeepVariant, RNA-Mutect2, Genotype prediction, Variant allele frequency (VAF)

1 Introduction

In this chapter, we present recent advances in bioinformatics, artificial intelligence (AI), and machine learning (ML) through a practical protocol that leverages single-cell RNA sequencing (scRNA-seq) data, with a particular emphasis on detecting rare variants in normal cells.

To highlight the value of AI/ML-driven gene analysis, we describe a practical bioinformatics protocol that compares a traditional method with an AI/ML-based approach for detecting somatic variants from scRNA-seq data. While variant calling is commonly used to study tumor evolution, in this chapter, we apply it to scRNA-seq data derived from a normal human tissue.

Variant calling within normal tissues is a challenging task, particularly when using scRNA-seq data. With scRNA-seq data, it is nearly

Y-h Taguchi (ed.), *AI/ML-Driven Gene Analysis*, Methods in Molecular Biology, vol. 3037,
https://doi.org/10.1007/978-1-0716-5284-8_12,

impossible to detect variants in normal tissue due to low expression levels, high dropout rates, technical noise, and allele-specific expression [1]. To detect variant calls despite this limitation, it is often necessary to extensively adjust parameters—though this can increase the risk of false positives.

To address the challenges inherent in variant calling from scRNA-seq data, we examine the characteristics of variant calls—such as variant types, read depth, and variant allele frequency (VAF) distributions—and explore strategies for filtering out noise [2].

Especially, the VAF interpretation in scRNA-seq is different from bulk DNA and RNA sequencing, because: (1) gene expression is stochastic, meaning allelic dropout affects VAF [3, 4]; (2) not all mutations are transcribed, leading to lower-than-expected VAF [5]; (3) coverage per cell is low, making VAF estimates noisier [2].

In scRNA-seq, VAF values can offer insights into:

- somatic mutations in single cells
- clonal vs. subclonal mutations
- expression biases due to allelic imbalance [6]
- technical artifacts such as dropout effects [3]

Table 1 shows the key differences in the interpretation of VAF values between bulk DNA-seq and scRNA-seq data [7–9] (*see* **Note 1**).

In the case of single-cell DNA sequencing (scDNA-seq), the interpretation of VAF is straightforward: VAF $\approx$ 1.0 and VAF $\approx$ 0.5 indicate homozygous and heterozygous variants at the site, respectively. According to previous studies [10–14], the expected VAF ranges in scRNA-seq are more variable than in scDNA-seq due to dropout effects and expression bias. Therefore, a more nuanced interpretation is required compared to scDNA-seq data (*see* **Note 2**).

For example, scRNA-seq does not capture all transcripts from a cell. This leads to artificial loss of heterozygous variants, shifting them toward VAF < 0.5 (allelic dropout affects). Unlike DNA-seq,

Table 1
VAF in bulk DNA-seq vs. scRNA-seq

Aspect	Bulk DNA-seq	scRNA-seq
VAF definition	Ratio of variant reads to total reads at a locus	Ratio of variant transcripts to total transcripts at a locus
Expected range	0.0–1.0	0.0–1.0 (but with greater variance)
Heterozygous mutation VAF	~50%	Highly variable (0%–50%) due to dropout
Subclonal mutation VAF	<50%	Much lower due to allelic expression bias
Technical noise	Low	High (dropout, amplification bias)

Table 2
Representative AI tools for somatic mutation detection

AI tool	Purpose	Technology
DeepVariant [16]	Deep learning–based variant calling	CNN
Clairvoyante [17]	Nanopore sequencing variant caller	Deep learning
SomaticSeq [18]	ML-based ensemble mutation caller	Random Forests, SVM
SCVI [19]	Single-cell sequencing denoising	Variational inference
PyClone-VI [20]	Clonal mutation analysis	Bayesian inference
StratoMod [21]	AI for filtering sequencing errors	Graph-based method

RNA expression levels affect variant detection. A highly expressed mutant transcript might skew toward 1.0, even if it is a heterozygous site (transcript-specific biases matter) (*see* **Note 3** for details).

To address these issues, applying AI/ML technologies to scRNA-seq data analysis for variant calling has become a straightforward protocol [15] (Table 2). Given the rapid expansion of AI-based methodologies in bioinformatics, it is beyond the scope of this chapter to provide a comprehensive overview. However, a brief selection of representative approaches is summarized in the Notes section (*see* **Notes 4–9**).

In this chapter, we use Google's DeepVariant [16] as a representative AI-based variant caller and compare its performance with RNA-Mutect2 [22], a "traditional" variant caller.

2 Materials and Methods

2.1 Algorithms of RNA-MuTect2 and DeepVariant

RNA-MuTect2 [22] is a variant caller specifically designed to detect somatic mutations from RNA sequencing (RNA-seq) data. It extends the widely used MuTect algorithm [23]—which was originally developed for DNA-seq—to reliably call variants in RNA-seq datasets, particularly for cancer genomics applications.

RNA-MuTect2 identifies somatic mutations as follows:

1. Preprocessing RNA-seq data: RNA-seq are aligned reads to a reference genome, typically with splice-aware aligners (e.g., STAR [24], HISAT2 [25]). Quality control, filtering, and removing duplicates are then performed to ensure high-quality input data.

2. Local realignment and base recalibration: Similar to DNA-based pipelines, RNA-MuTect often requires local realignment around indels and recalibration of base-quality scores to enhance accuracy.
3. Somatic mutation detection: Using the MuTect algorithm, aligned reads from tumor RNA-seq data are compared with matched-normal DNA or RNA samples to distinguish true somatic mutations from technical artifacts or germline variants. It statistically assesses read counts, strand bias, and sequencing errors to reliably identify somatic point mutations.
4. Variant filtering and annotation: Low-confidence variants, common sequencing errors, or germline variants are filtered out, and variants are annotated with gene/transcript information.

RNA-MuTect2 accounts for the unique characteristics of RNA-seq data (e.g., splicing and allele-specific expression), leverages proven statistical methods from DNA-based variant detection, is optimized for RNA-based data, and facilitates the identification of expressed somatic mutations relevant for functional studies, immunotherapy biomarker identification, or tumor evolution studies.

Typical applications include detecting somatic mutations in cancer research, identifying biomarkers from tumor RNA profiles, and integrating RNA-seq mutation calls with DNA-based variant analyses [22].

Google's DeepVariant [16] is a deep learning-based variant caller developed by Google that identifies genetic variants (single-nucleotide polymorphisms (SNPs) and small insertions or deletions (indels)) from sequencing data. Unlike traditional variant-calling algorithms that rely on explicit rules or statistical assumptions, DeepVariant utilizes neural networks [26] trained on high-quality datasets to interpret genomic data similarly to how image-recognition algorithms analyze images.

DeepVariant works as follows:

1. Read alignment: Input sequence reads (such as from whole-genome sequencing (WGS), whole-exome sequencing (WES), or targeted sequencing) are first aligned to a reference genome, producing a BAM file [27].
2. Image representation: DeepVariant transforms aligned reads at candidate variant sites into images (pileups: a novel representation of sequence data that transforms read alignments around candidate variant sites into image-like tensors [16]), encoding base qualities, mapping qualities, and read depths as pixel intensities.

3. Deep learning classification: It applies a convolutional neural network (CNN) [28] trained on labeled datasets to classify each candidate genomic position into variant/non-variant states.
4. Variant calling: Outputs high-quality variant calls in Variant Call Format (VCF) [29] and genomic VCF (gVCF) formats [30].

Advantages of DeepVariant are improved accuracy, often provides higher accuracy, generalizability, and versatility: i.e.,

- Improved accuracy: Often provides higher accuracy, sensitivity, and specificity compared to traditional variant callers.
- Generalizability: Robust across multiple sequencing technologies (Illumina, PacBio, Oxford Nanopore, etc.) and sequencing protocols (WGS, WES, targeted sequencing, RNA-seq).
- Versatility: Includes pretrained models specifically tailored for different sequencing methods (WGS, WES, PacBio, ONT).

Typical applications of DeepVariant are clinical genomics, population genetics, cancer genomics, and research involving genome editing validations. DeepVariant's combination of advanced machine learning and genomic expertise makes it a powerful tool for accurate and robust genetic analysis [16].

2.2 A Typical Protocol for RNA-MuTect2

RNA-MuTect2 is a variant caller based on GATK's MuTect2 [22], specifically adapted for detecting somatic mutations from RNA sequencing data. Below is a comprehensive explanation on how to install and use RNA-MuTect2.

As prerequisites, ensure you have the following dependencies installed:

- Java 8 or later
- GATK (Genome Analysis Toolkit v4.x) [31]
- Samtools (version ≥1.9 recommended) [32]
- BWA [33] or STAR [34] (alignment tools)
- Picard [35] (optional but recommended)

On Ubuntu, you may install dependencies as follows:

```
# Java installation (Ubuntu)
sudo apt-get install openjdk-8-jre-headless
# Samtools installation
sudo apt-get install samtools
# Picard installation (recommended)
conda install -c bioconda picard
```

Or it is easiest to use Conda [36] to manage bioinformatics software:

```
conda install -c bioconda gatk4
```

RNA-MuTect2 itself is primarily a set of modified parameters or pipelines based on standard MuTect2 from GATK. Typically, there is no standalone binary explicitly labeled "RNA-MuTect2"; rather, RNA-MuTect2 represents using MuTect2 with RNA-specific options or postprocessing adjustments.

If you want the workflow proposed in publications (such as Broad Institute recommendations [37] or related RNA-seq variant calling pipelines), the workflow usually relies on standard MuTect2 from GATK: Official GATK release (for MuTect2), https://github.com/broadinstitute/gatk/releases.
You may use the following commands without cloning:

```
wget https://github.com/broadinstitute/gatk/
releases/download/4.5.0.0/gatk-4.5.0.0.zip
unzip gatk-4.5.0.0.zip
cd gatk-4.5.0.0/
```

RNA-MuTect2 workflow usually follows these steps:

1. Mapping RNA-seq reads to a reference genome using STAR [24].
2. Postprocessing alignments (sorting, marking duplicates, and indexing).
3. Splitting'N'Trimming (optional but recommended)—using GATK SplitNCigarReads.
4. Calling somatic variants using MuTect2.
5. Filtering variants with FilterMutectCalls [30].

Typical commands for each step are:

1. Mapping RNA-seq reads to a reference genome using STAR:

```
STAR --runThreadN 8 \
--genomeDir /path/to/STAR/index \
--readFilesIn R1.fastq.gz R2.fastq.gz \
--readFilesCommand zcat \
--outFileNamePrefix sample_ \
--outSAMtype BAM SortedByCoordinate
```

Repeat similarly for the other samples.

2. Postprocessing alignments (sorting, marking duplicates, and indexing):

```
gatk MarkDuplicates \
-I sample_Aligned.sortedByCoord.out.bam \
-O sample_sorted_dedup.bam \
-M sample_dedup_metrics.txt
# Index BAM
samtools index sample_sorted_dedup.bam
```

Repeat for the other samples as well.

3. Splitting'N'Trimming (optional but recommended)—using GATK SplitNCigarReads:

```
gatk SplitNCigarReads \
-R reference.fasta \
-I sample_sorted_dedup.bam \
-O sample_split.bam
```

Repeat for the other samples as well.

4. Calling somatic variants using MuTect2. MuTect2 has two modes: tumor-normal and tumor-only. In our context, we use the tumor-only mode. Note that MuTect2 is primarily intended for tumor analysis, whereas we utilize it for analyzing normal cells:

```
gatk Mutect2 \
-R reference.fasta \
-I sample_split.bam \
-tumor SampleName \
--dont-use-soft-clipped-bases \
--output unfiltered.vcf.gz
```

The parameter `--dont-use-soft-clipped-bases` is highly recommended for RNA-seq data.

5. Filtering variants with FilterMutectCalls. Filter false positives:

```
gatk FilterMutectCalls \
-R reference.fasta \
-V unfiltered.vcf.gz \
-O filtered.vcf.gz
```

You may review your results as follows:

```
zcat filtered.vcf.gz | less
```

Or create a statistics report for the variant-calling metrics (*see* **Note 10**).

2.3 A Typical Protocol with DeepVariant

One of the simplest ways to implement DeepVariant is by using the prebuilt Docker [38] images distributed by Google. As a prerequisite, ensure Docker is installed on your system. For details, refer to https://www.docker.com/. You may check Docker installation in your shell:

```
docker --version
```

To pull the prebuilt DeepVariant Docker image from Google:

```
docker pull google/deepvariant:latest
```

If you need a specific version (recommended for reproducibility), specify it explicitly: e.g.,

```
docker pull google/deepvariant:1.4.0
```

You may need to execute the above commands as a superuser. You need the following files prepared and accessible:

- Reference genome FASTA (`reference.fasta` + `.fai` index file + `.dict` dictionary file)
- Input alignment file (`aligned_reads.bam` sorted and indexed `.bai` file)

Make sure they are accessible to Docker by placing them in an accessible directory, e.g.:

```
/home/user/deepvariant/
├── reference.fasta
├── reference.fasta.fai
├── reference.dict
├── aligned_reads.bam
└── aligned_reads.bam.bai
```

To run DeepVariant, execute the DeepVariant pipeline using Docker with the following command template:

```
BIN_VERSION="1.6.0" # specify your DeepVariant
version
MODEL_TYPE="WES" # choose from WGS, WES, PACBIO,
ONT, HYBRID_PACBIO_ILLUMINA


# Define input/output directories
INPUT_DIR="/home/user/deepvariant"
OUTPUT_DIR="/home/user/deepvariant/output"


mkdir -p ${OUTPUT_DIR}
docker run \
-v "${INPUT_DIR}":"/input" \
-v "${OUTPUT_DIR}":"/output" \
google/deepvariant:"${BIN_VERSION}" \
/opt/deepvariant/bin/run_deepvariant \
--model_type=${MODEL_TYPE} \
--ref=/input/reference.fasta \
--reads=/input/aligned_reads.bam \
--output_vcf=/output/output.vcf.gz \
--output_gvcf=/output/output.g.vcf.gz \
--num_shards=$(nproc)
```

Here, we use the WES DeepVariant model because:

- scRNA-seq data primarily capture expressed transcripts (exons) rather than the entire genome. The sequencing coverage resembles exome sequencing more than whole-genome sequencing.
- The WES DeepVariant model is optimized to handle irregular and targeted coverage, which is closer to what we would expect from RNA-seq experiments.

As additional recommendations, it is advisable to conduct pre- and postprocessing:

- Preprocessing: Before variant calling, ensure your scRNA-seq alignment data (BAM file) are sorted and indexed. Consider filtering reads based on mapping quality and removing PCR duplicates.
- Postprocessing: After variant calling, apply filtering based on coverage, allele frequency, or strand bias to reduce false positives commonly observed in RNA-seq.

For performance optimization, adjust `--num_shards` according to CPU cores available and use SSD storage for improved speed.

Ensure that BAM files are properly sorted and indexed, and that reference files (.fai and .dict) are generated using `samtools faidx` and `picard CreateSequenceDictionary`, respectively.

3 Interpretation of the Results

3.1 RNA-Mutect2 Outputs

Figure 1 shows a summary of variant type and depth distribution from RNA-Mutect2 output in normal tissue (tumor-only mode). The vast majority of detected variants are single-nucleotide polymorphisms (SNPs), with smaller but notable numbers of insertions and deletions (Fig. 1a). A very small number of complex variants are also observed. This distribution is typical of RNA variant calling, where SNPs are the most abundant and easiest to detect. Insertions and deletions are often underrepresented due to alignment challenges and read-coverage variability in RNA-seq.

Most variants are supported by relatively low read depth, with a sharp peak below 50 and a rapid drop-off at higher depths (Fig. 1b). The *x*-axis is capped at 1500 to remove outliers and focus on the bulk of the distribution. This is consistent with RNA-seq data, where gene expression levels vary widely, and many transcripts are present at low abundance. High read depth is rare and typically reflects highly expressed genes. This figure highlights the characteristics and limitations of variant calling from RNA-seq in normal tissue using RNA-Mutect2 in tumor-only mode, where matched-normal filtering and germline–somatic distinction are not applied.

Figure 2 shows variant allele frequency (VAF) distribution of heterozygous variants (0/x) in RNA-Mutect2 output under tumor-only mode in normal tissue. This histogram illustrates the distribution of alternate allele frequencies for variants called as heterozygous (0/x) in normal tissue using RNA-Mutect2 in tumor-only mode. A prominent peak near VAF = 1.0 suggests that many variants are supported almost exclusively by alternate reads. This may be attributed to monoallelic expression, allelic imbalance, or low expression of the reference allele, all of which are common in RNA-seq data from normal tissue.

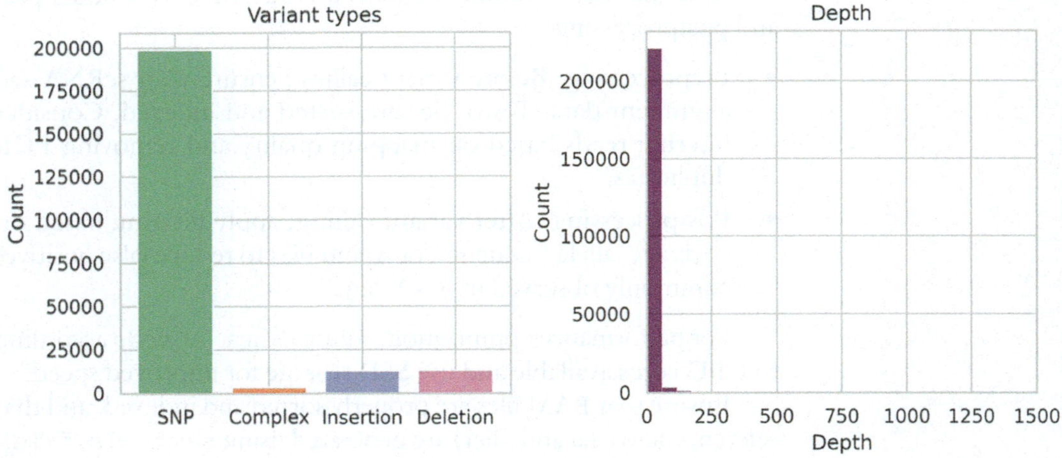

Fig. 1 Summary of variant calls from RNA-Mutect2 analysis. (**a**) Distribution of variant types shows that single-nucleotide polymorphisms (SNPs) constitute the vast majority of called variants, with smaller proportions of insertions, deletions, and complex events. (**b**) Read depth (DP) distribution at variant sites indicates that most variants are supported by low to moderate coverage, with a sharp drop-off above 200 reads and a cutoff at 1500

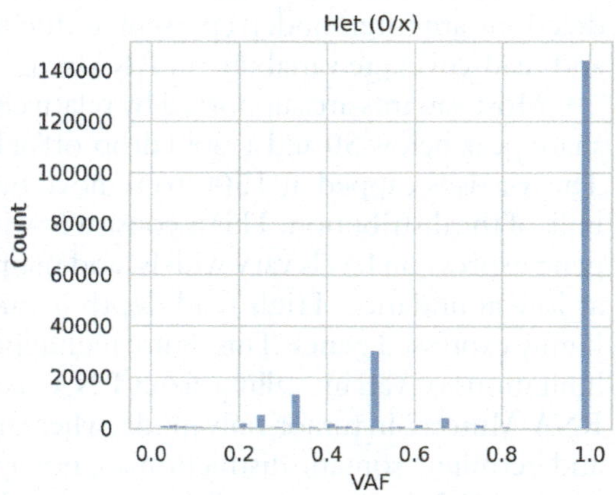

Fig. 2 Variant allele frequency (VAF) distribution of heterozygous variants (`0/x`) in RNA-Mutect2 output. The histogram shows a strong peak near VAF = 1.0, indicating that most detected variants have near-complete alternate allele support. This pattern is typical in RNA-seq data, where allele-specific expression, monoallelic transcription, or low expression of the reference allele can skew the VAF. Other heterozygous variants are distributed at lower VAFs, reflecting variability in transcript abundance and coverage. Only the Het (0/x) panel contains data; all other genotype classes (`0/0`, `1/1`, `x/y`, and `./.`) are empty (data not shown). This is common in tumor-only RNA-Mutect2 output, where genotyping information is limited and often restricted to heterozygous calls without a matched-normal sample

Notably, only the Het (0/x) panel contains data, while all other genotype classes (0/0, 1/1, x/y, and ./.) are absent (data not shown). This reflects a key limitation of RNA-Mutect2 in tumor-only mode: without a matched-normal sample and in the absence of DNA data, the tool primarily reports somatic-like heterozygous calls, without assigning confident genotypes for homozygous reference or alternate sites. This makes it difficult to distinguish between germline and somatic variants and can lead to apparent overrepresentation of high-VAF heterozygous calls, even in normal tissue.

In summary, this figure underscores the challenges of interpreting variant allele frequencies from tumor-only RNA-based variant-calling pipelines, especially in the context of normal samples where genotyping resolution is limited and VAFs may be biased by transcriptional dynamics.

Figure 3 shows an overview of substitution and indel characteristics in RNA-Mutect2 variant calls from normal tissue under tumor-only mode. This demonstrates that the RNA-Mutect2 pipeline in tumor-only mode on normal tissue captures a biologically plausible variant landscape, dominated by transitions and short indels. The variant characteristics are consistent with RNA-seq-specific biases and technical challenges, such as transcriptome complexity, allele-specific expression, and splicing artifacts.

Figure 3a represents biallelic base substitutions: Each panel shows the number of variants where a specific reference base (A, G, T, or C) was substituted by other bases. The most frequent transitions are A→G and T→C, which are common in both DNA and RNA due to biological mutational biases (e.g., deamination [39]) and technical artifacts. Transversions (e.g., A→C, G→T) are much less common. This pattern reflects expected substitution biology, with transitions generally more frequent than transversions.

Figure 3b represents transition/transversion (Ti/Tv) ratio [40]: This panel summarizes the total number of transitions (141,181) versus transversions (57,669), yielding a Ti/Tv ratio of 2.45. This value is consistent with what is typically observed in human RNA-seq data, suggesting good variant-calling quality. A higher Ti/Tv ratio is generally indicative of true biological signal, whereas lower ratios may suggest increased noise or false positives.

Figure 3c represents biallelic indel size distribution: This histogram shows the size distribution of biallelic insertions and deletions. Positive values on the *x*-axis represent insertions, where the alternate allele is longer than the reference. Negative values represent deletions, where the reference allele is longer than the alternate. This convention allows both types of indels to be shown on a single symmetric scale. Most indels are short (±1–2 bp), but the presence of longer deletions (e.g., −100 to −300 bp) may indicate alignment artifacts, incomplete transcript coverage, or splicing events being misinterpreted as deletions—an expected challenge in RNA-seq

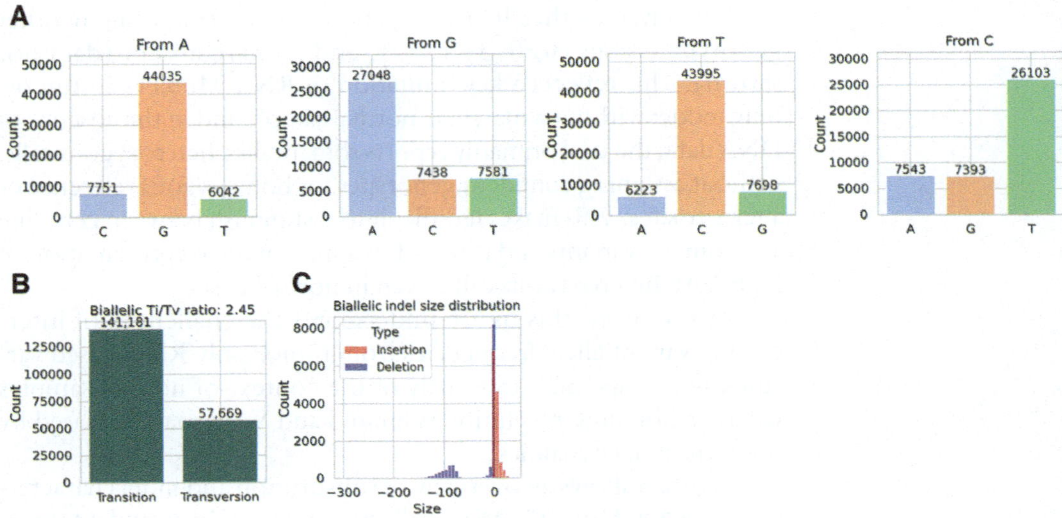

Fig. 3 Overview of substitution and indel patterns in RNA-Mutect2 variant calls from normal tissue in tumor-only mode. (**a**) Biallelic base substitutions from each reference base (A, G, T, C) to all possible alternative bases. Transitions (purine–purine or pyrimidine–pyrimidine changes) are generally more common than transversions, particularly A→G and T→C. (**b**) Transition/transversion (Ti/Tv) ratio across all biallelic SNPs is 2.45, which is within the expected biological range for RNA-seq data in human tissue, reflecting the predominance of transitions. (**c**) Size distribution of biallelic insertions and deletions (indels). Most indels are short, with a strong peak near ±1 bp, and deletions appear slightly more abundant than insertions. The presence of longer deletions (up to ~300 bp) suggests complex splicing or mapping artifacts common in RNA-seq variant calling. The negative values on the *x*-axis represent deletions, while positive values represent insertions

variant calling. These longer events should be interpreted cautiously, especially without matched DNA data.

3.2 DeepVariant Outputs

DeepVariant analyzes sequencing data to identify genetic variants—differences between a sample genome and a reference genome. The report gives a visual breakdown of variant types and quality.

Figure 4a shows the number of single-nucleotide polymorphisms (SNPs) and insertions/deletions (indels) found. The majority of variants are SNPs, which is expected. The presence of multiallelic variants and complex variants in small numbers is normal. A high number of reference calls (RefCalls) suggests many confidently non-variant sites. Figure 4b shows the distribution of sequencing depth per variant site. Most variants are supported by low-to-moderate coverage. A long tail toward high coverage is visible, but relatively few sites fall there. Figure 4c shows quality score (QUAL) [41] or the PHRED-scaled variant quality score [30]. A sharp peak near low QUAL values, tapering off toward higher scores. Most variants have low confidence by this metric. Depending on downstream use, you may want to filter out low-QUAL variants (e.g., QUAL < 20 or 30). Figure 4d shows genotype quality (GQ), a confidence measure—typically ranging from 0 to 99—for the predicted genotype. This histogram illustrates

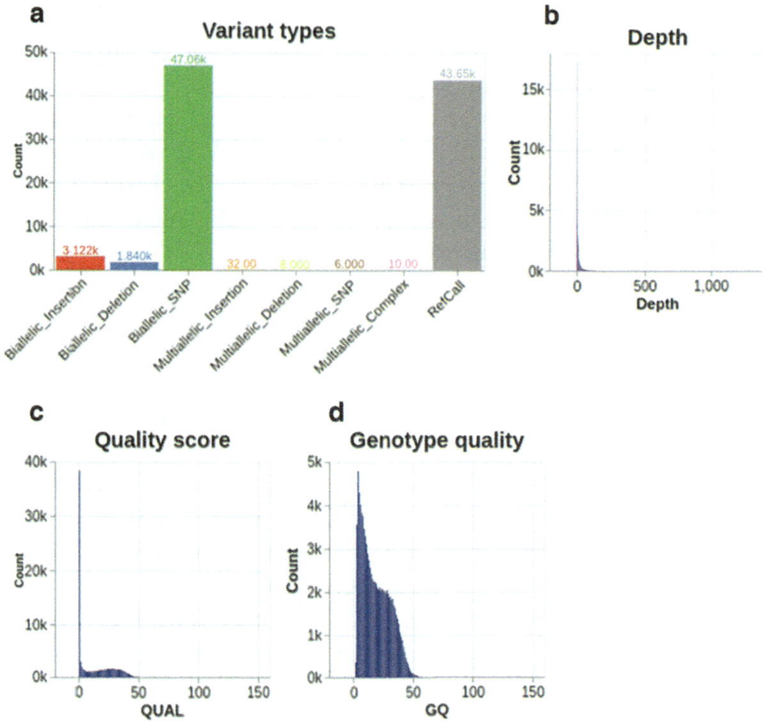

Fig. 4 Detected variant counts by DeepVariant. (**a**) Variant types. Biallelic SNPs (green, 47,060): most common variant type, representing single-base substitutions with two possible alleles; Biallelic insertions (red, 3122) and deletions (blue 1840): simple indels affecting one base or a few bases; Multiallelic variants: less frequent but more complex, involving insertions (brown, 32), deletions (yellow, 8000), SNPs (purple, 6000), and complex (brown, 10) with combinations of changes not easily classified as SNP/indel; RefCall (black, 43,650): positions assessed but matching the reference genome. (**b**) Histogram of sequencing depth (read coverage) per variant site: most sites have low to moderate depth. A long right tail indicates occasional high-coverage positions. (**c**) Distribution of QUAL (variant confidence score): most variants have low scores, with relatively few high-quality calls, indicating that cautious filtering may be required for high-confidence analysis. (**d**) Histogram of genotype quality (GQ): peaks at low GQ values and trails off with increasing GQ, suggesting a mixture of confident and uncertain genotype calls

genotype confidence values on a scale from 0 to 150. A prominent peak is observed at low GQ values, with the number of sites gradually decreasing as GQ increases. Only a small proportion of sites reach high GQ scores (above 90), suggesting some uncertainty in the genotype calls. Depending on the application, it may be advisable to filter out variants with GQ values below 20–30.

Figure 5 shows variant allele frequency (VAF) distributions across different genotype categories as output from DeepVariant calling pipeline. It is divided into two main sections: Main Genotypes

(Fig. 5a) and Other Genotypes (Fig. 5b). The Main Genotypes are the standard diploid genotype categories, i.e., Ref (0/0), Het (0/x), and Het (0/x).

In the Ref (0/0), these sites are called homozygous reference—i.e., no variant. VAF ~0 is expected (as only reference alleles are present). Most values cluster around 0, with a small number showing non-zero VAF—likely due to sequencing noise, misalignment, or artifacts.

The Het (0/x) consists of one reference allele and one alternate allele—heterozygous. Expected VAF is ~0.5. The observation has a strong peak around 0.5, with spread across the middle of the range—indicating real heterozygous calls, but also some variability due to coverage depth, allele bias, or sequencing noise.

The Hom (x/x) is a homozygous alternate genotype. Expected VAF is ~1.0 (i.e., all reads support the alternate allele). The observation has a sharp peak at 1.0, as expected—indicating confident homozygous variant calls.

In the Other Genotypes (Fig. 5b), there are less common or ambiguous categories. The Het - two variants (x/y) consists of two different alternate alleles (e.g., multiallelic variants). Expected

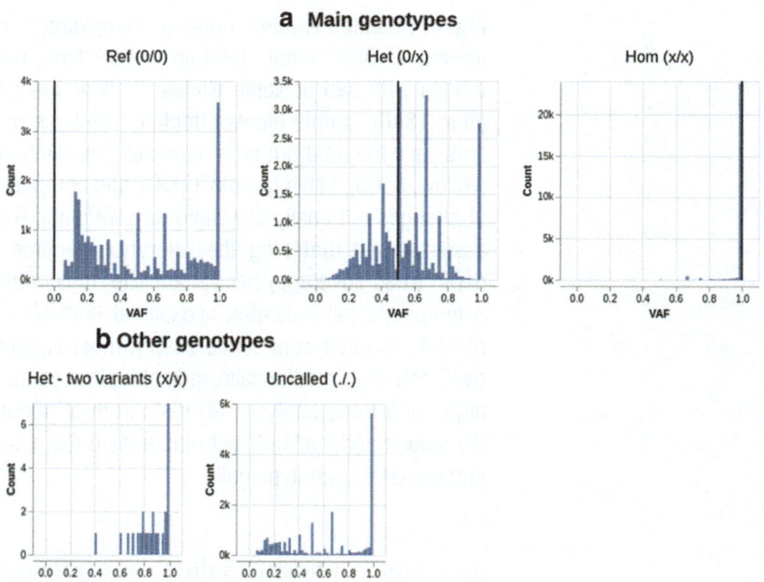

Fig. 5 Distribution of variant allele frequency (VAF) across genotype categories. (**a**) Main genotypes: For homozygous reference (Ref, 0/0), most VAF values cluster around 0; for heterozygous variants (Het, 0/x), VAF peaks near 0.5 as expected; and for homozygous alternate (Hom, x/x), a sharp peak is observed at VAF = 1.0. (**b**) Other genotypes: Multiallelic heterozygotes (x/y) display more variable VAF distributions due to differing allele proportions, while uncalled genotypes (./.) show a noisy pattern with a notable concentration at high VAF values, suggesting unresolved alternate alleles at those sites. This breakdown helps assess the reliability and characteristics of genotype calls

VAF depends on the read support of each variant allele. The observation is scattered distribution between 0.5 and 1.0, with very low counts— these are rare and often harder to call with high confidence.

The Uncalled (./.) is a genotype that could not be determined (missing or ambiguous). The observation is distribution that is noisy, with many values at high VAF—suggests uncertainty, possibly due to low depth or poor quality at those sites.

Overall, main genotype categories behave as expected: clear VAF peaks at 0.0 (Ref), 0.5 (Het), and 1.0 (Hom). Other genotypes are rare and show more variable or noisy VAF distributions.

Figure 6 presents a comprehensive overview of biallelic variant types, including base substitutions and indel sizes, which help assess the biological validity and technical quality of variant calls.

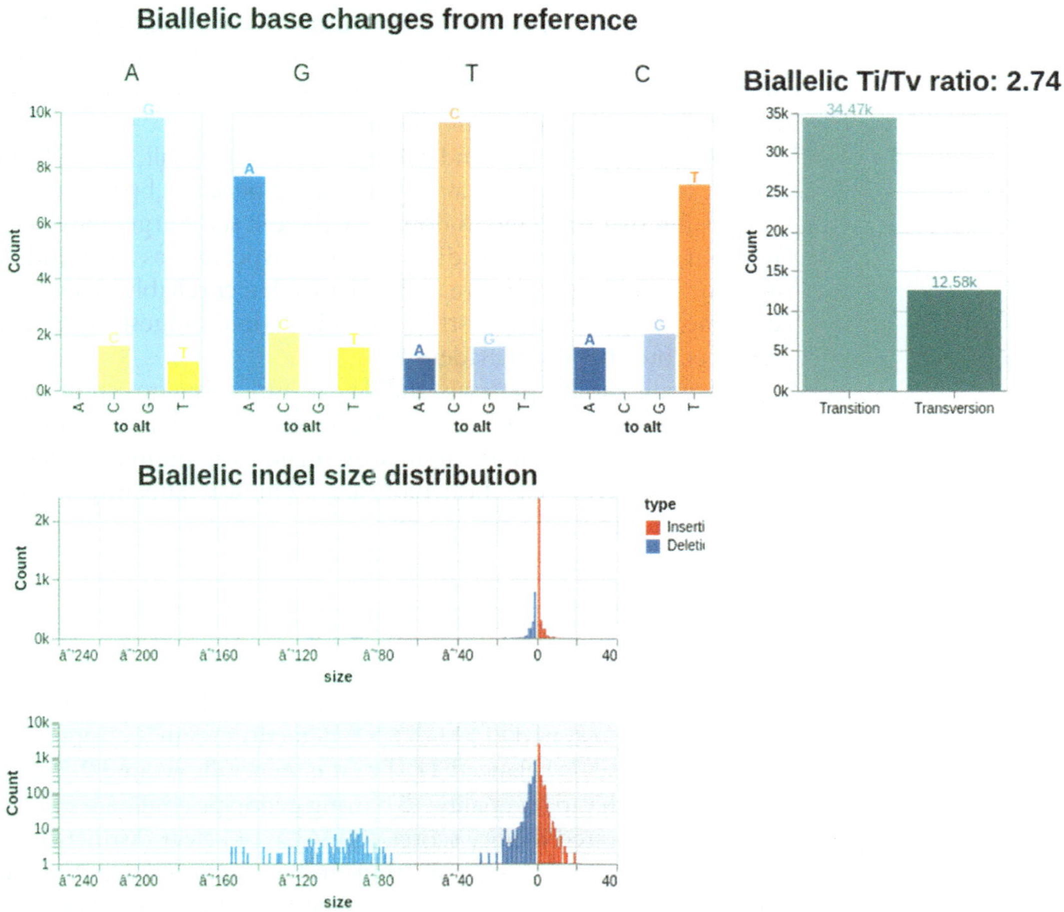

Fig. 6 Summary of biallelic variant types and indel characteristics. Left: Bar plots show the counts of biallelic base substitutions from each reference nucleotide (A, G, T, C) to alternate alleles. Transitions (e.g., A↔G, C↔T) dominate over transversions (other substitutions). Center: The transition-to-transversion (Ti/Tv) ratio is 2.74, indicating a strong prevalence of transitions, which is typical for high-quality variant calls in human genomes. Right: Biallelic indel size distributions are shown for insertions (red) and deletions (blue), using both linear (top) and log-scaled (bottom) *y*-axes. Most indels are short (±1 to ±5 bases), with a sharp enrichment near size 0, consistent with sequencing or alignment artifacts being well-controlled

The left four panels represent biallelic base changes from the reference. These panels show the number of times each reference base (A, G, T, C) was substituted with each of the other three possible bases. For each base, transitions (A↔G, C↔T) are far more frequent than transversions (A↔C/T, G↔C/T). This is expected in biological systems: transitions occur more frequently due to the chemical similarity between purines (A↔G) and between pyrimidines (C↔T). High transition rates are often associated with true biological variation, while excessive transversions may signal artifacts.

Center panel represents a Ti/Tv ratio = 2.74, with ~34.5k transitions and ~12.6k transversions. A Ti/Tv ratio around 2.0–3.0 is considered typical for human whole-genome or exome sequencing and suggests high-quality variant calls. A much lower ratio might indicate sequencing noise or miscalling; a much higher one could indicate over-stringent filtering or reference bias.

Right panels represent biallelic indel size distribution. These histograms show the frequency of insertion and deletion sizes: the top panel uses a linear scale on the *y*-axis. Bottom panel uses a log scale to better visualize rare or large indels.

Most insertions (red) and deletions (blue) are small, especially in the ±1 to ±5 bp range. There is a very sharp peak at 1 bp insertions, suggesting that small indels dominate the call set. Larger indels are rare but still present. This distribution is expected, as small indels are more common in nature and easier to detect reliably. A spike in extremely large or oddly distributed indels could suggest alignment artifacts, but that is not evident here.

Overall, variant patterns and Ti/Tv ratio are consistent with biologically plausible and technically sound variant calling. Indel size profile confirms that most variants are small, with minimal evidence of systematic artifacts. These plots are useful for validating variant call sets prior to downstream analysis (e.g., annotation or filtering).

4 Conclusions

DeepVariant, a deep learning–based variant caller developed by Google, demonstrated (1) high SNP detection accuracy, especially in biallelic sites; (2) balanced Ti/Tv ratio, generally around 2.7–2.8, suggesting high variant quality; (3) strong genotype confidence (GQ) and well-calibrated quality scores (QUAL); (4) clear distinction in variant types, with SNPs dominating, and well-defined depth distributions; (5) it produces clean VAF and GQ distributions, supporting precise downstream filtering.

In the meantime, RNA-Mutect2 is optimized for somatic variant calling in RNA-seq data: (1) In our context, it typically detects

Table 3
Advantages of DeepVariant's AI-based approach

Feature	DeepVariant	RNA-Mutect2
Technology	Deep learning (CNN over read pileups)	Bayesian/statistical modeling
Input types	WGS, WES, RNA (with preprocessing)	Primarily RNA-seq (tumor or tumor- normal)
Training-based	Trained on high-confidence reference genomes	Rule- and threshold-based
Variant representation	Accurate modeling of SNPs and indels	Optimized for somatic mutations
Genotype quality	Well-calibrated (GQ, QUAL)	Often limited (esp. in tumor-only RNA)
Output interpretability	High, via scoring metrics	Moderate, especially without matched normal

heterozygous variants (0/x) due to the lack of matched-normal information in tumor-only mode; (2) shows a bias toward high VAF (~1.0), likely due to monoallelic expression or allelic imbalance; (3) has limited genotype resolution; most variants are classified as 0/1 or remain uncalled (./.); and (4) complex variant types (insertions, deletions, and large deletions) are present but may include alignment artifacts, especially near splice junctions [42].

The comparison between DeepVariant and RNA-Mutect2 is summarized in Table 3.

Major advantages of the AI-driven approach (DeepVariant) are:

1. Better generalization:
   - Trained on massive datasets, DeepVariant learns nuanced patterns from sequencing data that are hard to hand-code.
   - It can distinguish sequencing noise from real variation, especially in low-depth or noisy regions.

2. Accurate genotyping:
   - Produces well-calibrated GQ scores [31] (*see* **Note 11**), even at difficult loci.
   - Unlike RNA-Mutect2, it can confidently classify 0/0, 0/1, and 1/1 genotypes.

3. Consistent Ti/Tv ratios:
   - DeepVariant tends to produce biologically realistic variant distributions, reducing the need for aggressive filtering.
4. Better indel handling:
   - Deep learning models improve indel accuracy, especially in repetitive or homopolymeric regions [43].
5. Cross-platform performance:
   - Works across platforms (Illumina, PacBio, ONT) and with WGS, WES, and RNA-seq when properly trained.

In conclusion, AI-based tools, such as DeepVariant, outperform traditional tools in genotype accuracy, variant confidence, and biological realism. While RNA-Mutect2 is tailored to RNA-seq contexts and excels in somatic variant detection without matched normals, it lacks genotype clarity and can suffer from RNA-specific artifacts. The integration of AI-based models into RNA-specific pipelines holds promise for combining the strengths of both.

As a future direction, reinforcement learning (RL) [44] may be useful for genomic decision-making [30], such as AI learning optimal variant-calling strategies. In clinical applications, federated learning for multicenter data is expected to enable secure AI training across hospitals without sharing patient data.

5 Notes

1. Somatic mutations generally exhibit lower VAF than germline variants, as they are present in a subset of cells rather than all cells in an individual. Somatic mutations are typically below 50% VAF, with most occurring in the 1%–40% range. High-VAF mutations (~50% or ~100%) are usually germline, unless there is strong evidence for loss of heterozygosity (LOH) [45, 46].
2. There are challenges in VAF interpretation for scRNA-seq, including dropout effects, gene expression bias, and low coverage per cell [47]. More specifically, we need to consider the following issues:
   - Dropout effects [47]: Not all transcripts are captured, leading to false negatives. A heterozygous mutation (expected VAF ~50%) may appear much lower (e.g., 5%–40%).
   - Gene expression bias: Some genes are preferentially transcribed from one allele (monoallelic expression), affecting VAF. For example, if only one allele is expressed, a heterozygous mutation can appear homozygous (VAF $\approx$ 1.0) [48].

- Low coverage per cell: Unlike bulk sequencing, where depth is high, scRNA-seq has few reads per variant site. This makes VAF estimates highly variable across cells [49].

3. The scRNA-seq suffers from reverse transcription errors, amplification bias, and mapping artifacts. In such case, unique molecular identifier (UMI)-based correction or error models (e.g., from Cell Ranger [50] or GATK RNA-Mutect2 [22]) may help improve variant calling. If we have matched bulk DNA-seq data, comparing VAF distributions helps distinguish true somatic mutations from scRNA-seq-specific artifacts.

   Considering those factors, a broader range of VAF distributions can be roughly interpreted as follows:

- VAF 0.0–0.4: Noise and dropouts [3, 47]
- scRNA-seq has significant allelic dropout, meaning some alleles fail to be captured due to low coverage and stochastic expression.
- False-positive low-frequency variants can result from sequencing errors, mapping artifacts, or PCR amplification bias.
- True low-VAF somatic mutations (such as clonal mosaic mutations) might also be present.

- VAF 0.4–0.8: Heterozygous variants [9]
- Bulk sequencing would show these variants at VAF ~0.5, but in scRNA-seq, expression bias and allelic imbalance (monoallelic expression, imprinting) cause deviations.
- If this range includes mutant-enriched transcripts, it could still represent true heterozygous sites.

- VAF 0.8–1.0: Homozygous variants/highly expressed alleles [2, 51]

- Many true homozygous sites appear here, but:
- Monoallelically expressed heterozygous sites (e.g., X-linked genes in males, genomic imprinting) might cluster here.
- Highly expressed mutant transcripts (e.g., nonsense-mediated decay (NMD) escapees: mRNAs that contain premature termination codons (PTCs) but are not efficiently degraded by the NMD pathway [52]) can also accumulate in this region.
- Technical artifacts such as mapping bias [53] or preferential PCR amplification [54] may inflate these numbers.

- These categories were established based on practical considerations rather than strict criteria. To determine their validity, statistical tests should be applied.

4. Using AI to improve somatic mutation detection: Upscaling and advanced approaches: AI and machine learning (ML) can significantly enhance the reliability of somatic mutation detection by improving data quality, filtering artifacts, and upscaling single-cell sequencing data [55]. Table 2 shows advanced techniques for reliable somatic mutation detection using AI.
5. Data upscaling [56] for improved mutation detection: Upscaling in this context refers to enhancing sequencing data quality by denoising, imputing missing values, and refining variant calling. AI can be applied in the following ways:

   A. AI-based data denoising for scRNA-seq and low-coverage data

   Deep learning models (e.g., DeepVariant, Clairvoyante) can correct sequencing errors and infer true mutations by learning patterns from high-quality datasets.
   For example, DeepVariant (Google) [16] uses convolutional neural networks (CNNs) to improve variant calling accuracy. Clairvoyante [57] is a deep learning model for nanopore sequencing.
   Single-cell Variational Inference (SCVI) [19] denoises scRNA-seq data, improving sensitivity for mutation detection.

   B. Super-resolution variant calling with generative models

   Generative adversarial networks (GANs) [58] and autoencoders can simulate high-depth sequencing reads from low-coverage data [59]. For application, if a region has only 5× coverage, AI can synthesize high-resolution predictions as if it were 30× or higher. For example, DeepSV [60] uses deep learning to reconstruct missing structural variation signals.
6. AI-powered somatic mutation detection pipelines
   AI models can refine traditional somatic mutation detection methods by integrating multiple evidence sources.

   A. CNN-based variant calling

   CNNs learn patterns from raw sequencing reads and distinguish true mutations from artifacts.
   The DeepVariant achieves high accuracy in somatic variant detection using CNN-based image classification.

   B. Transformer-based models for variant calling

   Transformer architectures (e.g., DNABERT [61]) can process genomic sequences more efficiently. For example, a transformer trained on tumor-normal variant calling can prioritize likely somatic variants.

C. Probabilistic graph-based mutation calling

Bayesian and Markov models can integrate VAF distributions, allele-specific expression data, mutational signatures. For example, SomaticSeq [62] combines multiple mutation callers using machine learning ensembles.

7. Integrating multiomics data for more reliable calls
   AI can increase reliability by incorporating multimodal data. For example, with RNA-seq + DNA-seq integration, AI detects allele-specific expression and validates mutations at the transcript level.
   With assay for transposase-accessible chromatin with high-throughput sequencing ATAC-Seq [63] + Hi-C [64] data, AI can confirm mutations in accessible chromatin regions.
   ATAC-Seq is a genomic technique used to study chromatin accessibility, which helps identify regulatory regions such as promoters, enhancers, and transcription factor binding sites.
   Since somatic mutations can occur in non-coding regulatory regions, ATAC-Seq helps determine which mutations are functionally relevant (mutations in active enhancers may drive cancer), chromatin accessibility that changes in tumor evolution (epigenetic alterations), and mutational hotspots in regulatory elements, refining variant classification.
   Hi-C is a chromosome conformation capture (3C) technique [65] that maps 3D genome organization by identifying physical interactions between distant genomic regions. This helps in understanding how chromatin is folded and how different genomic elements interact.
   Since many somatic mutations occur in non-coding regions, Hi-C helps determine which mutations affect chromatin looping (e.g., enhancer hijacking in cancer [66]), if a mutation alters gene regulation by changing TAD boundaries [67], and structural variations such as translocations, affecting oncogene activation.
   For example, graph neural networks (GNNs) [68] is for genomic networks (e.g., mutation co-occurrence in pathways). Self-supervised learning (SSL) [69] is to uncover hidden patterns in mutations across datasets.
8. AI-driven filtering to reduce false positives

A. AI for removing germline variants

Training AI models on databases such as gnomAD [70] to automatically exclude germline variants. For example, a neural network can learn the population allele frequency patterns to filter germline-like mutations.

B. AI to identify technical artifacts

AI can learn sequencing error profiles from strand bias (SB), low-quality reads, and PCR duplication artifacts. For example, StratoMod [21] identifies systematic sequencing errors.

9. AI for clonality estimation and evolutionary tracking
AI can infer tumor evolution using phylogenetic trees. Bayesian AI models estimate how somatic mutations accumulate in a population. For example, Example PyClone-VI [20] uses variational inference to estimate clonal structures.

10. The following Python code generates a statistics report for VCF files:

```
import vcfpy
import pandas as pd
import os


def analyze_vcf(vcf_file):
""" Generate a statistical summary of the given VCF
file. """
# Open the VCF file
reader = vcfpy.Reader.from_path(vcf_file)

# Initialize counters
total_variants = 0
snp_count = 0
indel_count = 0
multi_allelic_count = 0
chrom_counts = {}
af_values = []
genotype_counts = {"0/0": 0, "0/1": 0, "1/1": 0,
"./.": 0} # Common GTs
for record in reader:
total_variants += 1
# Count SNPs and Indels
if all(len(ref) == 1 and all(len(alt.value) == 1
for alt in record.ALT) for ref in record.REF):
snp_count += 1
else:
indel_count += 1
# Multi-allelic variant check
if len(record.ALT) > 1:
multi_allelic_count += 1
# Count variants per chromosome
chrom_counts[record.CHROM] = chrom_counts.
get(record.CHROM, 0) + 1
# Collect AF values if present
if "AF" in record.INFO:
af_values.extend(record.INFO["AF"])
# Count genotypes
for call in record.calls:
```

```
genotype = call.data.get("GT", "./.")
if genotype in genotype_counts:
genotype_counts[genotype] += 1
# Generate statistics report
stats = {
"Total Variants": total_variants,
"SNPs": snp_count,
"Indels": indel_count,
"Multi-Allelic Variants": multi_allelic_count,
"Chromosome-wise Variants": chrom_counts,
"Genotype Counts": genotype_counts
}
# Calculate AF statistics
if af_values:
af_series = pd.Series(af_values)
stats["Allele Frequency (AF) Stats"] = {
"Mean AF": af_series.mean(),
"Median AF": af_series.median(),
"Max AF": af_series.max(),
"Min AF": af_series.min(),
}
else:
stats["Allele Frequency (AF) Stats"] = "No AF
values found."
return stats
# Example Usage
vcf_file = "/path/to/your/file.vcf.gz" # Replace with
your VCF file path
if not os.path.exists(vcf_file):
raise FileNotFoundError(f"VCF file not found:
{vcf_file}")
# Run analysis and print statistics
vcf_stats = analyze_vcf(vcf_file)
for key, value in vcf_stats.items():
print(f"{key}: {value}")
```

This script uses `pysam`, `pandas`, and `vcfpy` to extract key statistics from a VCF file, such as:

- Total variants
- SNPs, indels, and multiallelic variants
- Chromosome-wise variant distribution
- Allele frequency (AF) statistics
- Genotype (GT) counts

Before running the script, you may need to install the necessary Python libraries:

```
pip install pandas pysam vcfpy
```

11. $GQ = -10 \log_{10}(P\ (\text{genotype is incorrect}))$.

Acknowledgments

This work was supported by the GAP Fund from RIKEN and KAKENHI (Grant No. 17H06399). The author thanks Eri Torichigai for her assistance.

Conflict of Interest The authors have no conflicts of interest to declare that are relevant to the content of this chapter.

References

1. Liu F, Zhang Y, Zhang L, Li Z, Fang Q, Gao R, Zhang Z (2019) Systematic comparative analysis of single-nucleotide variant detection methods from single-cell RNA sequencing data. Genome Biol 20(1):242. https://doi.org/10.1186/s13059-019-1863-4
2. Vu TN, Nguyen H-N, Calza S, Kalari KR, Wang L, Pawitan Y (2019) Cell-level somatic mutation detection from single-cell RNA sequencing. Bioinformatics 35(22):4679–4687. https://doi.org/10.1093/bioinformatics/btz288
3. Petti AA, Williams SR, Miller CA, Fiddes IT, Srivatsan SN, Chen DY, Fronick CC, Fulton RS, Church DM, Ley TJ (2019) A general approach for detecting expressed mutations in AML cells using single cell RNA-sequencing. Nat Commun 10(1):3660. https://doi.org/10.1038/s41467-019-11591-1
4. Jiang Y, Zhang NR, Li M (2017) SCALE: modeling allele-specific gene expression by single-cell RNA sequencing. Genome Biol 18(1):74. https://doi.org/10.1186/s13059-017-1200-8
5. Marot-Lassauzaie V, Beneyto-Calabuig S, Obermayer B, Velten L, Beule D, Haghverdi L (2024) Identifying cancer cells from calling single-nucleotide variants in scRNA-seq data. Bioinformatics 40(9), btae512. https://doi.org/10.1093/bioinformatics/btae512
6. Qi G, Strober BJ, Popp JM, Keener R, Ji H, Battle A (2023) Single-cell allele-specific expression analysis reveals dynamic and cell-type-specific regulatory effects. Nat Commun 14(1):6317. https://doi.org/10.1038/s41467-023-42016-9
7. Edwards N, et al. (2023) SCExecute: custom cell barcode-stratified analyses of scRNA-seq data. Bioinformatics 39(1), btac768. https://doi.org/10.1093/bioinformatics/btac768
8. Navin N, Kendall J, Troge J, Andrews P, Rodgers L, McIndoo J, Cook K, Stepansky A, Levy D, Esposito D, Muthuswamy L, Krasnitz A, McCombie WR, Hicks J, Wigler M (2011) Tumour evolution inferred by single-cell sequencing. Nature 472(7341):90–94. https://doi.org/10.1038/nature09807
9. Prashant NM, Liu H, Bousounis P, Spurr L, Alomran N, Ibeawuchi H, Sein J, Reece-Stremtan D, Horvath A (2020) Estimating the allele-specific expression of SNVs from 10× genomics single-cell RNA-sequencing data. Genes (Basel) 11(3):240. https://doi.org/10.3390/genes11030240
10. Kim JK, Marioni JC (2013) Inferring the kinetics of stochastic gene expression from single-cell RNA-sequencing data. Genome Biol 14(1):R7. https://doi.org/10.1186/gb-2013-14-1-r7
11. Reinius B, Sandberg R (2015) Random monoallelic expression of autosomal genes: stochastic transcription and allele-level regulation. Nat Rev Genet 16(11):653–664. https://doi.org/10.1038/nrg3888
12. Huang Y, McCarthy DJ, Stegle O (2018) SAVER: gene expression recovery for single-cell RNA sequencing. Nat Methods 15(7):539–542. https://doi.org/10.1038/s41592-018-0033-z
13. Zappia L, Phipson B, Oshlack A (2018) Exploring the single-cell RNA-seq analysis landscape with the scRNA-tools database. PLoS Comput Biol 14(6):e1006245. https://doi.org/10.1371/journal.pcbi.1006245
14. van Dijk D, Sharma R, Nainys J, Yim K, Kathail P, Carr AJ, Burdziak C, Moon KR, Chaffer CL, Pattabiraman D, Bierie B, Mazutis L, Wolf G, Krishnaswamy S, Pe'er D (2018) Recovering gene interactions from single-cell data using data diffusion. Cell 174(3):716–729.e727. https://doi.org/10.1016/j.cell.2018.05.061
15. Dou J, Tan Y, Kock KH, Wang J, Cheng X, Tan LM, Han KY, Hon C-C, Park W-Y, Shin JW, Jin H, Wang Y, Chen H, Ding L, Prabhakar S, Navin N, Chen R, Chen K (2024) Single-nucleotide variant calling in single-cell sequencing data with Monopogen. Nat Biotechnol 42(5):803–812. https://doi.org/10.1038/s41587-023-01873-x
16. Poplin R, Chang P-C, Alexander D, Schwartz S, Colthurst T, Ku A, Newburger D, Dijamco J, Nguyen N, Afshar PT, Gross SS, Dorfman L, McLean CY, DePristo MA (2018) A universal

SNP and small-indel variant caller using deep neural networks. Nat Biotechnol 36(10):983–987. https://doi.org/10.1038/nbt.4235
17. Luo R, Sedlazeck FJ, Lam T-W, Schatz MC (2018) Clairvoyante: a multi-task convolutional deep neural network for variant calling in Single Molecule Sequencing. bioRxiv:310458. 10.1101/310458
18. Fang LT (2020) SomaticSeq: an ensemble and machine learning method to detect somatic mutations. Methods Mol Biol 2120:47–70. https://doi.org/10.1007/978-1-0716-0327-7_4
19. Lopez R, Regier J, Cole MB, Jordan MI, Yosef N (2018) Deep generative modeling for single-cell transcriptomics. Nat Methods 15(12):1053–1058. https://doi.org/10.1038/s41592-018-0229-2
20. Gillis S, Roth A (2020) PyClone-VI: scalable inference of clonal population structures using whole genome data. BMC Bioinformatics 21(1):571. https://doi.org/10.1186/s12859-020-03919-2
21. Dwarshuis N, Tonner P, Olson ND, Sedlazeck FJ, Wagner J, Zook JM (2024) StratoMod: predicting sequencing and variant calling errors with interpretable machine learning. Commun Biol 7(1):1316. https://doi.org/10.1038/s42003-024-06981-1
22. Benjamin D, Sato K, Cibulskis K, Getz G, Stewart C, Lichtenstein L (2019) Calling somatic SNVs and indels with Mutect2. bioRxiv
23. Sheng Q, Zhao S, Li CI, Shyr Y, Guo Y (2016) Practicability of detecting somatic point mutation from RNA high throughput sequencing data. Genomics 107(5):163–169. https://doi.org/10.1016/j.ygeno.2016.03.006
24. Dobin A, Davis CA, Schlesinger F, Drenkow J, Zaleski C, Jha S, Batut P, Chaisson M, Gingeras TR (2012) STAR: ultrafast universal RNA-seq aligner. Bioinformatics 29(1):15–21. https://doi.org/10.1093/bioinformatics/bts635
25. Kim D, Paggi JM, Park C, Bennett C, Salzberg SL (2019) Graph-based genome alignment and genotyping with HISAT2 and HISAT-genotype. Nat Biotechnol 37(8):907–915. https://doi.org/10.1038/s41587-019-0201-4
26. Rumelhart DE, Hinton GE, Williams RJ (1986) Learning representations by back-propagating errors. Nature 323(6088):533–536. https://doi.org/10.1038/323533a0
27. Li H, Handsaker B, Wysoker A, Fennell T, Ruan J, Homer N, Marth G, Abecasis G, Durbin R (2009) The Sequence Alignment/Map format and SAMtools. Bioinformatics 25(16):2078–2079. https://doi.org/10.1093/bioinformatics/btp352
28. Lecun Y, Bottou L, Bengio Y, Haffner P (1998) Gradient-based learning applied to document recognition. Proc IEEE 86(11):2278–2324. https://doi.org/10.1109/5.726791
29. Danecek P, Auton A, Abecasis G, Albers CA, Banks E, DePristo MA, Handsaker RE, Lunter G, Marth GT, Sherry ST, McVean G, Durbin R, Genomes Project Analysis G (2011) The variant call format and VCFtools. Bioinformatics (Oxford, England) 27(15):2156–2158. https://doi.org/10.1093/bioinformatics/btr330
30. DePristo MA, Banks E, Poplin R, Garimella KV, Maguire JR, Hartl C, Philippakis AA, del Angel G, Rivas MA, Hanna M, McKenna A, Fennell TJ, Kernytsky AM, Sivachenko AY, Cibulskis K, Gabriel SB, Altshuler D, Daly MJ (2011) A framework for variation discovery and genotyping using next-generation DNA sequencing data. Nat Genet 43(5):491–498. https://doi.org/10.1038/ng.806
31. McKenna A, Hanna M, Banks E, Sivachenko A, Cibulskis K, Kernytsky A, Garimella K, Altshuler D, Gabriel S, Daly M, DePristo MA (2010) The Genome Analysis Toolkit: a MapReduce framework for analyzing next-generation DNA sequencing data. Genome Res 20(9):1297–1303. https://doi.org/10.1101/gr.107524.110
32. The SAM/BAM Format Specification Working Group (2020) Sequence alignment/map format specification. https://samtools.github.io/hts-specs/SAMv1.pdf. Accessed 29 2020
33. Li H, Durbin R (2009) Fast and accurate short read alignment with Burrows-Wheeler transform. Bioinformatics 25(14):1754–1760. https://doi.org/10.1093/bioinformatics/btp324
34. Dobin A, Gingeras TR (2015) Mapping RNA-seq Reads with STAR. Curr Protoc Bioinformatics 51:11.14.11–11.14.19. https://doi.org/10.1002/0471250953.bi1114s51
35. Broad I (2019) Picard Toolkit. Broad Institute
36. Anaconda I (2012) Conda: Package, dependency and environment management for any language
37. Van der Auwera GA, Carneiro MO, Hartl C, Poplin R, Del Angel G, Levy-Moonshine A, Jordan T, Shakir K, Roazen D, Thibault J, Banks E, Garimella KV, Altshuler D, Gabriel S, DePristo MA (2013) From FastQ data to high confidence variant calls: the Genome Analysis Toolkit best practices pipeline. Curr Protoc Bioinformatics 43(1110):11.10.11–11.10.33. https://doi.org/10.1002/0471250953.bi1110s43
38. Merkel D (2014) Docker: lightweight Linux containers for consistent development and deployment. Linux J 2014(239):Article 2
39. Coulondre C, Miller JH, Farabaugh PJ, Gilbert W (1978) Molecular basis of base substitution hotspots in Escherichia coli. Nature

274(5673):775–780. https://doi.org/10.1038/274775a0
40. Kimura M (1980) A simple method for estimating evolutionary rates of base substitutions through comparative studies of nucleotide sequences. J Mol Evol 16(2):111–120. https://doi.org/10.1007/BF01731581
41. Ewing B, Green P (1998) Base-calling of automated sequencer traces using phred. II. Error probabilities. Genome Res 8(3):186–194
42. Engström PG, Steijger T, Sipos B, Grant GR, Kahles A, Alioto T, Behr J, Bertone P, Bohnert R, Campagna D, Davis CA, Dobin A, Engström PG, Gingeras TR, Goldman N, Grant GR, Guigó R, Harrow J, Hubbard TJ, Jean G, Kahles A, Kosarev P, Li S, Liu J, Mason CE, Molodtsov V, Ning Z, Ponstingl H, Prins JF, Rätsch G, Ribeca P, Seledtsov I, Sipos B, Solovyev V, Steijger T, Valle G, Vitulo N, Wang K, Wu TD, Zeller G, Rätsch G, Goldman N, Hubbard TJ, Harrow J, Guigó R, Bertone P, The RC (2013) Systematic evaluation of spliced alignment programs for RNA-seq data. Nat Methods 10(12):1185–1191. https://doi.org/10.1038/nmeth.2722
43. Dechering KJ, Cuelenaere K, Konings RN, Leunissen JA (1998) Distinct frequency-distributions of homopolymeric DNA tracts in different genomes. Nucleic Acids Res 26(17):4056–4062. https://doi.org/10.1093/nar/26.17.4056
44. Sutton RS, Barto AG (1998) Reinforcement learning: an introduction.
45. Constance B, Wencke W, Stephan H, Sven T, Manja M, Wolfgang K, Torsten H, Claudia H (2019) "Somatic" and "pathogenic" - is the classification strategy applicable in times of large-scale sequencing?. Haematologica 104(8):1515–1520. https://doi.org/10.3324/haematol.2019.218917
46. Jalloul N, Gomy I, Stokes S, Gusev A, Johnson BE, Lindeman NI, Macconaill L, Ganesan S, Garber JE, Khiabanian H (2021) Germline testing data validate inferences of mutational status for variants detected from tumor-only sequencing. JCO Precis Oncol 5:1749–1757. https://doi.org/10.1200/PO.21.00279
47. Qiu P (2020) Embracing the dropouts in single-cell RNA-seq analysis. Nat Commun 11: 1169. https://doi.org/10.1038/s41467-020-14976-9
48. Nag A, Savova V, Fung HL, Miron A, Yuan GC, Zhang K, Gimelbrant AA (2013) Chromatin signature of widespread monoallelic expression. eLife 2:e01256. https://doi.org/10.7554/eLife.01256
49. Pollen AA, Nowakowski TJ, Shuga J, Wang X, Leyrat AA, Lui JH, Li N, Szpankowski L, Fowler B, Chen P, Ramalingam N, Sun G, Thu M, Norris M, Lebofsky R, Toppani D, Kemp DW, Wong M, Clerkson B, Jones BN, Wu S, Knutsson L, Alvarado B, Wang J, Weaver LS, May AP, Jones RC, Unger MA, Kriegstein AR, West JAA (2014) Low-coverage single-cell mRNA sequencing reveals cellular heterogeneity and activated signaling pathways in developing cerebral cortex. Nat Biotechnol 32(10):1053–1058. https://doi.org/10.1038/nbt.2967
50. Zheng GXY, Terry JM, Belgrader P, Ryvkin P, Bent ZW, Wilson R, Ziraldo SB, Wheeler TD, McDermott GP, Zhu J, Gregory MT, Shuga J, Montesclaros L, Underwood JG, Masquelier DA, Nishimura SY, Schnall-Levin M, Wyatt PW, Hindson CM, Bharadwaj R, Wong A, Ness KD, Beppu LW, Deegan DF, Collier S, Nesselbeck S, McCracken C, Pothula K, Hamby ME, Bowden AK, Sinha A, Tuttle PD, Yuan R, Jones RC, Mack D, Eastburn DJ, Fredrikson KT, Hindson BJ, Saxonov S, Stevanovic M, Bielas JH (2017) Massively parallel digital transcriptional profiling of single cells. Nat Commun 8: 14049. https://doi.org/10.1038/ncomms14049
51. Gimelbrant A, Hutchinson JN, Thompson BR, Chess A (2007) Widespread monoallelic expression on human autosomes. Science 318(5853):1136–1140. https://doi.org/10.1126/science.1148910
52. Dyle MC, Kolakada D, Cortazar MA, Jagannathan S (2020) How to get away with nonsense: mechanisms and consequences of escape from nonsense-mediated RNA decay. Wiley Interdiscip Rev: RNA 11(1):e1560. https://doi.org/10.1002/wrna.1560
53. Schwartz S, Oren R, Ast G (2011) Detection and removal of biases in the analysis of next-generation sequencing reads. PLoS One 6(1):e16685. https://doi.org/10.1371/journal.pone.0016685
54. Walsh PS, Erlich HA, Higuchi R (1992) Preferential PCR amplification of alleles: mechanisms and solutions. PCR Methods Appl 1(4):241–250. https://doi.org/10.1101/gr.1.4.241
55. Liu X, Chapple RH, Bennett D, Wright WC, Sanjali A, Culp E, Zhang Y, Pan M, Geeleher P (2025) CSI-GEP: A GPU-based unsupervised machine learning approach for recovering gene expression programs in atlas-scale single-cell RNA-seq data. Cell Genom 5(1):100739. https://doi.org/10.1016/j.xgen.2024.100739
56. Dong C, Loy CC, He K, Tang X (2015) Image super-resolution using deep convolutional networks. arXiv preprint arXiv:1501.00092
57. Luo R, Sedlazeck FJ, Lam T-W, Schatz MC (2019) A multi-task convolutional deep neural network for variant calling in single molecule

sequencing. Nat Commun 10(1):998. https://doi.org/10.1038/s41467-019-09025-z
58. Goodfellow IJ, Pouget-Abadie J, Mirza M, Xu B, Warde-Farley D, Ozair S, Courville A, Bengio Y (2014) Generative adversarial networks
59. Han BW, Yang X, Qu SF, Guo ZW, Huang LM, Li K, Ouyang GJ, Cai GX, Xiao WW, Weng RT, Xu S, Huang J, Yang XX, Wu YS (2021) A deep-learning pipeline for TSS coverage imputation from shallow cell-free DNA Sequencing. Front Med (Lausanne) 8:684238. https://doi.org/10.3389/fmed.2021.684238
60. Cai L, Wu Y, Gao J (2019) DeepSV: accurate calling of genomic deletions from high-throughput sequencing data using deep convolutional neural network. BMC Bioinformatics 20(1):665. https://doi.org/10.1186/s12859-019-3299-y
61. Ji Y, Zhou Z, Liu H, Davuluri RV (2021) DNABERT: pre-trained Bidirectional Encoder Representations from Transformers model for DNA-language in genome. Bioinformatics 37(15):2112–2120. https://doi.org/10.1093/bioinformatics/btab083
62. Fang LT, Afshar PT, Chhibber A, Mohiyuddin M, Fan Y, Mu JC, Gibeling G, Barr S, Asadi NB, Gerstein MB, Koboldt DC, Wang W, Wong WH, Lam HY (2015) An ensemble approach to accurately detect somatic mutations using SomaticSeq. Genome Biol 16: 197. https://doi.org/10.1186/s13059-015-0758-2
63. Buenrostro JD, Giresi PG, Zaba LC, Chang HY, Greenleaf WJ (2013) Transposition of native chromatin for fast and sensitive epigenomic profiling of open chromatin, DNA-binding proteins and nucleosome position. Nat Methods 10(12):1213–1218. https://doi.org/10.1038/nmeth.2688
64. Lieberman-Aiden E, van Berkum NL, Williams L, Imakaev M, Ragoczy T, Telling A, Amit I, Lajoie BR, Sabo PJ, Dorschner MO, Sandstrom R, Bernstein B, Bender MA, Groudine M, Gnirke A, Stamatoyannopoulos J, Mirny LA, Lander ES, Dekker J (2009) Comprehensive mapping of long-range interactions reveals folding principles of the human genome. Science 326(5950):289–293. https://doi.org/10.1126/science.1181369
65. Dekker J, Rippe K, Dekker M, Kleckner N (2002) Capturing Chromosome Conformation. Science 295(5558):1306–1311. https://doi.org/10.1126/science.1067799
66. Northcott PA, Lee C, Zichner T, Stütz AM, Erkek S, Kawauchi D, Shih DJH, Hovestadt V, Zapatka M, Sturm D, Jones DTW, Kool M, Remke M, Cavalli FMG, Zuyderduyn S, Bader GD, VandenBerg S, Esparza LA, Ryzhova M, Wang W, Wittmann A, Stark S, Sieber L, Seker-Cin H, Linke L, Kratochwil F, Jäger N, Buchhalter I, Imbusch CD, Zipprich G, Raeder B, Schmidt S, Diessl N, Wolf S, Wiemann S, Brors B, Lawerenz C, Eils J, Warnatz H-J, Risch T, Yaspo M-L, Weber UD, Bartholomae CC, von Kalle C, Turányi E, Hauser P, Sanden E, Darabi A, Siesjö P, Sterba J, Zitterbart K, Sumerauer D, van Sluis P, Versteeg R, Volckmann R, Koster J, Schuhmann MU, Ebinger M, Grimes HL, Robinson GW, Gajjar A, Mynarek M, von Hoff K, Rutkowski S, Pietsch T, Scheurlen W, Felsberg J, Reifenberger G, Kulozik AE, von Deimling A, Witt O, Eils R, Gilbertson RJ, Korshunov A, Taylor MD, Lichter P, Korbel JO, Wechsler-Reya RJ, Pfister SM (2014) Enhancer hijacking activates GFI1 family oncogenes in medulloblastoma. Nature 511(7510):428–434. https://doi.org/10.1038/nature13379
67. Dixon JR, Selvaraj S, Yue F, Kim A, Li Y, Shen Y, Hu M, Liu JS, Ren B (2012) Topological domains in mammalian genomes identified by analysis of chromatin interactions. Nature 485(7398):376–380. https://doi.org/10.1038/nature11082
68. Scarselli F, Gori M, Tsoi AC, Hagenbuchner M, Monfardini G (2009) The Graph Neural Network Model. IEEE Trans Neural Netw 20(1):61–80. https://doi.org/10.1109/TNN.2008.2005605
69. Doersch C, Gupta A, Efros AA (2016) Unsupervised visual representation learning by context prediction
70. Karczewski KJ, Francioli LC, Tiao G, Cummings BB, Alföldi J, Wang Q, Collins RL, Laricchia KM, Ganna A, Birnbaum DP, Gauthier LD, Brand H, Solomonson M, Watts NA, Rhodes D, Singer-Berk M, England EM, Seaby EG, Kosmicki JA, Walters RK, Tashman K, Farjoun Y, Banks E, Poterba T, Wang A, Seed C, Whiffin N, Chong JX, Samocha KE, Pierce-Hoffman E, Zappala Z, O'Donnell-Luria AH, Minikel EV, Weisburd B, Lek M, Ware JS, Vittal C, Armean IM, Bergelson L, Cibulskis K, Connolly KM, Covarrubias M, Donnelly S, Ferriera S, Gabriel S, Gentry J, Gupta N, Jeandet T, Kaplan D, Llanwarne C, Munshi R, Novod S, Petrillo N, Roazen D, Ruano-Rubio V, Saltzman A, Schleicher M, Soto J, Tibbetts K, Tolonen C, Wade G, Talkowski ME, Aguilar Salinas CA, Ahmad T, Albert CM, Ardissino D, Atzmon G, Barnard J, Beaugerie L, Benjamin EJ, Boehnke M, Bonnycastle LL, Bottinger EP, Bowden DW, Bown MJ, Chambers JC, Chan JC, Chasman D, Cho J, Chung MK, Cohen B, Correa A, Dabelea D, Daly MJ, Darbar D, Duggirala R, Dupuis J, Ellinor PT, Elosua R, Erdmann J, Esko T, Färkkilä M, Florez J, Franke A, Getz G, Glaser B, Glatt SJ, Goldstein D, Gonzalez C, Groop L, Haiman C, Hanis C, Harms M,

Hiltunen M, Holi MM, Hultman CM, Kallela M, Kaprio J, Kathiresan S, Kim B-J, Kim YJ, Kirov G, Kooner J, Koskinen S, Krumholz HM, Kugathasan S, Kwak SH, Laakso M, Lehtimäki T, Loos RJF, Lubitz SA, Ma RCW, MacArthur DG, Marrugat J, Mattila KM, McCarroll S, McCarthy MI, McGovern D, McPherson R, Meigs JB, Melander O, Metspalu A, Neale BM, Nilsson PM, O'Donovan MC, Ongur D, Orozco L, Owen MJ, Palmer CNA, Palotie A, Park KS, Pato C, Pulver AE, Rahman N, Remes AM, Rioux JD, Ripatti S, Roden DM, Saleheen D, Salomaa V, Samani NJ, Scharf J, Schunkert H, Shoemaker MB, Sklar P, Soininen H, Sokol H, Spector T, Sullivan PF, Suvisaari J, Tai ES, Teo YY, Tiinamaija T, Tsuang M, Turner D, Tusie-Luna T, Vartiainen E, Vawter MP, Ware JS, Watkins H, Weersma RK, Wessman M, Wilson JG, Xavier RJ, Neale BM, Daly MJ, MacArthur DG, Genome Aggregation Database C (2020) The mutational constraint spectrum quantified from variation in 141,456 humans. Nature 581(7809):434–443. https://doi.org/10.1038/s41586-020-2308-7

Chapter 13

Copy Number Variation Analysis

Haydee Artaza

Abstract

Copy number variants (CNVs) considerably influence the human genome and may play a role in disease development. Data produced by high-throughput SNP genotyping platforms can be used for CNV detection. Here, we present a study case, including code, for the detection of CNVs, quality assessment, and identification of rare CNVs.

Keywords CNVs detection, Rare CNVs, PennCNV, Plink, Pathways

1 Introduction

Copy Number Variations (CNVs) represent a form of structural variation within the genome. This phenomenon involves the alternation in the number of copies of a particular DNA segment, leading to the occurrence of deletions and duplications across the genome. CNVs are a significant source of genetic diversity between individuals and play a crucial role in numerous complex diseases, including mental illness, developmental disorders, and cancer [1, 2].

Diverse technologies for the detection of CNVs have been established, including quantitative polymerase chain reaction (qPCR) [3] and multiplex ligation-dependent probe amplification (MLPA) [4], both of which are targeted gene panel methods. Subsequently, microarray-based methods such as array-CGH (comparative genomic hybridization) and single nucleotide polymorphism (SNP)-array have enabled the investigation of CNVs, offering significant advancements due to their genome-wide approach [5, 6].

In this work, we present the fundamental analysis of rare CNV using the genotyping data from the SNP array, PennCNV [7], and Plink [8] for CNV detection. This process includes conducting the quality assessment and identifying rare CNVs implicated in a specific disorder. To illustrate this, we use a specific case study involving the

Y-h Taguchi (ed.), *AI/ML-Driven Gene Analysis*, Methods in Molecular Biology, vol. 3037,
https://doi.org/10.1007/978-1-0716-5284-8_13,

detection, quality control (QC), and rare CNVs analysis in a subset of individuals with pediatric obesity, analysed in a prior study [5]. This previous study was selected due to the availability of free data and its suitability as a case study for this work. We do not intend to replicate this study.

This analysis assumes the reader is skilled in using Linux-based operating systems.

2 Materials

All necessary code and resources for conducting this analysis are included within the files provided by this work:

1. Raw data from Gene Expression Omnibus (GEO): GSE101417.
2. Resources (see Sect. 2.2).
3. Calling and quality control (QC) script code.
4. Rare CNV script code.

2.1 Samples

The genotyping data was downloaded from https://www.ncbi.nlm.nih.gov/geo/query/acc.cgi?acc=GSE101418. This dataset comprises 31 genotyped data, obtained using Illumina HumanOmni2.5 platform.

2.2 Other Resources

1. For the extraction of rare CNVs, we used the Gold Strand Variants file for GRCh37, which was download from Database of Genomic Variants (DGV) https://dgv.tcag.ca/dgv/docs/DGV.GS.March2016.50percent.GainLossSep.Final.hg19.gff3.
2. The gene annotation for the entire genome was downloaded from the Plink resources page https://www.cog-genomics.org/plink/1.9/resources.
3. Files used by PennCNV for CNV detection are provided within the files included in this analysis.

2.3 Preparing the Environment for Code Execution

1. Download the project from test.tar.gz. The structure should be the next:

```
├── GSE101417_RAW.tar
├── qc_CNV_analysis
│   ├── qc_pipeline.sh
│   ├── qc_plots.R
│   └── rareCNV_pipeline.sh
└── resources
```

2. CNV detection and quality control:
   - Uncompress genotyping data in your base directory (“.” in point 1):

     mkdir GSE101417_RAW

     tar xvf GSE101417_RAW.tar -C GSE101417_RAW
   - Define the base directory for work by assigning it to the ***$basedir*** variable inside *qc_pipeline.sh* script included on qc_CNV_analysis directory.
   - Run the script for calling and quality control (QC):.
     /qc_pipeline.sh
   - Results generated by the previous script will be found in the qc_results directory.

3. Rare CNVs analysis:
   - Specify the path to Plink executable in the ***$plink*** variable within the *rareCNV_pipeline.sh* script included in the qc_CNV_analysis directory.
   - Define the base directory for work by assigning it to the ***$basedir*** variable inside *rareCNV_pipeline.sh* script.
   - Run the script for rare CNVs analysis:.
     /rareCNV_pipeline.sh
   - Results generated by the previous script will be found in the rareCNV_results directory.

3 Methods

The analysis consists of two sub-analysis: (1) detections and quality control of CNVs, and (2) identifications of rare CNVs. The code presented in this section is included in the material provided, as shown in Sect. 2.

3.1 CNV Detection and Quality Control (QC)

1. CNV calling is performed using PennCNV version 1.0.5. CNVs are identified from the genotyping data of 31 individuals with pediatric obesity. The SNP-array genotyping signal intensity values, Log R Ratio (LRR), and B Allele Frequency (BAF), are extracted from the HumanOmni2.5 report (*see* **Note 1**):

```
#Preparing input signal intensity files from Illumina
Report
split_illumina_report.pl \
    -numeric \
    -prefix  $intensitydir/  $rawdatadir/GSE101417_
     report.txt
```

The command *split_illumina_report.pl* generates a file for each sample, containing the signal intensity for each SNP. The *--numeric* parameter allows for the generation of a numeric ID name for each file associated-sample, which helps to anonymize the original IDs when working with sensitive data samples.

2. PFB (Population frequency of B allele) file and the GCModel files are generated since PennCNV relies on these for accurate CNV detection:

```
# Get PBF file using PennCNV
commandcompile_pfb.pl \
  -listfile $conversiondir/list_intensity_files.txt \
  -snpposfile $conversiondir/SNPfile.txt \
  -output $conversiondir/GSE101417.pfb
# Get GC model file using PennCNV command
cal_gc_snp.pl \
    $resourcesdir/hg19.gc5Base.txt $conversiondir/
    SNPfile.txt\-output $conversiondir/GSE101417.
    hg19.gcmodel
```

The *compile_pfb.pl* generates the PBF model using the list of signal intensity files (--listfile) and all SNPs positions (--snpposfile). Similarly, the command *cal_gc_snp.pl* calculate GC content surrounding each marker, using the UCSC GC annotation file and the all SNPs positions. The --out argument specifies the output path.

3. After obtaining PBF and GC content model, the calling of CNVs is carried out as follows:

```
detect_cnv.pl \
  -test \
  -conf \
  -hmm $resourcesdir/hhall.hmm \
  -pfb $conversiondir/GSE101417.pfb \
  -directory $intensitydir \
  -list $conversiondir/list_intensity_files.txt \
  -log $callingdir/sampleall.log \
  -out $callingdir/sampleall.rawcn \
  -gcmodel $conversiondir/GSE101417.hg19.gcmodel
```

The arguments --test is used to generate CNV calls. The --hmmfile argument uses the generic HMM model file (hhall.hmm), along with the previous generated PFB and GC models. The --list argument specifies the list of samples CNV generation, the --log argument indicates the log file, and the --out argument specifies the output CNV calls.
For the 31 samples, a total of 1644 calls were obtained as a result of the calling process.

4. Following the detection of CNVs, a standard quality procedure is conducted to evaluate the quality at both the sample level and call level.
5. At the call level, CNV calls detected in challenging genomic regions such as the regions near the centromeres and the telomeres are considered spurious and are removed:

```
# Cleaning spurious regions
scan_region.pl \
    $callingdir/sampleall.rawcn \
    $resourcesdir/immunoglobulin_penncnv.txt \
    -minqueryfrac 0.5 > $cleandir/immunoglobulin.
    regions

scan_region.pl \
    $cleandir/immonuglobulin.clean.rawcn \
    $resourcesdir/centromere_telomere_penncnv.txt \
    -minqueryfrac 0.5 > $cleandir/centromere_telomere.
    regions
```

The files immunoglobulin_penncnv.txt and centromere_telomere_penncnv.txt contain the positions of telomeres and centromeres, respectively, in the format chr:bp1-bp2.

6. At sample level, the SNP-array genotyping signal intensity values, LRR_SD (standard deviation of the LRR), BAF_drift (B Allele Frequency drift which summarize the proportion of BAF values falling out of the expected: 0, 0.5 and 1), WF (Waviness Factor, which measure the strength of waviness in a given sample), and NumCNVs (number of called CNVs per sample) for all markers in all samples is evaluated:

```
# Filtering calls by LRR_SD, BAF_drift, WF, NumCNV
qcnumcnv=54
wf=0.05
qcbafdrift=0.01
qclrrsd=0.3

filter_cnv.pl $cleandir/centromere_telomere.clean.
rawcn \
    -qcnumcnv $qcnumcnv \
    -qcwf $wf \
    -qcbafdrift $qcbafdrift \
    -qclrrsd $qclrrsd \
    -qclogfile $callingdir/sampleall.log \
    -qcpassout $cleandir/samples_clean_qcpass.list \
    -qcsumout $cleandir/samples_clean_qcsum.list \
    -output $cleandir/samples_clean_qcpass.rawcn
```

The *filter_cnv.pl* command analyzes the sampleall.log log file (--qclogfile), which was previously generated in the CNV detection process. It identifies all samples with LRR_SD less than specific value at *qclrrsd*, BAF_drift less than qcbafdrift, WF less than *wf*, and NumCNV less than *qcnumcnv*. Samples that pass the QC are written to the *samples_clean_qcpass.list* file, and the CNV calls for these samples are written to the *samples_clean_qcpass.rawcn* file. Additionally, the QC summary for all samples is written to the sampleall.qcsum file.

7. The performance of these quality metrics in samples meeting or failing the exclusion criteria can be inspected using various plots. These plots assist in determining the appropriate study-specific threshold values (see Figs. 1 and 2).

8. For this case study, we will set the default QC criteria for the next analysis as follows: LRR_SD < 0.3, BAF_drift < 0.01 and |WF| < 0.05. Additionally, we establish the NumCNVs < 54 (*see* **Note 2**).

9. Finally, adjacent CNV calls are merged to address the tendency of artificially fragmenting larger CNVs into smaller segments during the calling process. This procedure results in a set of high-quality CNVs, which will be used for the investigation of rare CNVs:

```
# Merging adjacent CNV calls
clean_cnv.pl \
  -fraction 0.5 \
    -bp \
    -signalfile $conversiondir/GSE101417.pfb \
```

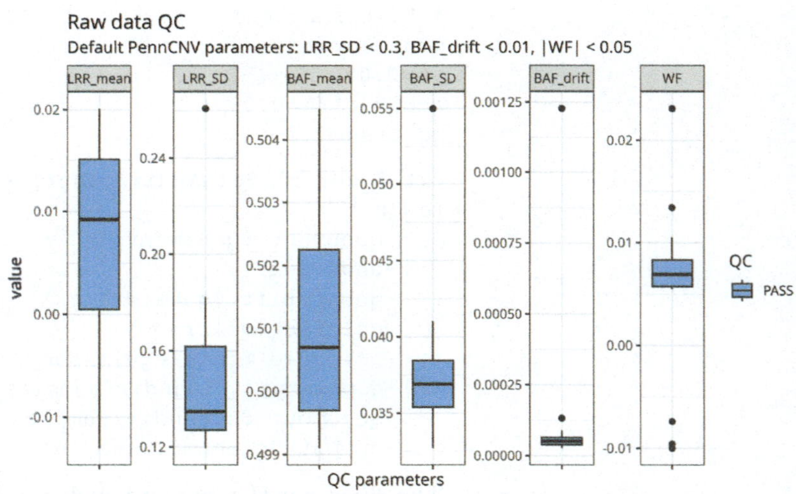

Fig. 1 Sample quality parameters. Blue boxes show samples that pass the quality control based on the PennCNV parameters: LRR_SD < 0.3, BAF_drift < 0.01 and |WF| < 0.05. For this specific small set of samples, the quality is good according to the previous thresholds, and all samples passed the QC criteria. However, with more stringent criteria, many samples could be excluded

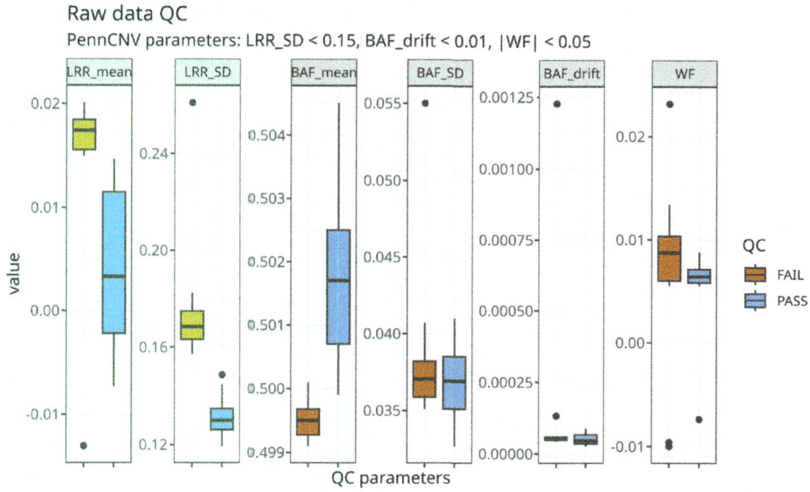

Fig. 2 Sample quality with stringent parameters. Red boxes show samples, which fail the inclusion criteria based on the PennCNV QC threshold (LRR_SD < 0.15 & BAF_drift < 0.01 & |WF| < 0.05). Blue boxes show samples that pass the quality control. This plot shows the metrics for the same set of samples presented at Fig. 1 but with more stringent criteria for LRR standard deviation

```
  combineseg \
  $cleandir/samples_clean_qcpass.rawcn \
-output $cleandir/samples_clean_qcpass.merged.rawcn
```

The *command clean_cnv.pl* merged adjacent CNVs, --fraction parameter defines the maximum fraction of gap divided by combined CNV, --bp parameter uses base pairs to calculate fraction (by default, it uses the number of SNPs/markers within the call). For this use case, we merged the CNVs using a fraction of less than 50%. However, for a larger number of CNVs in a larger sample size, this process could be repeated for best precision [9].

10. Upon completion of the quality assessment, a total of 26 samples (within *samples_clean_qcpass.list* file) and 1019 calls (within *samples_clean_qcpass.merged.rawcn* file) will be included for the identification of rare CNVs in individuals with pediatric obesity.

3.2 Identifications of Rrare CNVs

1. After the CNV detection and QC analysis, the samples and calls in PennCNV format are first converted to Plink files: fam, cnv and map (code is included in the *rareCNV_pipeline.sh* file) (*see* **Note 3**).
2. Small CNV calls are often challenging to detect reliably using SNP arrays [10, 11]. Based on the original study for the dataset in this case study, we only retain CNVs

larger than 10 kb and covered by more than five probes (*see* **Note 4**):

```
SNPs=5
cnvKB=10
# Generating files with CNVs bigger than $cnvKB Kb
and $SNPs SNPs
$plink \
    --cfile $conversiondir/$prefix"_all" \
    --cnv-kb $cnvKB \
    --cnv-sites $SNPs \
    --out $conversiondir/$prefix"_final" \
    --cnv-write \
    --allow-no-sex \
    --noweb
```

The above Plink command reads the calls, samples and map files (--cfile), filtering data based on CNV length and number of probes (--cnv-kb and --cnv-sites).

3. To concentrate on rare CNVs, deletions and duplications, we excluded all CNVs that exhibited at least a 50% overlap with a common CNV, with frequency >1% in the database of genomic variants (DGV) [12] (*see* **Note 5**):

```
$plink \
    --cfile $conversiondir/$prefix"_final" \
    --cnv-exclude $resourcesdir/DGV_gold_common_
dels.tsv \
    --cnv-overlap 0.50 \
    --cnv-del \
    --out $rarecnvsdir/$prefix"_rare_dels" \
    --cnv-write \
    --allow-no-sex \
    --noweb
```

The --cnv-exclude parameter filters out CNVs overlapping at least 50% (--cnv-overlap) of the regions of common variants. In this specific command, deletions (--cnv-del) are extracted. Similar command is executed for duplications.

4. A total of 242 rare deletions (within *study_rare_dels.cnv* file) and 173 rare duplications (within *study_rare_dups.cnv* file) were extracted for use in identifying rare CNVs in pediatric obesity samples.

5. Next, we evaluate the genome regions overlapped by the rare CNVs:

```
$plink \
    --cfile $rarecnvsdir/$prefix"_rare_dels" \
    --cnv-intersect $resourcesdir/glist-hg19.dat \
```

```
--cnv-region-overlap 0.01 \
--cnv-border 20 \
--noweb \
--cnv-verbose-report-regions \
--allow-no-sex \
--out $intersectdir/$prefix"_rare_dels_intersect"
```

The --cnv-intersect parameter evaluates the intersected region based on the proportion of the region that is affected by CNV (--cnv-region-overlap). The file *glist-hg19.dat* contains the human genome annotation (genes coordinates). The parameter --cnv-border adds a kb border around each region. This Plink command generates a file (**.reg*) containing the information on the affected regions and the list of sample-CNs affecting those regions.

6. The subsequent steps entailed the identification of potentially pathogenic rare CNVs in alignment with the specific objectives of the study. The original study prioritized rare CNVs based on previously reported CNVs in obesity research, overlaps with CNVs in DECIPHER database for obesity [13], and CNVs affecting genomic locus involved in energy homeostasis or related processes, among other criteria. Based on the prior identifications of rare CNVs, we found several CNVs included in the original study, as is shown in Table 1, though limited by the number of samples analyzed (*see* **Note 6**).
7. Alternative approach to evaluate the potential role of CNVs in risk disease could involve:

   - Investigating all genes affected by rare CNVs using tools for functional annotation, enrichment analyses of gene lists, and pathway analysis. These tools include DAVID (Database for Annotation, Visualization, and Integrated Discovery) [14], KEGG (Kyoto Encyclopedia of Genes and Genomes) [15], among others. They could help identify the biological roles of genes affected by rare CNVs, determine their involvement in specific pathways or biological processes, and find any enrichment of particular functions or pathways. For instance, by selecting all the genes affected by rare deletions (included in the **.reg* file previously obtained in Sect. 3.2, point 5), we used DAVID webserver and its functional annotation cluster option (with default parameters), to obtain the list of pathways where these genes are involved. As a result, we obtained, as part of an extensive list, the KEGG pathway for Ascorbate and Aldarate Metabolism, a crucial carbohydrate metabolic pathway that combats oxidative damage in cells [16] (see Fig. 3). Two deletions (17:19499229-19537470) upstream of the *ALDH3A2* gene were observed

Table 1
Clinically relevant and potentially clinically relevant CNVs, as identified by [28], and confirmed in this analysis

Coordinates (hg19)##Chr:bp1-bp2	CNV Type	Size (kb)	Genes	Relevant clinical details
22:20733495-21464479	Dup	731	**PI4KA**, CRKL, THAP7, SLC7A4, SNAP29, MED15, AIFM3, LZTR1, SERPIND1, P2RX6, SCARF2, ZNF74	Endocrine disorders [29, 30]
6:25674509-25736678	Dup	62	**SCGN**, HIST1H2AA, HIST1H2BA	Role in appetite [31]
7:157306440-157370645	Dup	64	**PTPRN2**	Involved in insulin secretion processes and obesity [32, 33]
10: 62998362-67398310	Del	4400	**ARID5B**, C10orf107, EGR2, RTKN2, ZNF365, TMEM26, JMJD1C, ADO, REEP3, NRBF2	Role in adipocyte development and normal lipid metabolism [34, 35]

in our results. The DECIPHER database indicates that four patients are affected by this deletion, which is associated with an obesity phenotype. However, only one case was considered likely pathogenic (DECIPHER ID patients: 1643, 249307, 251420, 400878).

- A targeted alternative approach could involve selecting a specific subset of genes involved in a pathway of interest and examining the function of the genes overlapped by CNVs in the specific study (*see* **Note 7**).
- Classifying the potential effects of CNVs at the transcript level investigating their impact on gene expression. CNVs affecting an enhancer or promoter sequence may alter transcription level. Duplicated and, specially, deleted sequences may disrupt gene structure and functionality.
- In the case of case-control studies, performing a burden CNV analysis by examining CNVs in both patients and healthy control individuals could elucidate the role of CNVs in the pathogenesis of specific disease, as suggested in literature [9, 17–19].

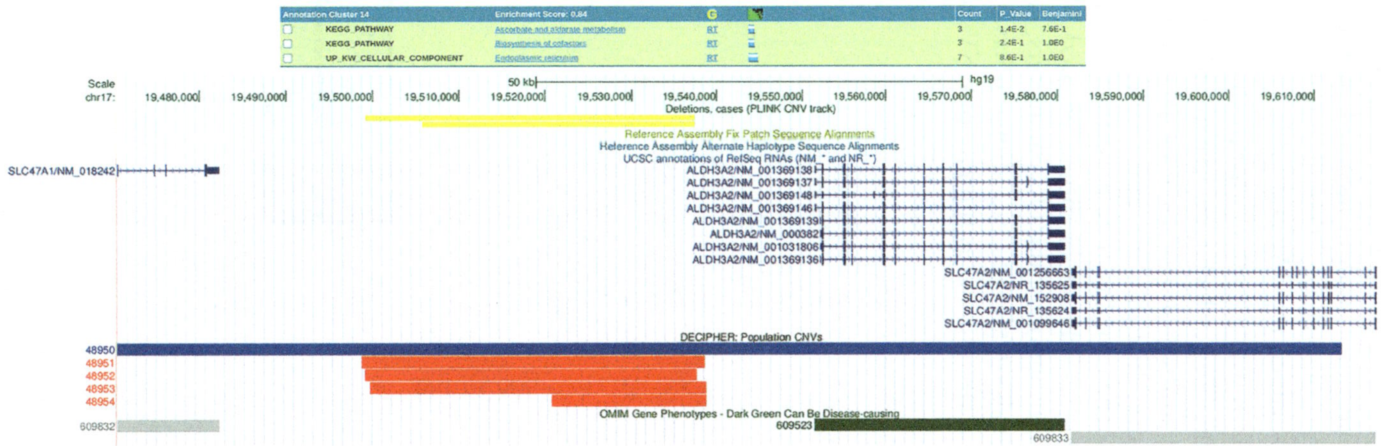

Fig. 3 David webserver for functional annotation analysis. Pathway annotation for genes affected by rare deletions in pediatric obesity samples identified the KEGG pathway Ascorbate and Aldarate Metabolism as a candidate cluster. Below the David results, the region chr17:19,470,519-19,617,322 from Genome Browser displays four deletions (indicated by red thick rectangles) registered in the DECIPHER database as associated with the obesity phenotype. Two deletions (indicated by red thin rectangles at the top) were observed in our case study

4 Notes

1. For this case study, the entire report file was generated from the individual reports included in the GSE101417 project (*.processed.txt.gz). This file must contain the sample IDs, SNPs names, the BAF and LRR.
2. Previous studies indicate that the number of CNVs per sample (NumCNVs), which is associated with the DNA quality, is sensitive to the platform used for data genotyping [20, 21]. For instance, the PennCNV tutorial mentions that Affymetrix platform data contains more noise than Illumina data, and a more lenient QC threshold should be used. We suggest checking the distribution of the QC parameters, including NumCNVs, across all samples and excluding outliers. Figures 4 and 5 show the distribution of the number of CNVs in this set of samples.

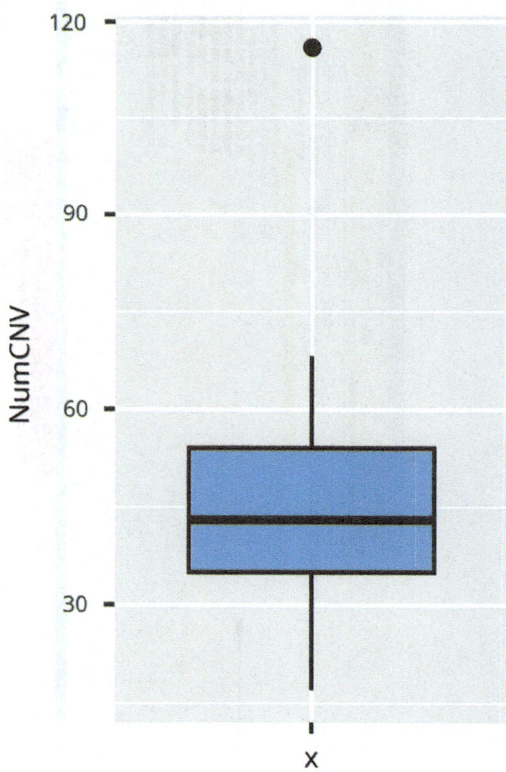

Fig. 4 The distribution of the number of CNVs per sample. Samples with an excessive number of CNVs should be considered for exclusion because it can indicate low data quality. For this set of samples, the statistics show, sample size = 31, minimum = 17, Q1 = 35, median = 43, mean = 45.65, Q3 = 54, maximum (outlier) = 116. We select the upper quartile (Q3) as the filter threshold

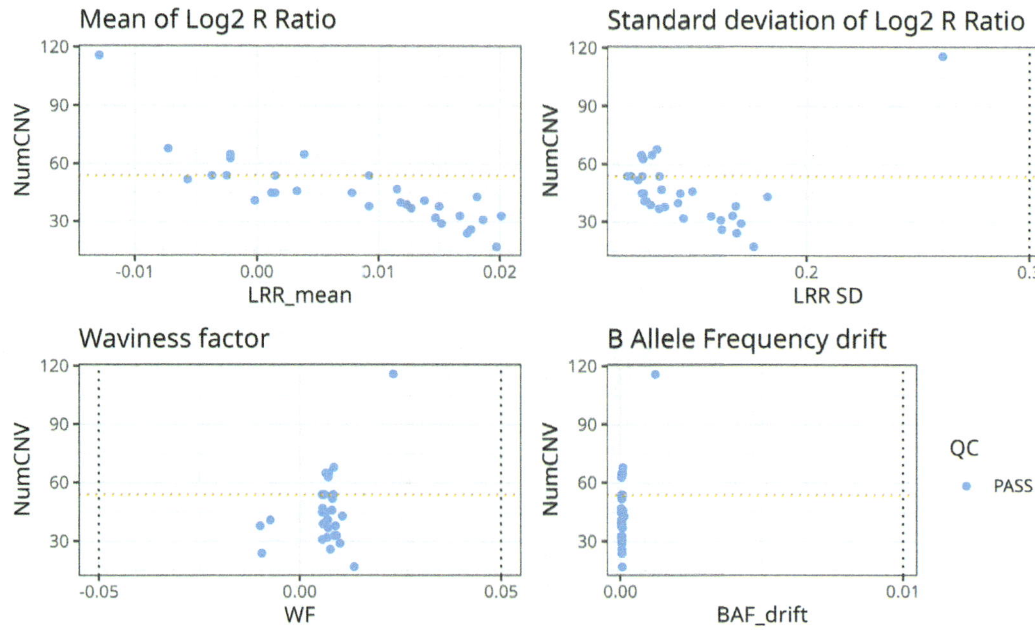

Fig. 5 PennCNV statistics and distribution of the number of CNVs per sample. Although all samples passed the quality control based on PennCNV statistics, the threshold for the number of CNVs per sample (NumCNV) is used as an exclusion criterion for DNA of poor quality. For the set of samples in this work, yellow dashed lines delimit the NumCNV threshold

3. Plink files required for CNV analysis include fam, cnv and map format files. FAM file should contains: Family ID ("FID"), Within-family ID ("IID"; cannot be "0"), Within-family ID of father ("0" if father isn't in dataset), Within-family ID of mother ("0" if mother isn't in dataset), Sex code ("1" = male, "2"= female, "0"= unknown), and Phenotype value ("1" = control, "2" = case, "-9"/"0"/non-numeric = missing data if case/control). Since we do not have all this information available, we are including default values. The CNV file format contains: FID and IID as in fam file, along with CHR, BP1, BP2, TYPE, SCORE, and SITES, which are obtained from rawcn file. The MAP file is created using the Plink command with the --cnv-make-map parameter. All this code is included in the *rareCNV_pipeline.sh* file.
4. Given that our case study involves a subset of samples from a previous study, we are employing the same values to filter CNVs by length and probe to achieve comparable results. However, the optimal CNV size for minimizing false calls using SNP array platforms, including the HumanOmni2.5 platform, can vary. Generally, CNVs larger than 50 kilobases (kb) are more reliably detected, whereas smaller CNVs, particularly those less

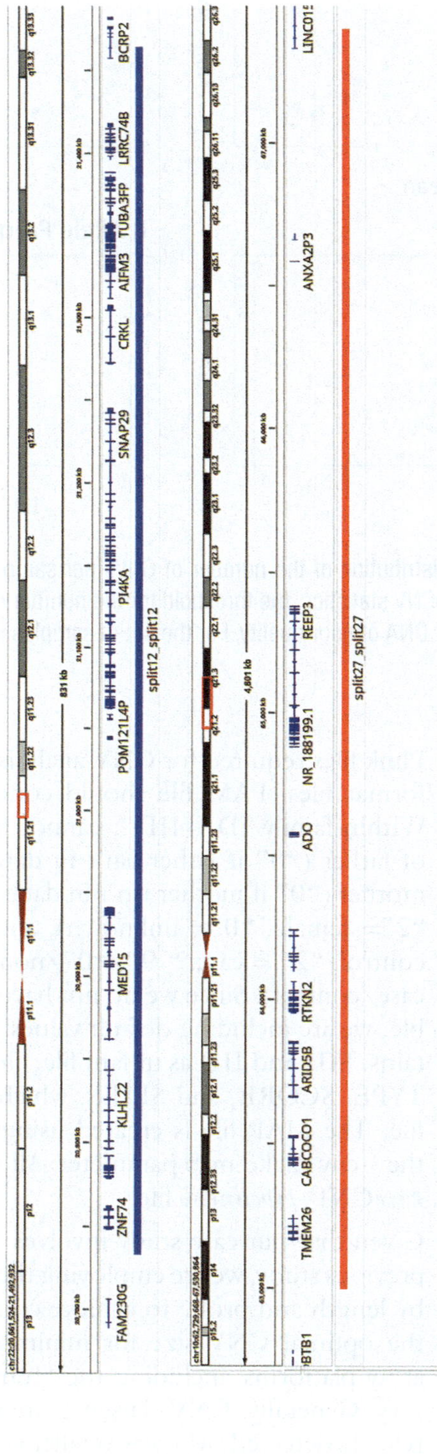

Fig. 6 Visualization of two rare CNVs, including a duplication at chr22:20733495-21464479 and a deletion at chr10:62998362-67398310, using the Integrative Genomics Viewer (IGV)

than 10 kb, are challenging to detect accurately due to the limitations of SNP array resolution [22–24].

5. In the absence of control samples, we are referencing CNV frequency information from the Database of Genomic Variants (DGV) Gold Standard to identify common variants and extract rare CNVs in the dataset for this study case. Two files, *DGV_gold_common_dels.tsv* and *DGV_gold_common_dups.tsv*, containing information on CNV position, type, and frequency (%), are provided in the resources directory of this project.
6. Rare CNVs can be visually presented using graphical interface tools such as Integrative Genomics Viewer (IGV) [25] or UCSC Genome Browser [26] using the custom tracks option. BED format files are generated in the code for this project to facilitate this visualization. Figure 6 illustrates two largest rare CNVs from Table 1.
7. We downloaded the early-onset diabetes panel (V4.0), restricted to green status genes, from Genomics England PanelApp [27], which provides panels with a list of genes related to human disorders. Using this list of genes, we employed Plink (with the --cnv-intersect parameter) to identify the rare CNVs previously obtained that overlap these regions. Due to the small sample size and the focus on rare CNVs, no results were found. The code for this analysis is included at *rareCNV_pipeline.sh*.

Conflict of Interest

The authors have no conflicts of interest to declare that are relevant to the content of this chapter.

References

1. Hastings PJ, Lupski JR, Rosenberg SM, Ira G (2009) Mechanisms of change in gene copy number. Nat Rev Genet 10:551–564. https://doi.org/10.1038/nrg2593
2. Li YR, Glessner JT, Coe BP, Li J, Mohebnasab M, Chang X, Connolly J, Kao C, Wei Z, Bradfield J et al (2020) Rare copy number variants in over 100,000 European ancestry subjects reveal multiple disease associations. Nat Commun 11:255. https://doi.org/10.1038/s41467-019-13624-1
3. Higuchi R, Fockler C, Dollinger G, Watson R (1993) Kinetic PCR analysis: real-time monitoring of DNA amplification reactions. Biotechnol 11:1026–1030. https://doi.org/10.1038/nbt0993-1026
4. Schouten JP, McElgunn CJ, Waaijer R, Zwijnenburg D, Diepvens F, Pals G (2002) Relative quantification of 40 nucleic acid sequences by multiplex ligation-dependent probe amplification. Nucleic Acids Res 30:e57. https://doi.org/10.1093/nar/gnf056
5. Zarrei M, MacDonald JR, Merico D, Scherer SW (2015) A copy number variation map of the human genome. Nat Rev Genet 16:172–183. https://doi.org/10.1038/nrg3871
6. Lavrichenko K, Johansson S, Jonassen I (2021) Comprehensive characterization of copy number variation (CNV) called from array, long- and short-read data. BMC Genom 22: 826. https://doi.org/10.1186/s12864-021-08082-3

7. de Araújo Lima L, Wang K (2017) PennCNV in whole-genome sequencing data. BMC Bioinform 18: 383. https://doi.org/10.1186/s12859-017-1802-x
8. Chang CC, Chow CC, Tellier LC, Vattikuti S, Purcell SM, Lee JJ (2015) Second-generation PLINK: rising to the challenge of larger and richer datasets. Gigascience 4: 7. https://doi.org/10.1186/s13742-015-0047-8
9. Artaza H, Eriksson D, Lavrichenko K, Aranda-Guillén M, Bratland E, Vaudel M, Knappskog P, Husebye ES, Bensing S, Wolff ASB et al (2024) Rare copy number variation in autoimmune Addison's disease. Front Immunol 15: 1374499. https://doi.org/10.3389/fimmu.2024.1374499
10. Marenne G, Rodríguez-Santiago B, Closas MG, Pérez-Jurado L, Rothman N, Rico D, Pita G, Pisano DG, Kogevinas M, Silverman DT et al (2011) Assessment of copy number variation using the illumina infinium 1M SNP-array: a comparison of methodological approaches in the Spanish Bladder Cancer/EPICURO study. Hum Mutat 32:240–248. https://doi.org/10.1002/humu.21398
11. Pinto D, Darvishi K, Shi X, Rajan D, Rigler D, Fitzgerald T, Lionel AC, Thiruvahindrapuram B, MacDonald JR, Mills R et al (2011) Comprehensive assessment of array-based platforms and calling algorithms for detection of copy number variants. Nat Biotechnol 29:512–520. https://doi.org/10.1038/nbt.1852
12. MacDonald JR, Ziman R, Yuen RKC, Feuk L, Scherer SW (2014) The Database of Genomic Variants: a curated collection of structural variation in the human genome. Nucleic Acids Res 42:D986–D992. https://doi.org/10.1093/nar/gkt958
13. Bragin E, Chatzimichali EA, Wright CF, Hurles ME, Firth HV, Bevan AP, Swaminathan GJ (2014) DECIPHER: database for the interpretation of phenotype-linked plausibly pathogenic sequence and copy-number variation. Nucleic Acids Res 42:D993–D1000. https://doi.org/10.1093/nar/gkt937
14. Sherman BT, Hao M, Qiu J, Jiao X, Baseler MW, Lane HC, Imamichi T, Chang W (2022) DAVID: a web server for functional enrichment analysis and functional annotation of gene lists (2021 update). Nucleic Acids Res 50:W216–W221. https://doi.org/10.1093/nar/gkac194
15. Kanehisa M, Goto S (2000) KEGG: Kyoto Encyclopedia of Genes and Genomes. Nucleic Acids Res 28:27–30
16. Peng L, Chen L, Wan J, Liu W, Lou S, Shen Z (2023) Single-cell transcriptomic landscape of immunometabolism reveals intervention candidates of ascorbate and aldarate metabolism, fatty-acid degradation and PUFA metabolism of T-cell subsets in healthy controls, psoriasis and psoriatic arthritis. Front Immunol 14:1179877.https://doi.org/10.3389/fimmu.2023.1179877
17. The Wellcome Trust Case Control Consortium (2010) Genome-wide association study of CNVs in 16,000 cases of eight common diseases and 3,000 shared controls. Nature 464:713–720. https://doi.org/10.1038/nature08979
18. Wheeler E, Huang N, Bochukova EG, Keogh JM, Lindsay S, Garg S, Henning E, Blackburn H, Loos RJF, Wareham NJ et al (2013) Genome-wide SNP and CNV analysis identifies common and low-frequency variants associated with severe early-onset obesity. Nat Genet 45:513–517. https://doi.org/10.1038/ng.2607
19. Aguirre M, Rivas MA, Priest J (2019) Phenome-wide burden of copy-number variation in the UK Biobank. Am J Hum Genet 105:373–383. https://doi.org/10.1016/j.ajhg.2019.07.001
20. Lin C-F, Naj AC, Wang L-S (2013) Analyzing copy number variation using SNP array data: protocols for calling CNV and association tests. Curr Protoc Hum Genet 79(Unit-1):27. https://doi.org/10.1002/0471142905.hg0127s79
21. Artaza H, Lavrichenko K, Wolff ASB, Røyrvik EC, Vaudel M, Johansson S (2024) Rare Copy Number Variant analysis in case-control studies using SNP Array Data: a scalable and automated data analysis pipeline. 2024.03.13.584428. https://doi.org/10.1101/2024.03.13.584428
22. Haraksingh RR, Abyzov A, Urban AE (2017) Comprehensive performance comparison of high-resolution array platforms for genome-wide Copy Number Variation (CNV) analysis in humans. BMC Genom 18: 321. https://doi.org/10.1186/s12864-017-3658-x
23. Zampaglione E, Kinde B, Place EM, Navarro-Gomez D, Maher M, Jamshidi F, Nassiri S, Mazzone JA, Finn C, Schlegel D et al (2020) Copy-number variation contributes 9% of pathogenicity in the inherited retinal degenerations. Genet Med 22:1079–1087. https://doi.org/10.1038/s41436-020-0759-8
24. van Baardwijk MN, Heijnen LSEM, Zhao H, Baudis M, Stubbs AP (2024) A systematic benchmark of copy number variation detection tools for high density SNP genotyping arrays. Genomics 116:110962. https://doi.org/10.1016/j.ygeno.2024.110962
25. Robinson JT, Thorvaldsdóttir H, Winckler W, Guttman M, Lander ES, Getz G, Mesirov JP (2011) Integrative Genomics Viewer. Nat Biotechnol 29:24. https://doi.org/10.1038/nbt.1754
26. Perez G, Barber GP, Benet-Pages A, Casper J, Clawson H, Diekhans M, Fischer C, Gonzalez

JN, Hinrichs AS, Lee CM et al (2024) The UCSC Genome Browser database: 2025 update. Nucleic Acids Res 53:D1243–D1249. https://doi.org/10.1093/nar/gkae974
27. Martin AR, Williams E, Foulger RE, Leigh S, Daugherty LC, Niblock O, Leong IUS, Smith KR, Gerasimenko O, Haraldsdottir E et al (2019) PanelApp crowdsources expert knowledge to establish consensus diagnostic gene panels. Nat Genet 51:1560–1565. https://doi.org/10.1038/s41588-019-0528-2
28. Selvanayagam T, Walker S, Gazzellone MJ, Kellam B, Cytrynbaum C, Stavropoulos DJ, Li P, Birken CS, Hamilton J, Weksberg R et al (2018) Genome-wide copy number variation analysis identifies novel candidate loci associated with pediatric obesity. Eur J Hum Genet 26:1588–1596. https://doi.org/10.1038/s41431-018-0189-0
29. Ensenauer RE, Adeyinka A, Flynn HC, Michels VV, Lindor NM, Dawson DB, Thorland EC, Lorentz CP, Goldstein JL, McDonald MT et al (2003) Microduplication 22q11.2, an emerging syndrome: clinical, cytogenetic, and molecular analysis of thirteen patients. Am J Hum Genet 73:1027–1040
30. Bhattarai D, McGinn DE, Crowley TB, Giunta V, Gaiser K, Zackai EH, Emanuel BS, Heimall J, Jyonouchi S, Lee J et al (2023) Immunologic, Molecular, and Clinical Profile of Patients with Chromosome 22q11.2 Duplications. J Clin Immunol 43:794–807. https://doi.org/10.1007/s10875-023-01443-5
31. Gyengesi E, Paxinos G, Andrews ZB (2012) Oxidative stress in the hypothalamus: the importance of calcium signaling and mitochondrial ROS in body weight regulation. Curr Neuropharmacol 10:344–353. https://doi.org/10.2174/157015912804143496
32. Cai T, Hirai H, Zhang G, Zhang M, Takahashi N, Kasai H, Satin LS, Leapman RD, Notkins AL (2011) Deletion of IA-2 and/or IA-2β decreases insulin secretion by reducing the number of dense core vesicles. Diabetologia 54:2347–2357. https://doi.org/10.1007/s00125-011-2221-6
33. Chen P-Y, Chu A, Liao W-W, Rubbi L, Janzen C, Hsu F-M, Thamotharan S, Ganguly A, Lam L, Montoya D et al (2018) Prenatal growth patterns and birthweight are associated with differential DNA methylation and gene expression of cardiometabolic risk genes in human placentas: a discovery-based approach. Reprod Sci 25:523–539. https://doi.org/10.1177/1933719117716779
34. Yamakawa T, Sugimoto K, Whitson RH, Itakura K (2010) Modulator recognition factor-2 regulates triglyceride metabolism in adipocytes. Biochem Biophys Res Commun 391:277–281. https://doi.org/10.1016/j.bbrc.2009.11.049
35. Claussnitzer M, Dankel SN, Kim K-H, Quon G, Meuleman W, Haugen C, Glunk V, Sousa IS, Beaudry JL, Puviindran V et al (2015) FTO obesity variant circuitry and adipocyte browning in humans. N Engl J Med 373:895–907. https://doi.org/10.1056/NEJMoa1502214

Chapter 14

Graph-Based Gene Embedding

Henry Cousins

Abstract

Gene embeddings, concise numerical descriptions of complex genetic relationships, are powerful tools for predicting unknown functions of genes and drugs. The application of graph-specific representation learning algorithms on large biological network databases allows for the efficient computation of highly expressive gene embeddings. This chapter provides an explanation of the end-to-end calculation of such embeddings, with a focus on the most widely used and generally applicable datasets and algorithms.

Keywords Gene embedding, Machine learning, Bioinformatics, Protein–protein interactions, Network biology

1 Introduction

Gene embedding refers to the representation of gene products such that quantitative likeness corresponds to functional likeness. Specifically, gene embedding methods generate numerical vectors, themselves called embeddings, whose mathematical similarity connotes some degree of shared biology [1]. Conceptually, in a useful embedding space, the respective embeddings for a specific ligand and its corresponding receptor will be more similar than expected by chance, reflecting functional overlap. Moreover, the vector difference between such embeddings will be similar for different ligand-receptor pairs, reflecting also a conception of general functional distinctions. Embedding methods aim to achieve such expressivity while retaining conciseness, distilling complex functional data into a comparatively low-dimensional, practical space [2].

Gene embedding methods require training on well-structured datasets of gene function, but their generalizability depends on large volumes of disparate data types [3]. Network or graph-based methods have consequently emerged as uniquely useful in this regard. Such approaches combine two important advances: first, the development of large gene and protein interaction databases with intrinsic network structures, and second, the creation of representation learning

Y-h Taguchi (ed.), *AI/ML-Driven Gene Analysis*, Methods in Molecular Biology, vol. 3037,
https://doi.org/10.1007/978-1-0716-5284-8_14,

methods that operate directly on network topologies [4]. Biological interaction networks are both well-structured and broad, enabling rich functional representations while retaining generalizability for various inference tasks [5].

Embeddings derived from network structures have proven useful in a wide collection of applications. They can be applied directly to identify functionally related gene clusters, which is particularly useful in analyzing gene expression patterns, or to infer pathogenicity of less studied genes, which has been applied in conditions ranging from cancer to Alzheimer's disease [6–8]. Alternatively, they can form a basis for task-specific bioinformatic pipelines, such as drug-repurposing efforts or driver gene prediction models [9, 10].

This chapter aims to provide an introduction to performing graph-based gene embedding, with a focus on the most commonly used databases and algorithms. It focuses on the generation of the embeddings themselves, rather than on downstream use cases. Many applications will benefit from specialized models and task-specific fine-tuning, regarding which the curious reader is better advised to consult the most current literature.

2 Materials

2.1 Hardware Considerations

Graph-based gene embedding pipelines, in comparison to transformer-based methods, can be easily adapted to hardware constraints. Graphics processing unit (GPU) memory is advantageous for deep-learning approaches, such as graph convolutional networks (GCNs), but central processing unit (CPU) architectures are often sufficient for random-walk methods. This distinction will be further explained below. Memory requirements are challenging to estimate a priori but can be compared to known pipelines on the basis of total edge count and embedding size (*see* **Note 1**).

2.2 Software Considerations

Gene embedding pipelines are most commonly built in a Python 3 environment. Familiarity with PyTorch or TensorFlow is helpful for debugging but not strictly required for the implementation of the algorithms described in this chapter. Most analyses described in this chapter can be conducted using the SciPy and scikit-learn libraries [11, 12].

2.3 Terminology

This chapter discusses graphs corresponding to a set of nodes and edges, which may be associated with features or weights. Generally, nodes correspond to biological entities, such as gene products, and edges correspond to biological associations, such as physical interactions. In homogenous graphs, all nodes are of a common type, while heterogeneous graphs contain multiple node types.

3 Methods

3.1 Network Construction

The primary choice in a gene embedding schema is the selection of a biological network database to represent. Protein-protein interaction (PPI) networks are commonly used, owing to their versatility and scale. PPI networks are homogeneous networks, often weighted, that intend to illustrate physical interactions between gene products. While they may be constructed at any scale, general-purpose gene embedding approaches rely on the largest such networks, which are curated from large sets of literature.

Several such networks are available, including STRING, Reactome, and IntAct [13–15]. These networks have considerable variation in their representation of different protein classes, which should be an important consideration at this stage. Each of these PPI networks is maintained as a standalone database and should be obtained directly from the main repository where possible, as frequent updates to the networks require accurate versioning.

Multimodal networks are heterogeneous graphs that describe literature-derived relationships between genes and non-gene entities, such as drugs or diseases. They may be preferable if the embeddings are intended for higher-order inference tasks, such as drug-repurposing studies or disease-specific pathogenicity, with the drawback that semantic relationships in the graph can considerably bias node embeddings away from fundamental biochemical relationships. PrimeKG and GNBR are two popular multimodal biological networks and are publicly available through their respective citations [16, 17].

3.2 Network Refinement

Many networks, including STRING, have edge weights, which may be filtered either to remove low-confidence interactions or to create an unweighted graph. It is generally recommended to remove low-confidence edges, which add significant computing overhead with marginal benefit to embedding accuracy (*see* **Note 2**).

Consideration should also be given to filtering by the evidence source for edge data, which is annotated in most literature-derived databases. Important distinctions include between biophysical and genetic associations and between measured and imputed interactions (*see* **Note 3**).

3.3 Graph Representations

Most commonly, raw network data is obtained from the source as a tabular list of edges and corresponding weights, if applicable. This must be converted into a graph structure. Dedicated graph representation libraries such as NetworkX are preferred at this stage, given the need for downstream compatibility with embedding algorithms [18]. Specialized network plotting tools like PyVis are useful for visualization, although standalone platforms like Cytoscape may offer additional functionality [19, 20].

3.4 Embedding Methods

Following the construction of the network, an appropriate embedding algorithm must be selected. Two categories of algorithms deserve particular consideration at this stage. Random-walk methods, such as node2vec, are widely used for their relative efficiency during training, while still enabling good representation of local network relationships [21]. They may be preferred in the setting of very large graphs or limited computing resources and are best suited to homogeneous graphs without node features (*see* **Note 4**). Alternatively, deep-learning approaches, such as GCNs, are more flexible in their ability to represent different network structures, such as heterogeneous graphs with node features [22]. However, computing requirements during training can be extensive for deep-learning methods and may be prohibitive for very large datasets.

For the most popular algorithms, such as node2vec or GCNs, a number of libraries enable streamlined integration into bioinformatic workflows. PyTorch Geometric is among the most popular libraries, but many alternatives may be considered if hardware constraints are an issue or if a particular architecture framework, such as TensorFlow, is specifically preferred [23].

3.5 Parameter Tuning

During construction of the embedding pipeline, it is good practice to identify and optimize key model parameters. This is valuable both to ensure maximal biological relevance of the embeddings and to understand the underlying sensitivity of the embeddings to parameter selection. A non-exhaustive list of such parameters includes confidence score threshold for PPI network construction, embedding size, length, and number of walks for random-walk approaches, and learning rate for deep-learning approaches. Simple grid searches remain very useful in this regard (*see* **Note 5**).

3.6 Validation Approaches

Evaluating the performance of embedding methods is fundamentally challenging owing to the lack of objective labels against which to compare. A good starting point is to confirm that the desired attributes of the original network are captured in the embedding space. For instance, if capturing local protein-protein interactions is a priority, calculating the association between inter-embedding distance and intra-network edgewise distance can provide an estimate of the model's resolution. For general-purpose applications, it is also useful to quantify the clustering tendency of embeddings with respect to known gene categories. For instance, calculating a silhouette score for the embeddings in relation to known gene ontology categories provides some external validation of biological relevance.

4 Notes

1. For the networks and algorithms discussed in this chapter, it is reasonable to provision a minimum memory requirement of 5GB. Requirements for embedding full PPI networks with larger embedding sizes can easily exceed 50GB.
2. In STRING, confidence scores greater than 0.7 are generally considered "high confidence," and scores above 0.9 connote "highest confidence." However, it may in many cases be more practical to treat the confidence score threshold as a hyperparameter that should be optimized based on available computing resources. Increasing the confidence score threshold can dramatically reduce memory requirements.
3. The extent to which these distinctions matter in practice is somewhat unclear. To a large extent, bioinformatic insights into protein interactions rely on indirect genetic observations, including coexpression and coevolutionary analyses, rendering distinctions between proteins and their corresponding genes harder to interpret. Consequently, many biological network datasets employ the terms "gene" and "protein" somewhat interchangeably. The most expressive embeddings in the field seem to benefit from networks with a variety of experimental sources. However, one might conjecture that an application focused on artificial use cases for proteins, for instance, might benefit from a network focused exclusively on biophysical interactions.
4. It is possible to account for node features while using a random-walk method, but, especially when using high-dimensional features, it is usually recommended to consider deep-learning methods first-line for this task.
5. Hyperparameter tuning can be challenging for embedding methods due to the lack of clear metrics of model performance. Unless an application has well-defined labels by which to benchmark embedding relevance directly, it may be more appropriate to focus on a smaller number of biologically relevant sensitivity analyses (e.g., clustering tendency of embeddings as a function of network size).

Conflict of Interest

The authors have no conflicts of interest to declare that are relevant to the content of this chapter.

References

1. Nayar G, Altman RB (2024) Heterogeneous network approaches to protein pathway prediction. Comput Struct Biotechnol J 23:2727–2739
2. Brechtmann F, Bechtler T, Londhe S et al (2023) Evaluation of input data modality choices on functional gene embeddings. NAR Genom Bioinform 5:lqad095
3. Su C, Tong J, Zhu Y et al (2020) Network embedding in biomedical data science. Brief Bioinform 21:182–197
4. Yue X, Wang Z, Huang J et al (2020) Graph embedding on biomedical networks: methods, applications and evaluations. Bioinformatics 36:1241–1251
5. Miryala SK, Anbarasu A, Ramaiah S (2018) Discerning molecular interactions: a comprehensive review on biomolecular interaction databases and network analysis tools. Gene 642:84–94
6. Wang S, Flynn ER, Altman RB (2020) Gaussian embedding for large-scale gene set analysis. Nat Mach Intell 2:387–395
7. Doria-Belenguer S, Xenos A, Ceddia G et al (2023) A functional analysis of omic network embedding spaces reveals key altered functions in cancer. Bioinformatics 39:btad281
8. Lagisetty Y, Bourquard T, Al-Ramahi I et al (2022) Identification of risk genes for Alzheimer's disease by gene embedding. Cell Genom 2:100162
9. Liu Y, Guo Y, Liu X et al (2021) Pathogenic gene prediction based on network embedding. Brief Bioinform 22:bbaa353
10. Sosa DN, Derry A, Guo M et al (2020) A literature-based knowledge graph embedding method for identifying drug repurposing opportunities in rare diseases. Pac Symp Biocomput 25:463–474
11. Virtanen P, Gommers R, Oliphant TE et al (2020) SciPy 1.0: fundamental algorithms for scientific computing in Python. Nat Methods 17:261–272
12. Pedregosa F, Varoquaux G, Gramfort A et al (2011) Scikit-learn: machine learning in Python. J Mach Learn Res 12:2825–2830
13. Szklarczyk D, Kirsch R, Koutrouli M et al (2023) The STRING database in 2023: protein-protein association networks and functional enrichment analyses for any sequenced genome of interest. Nucleic Acids Res 51:D638–D646
14. Milacic M, Beavers D, Conley P et al (2024) The reactome pathway knowledgebase 2024. Nucleic Acids Res 52:D672–D678
15. del Toro N, Shrivastava A, Ragueneau E et al (2022) The IntAct database: efficient access to fine-grained molecular interaction data. Nucleic Acids Res 50:D648–D653
16. Chandak P, Huang K, Zitnik M (2023) Building a knowledge graph to enable precision medicine. Sci Data 10: 67
17. Percha B, Altman RB (2018) A global network of biomedical relationships derived from text. Bioinformatics 34:2614–2624
18. Hagberg A, Swart PJ, and Schult DA (2008) Exploring network structure, dynamics, and function using networkX. In: Proceedings of the 7th Python in science conference, Pasadena, CA, USA, pp 11–16
19. Perrone G, Unpingco J, Lu H (2020) Network visualizations with Pyvis and VisJS. In: 19th Python in science conference. Austin, TX, USA, pp 58–62
20. Shannon P, Markiel A, Ozier O et al (2003) Cytoscape: a software environment for integrated models of biomolecular interaction networks. Genome Res 13:2498–2504
21. Grover A, Leskovec J (2016) node2vec: scalable feature learning for networks. In: Proceedings of the 22nd ACM SIGKDD international conference on knowledge discovery and data mining. Association for Computing Machinery, New York, NY, USA, pp 855–864
22. Kipf TN, Welling M (2017) Semi-supervised classification with graph convolutional networks. In: International conference on learning representations, Toulon, France
23. Fey M, Lenssen JE (2019) Fast graph representation learning with PyTorch geometric. In: International conference on learning representations, New Orleans, LA, USA

Subject Index

Y-h Taguchi (ed.), *AI/ML-Driven Gene Analysis*, Methods in Molecular Biology, vol. 3037,
https://doi.org/10.1007/978-1-0716-5284-8,

The manufacturer's authorised representative in the EU is Springer Nature Customer Service Centre GmbH, Europaplatz 3, 69115 Heidelberg, Germany. If you have any concerns regarding our products, please contact ProductSafety@springernature.com

Printed and bound by CPI Group (UK) Ltd, Croydon, CR0 4YY
15/09/2026
02217000-0003